COLLECTED PAPERS, VOLUME I: MIND AND LANGUAGE, 1972–2010

Collected Papers, Volume 1

MIND AND LANGUAGE, 1972–2010

Stephen Stich

OXFORD

UNIVERSITY PRESS

Oxford University Press, Inc., publishes works that further
Oxford University's objective of excellence
in research, scholarship, and education.

Oxford   New York
Auckland   Cape Town   Dar es Salaam   Hong Kong   Karachi
Kuala Lumpur   Madrid   Melbourne   Mexico City   Nairobi
New Delhi   Shanghai   Taipei   Toronto

With offices in
Argentina   Austria   Brazil   Chile   Czech Republic   France   Greece
Guatemala   Hungary   Italy   Japan   Poland   Portugal   Singapore
South Korea   Switzerland   Thailand   Turkey   Ukraine   Vietnam

Copyright © 2011 by Oxford University Press, Inc.

Published by Oxford University Press, Inc.
198 Madison Avenue, New York, New York 10016

www.oup.com

Library of Congress Cataloging-in-Publication Data
Stich, Stephen P.
[Selections. 2011]
Collected papers / by Stephen Stich.
   v.   cm.
Includes bibliographical references.
Contents: v. 1. Mind and language, 1972–2010
ISBN 978-0-19-973410-8 (v. 1 : alk. paper)
I. Title.
B945.S7551   2011
191–dc22   2010013600

1 3 5 7 9 8 6 4 2

Printed in the United States of America
on acid-free paper

To Noam Chomsky and to the memory of Van Quine

Contents

Acknowledgments

I am grateful to my co-authors and to the original publishers for granting permission to reprint these essays. The original publication of each essay is listed below.

1. Stephen P. Stich, "Grammar, Psychology and Indeterminacy," *Journal of Philosophy*, LXIX, 22, 1972. Pp. 799–818.

2. Stephen P. Stich, "The Idea of Innateness," in S.P. Stich, ed., *Innate Ideas* (Berkeley & London: University of California Press) 1975. Pp. 1–22.

3. Stephen P. Stich, "Beliefs and Subdoxastic States," *Philosophy of Science*, 45, 4, 1978. Pp. 499–518.

4. Stephen P. Stich, "Autonomous Psychology and the Belief–Desire Thesis," *The Monist*, Special Number on the Philosophy and Psychology of Cognition, 61, 4, 1978. Pp. 573–591.

5. Stephen P. Stich, "Dennett on Intentional Systems," *Philosophical Topics*, 12, 1, 1981. Pp. 39–62.

6. William Ramsey, Stephen P. Stich, and Joseph Garon, "Connectionism, Eliminativism and the Future of Folk Psychology," *Philosophical Perspectives, 4: Action Theory and Philosophy of Mind*, 1990. Pp. 499–533.

7. William Ramsey and Stephen P. Stich, "Connectionism and Three Levels of Nativism," *Synthese*, 82, 2, 1990. Pp. 177–205.

8. Stephen P. Stich, "Narrow Content Meets Fat Syntax," in *Meaning in Mind: Fodor and His Critics*, ed. by Barry Loewer and Georges Rey (Oxford: Basil Blackwell), 1991. Pp. 239–254.

9. Stephen P. Stich and Shaun Nichols, "Folk Psychology: Simulation or Tacit Theory," *Mind and Language*, 7, 1&2, 1992. Pp. 29–65.

10. Stephen P. Stich and Stephen Laurence, "Intentionality and Naturalism," *Midwest Studies in Philosophy*, v. 19, *Naturalism*, ed. by Peter A. French, Theodore E. Uehling, Jr. (University of Notre Dame Press), 1994. Pp. 159–182.

11. Stephen P. Stich and Ian Ravenscroft, "What *Is* Folk Psychology?" *Cognition*, 50, 1–3, 1994. Pp. 447–468.

12. Michael Bishop and Stephen P. Stich, "The Flight to Reference, or How *Not* to Make Progress in the Philosophy of Science," *Philosophy of Science*, 65, 1, March. 1998. Pp. 33–49.

13. Ron Mallon and Stephen Stich, "The Odd Couple: The Compatibility of Social Construction and Evolutionary Psychology," *Philosophy of Science*, 67 (March, 2000). Pp. 133–154.

14. Dominic Murphy and Stephen Stich, "Darwin in the Madhouse: Evolutionary Psychology and the Classification of Mental Disorders," in Peter Carruthers and Andrew Chamberlain, eds., *Evolution and the Human Mind: Modularity, Language and Meta-Cognition*, (Cambridge: Cambridge University Press) 2000. Pp. 62–92.

15. Stephen Stich and Shaun Nichols, "Folk Psychology," in Stephen Stich and Ted Warfield, eds., *The Blackwell Guide to Philosophy of Mind* (Oxford: Blackwell Publishing), 2003. Pp. 235–255.

16. Edouard Machery, Ron Mallon, Shaun Nichols, and Stephen Stich, "Semantics, Cross-cultural Style," *Cognition*, 92, 2004. Pp. B1–B12.

17. Ron Mallon, Edouard Machery, Shaun Nichols, and Stephen Stich, "Against Arguments from Reference," *Philosophy and Phenomenological Research*, LXXIX, 2, 2009. Pp. 332–356.

Introduction

THE ESSAYS COLLECTED here are arranged chronologically, and they span almost four decades. The earliest, "Grammar, Psychology, and Indeterminacy" (chapter 1), was published in 1972 and the most recent, "Against Arguments from Reference" (chapter 17), appeared in 2009. They discuss a wide range of topics including grammar, innateness, reference, folk psychology, eliminativism, connectionism, evolutionary psychology, simulation theory, social construction, and psychopathology. One way to characterize the volume is that it is a collection of essays on topics in the philosophy of mind and the philosophy of language that happen to have caught my interest. And there is much truth in that. In assembling the volume, I read through most of the papers I had published in the last forty-plus years (an exercise that I most definitely do not recommend!) and selected the essays dealing with mind and language that I thought might be worth reprinting in this collection. A second volume will contain essays on epistemology, rationality, and morality. But there is more unity to the essays in this volume than that might suggest. Just about all the work assembled here can, in one way or another, be traced back to two bountiful streams of philosophical thought and debate that did much to shape the philosophical landscape of the last half-century. In this brief introductory essay, I'll try to characterize these two streams, locate the essays in the philosophical terrain that they created, and say a bit about how these streams joined up with other tributaries that appeared as the twentieth century drew to a close.

THE VIABILITY OF THE COMMONSENSE CONCEPTION OF THE MIND

The first theme that unifies many of these essays is the debate over the viability of the commonsense conception of the mind. Like many extended and multifaceted debates, this one has a number of sources. William James, Sigmund Freud, and other central figures in the emergence of scientific psychology assumed that the science they were building would adopt and adapt the conceptual resources of commonsense psychology. It would study mental states like beliefs, desires, emotions, and sensations, perhaps discovering remarkable and unexpected facts about them—like Freud's (putative) discovery that many of our most important beliefs and desires are unconscious. But psychological behaviorists like John Watson and B. F. Skinner would have none of this. In their more cautious writings, the behaviorists urged that scientific psychology should eschew the posits of commonsense psychology for methodological reasons, and in their less cautious writings they suggested that most of the mental states that were spoken of in commonsense psychology did not exist at all.

In the middle years of the twentieth century, Skinner's friend and Harvard colleague W. V. Quine offered a new cluster of arguments against invoking beliefs, desires, and other propositional attitudes in scientific psychology. Put very crudely, the argument went something like this: Propositional attitudes are individuated by their propositional content. You and I share the same belief if and only if we each believe that p, where p is some specific proposition. But propositions, Quine insisted, are "creatures of darkness" (Quine 1956, § II). To individuate them and to determine whether a pair of utterances or a pair of content sentences express one proposition or two, we would need a notion of meaning that enabled us to distinguish analytic sentences from synthetic sentences. And there was, Quine argued, no such notion.

At about the same time, the work of Wilfred Sellars was laying the foundation for a related assault on the invocation of propositional attitudes in scientific psychology. In his seminal essay, "Empiricism and the Philosophy of Mind" (1956), Sellars introduced the idea that common terms for mental states could be viewed as theoretical terms in a commonsense theory constructed with the goal of explaining behavior. Sellars himself was no foe of the posits of this commonsense theory; indeed, he describes Jones, the mythical creator of the theory, as a genius.[1] But a number of philosophers influenced by Sellars, most notably Richard Rorty and Paul Churchland, went on to suggest that the mythical Jones might be less of a genius than Sellars supposed. These philosophers maintained that Jones's theory—commonsense (or "folk") psychology—was turning out to be a seriously mistaken theory, and that is a good reason to conclude that the mental states that the theory posits do not really exist. This was the core argument for the view that came to be known as "eliminativism."

---

1. For more on Sellars's myth, see chapter 15, "Folk Psychology."

My first contribution to this literature grew out of what I took to be a very simple idea. In the early 1970s, the view that became known as "semantic externalism" was becoming a hot topic in philosophy. Kripke (1972) and Putnam (1975) both defended the idea that the reference of a term depends on the term's causal history, and from this Putnam famously concluded that "meaning just ain't in the head." But it struck me that if meanings ain't in the head, then, since beliefs are individuated by their meaning or content, beliefs ain't either. A bit more precisely, there could be physically identical people who had beliefs with different contents. And if one assumed, as I did, that the states invoked in the explanation of behavior ought to be shared by all of a person's physical replicas, it followed that beliefs should not be invoked in the explanation of behavior. That, in a nutshell, is the argument set out in "Autonomous Psychology and the Belief–Desire Thesis" (chapter 4). This was, to put it mildly, not the last word on the topic. Jerry Fodor, who thought that "if commonsense intentional psychology really were to collapse, that would be, beyond comparison, the greatest intellectual catastrophe in the history of our species" (Fodor 1987, xii), proposed that we might "mitigate the panic" by replacing the commonsense notion of content with a close relative, which he dubbed "narrow content." However, I was not persuaded that narrow content was up to the task, and in "Narrow Content Meets Fat Syntax" (chapter 8), I say why.

Fodor was not the only important philosopher who was alarmed by the specter of eliminativism. Dan Dennett had been a pioneer in raising the concern that if eliminativism were true, it would do irreparable harm to our conception of ourselves as moral agents (Dennett 1978, Ch. 14). But Dennett's strategy for rescuing commonsense psychology was very different from Fodor's. Dennett maintained that commonsense psychology could not be overthrown by findings about the states and processes that cause behavior, because commonsense psychology says little or nothing about such states. Rather, he argued, commonsense psychology is a sort of "instrumentalistic calculus" that could be captured and rendered more precise by what he called "intentional systems theory." Once again, I was not persuaded, and in "Dennett on Intentional Systems" (chapter 5), I set out my reasons.

In his contribution to *Stich and His Critics* (Murphy and Bishop 2009), my friend Michael Devitt refers to me (approvingly, I think) as an "enfant terrible," and in a blurb on the back cover of that book my frequent collaborator, John Doris, calls me philosophy of mind's "provocateur-in-chief." I'm afraid I must plead guilty to these charges. I often find myself inclined to defend provocative positions, and part of the fun is that they *are* provocative. So in the early 1980s, while I was on the faculty at the University of Maryland, I decided to write a book setting out what I took to be the strongest case for eliminativism. Much to my amazement, that book, *From Folk Psychology to Cognitive Science* (1983), is still in print. While I was writing the book, the Parallel Distributed Processing (PDP) group at the University of California, San Diego, led by Dave Rumelhart and James McClelland, was developing connectionism—an important new way of thinking about computation in general and mental computation in particular. When I moved to

UCSD in 1986, I knew next to nothing about connectionism. But that changed very quickly, since the work of the PDP group was generating a great deal of intellectual excitement on campus and around the world. In discussions with Bill Ramsey, who was then a philosophy grad student, and Joey Garon, a gifted cognitive science undergraduate major, a new argument for eliminativism emerged, albeit a conditional one. It was, we thought, too early to say whether successful connectionist models could be built for important parts of the human memory or belief system. But if they could, eliminativism about propositional attitudes would turn out to be correct. The argument for that conditional is elaborated in "Connectionism, Eliminativism, and the Future of Folk Psychology" (chapter 6).

Defending eliminativism was great fun while it lasted. But the fun was brought to an end by that notorious spoilsport, William Lycan, who pointed out that even if it is true that commonsense psychology is mistaken, it does not follow that the mental states invoked by commonsense psychology do not exist. To get that conclusion, an additional premise is needed and, Lycan noted, the premise most often assumed by me and by other eliminativists was some version of a description theory of reference. That, however, is hardly an assumption that can be made without argument, since Putnam, Kripke, and others had offered and defended a quite different "causal-historical" picture of how reference works. And if that account of reference is correct, then the conclusion of the eliminativists' argument does not follow from their premises. So it looked like assessing the plausibility of the eliminativist argument would require determining which account of reference is the right one for commonsense psychological terms like 'belief' and 'desire.' Thinking about that question led me to a number of very surprising conclusions, some of which are almost as provocative as eliminativism itself.

The first step was to ask what counts as getting a theory of reference right. Though philosophers had rarely addressed that question explicitly, much of the literature suggested that the goal of the project was to describe a word-world relationship, call it R, that would capture people's (or perhaps just philosophers') *intuitions* about reference. Word-world relationships are just mappings, and there are endlessly many of them. Some (call them R* and R**) may differ just a smidgen from R; they map most terms to the same objects as R and depart from R in just a few cases. Others (R***, R****, etc.) depart from R in *lots* of cases. In "The Flight to Reference" (chapter 12), Mike Bishop and I argue that in order to invoke reference to fill the gap between the premises of the eliminativist argument and its conclusion, the reference relation will have to sustain "semantic assent"—it will have to make instances of the following schema true:

(x) Fx iff 'F___' refers to x.

But why should we think that R, the word-world mapping that happens to be most compatible with some group's intuitions, will do the trick? Or, to put the question in a different way, why should we think that the word-world mapping sanctioned by *reference intuitions* really is *reference*? In the title essay of *Deconstructing the Mind* (1996), which is an extended account of my disenchantment with eliminativism, I posed a rather complex and obscure version of this question and argued, even more obscurely I'm told, that there was no good answer to be had. A few years later, Mike Bishop and I collaborated on what we thought was a much clearer version of the argument. That's the central argument to be found in "The Flight to Reference."

The argument in "The Flight to Reference" makes no appeal to empirical findings about reference intuitions. All it needs is the obvious fact that no matter what word-world mapping, R, best captures "our" reference intuitions, there will be lots of other word-world mappings—some of them very similar to R, some not—that do less well at capturing our intuitions. But shortly after "The Flight to Reference" appeared, a remarkable idea began to gain currency in some philosophical circles. For many years, people working in the philosophy of mind, the philosophy of language, and various branches of the philosophy of science had been *consumers* of empirical findings. They read and cited the papers of colleagues who did empirical research, and explored the ways in which empirical findings might be relevant for a variety of philosophical claims. But there were obvious limits imposed by the fact that philosophers were consumers of empirical findings that others had reported. For our colleagues in other departments have their own priorities, shaped by the needs and interests of their own disciplines. And it was often the case that the empirical study that would be most useful in advancing some philosophical debate was a study that no one in another department was interested in doing. Frustrated by the fact that we could not persuade our busy psychologist colleagues to do the studies *we* wanted them to do, Shaun Nichols, Jonathan Weinberg, and I decided we would do them ourselves. Others, notably Joshua Green and Joshua Knobe at Princeton, made the same decision at about the same time. Thus it was that the experimental philosophy movement was born. The first studies that I had a hand in, in collaboration with Nichols and Weinberg, were aimed at determining whether there is demographic variation in epistemic intuitions. That's a topic I'll take up in the Introduction to the second volume of these essays. But soon enough someone suggested that we should also look at intuitions about reference. The result was "Semantics Cross-Cultural Style" (chapter 16) coauthored with Edouard Machery, Ron Mallon, and Shaun Nichols. What we found was that for one well-known philosophical thought experiment—Kripke's Gödel/Schmidt case—the intuitions of English-speaking subjects in New Jersey, whose cultural background was Western European, were significantly different from the intuitions of English-speaking Chinese subjects in Hong Kong. It is only a small study; much more remains to be done. But if the finding is robust, as some subsequent work suggests it is,[2] it leads to a new and important argument against the strategy that Bishop and I called "the flight to reference." For if the right theory of reference is the one

---

2. See Machery, Olivola, and de Blanc 2009; Machery 2011; Deutsch et al., in preparation.

that captures reference intuitions, and reference intuitions differ across cultures, then it looks like we'll have to accept different accounts of reference for people with different cultural backgrounds, even though they speak what is ordinarily thought to be the same language. The implications of this head-spinning idea are explored at some length in "Against Arguments from Reference" (chapter 17), coauthored with Mallon, Machery, and Nichols.

As I noted earlier, it was Lycan's challenge that initially prompted my disillusionment with eliminativism. But once the argument for eliminativism started to unravel, I began to see problems in lots of places. As Shaun Nichols and I note in "Folk Psychology" (chapter 15), Sellars's contention that ordinary mental state terms can be viewed as theoretical terms of a folk theory is a central idea in one version of functionalism in the philosophy of mind. It also plays a central role in most arguments both for and against eliminativism. However, as Ian Ravenscroft and I argue in "What *Is* Folk Psychology?" (chapter 11), there are a number of quite different ways to unpack the idea that there is a folk psychological theory associated with our commonsense capacity to use mental state terms. Moreover, on what is perhaps the most natural cluster of interpretations of this idea—the cluster that Ravenscroft and I call "internal accounts"—the eliminativists are making a risky bet about the way in which folk psychological information is stored in the mind. They are betting that it is stored in a system that consists (at least in part) in sentence-like principles or generalizations, or in a mental model or connectionist network that maps onto a set of propositions in a unique and well-motivated way. If the eliminativists lose this empirical bet, then their argument collapses right at the beginning. For if folk psychological information is not stored in sentence-like principles or in a mental model or connectionist network that maps onto a set of propositions in a unique and well-motivated way, then folk psychology *can't* turn out to be mistaken, since it's not the sort of thing that can be *either true or false*.

From its inception, cognitive science has been concerned to explain complex cognitive skills or capacities, like producing and understanding natural language, or playing a good game of chess. The explanatory strategy most frequently invoked in these projects is to assume that people's performance in these tasks is guided (at least in part) by an internalized body of information—a collection of rules and principles that provide a recipe or program for executing the skill in question. As Ravenscroft and I note, the "folk psychological capacity" to attribute mental states to others, to predict their behavior, and to explain their behavior by appeal to their mental states is yet another example of the sort of complex capacity that might be explained in this way. So, not surprisingly, many philosophers involved in the eliminativism debate assumed that this folk psychological capacity was subserved by a tacit theory, and starting in the mid-1980s, a growing number of psychologists adopted this "theory-theory" approach. However, at about the same time, philosophers Jane Heal, Robert Gordon, and Alvin Goldman suggested a quite different way in which our folk psychological capacities might be explained. Rather than relying on an internally represented, informationally rich, folk psychological theory, our folk psychological capacities might be explained by a process of off-line simulation in which we use our own psychology as a model for the psychology of the person whose behavior we are predicting or explaining. As the defenders of simulation theory were quick to point out, their theory has important implications for the eliminativism debate—implications that are similar to those that Ravenscroft and I noted for some connectionist and purely rule-based accounts of folk psychology. If simulation theory is correct, then our folk psychological capacities are not subserved by a tacit theory, thus they could not be subserved by a *false* tacit theory. And once again, it seems that the eliminativist argument is scuttled before it can get started. Of course, neither eliminativists nor their opponents need worry about this unless simulation theory *is* correct. Shaun Nichols and I were not much impressed by the case simulation theorists offered in their first attempts to defend their theory. "Folk Psychology: Simulation or Tacit Theory?" (chapter 9) is our critique of the early efforts to defend simulation theory.

This was, however, only the first exchange in a long and fruitful debate. In the years that followed, defenders of simulation theory offered new evidence and new arguments. Some of them, most notably Robert Gordon, continued to insist that a tacit theory played almost no role in explaining our folk psychological capacities. Alvin Goldman, on the other hand, allowed that theory might play some role in explaining our folk psychological skills, though he continued to put the "emphasis on the simulation component" (Goldman 2006, 21). Nichols and I also moved in the direction of a hybrid account, though we continue to believe that there are quite central aspects of our folk psychological (or "mindreading") skills that can't be explained by simulation. We make the case for this in "Folk Psychology" (chapter 15) and elaborate on the theme in our book, *Mindreading* (2003).

The first premise in the eliminativists' argument is that commonsense mental states like beliefs and desires can be viewed as posits of a commonsense theory, and that terms like 'belief' and 'desire' can be viewed as theoretical terms in this folk theory. The second premise is that folk psychology is a seriously mistaken theory. In my ongoing reassessment of the case for eliminativism, after Lycan woke me from my dogmatic slumbers, I came to think that some of the arguments aimed at establishing the second premise were much more problematic than I had once thought. According to Jerry Fodor, "the deepest motivation for intentional irrealism [the view that intentional states don't exist] derives . . . from a certain ontological intuition: that there is no place for intentional categories in a physicalistic view of the world; that the intentional can't be *naturalized*." (Fodor 1987, 97) Though at one time I think I shared that intuition, I became increasingly skeptical. In the philosophical literature at that time, there was no shortage of attempts to "naturalize" the intentional. But, as Stephen Laurence and I argue in "Intentionality and Naturalism" (chapter 10), these projects appear to endorse a variety of quite different views about what is required to "naturalize intentional categories." Moreover, on most of these accounts, the fact—if it is a fact—that intentional categories cannot be naturalized would be no cause for alarm, since there is no reason to think that intentional irrealism, or anything else that's worth worrying about, would follow. There is one exception to this, one account of naturalizing on which, if it turns out that intentional categories cannot be naturalized, alarming consequences would indeed follow. But, Laurence and I argue, if *that* is what naturalizing comes to, then there is not the slightest reason to think that the intentional can't be naturalized.

THE NATURE AND THE PHILOSOPHICAL IMPLICATIONS OF COGNITIVE SCIENCE

I noted earlier that much of the work in this volume is situated in two important streams of philosophical reflection. In the first of these streams, the viability of commonsense psychology is the central issue. That one is a stream with many important sources. In the second stream, the focus is on the philosophical implications of research in cognitive science that, in the last half century, has transformed both our understanding of the mind and the ways in which the mind is studied. While many people have contributed to this line of philosophical inquiry, it is the work of Noam Chomsky that got it started. I first encountered that work in 1965 when, as a graduate student at Princeton, I received an unexpected letter. Chomsky was going to give the Christian Gauss Lectures at Princeton, the letter announced, attendance was by invitation only, and I was invited. It was, to put it mildly, a surprising invitation, since I had barely heard of Chomsky and knew next to nothing about his work. Indeed, I have long suspected that the invitation was the result of a clerical error. But if so, it was an error that changed my life. The lectures were spellbinding. In a confident, almost nonchalant style, Chomsky set out some of the basic ideas and findings of the new "transformational generative grammar" that he had been developing and then, amazingly, went on to argue that from the facts about the grammar of English and a few other languages we could make a plausible case that the human mind was chockablock with innate ideas and innate knowledge. Contrary to what just about every philosopher I had ever met believed at that time, Chomsky argued that Plato, Descartes, and Leibniz were right about the mind, and that Locke, Hume, and the Logical Positivists were wrong! Though I had come to Princeton thinking that I would write a dissertation on some current issue in the philosophy of science—explanation, perhaps, or confirmation—by the time the Gauss Lectures were over, I had changed my mind. What I wanted to do was understand how this new science that Chomsky was creating worked and grapple with his astounding claim that it could resolve a debate that had been central to philosophy since antiquity.

The first step was to say, as clearly and explicitly as I could, what the goals of generative grammar are, what claims generative grammatical theories make, and what evidence is used to support those claims. "Grammar, Psychology, and Indeterminacy" (chapter 1) was my first attempt to do this. I thought long and hard about whether to include that paper in this collection because, while many of the papers in this volume contain claims or arguments that I would no longer endorse without qualifications, the blooper in "Grammar, Psychology, and Indeterminacy" is a doozy. When I wrote that paper,[3] I and many other philosophers were skeptical about the idea of invoking internal representations in psychological theories. Though there was, no doubt, a variety of reasons for this skepticism, the most persuasive, at least for me, was the concern that theories invoking internal representations made no explanatory progress, since representations need to be interpreted, and that required a homunculus to do the interpreting. But in a pair of important and influential papers, Jerry Fodor (1968) and Dan Dennett (1978) argued that positing a homunculus was a problem only if the homunculus was as intelligent as the agent whose behavior was being explained. If the intelligent behavior of an agent could be explained by invoking stupid homunculi, progress was being made. And we could make further progress by positing even dumber homunculi to explain how the first level of stupid homunculi did their work. I found Dennett's version of this picture particularly compelling since he pointed out that this was exactly what was being done, rather impressively, in the emerging field of artificial intelligence, where the process comes to an end with homunculi that are so stupid that they can be replaced by a simple machine, like an and-gate or an or-gate. Dennett went on to argue that this was also an excellent strategy for psychology—a strategy that was being actively pursued by a growing cohort of psychologists who would come to identify themselves as "cognitive scientists." Ultimately, I decided that there is enough of interest in "Grammar, Psychology, and Indeterminacy" to justify its inclusion in this collection. But please take the stuff on internal representation with a *big* grain of salt.

The next task was to understand just what was being claimed by theorists, like Plato, Descartes, and Chomsky, who claimed that a great deal of knowledge is *innate*. In "The Idea of Innateness" (chapter 2), I offered two tentative analyses, one inspired by Descartes, the other by Plato. But in the years that followed, many philosophers argued that neither of my accounts succeeded in capturing either the commonsense notion of innateness or the notion that was being invoked by Chomsky and the growing group of empirical researchers inspired by him who were uncovering remarkable facts about our innate cognitive endowment. In a recent paper, Fiona Cowie (2009) offers a brief overview of the literature aimed at analyzing the concept of innateness that emerged after my early efforts, and reports that there are now twenty-five accounts, *all* of which fall victim to fairly compelling counter-examples. In light of this, some philosophers, most notably Paul Griffiths (2002), have argued that we should simply jettison the notion of innateness and replace it with more scientifically respectable concepts like canalization, species typicality and adaptation. Though I definitely saw the appeal of Griffiths's proposal, I could never quite bring myself to adopt it, and Cowie, rightly, sees a puzzle lurking here.

---

3. Though it was published in 1972, the paper was written in 1967.

Normally not one to pass up the opportunity to hound treasured 'folk' notions (like belief, truth and rationality), Stich has nonetheless remained a champion of the innate—not in the sense that he has explicitly defended any particular nativist thesis, but in the sense that he seems quite committed to the concept's remaining part of the discourse of cognitive science. He has sponsored conferences on innateness, and edited books on innateness . . . , and written influential papers exploring the boundaries of the concept. . . . (2002, 75)

One of those papers is "Connectionism and Three Levels of Nativism" (chapter 7) in which Bill Ramsey and I explore, and ultimately reject, the widespread view that connectionism poses a fundamental challenge for nativist views like Chomsky's. As for Cowie's puzzle, well, I had no good justification for resisting Griffiths's proposal. But fortunately Cowie has provided one. In her insightful and important paper she argues

[F]irst, that it is quite common in science for investigators to continue using concepts that everyone knows to be inadequate—ambiguous, vague, incomplete, perhaps even incoherent. . . . [S]econdly, that this practice seems de facto to be part and parcel of the development of new, better ways of conceiving the world. . . . [T]hird, that there are philosophical (not just historical) reasons to expect this to be the case. (2002, 90)

The lesson she draws from this is that "it is a bad idea on both pragmatic and philosophical grounds to eliminate bad concepts—like 'innateness'—until better ones are found" and that "one's philosophical prudishness should give way to vulgar pragmatism" (2002, 90, 97). Thanks, Fiona. I couldn't agree more!

Like many others whose thinking was indelibly influenced by Chomsky, my interest in the cognitive processes underlying language use and language acquisition led to a curiosity about the cognitive mechanisms subserving other aspects of cognition. My first foray into cognition beyond language was "Beliefs and Subdoxastic States" (chapter 3) in which I drew attention to an important distinction between two sorts of contentful psychological states, a distinction that, I argued, much of cognitive psychology had been neglecting. The notion of "subdoxastic states" that I develop in the paper was a precursor of Fodor's enormously influential notion of a mental module.[4] Other papers, which explore the cognitive processes underlying reasoning and moral judgment, will be included in the second volume of these essays.

In the last decade of the twentieth century, Chomsky's nativism and Fodor's notion of modularity (or something like it) were taken on board by a group of psychologists and anthropologists who had been deeply influenced by the style of evolutionary thinking that E. O. Wilson and other sociobiologists had popularized—and made very controversial—two decades earlier. The result was the sort of "evolutionary psychology"

4. Fodor (1983, 88 ff).

championed by Leda Cosmides, John Tooby, Steven Pinker, and many others. It was widely thought that evolutionary psychology is at odds with even the sensible strands of social constructionist thinking about human kinds. But Ron Mallon and I thought otherwise. In the debate over the nature of emotions, what looks like a clash of empirical theories, we thought, is actually a philosophical dispute about the reference of ordinary terms for emotions. Once this is recognized, it is easy to see how, with a bit of technical terminology, both evolutionary psychologists and social constructionists can say everything they really want to say; their theories are complementary rather than incompatible. The argument for this view, which provoked a fair amount of ire from *both* social constructionists and evolutionary psychologists, is set out in "The Odd Couple: The Compatibility of Social Construction and Evolutionary Psychology" (chapter 13).

Though evolutionary psychology is primarily concerned with normal psychological phenomena like perception, social exchange, mate choice, and gender roles, some theorists believe that it also offers insight into psychopathologies of various sorts. In "Darwin in the Madhouse" (chapter 14), Dominic Murphy and I argue that taking evolutionary perspective may be useful in thinking about the vexed question of how mental disorders should be classified. Indeed, from this perspective, it looks like some conditions that are currently classified as disorders may not be disorders at all.

This completes my brief guide to what the reader will find in the pages that follow. It remains to say something about authorship. Though it is my name that appears on the title page, nine other authors have contributed to one or more of these papers. In every case, our collaborations began when my coauthors were my students. But in many cases, they have continued right up to the present. I have been enormously fortunate to have had the opportunity to work with, and learn from, these exceptionally gifted, enthusiastic and productive younger scholars, and even more fortunate to have them as friends.

REFERENCES

Cowie, F. 2009. Why isn't Stich an ElimiNativist? In *Stich and his critics*, ed. D. Murphy and M. Bishop, 74–100. Chichester, UK: Wiley-Blackwell.

Dennett, D. 1978. Artificial Intelligence as philosophy and psychology. In *Brainstorms*. Cambridge, MA: Bradford Books / MIT Press.

Deutsch, M., C. Carroll, J. Sytsma, and E. Machery. In preparation. Speaker's reference and cross-cultural semantics.

Fodor, J. 1968. The appeal to tacit knowledge in psychological explanation. *Journal of Philosophy*, 65.

Fodor, J. 1983. *The modularity of mind*. Cambridge, MA: Bradford Books / MIT Press.

Fodor, J. 1987. *Psychosemantics*. Cambridge, MA: Bradford Books / MIT Press.

Goldman, A. 2006. *Simulating minds: The philosophy, psychology, and neuroscience of mindreading*. New York: Oxford University Press.

Griffiths, P. 2002. What is innateness? *The Monist* 85, no. 1: 70–85.

Kripke, S. 1972. Naming and necessity. In *Semantics of natural language*, ed. D. Davidson and G. Harman, 253–355. Dordrecht, The Netherlands: Reidel.

Machery, E. 2011. Variation in intuitions about reference and ontological disagreements. In *A companion to relativism*, ed. S. D. Hales. New York: Blackwell.

Machery, E., C. Y. Olivola, and M. de Blanc. 2009. Linguistic and metalinguistic intuitions in the philosophy of language. *Analysis* 69: 689–694.

Murphy, D., and M. Bishop, eds. 2009. *Stich and his critics*. Chichester, UK: Wiley-Blackwell.

Putnam, H. 1975. The meaning of "meaning." In *Language, Mind, and Knowledge*, edited by K. Gunderson. Vol. 7 of *Minnesota Studies in the Philosophy of Science*, ed. H. Feigl and G. Maxwell. Minneapolis: University of Minnesota Press.

Quine, W. V. 1956. Quantifiers and propositional attitudes. *Journal of Philosophy* 53, no. 5: 177–187.

Sellars, W. 1956. Empiricism and the philosophy of mind. In *The foundations of science and the concepts of psychology and psychoanalysis*, edited by H. Feigl and M. Scriven. Vol. 1 of *Minnesota studies in the philosophy of science*, 253–329. Minneapolis: University of Minnesota Press.

Stich, S. 1983. *From folk psychology to cognitive science*. Cambridge, MA: Bradford Books / MIT Press.

Stich, S. 1996. *Deconstructing the mind*. New York: Oxford University Press.

COLLECTED PAPERS, VOLUME 1: MIND AND LANGUAGE, 1972–2010

> Significance is the trait with respect to which
> the subject matter of linguistics is studied
> by the grammarian.
> Pending a satisfactory explanation of the
> notion of meaning, linguists in semantic
> fields are in the position of not knowing
> what they are talking about.
>
> —W. V. QUINE

1

GRAMMAR, PSYCHOLOGY, AND INDETERMINACY

ACCORDING TO QUINE, the linguist qua grammarian does not know what he is talking about. The goal of this essay is to tell him. My aim is to provide an account of what the grammarian is saying of an expression when he says it is grammatical, or a noun phrase, or ambiguous, or the subject of a certain sentence. More generally, I want to give an account of the nature of a generative grammatical theory of a language—of the data for such a theory, the relation between the theory and the data, and the relation between the theory and a speaker of the language.

I

Prominent among a linguist's pronouncements are attributions of grammaticality. What are we saying about a sentence when we say it is grammatical? One strategy for answering this question is to attend to the work of the grammarian. To be grammatical, a sentence must have those characteristics which the grammarian seeks in deciding whether a sentence is grammatical. So a reconstruction of the grammarian's work is a likely path to an explication of 'grammatical.' This is the strategy adopted by Quine,[1] and it will be of value to study his remarks in some detail. On Quine's account, *significance* rather than *grammaticality* "is the trait with respect to which the subject matter of linguistics is studied by the grammarian" (48). If the two are different, there is some inclination to take

---

1. *From a Logical Point of View*, 2d ed., revised (New York: Harper & Row, 1963), essay III.

the grammarian at his name. So let us see what can be learned by taking Quine's proposal as an explication of *grammaticality*.

The problem for the grammarian may be posed as the segregating of a class K of sequences that we will call *grammatical*. On Quine's view, he attends to four nested classes of sequences, H, I, J, and K.

> H is the class of observed sequences, excluding any which are ruled inappropriate in the sense of being non-linguistic or belonging to alien dialects. I is the class of all such observed sequences and all that ever will happen to be professionally observed, excluding again those which are ruled inappropriate. J is the class of all sequences ever occurring, now or in the past or future, within or without professional observation—excluding, again, only those which are ruled inappropriate. K, finally, is the infinite class of all those sequences, with the exclusion of the inappropriate ones as usual, which *could* be uttered without bizarreness reactions. K is the class which the grammarian wants to approximate *in* his formal reconstruction (53).

The linguist's data are H, and he checks his predictions against I minus H hoping that this will be a representative sample of J. It is when we come to K that philosophical eyebrows are raised; for what is the force of the 'could' which extends the class beyond J, commonly infinitely beyond? Quine's answer is that, besides H and future checks against I, the 'could' is the reflection of the scientist's appeal to simplicity. "Our basis for saying what 'could' be generally consists . . . in what *is* plus simplicity of the laws whereby we describe and extrapolate what is" (54).

Quine's proposal shares with other operational definitions the virtue of objectivity. Yet his solution is beset with problems. For Quine's procedure just does not pick out anything like the class we would pre-systematically hold to be grammatical—and this because his account fails to portray what the grammarian *actually does*. To see this, consider the case of a Quinean linguist ignorant of English setting out to segregate grammatical English sequences. He starts with H, the class of sequences he observes. But H, in addition to samples of what we would pre-systematically hold to be grammatical sequences, contains all manner of false starts, "lost thoughts," peculiar pauses ('aahhhh'!) and, unless he is uncommonly fortunate, a liberal sprinkling of blatantly incoherent speech. Yet Quine, if we take him literally, would have H included as a subset of K. What the resulting projection might be is hard to imagine. But K, so constructed, would not be the class of grammatical sequences in English.

It might be thought that, appealing to simplicity, the linguist could toss out an occasional member of H, much as he excludes from H what he takes to be nonlinguistic noise or intrusion from another tongue. But an hour spent attending carefully to unreflective speech will dispel this notion. There is simply too much to exclude.[2]

---

2. Much the same point is made by Jerrold Katz and Jerry Fodor in "What's Wrong with the Philosophy of Language?," *Inquiry*, v (1962): 197–237.

Quine succeeds in muddying the waters a bit by sprinkling the restriction that the sentences to be studied are those which could be uttered "without bizarreness reactions." It is not clear whether he takes such sentences to be excluded from *H* and *I* by virtue of their being observed *in situ* or whether he would have *H* and *I* further filtered. But it seems clear that, in either case, either this move is inadequate or it begs the question. If by 'bizarreness' Quine means *bizarreness*, then the exclusion will hardly accomplish his purpose. For many sorts of sequences that we would want to exclude from *K* (those with 'aahhh's' interspersed, for example, or those which change subject mid-sentence) are uttered all the time without bizarreness reactions. And many sentences we would want to include in *K* would surely evoke the strongest of bizarreness reactions. Indeed, though *K* will be infinite, only members of a finite subset could be uttered without evoking a bizarreness reaction. Sentences that take more than six months to utter are bizarre. If, however, the reaction Quine has in mind is the reaction (whatever it may be) characteristically displayed when an ungrammatical sequence is uttered, then, until he has provided some account of how this reaction is to be recognized, he has begged the question.[3]

II

Taking Quine's proposal as an explication of grammaticality has led to an impasse. In seeking our way around it we might do well to return to Quine's original insight and attend more closely to what the grammarian actually does. From the first, the generative grammarian has relied heavily on the fact that, with a modicum of instruction, speakers can be brought to make all manner of judgments about their language. In particular, they can be brought to make firm judgments on the oddness or acceptability of indefinitely many sequences. Provided with a few examples, speakers can go on to judge new sequences in point of grammaticality, and do so with considerable consistency for large numbers of cases. This suggests that we might try to remedy the difficulties with Quine's proposal by substituting *intuitive judgments* for observed utterances. On the revised account, *H* would be the class of those sequences which to date have been considered and judged to be grammatical. *I* would be the class of sequences ever reflected upon and judged clearly grammatical. And *K* is the infinite class projected along simplest lines from *H* and checked against *I*.

This modified account nicely circumvents the major shortcoming we found in Quine's proposal. Read literally, Quine's method did not pick out the class of sequences we would pre-systematically call grammatical. The class *H* on which his projection was based

---

3. Significance is likely a more inclusive notion than grammaticality, more liberal in the constructions it will allow and tolerating a richer sprinkling of 'aahhh's,' 'I mean's,' and 'you know's.' Thus perhaps Quine's proposal does rather better when taken as advertised. But whatever its interest, significance as characterized by Quine is not the property studied by grammarians of a generative bent.

was already tainted with ungrammatical sequences. Our modified version avoids this difficulty by basing its projection on sequences intuitively taken to be grammatical. The projected class K can still miss the mark, failing to be compatible with I minus H. But this potential failure is the normal inductive one.[4]

We can now make a plausible first pass at depicting the grammarian's work. He proceeds by eliciting intuitive judgments about which sequences are in the informant's language and which are not. He then projects these clear cases along simplest lines, checking his projected class against speakers' intuitions. Thus the task of the generative grammarian may be viewed as that of constructing a system of rules and a definition of 'generate' that define a terminal language containing phonetic representations for all the sequences judged by speakers to be clearly acceptable and containing no sequence judged to be clearly unacceptable. The sequences about which speakers have no firm or consistent intuitions can be relegated to the class of "don't cares" and decided by the simplest grammar that handles the clear cases.

Yet as it stands the account still will not do. One fault is its myopic concentration on intuitions. Speakers' judgments about acceptability are the most important data for the grammarian. But they are not his only data, nor are they immune from being corrected or ignored. The attentive grammarian will attend to many aspects of his subjects' behavior in addition to their response to questions about sentences' acceptability. And a proper explication of the grammarian's job must provide some account of the role these additional data play.

Perhaps the most important sort of evidence for the grammarian besides intuitions of acceptability is the actual unreflective speech of his subjects. An informant's protest that a given sequence is unacceptable may be ignored if he is caught in the act, regularly uttering unpremeditatedly what, on meditation, he alleges he doesn't say. In addition to actual speech, there is a host of further clues for the grammarian. Stress patterns, facts about how sentences are heard and data on short-term verbal recall are among them.[5] Others might be mentioned. To what use does the grammarian put this further evidence? Principally, I suggest, to shore up the evidence provided by speakers' intuitive judgments or to justify his neglect of them. A sentence whose acceptability to speakers is in some doubt will, with good conscience, be generated by a grammar if it ranks high in the other tests. And, on the other side, a sentence that has the blessings of speakers may be rejected—not generated by the grammar—if it fails to display the other characteristics of grammatical sequences.

We now have one justification the grammarian may use for rejecting speakers' intuitions. There is another. And consideration of it will lead to a fundamental revision of our

---

4. Note that Quine's "bizarreness reactions" could be taken as negative judgments when the subject is queried about a sequence's acceptability. If this is Quine's intention, his proposal and the present account converge.

5. Cf. George A. Miller and Stephen Isard, "Some Perceptual Consequences of Linguistic Rules," *Journal of Verbal Learning and Verbal Behavior*, II (1963): 217–228.

account of grammaticality. Intuitive oddness may be explained by many factors. Some sentences seem odd because they are pragmatically odd, describing a situation that is bizarre. Others, perhaps, may be rejected as obscene or taboo. Most importantly, sentences may seem odd because they are simply too long and complicated. If the grammarian suspects that any of these factors explain speakers' rejection of a sentence, he may classify it as grammatical *even though it lacks all the characteristics in the cluster associated with grammaticality.*

Note that at this juncture two notions we have been conflating part company. Thus far I have been interchanging 'acceptability' and 'grammaticality' with studied equivocation. Intuitions of acceptability and the cluster of further characteristics usually accompanying sentences judged acceptable have been taken as (more or less) necessary and sufficient conditions for grammaticality. But the picture changes when a sentence may be classed as grammatical in spite of failing each relevant test. The motivation for separating acceptability and grammaticality is *broad theoretic simplicity*. It is simpler to generate an infinite class including the acceptable sentences than it is to draw a boundary around just those sentences which rank high in the several tests for acceptability. But in thus choosing the simpler task we must assume that some further theory or theories will account for those grammatical sentences which are unacceptable. And we must also assume that the new theory combined with a grammatical theory will together be simpler than any theory attempting directly to generate all and only the acceptable sequences. In short, we are venturing that the best theory to account for *all* the data will include a grammar of infinite generative capacity. This is hardly a step to be taken lightly. For in allowing his grammar to generate an infinite number of sentences, the grammarian is countenancing as grammatical an infinite number of sentences that fail each test of acceptability. It might be thought that such prodigality could be avoided by simply cutting off the class of sentences generated by a grammar at an appropriately high point. But this is not the case. For there is no natural point to draw the line—no point at which the addition of another conjunct or another clause regularly changes a clearly acceptable sentence into a clearly unacceptable one. Nor would it do to pick an *arbitrary* high cut-off point. This would leave the grammarian as before with generated sentences that are unacceptable. And any account of *why* these sentences were unacceptable would likely also account for the sequences beyond the arbitrary cut-off point.

By now it is evident that grammaticality is best viewed as a *theoretical* notion. Like other theoretical notions, it is related to relevant data in several and complex ways. Simple grammatical sentences generally have several or all of the cluster of characteristics typical of acceptable sequences. More complex grammatical sentences may share none of these characteristics. They are grammatical in virtue of being generated by the grammar that most simply generates all the clearly acceptable sentences and holds the best promise of fitting into a simple total theory of acceptability.

There is, thus, a conjecture built into a proposed grammar—the conjecture that this generative system will fit comfortably into a total theory that accounts for all the data.

In this respect a grammar is similar to the theory of ideal gases. The ideal-gas laws do a good job at predicting the behavior of light gases at high temperatures and low pressures. In less favorable cases, the laws predict poorly. They were acceptable in the hope, later fulfilled, that further laws could be found to explain the difference between the behavior of real gases and the predicted behavior of ideal ones. The adoption of a given grammar or form of grammar might be viewed as setting up a "paradigm"[6] or framework for future investigation. The grammar serves to divide those phenomena still needing explanation (viz., unacceptable grammatical sequences) from those already adequately handled.

In our portrait of the grammarian's job, the emphasis has shifted from the concept of grammaticality to the notion of a correct grammar. A sequence is grammatical if and only if it is generated by a correct grammar for the language in question. And a grammar is correct only if it excels in the virtues lately adumbrated. But there are higher virtues to which a grammar may aspire, and more data to be reckoned with. So far we have taken into account data about speakers' intuitions of acceptability and data about a cluster of further characteristics common among acceptable sequences. But we have hardly exhausted the speaker's intuitions about matters linguistic. There is a host of other properties of sentences and their parts about which speakers have firm intuitions. With a bit of training speakers can judge pairs of sentences to be related as active and passive, or as affirmative and negative. They can pick out parts of speech, detect subjects and objects, and spot syntactic ambiguities. The list of these grammatical intuitions could easily be extended. A grammatical theory will not only try to specify which sequences are acceptable; it will also try to specify the grammatical properties and relations of sentences as intuited by speakers. As in the case of intuitions of acceptability, the grammatical theory will be expected to agree with grammatical intuitions only for relatively short and simple sentences. The theory is an idealization, and, as before, we permit it to deviate from the intuited data in the expectation that further theory will account for the differences.

III

It might seem our job is finished. We set ourselves to giving an account of the grammarian's doings in building a grammar, and this we have done. But the reader conversant with competing accounts[7] will expect more. For, commonly, such accounts go on to talk of

---

6. In a sense that may be intended by T. S. Kuhn, *The Structure of Scientific Revolutions* (Chicago: University Press, 1962).

7. For example, those in Noam Chomsky, "Current Issues in Linguistic Theory," in Fodor and Katz, eds., *The Structure of Language* (Englewood Cliffs, N.J.: Prentice-Hall, 1964); in Chomsky, *Aspects of the Theory of Syntax* (Cambridge, Mass.: MIT Press, 1965), ch. 1; and Katz, *The Philosophy of Language* (New York: Harper & Row, 1966).

linguistic theory, acquisition models, evaluation measures and other notions related to the question of how a speaker acquires his grammar. Moreover the discussion of these notions is not a simple addition to the account of the grammarian's work in constructing a grammar. Rather it is an intrinsic part of that account. Yet why this is so is far from obvious. Constructing a theory of grammar acquisition is surely a fascinating project and one which would naturally catch a grammarian's eye. But, at first blush at least, it would seem to be a new project, largely distinct from the job of constructing grammars for individual languages. Why, then, do Chomsky and others view the study of acquisition as intrinsic to the construction of grammars for individual languages? This is the riddle that will occupy us in the present section. In the course of untangling it we will come upon some unexpected facts about grammar and its place among the sciences.

Let me begin with a puzzle. A grammar of English will generate structural descriptions for English sentences in the form of phrase markers or labeled bracketings. The labels on these brackets will be the familiar NP, VP etc. But now imagine a perverse variant of our grammar created by systematically interchanging the symbols NP and VP throughout the theory. If the change is thoroughgoing (made in all appropriate generative rules and definitions), then presumably the original theory and the variant will make exactly the same predictions about intuitions, etc. So the two would appear to be empirically indistinguishable. On what basis, then, are we to select one over the other?

To underscore the puzzle, consider a grammarian attending to the hitherto neglected tongue of some appropriately exploited and unlettered people. His grammar will likely end up generating labeled bracketings among whose labels are the familiar NP and VP. But what justification can there be for this grammar as constrasted with a variant interchanging NP and VP throughout, or yet another variant in which NP and VP are systematically replaced with a pair of symbols that occur nowhere in any grammar of English?[8]

There is a related puzzle that focuses not on the vocabulary of a grammar but on its rules. Consider any grammar or fragment of a grammar for English. With the grammar at hand it requires only modest ingenuity to produce a variant set of rules and definitions whose consequences (the entailed claims about grammaticality, grammatical relations and the rest) are identical with those of the original. Among the variants that might be produced some will differ only trivially, adding a superfluous rule perhaps, or capturing a generalization in two rules rather than one. But other variants exist which differ quite radically from the original.[9] A grammar is but an axiomatized theory, and it is a truism that a theory that can be axiomatized at all can be axiomatized in radically different ways. Yet each of these variants makes identical claims about the grammarian's data—not only the data on hand, but *all* the data he might acquire. They may, of course, predict

---

8. Much the same puzzle is hinted at by Quine in "Methodological Reflections on Current Linguistic Theory," *Synthese*, XXI, 3/4 (October 1970): 386–398, pp. 390 ff.

9. Such variants often require considerable effort to construct. Nor is it always a trivial matter to prove the equivalence of a pair of grammars.

incorrectly on a given point; but if one variant predicts incorrectly they all will. How then is the grammarian to decide among them?

The point of these puzzles is that grammar is afflicted with an embarrassment of riches. It is a task demanding wit and perseverance to construct a grammar that correctly captures a broad range of speakers' intuitions. Yet when the job has been done there are indefinitely many variants each of which captures the known intuitions equally well and predicts unprobed intuitions equally well (or poorly). Somehow the grammarian does come up with a single theory. What principle can he use to guide his choice?

It is in attempting to answer this question that the study of acquisition looms large in Chomsky's writings. But exactly how a theory of grammar acquisition is supposed to motivate a choice among alternative grammars is far from clear. Part of the obscurity, I suspect, stems from the fact that Chomsky, perhaps without realizing it, pursues two rather different strategies in relating the study of acquisition to the problem of choosing among alternative grammars. One of these strategies, I will contend, is thoroughly misguided and rests on a mistaken picture of what grammar is. The other is quite compatible with the account of grammar developed above and suggests an illuminating solution to the puzzles of alternative grammars. Our first project will be to dissect out these alternatives for closer inspection.

Before we begin, some terminology will be helpful. Let us call a grammar *descriptively adequate* for a given language if it correctly captures the intuitions of the speakers of the language (and the rest of the grammarian's data) within the limits of accuracy allowed by idealization. The grammarian's embarrassment of riches arises from the fact that for each descriptively adequate grammar of a language there are indefinitely many alternatives all of which are also descriptively adequate.

Now the strategy I would disparage unfolds like this:[10] When a child learns a language, he learns a descriptively adequate grammar *(dag)*. He somehow "internally represents" the rules of the grammar. So if we could discover which set of rules the child has "internalized" we would be able to choose a right one from among the *dags* of the child's language. The right one is simply that grammar which the child has in fact internally represented. The study of acquisition will be designed to give us a lead on which descriptively adequate grammar the child has learned.

Let us reflect on what the child must do to acquire his grammar. The learner is exposed to what Chomsky calls *primary linguistic data (pld)* which "include examples of linguistic performance that are taken to be well formed sentences, and may include also examples designated as non-sentences, and no doubt much other information of the sort that is required for language learning, whatever this may be" (*ibid.*, p. 25). When he has succeeded in learning his language the child will have internalized a *dag*. In two rather

---

10. I think this strategy is often suggested by what Chomsky says (e.g., in *Aspects of the Theory of Syntax*, pp. 24–27 and elsewhere). But my concern here is to scotch the view, not to fix the blame. So I will not bother to document details of its parentage.

different ways this grammar will specify more information about the language than is to be gleaned from the *pld*. First, the *pld* contain a modest sample of the grammatical sentences of the language; the grammar acquired generates all the grammatical sentences. Second, the *pld* contain little or no information about the structural descriptions of sentences and the grammatical relations among them; the grammar assigns structural descriptions to each grammatical sentence and entails all the appropriate facts about grammatical relations. Thus a theory of grammar acquisition must explain how the child can acquire and internalize a grammar that is significantly more informative about the sentences of the language than the *pld* he has been exposed to.

How might we build a theory that accounts for the child's accomplishment? What we seek is a model (or function) which, when given a complete account of the *pld* available to the child as input (or argument), will produce, as output (or value), the *dag* that the child acquires. Our problem is to design the model with sufficient structure so that it can correctly project from the limited *pld* to the full grammar of the language from which the data are drawn. What sort of information should the model contain?

Suppose it were discovered that certain features were shared by all known *dags*. If the grammars that shared the features were sufficiently numerous and diverse we might reasonably hypothesize that these features were universal among *dags* of natural language. We would, in effect, be hypothesizing that there is a restricted set of grammars that humans can in fact learn (in the normal way). Were such universal features to be found, our strategy suggests that we take account of them in our acquisition model. Since the output of the model must be a *dag*, we would want to build our model in such a way that the possible outputs (the range of the acquisition function) each had the features that were universal to all *dags*. We would thus take the specification of universal features to define the class of *humanly possible grammars (hpgs)*. The task of the acquisition model is to discover the correct grammar, the grammar of the language the child is actually exposed to, from among the humanly possible grammars.

There is great gain for the builder of an acquisition theory in discovering as rich a set of universal features as possible. For the stronger the restrictions on the *hpgs*, the smaller the class of such grammars will be. Thus the easier the task relegated to the other parts of the model. What remains for the rest of the model is to compare the *pld* with the class of *hpgs* and exclude those possible grammars which are incompatible with the data.

Now it might happen that the universal features we discover so narrow down the class of *hpgs* that only one *hpg* is compatible with the *pld*.[11] If this is commonly the case, our acquisition theory need contain only a specification of *hpgs* and a device for excluding those *hpgs* which are incompatible with the *pld*. If, however, there are several *hpgs* compatible with all the data the child has accumulated by the time acquisition is essentially complete, we will have to seek some further principle of selection. The principle, the

---

11. Chomsky suggests this possibility, *ibid.*, pp. 36–37.

strategy suggests, is to be found in an evaluation measure or weighting of *hpgs*. Some of the *hpgs* that are compatible with all the *pld* will still fail to be descriptively adequate for the child's language. Some of these may simply project incorrectly beyond the sample of the language available to the child. They will then classify as grammatical sequences that are not grammatical. Others, while projecting correctly, may miss the mark on structural descriptions or grammatical relations, specifying that sentences are related in ways other than the ways speakers in fact intuit them to be related. So what we seek in our evaluation measure is some ranking of *hpgs* that has the following property: when we exclude from the *hpgs* those grammars which are incompatible with the *pld*, the highest ranked of the *remaining* grammars is a descriptively adequate grammar of the language the child acquires. The acquisition model would then proceed by first eliminating those *hpgs* which are not compatible with the *pld*, then selecting from among those which remain the one that is highest ranked. The grammar selected is unique among *dags*, for it is chosen by a model that explains how a child might go about acquiring the grammar he does acquire. It is this "explanatorily adequate" grammar which the child actually internalizes and which the linguist seeks to uncover.

A more detailed account of the strategy we are sketching might now go on to worry about how the appropriate evaluation measure could be discovered or what we can say about linguistic universals in the light of present knowledge. But this will not be our course. For I think we have said enough to see that the strategy is wholly wrongheaded. To begin, let us consider the possibility, mentioned briefly a paragraph back, that the universals so constrict the class of *hpgs* that only one *hpg* will be compatible with the *pld*. A moment's reflection will reveal that this is not a real possibility at all. For recall the pair of puzzles that initially prodded our interest in acquisition models. Each puzzle pointed to the superabundance of descriptively adequate grammars for any natural language. For every *dag* there are alternatives which are also descriptively adequate. But the linguistic universals were taken to be properties of all *dags*.[12] Thus each *dag* for every natural language will be among the *hpgs*. So if any *dag* is compatible with the *pld*, all its alternatives will be as well. And we have made no progress at selecting a single *dag* as the right one.

What is more, the hunt for an evaluation measure is of no real value in narrowing down the class of *dags*. The job that was set for the evaluation measure was not a trivial one. Given any body of *pld*, the evaluation measure had to rank as highest among the *hpgs* which are compatible with the *pld* a *dag* of the language from which the data are drawn. Finding such a measure would likely be a task of considerable difficulty. But, and this is

---

12. It is essential that the linguistic universals be taken as the properties common to each descriptively adequate grammar of every natural language. An alternative notion that took the linguistic universals as the features common to each of the actually internalized grammars of every natural language would be useless in the present context, since our project is to discover which among the *dags* of a given language is internalized. And until we *know* which grammars are internalized we cannot discover which features are universal to such grammars.

the crucial point, once such a measure *has* been found there will be indefinitely many alternative measures which select different *dags* for the same body of *pld*. If the sub-class of *hpgs* compatible with a given body of *pld* contains *one dag* of the language of which the data are a sample, it will contain many. Thus if we can design a measure which ranks any one of these *dags* highest in the sub-class, there will be another measure which ranks a different *dag* highest.[13] But whatever justification there is for holding the *dag* selected by one measure to be the grammar actually internalized is equally justification for holding that the other is. And we are back where we started, with too many *dags* each with equal claim to be the "right one."

The second strategy for solving the problem, the strategy I would endorse, sets out in quite a different direction from the first. It docs not propose to select among *dags* by finding the one actually internalized. Indeed it is compatible with (but does not entail) the view that *no* grammar is, in any illuminating sense, internally represented in the speaker's mind or brain, and that there is no good sense to be made of the notion of "internal representation." The second strategy approaches the multiplicity of *dag* as a practical problem for the working linguist. At numerous junctures a linguist may find himself with data to account for and a variety of ways of doing so. Among the alternatives, more than one will handle all the data available and will coincide in their predictions about facts as yet unrecorded. How is the linguist to choose? What the linguist seeks, according to this strategy, is not the grammar actually in the head (whatever that may mean) but some motivated way to select among *dags*.

The motivation is to be found through the study of acquisition models, though the goals of an acquisition model must be reinterpreted. If we suspend interest in which grammar is "internally represented" we need no longer demand of an acquisition model that, for a given body of *pld*, it produce as output a grammar that a learner exposed to the data would internalize. Instead, we ask only that the acquisition model have as output *some* grammar that is true of the accomplished speaker (i.e., some grammar that correctly describes the sentences acceptable to him, his intuitions about grammatical relations, etc.). But let it not be thought that this is a trivial task. Such a model would be able to specify a grammar true of the speaker given only the (relatively scant) primary linguistic data to which the speaker was exposed. To do this would be a monumentally impressive feat realizable, for the foreseeable future, only in linguistic science fiction.

How can such a model be built? In attending to the more demanding model of the first strategy, our first move was to linguistic universals, the properties shared by all *dags*. The analogous role in the present strategy can be played by properties less difficult to discover.

---

13. As is the case with alternative *dags*, some alternative measure functions will be trivially cooked up variants of the original. (E.g., simply select an arbitrary *dag* of the language from which the *pld is* drawn and place it highest under the evaluation measure, leaving the rest of the measure unchanged.) Others will exist which differ from the original in more substantial ways.

For suppose we have a single descriptively adequate grammar of a particular natural language. Might it not be reasonable to take as many properties of that grammar as possible as "quasi-universals"? "Quasi-universal" properties play just the role that universals did in the first strategy—they constrain the output of the acquisition model. The quasi-universals, then, define a class of "quasi-humanly possible grammars" which are the only possible outputs of the acquisition model. The terminology is adopted to stress the parallel with the first strategy. But there are important differences. For quasi-universals are in no sense universals—there is no claim that all *dags* must share them. Nor does the class of quasi-humanly possible grammars pretend to exhaust the class of grammars that humans can learn;[14] it simply coincides with the possible outputs of the acquisition model.

As was the case at the analogous point in the first strategy, there is profit in taking the quasi-universals to be as strong as we can. For the stronger the quasi-universals, the smaller the class of quasi-*hpgs* and thus the easier the task that remains for the rest of the model. Indeed, it would not be unreasonable as a first guess to take *all* the properties of the single *dag* as quasi-universals.[15] But this clearly will not do. For then the output class of the acquisition model would have but a single member. Rather, our principle in deciding whether to take features of our single *dag* as quasi-universal is this: take as quasi-universal as many features of the *dag* as possible, provided only that the resultant class of quasi-*hpgs* contains at least one quasi-*hpg* for each natural language. The remainder of the model will contain (at least) a component testing the compatibility of quasi-*hpgs* with the accumulated *pld*. Note that, on this second strategy, it is indeed possible that the quasi-universals so narrow down the class of quasi-*hpgs* that only one *hpg* will be compatible with any given body of *pld*. If this is the case, then a specification of the quasi-universals and a compatibility-testing device of the sort lately considered would complete an acquisition model. But if we cannot discover quasi-universals of this strength, we will again resort to an evaluation measure. As with the first strategy, what we seek is a ranking of quasi-*hpgs* which, when we exclude from the quasi-*hpgs* those grammars incompatible with a given body of *pld*, ranks highest among the remaining quasi-*hpgs* a grammar that is descriptively adequate for the language from which the *pld* was drawn. Since we are making no claim that the selected grammar is "actually internalized" we need not be concerned that there may be several such evaluation measures. Our project is the highly nontrivial project of producing a model that takes *pld* as input and yields an appropriate *dag* as output. *Any* evaluation measure that does the trick will be suitable.

14. Indeed, if we abandon the notion of internal representation, it is no longer clear that it makes sense to speak of a child "learning" a grammar. When the child succeeds in mastering his mother tongue, each *dag* of that tongue is true of him. But he surely has not learned *all* these *dags*. What, then, is the "cash value" of the claim that he has learned any one of them?

15. During the John Locke Lectures at Oxford in 1969, Chomsky suggested that were a Martian linguist to come to earth in the midst of an English-speaking community, his most reasonable first hypothesis would be that the ability to speak English is entirely innate. I suspect that Chomsky's remark and the present observation are directed at basically the same point.

The outline we have given of the construction of an acquisition model is, in a crucial respect, misleading. For it suggests that the model builder is bound irrevocably by the first *dag* he constructs. He takes as quasi-universal as many properties of this grammar as he can get away with, weakening the quasi-universals only when he comes upon some language no *dag* of which would be included among the quasi-*hpgs* if the stronger quasi-universals are retained. Actually, of course, matters are much more flexible. There is room for substantial feedback in both directions as work proceeds on the model and on individual grammars. The overriding concern is to make both the individual grammars and the acquisition model as simple and as powerful as possible. If at a given juncture it is found that adhering to the working hypothesis about the acquisition model will substantially complicate construction of grammars for one or more languages, he will try to alter the model, even if this may require altering or abandoning the original grammar from which the earliest hypothesis about quasi-universals was drawn. And, on the other side, if in constructing a particular *dag* a certain choice of how to proceed would accord well with the working hypothesis about the acquisition model, then he will be inclined to make that choice even if the resulting grammar is somewhat less elegant than another which would result from an alternative choice. There is no circularity here, or at least, to crib a phrase, the circularity is virtuous. Through this process of mutual adjustment progress on the acquisition model and on particular grammars can take place simultaneously.

Notice, now, that the strategy we have been detailing will solve the puzzles with which we began. An acquisition model provides motivation for selecting one *dag* over another, though both do equally well at predicting intuitions and such. The grammar to be chosen is that which accords with the quasi-universals. And, if several do, the grammar chosen is the one the evaluation measure ranks highest. Thus the grammar chosen will be preferred to its descriptively adequate competitors because it is more closely parallel to successful grammars for other languages and integrates more successfully into a model of grammar acquisition.

The account we have given of the second strategy has the further virtue of according well with actual linguistic practice. It is simply not the case that, when speculating about "linguistic universals," Chomsky and his followers set out to survey a broad range of languages and collect those features common to all the grammars. Rather, speculation is based on the study of a single language, or at best a few closely related languages. A feature of a grammar will be tentatively taken as "universal" if it is sufficiently abstract (or nonidiosyncratic) to make it plausible that the feature could be readily incorporated into a grammar of every natural language. If "universals" are taken to be features common to all *dags*, this speculation about universals would be quite mad. But in the light of the second strategy the speculation appears as a thoroughly reasonable way to proceed.

An element of indeterminacy still lurks in our second strategy. And if I am right in identifying this strategy with the generative grammarian's practice, then the indeterminacy infuses his theory as well. In constructing an acquisition model, the first few plausible (approximations of) descriptively adequate grammars have a profound influence. For it is the abstract features of these grammars which are taken as quasi-universals. Yet the selection of these first *dags* over indefinitely many alternatives is completely unmotivated by any linguistic evidence. Which *dag* is first constructed is largely a matter of historical accident. But the accident casts its shadow over all future work. The acquisition model serves to direct future research into the channel forged by these first grammars, even though there are indefinitely many other possible channels available. Nor does the flexibility we stressed three paragraphs back eliminate the indeterminacy. There we noted that, if an original choice of quasi-universals led to overwhelming difficulties in constructing a grammar for some previously neglected language, the universals might be patched and the early grammars that suggested them might be abandoned. But the new choice of quasi-universals has no more claim to uniqueness than the old. For they too will be abstracted from *dags* that were selected over competitors largely by virtue of historical accident.

To the appropriately conditioned reader this indeterminacy will appear familiar enough. It bears strong analogy with Quine's thesis of the indeterminacy of translation.[16] Quine's analytical hypotheses, like the first *dags*, are underdetermined by the data. The selection of one *dag* or one set of analytical hypotheses is largely a matter of cultural bias or historical accident. But once a *dag* or a set of analytical hypotheses has been formulated, it has profound effects on the remainder of the translation theory (for analytical hypotheses), or on the acquisition model and *dags* for other languages. Both analytical hypotheses and early *dags* are susceptible to later tampering; but neither a patched *dag* nor a patched analytical hypothesis has any more claim to uniqueness than the originals.

My departure from Quine comes on the score of the *implications* of the indeterminacy. Were Quine to grant that grammars and translation manuals share a sort of indeterminacy,[17] he would presumably conclude that for grammars, as for translations, modulo the indeterminacy, there is nothing to be right about. On this view there is no saying that one *dag* of a language is more correct than another, except relative to a given set of quasi-universals. Yet the selection of quasi-universals, like the selection of analytical hypotheses, is in part quite arbitrary. My dissent comes in the step that passes from recognition of arbitrariness in quasi-universals or analytical hypotheses to the claim that there is (modulo the indeterminacy) nothing to be right about. For I think that, *pace* Quine, the same indeterminacy could be shown lurking in the foundations of every empirical science. Grammar and translation are not to be distinguished, in this quarter, from psychology or biology or physics. If we are disinclined to say that in all science, modulo

---

16. Cf. "Speaking of Objects," *Proceedings and Addresses of the American Philosophical Association*, XXXI (1957/8): 5–22; "Meaning and Translation," in Fodor and Katz, *The Structure of Language, op. cit.*; *Word and Object* (Cambridge, Mass.: MIT Press, 1960), ch. II; and *"Ontological Relativity," Journal of Philosophy*, LXV, 7 (April 4, 1968): 185–212, reprinted in *Ontological Relativity, and Other Essays* (New York: Columbia, 1969).

17. There is evidence that he would. Cf. "Methodological Reflections . . .," *op. cit.*

the indeterminacy, there is nothing to be right about, it is because the theories we are willing to allow as correct are those whose arbitrary features have the sanction of tradition. But all this is to stake out my dissent, not to defend it. The defense is a project I must postpone until another occasion.

IV

Our sketch of the grammarian's doings is all but complete. We have surveyed the data to which he attends and indicated the nature of the theory he builds upon his data. It remains to say something of the interest of the grammarian's theory and to set out the relation between his theory and the speakers whose intuitions and behavior are his data.

As I have depicted it, a grammar is a modest portion of a psychological theory about the speaker. It describes certain language-specific facts: facts about the acceptability of expressions to speakers and facts about an ability or capacity speakers have for judging and classifying expressions as having or lacking grammatical properties and relations.

The modesty of a grammar, on my account, stands in stark contrast to more flamboyant portraits. On Jerrold Katz's view, a grammar is a theory in physiological psychology whose components are strongly isomorphic to the fine structure of the brain. "The linguistic description and the procedures of sentence production and recognition," according to Katz, "must correspond to independent mechanisms in the brain. Componential distinctions between the syntactic, phonological, and semantic components must rest on relevant differences between three neural submechanisms of the mechanism which stores the linguistic description. The rules of each component must have their psychological reality in the input-output operations of the computing machinery of this mechanism."[18] Though Katz's claims about grammar are more expansive than those I have made, the evidence he uses to confirm a grammar is of a piece with the evidence indicated in my account. Thus it remains something of a mystery how the grammarian has learned as much as Katz would have him know about the structure of the brain, having left the skulls of his subjects intact.

Less imaginative than Katz's view, but still not so sparse as mine, is a story about grammar put forward by Chomsky.[19] On this account a grammar describes the speaker's "competence"—his knowledge of his language. The speaker is held to have a large and complex fund of knowledge of the rules of his grammar. The grammarian's theory mirrors or describes the knowledge that the speaker has "internalized" and "internally represented." Chomsky's view is intriguing, though an explicit unpacking of the metaphors of "internalization," "representation," and the rest can prove an exasperating task. My own view is that the notion of competence is explanatorily vacuous and that attributing

---

18. "Mentalism in Linguistics," *Language*, XL, 2 (April/June 1964): 124–137, p. 133.
19. In *Aspects of the Theory of Syntax, op. cit.*, and elsewhere.

knowledge of a grammar to a speaker is little more plausible than attributing knowledge of the laws of physics to a projectile whose behavior they predict. But the issues are complex, and I have aired my views at length elsewhere.[20] I will not rehash them here. What is important to our present project is the observation that, on the account of grammar and acquisition models we have constructed, no knowledge claim is *needed*. A grammar is a theory describing the facts of acceptability and intuition; a grammar-acquisition model is a theory specifying a grammar which comes to be true of a child, as a function of the linguistic environment in which he is placed. Grammar and the theory of grammar acquisition are bits of psychological theory.

If our account of the grammarian's activity is accurate, then it is perhaps misleading to describe him as constructing a theory of the language of his subjects. Rather he is building a description of the facts of acceptability and linguistic intuition. A theory of a language seriously worthy of the name would provide some insight into what it is to *understand* a sentence, how sentences can be used to communicate and to deal more effectively with the world, and into a host of related questions that we have yet to learn to ask in illuminating ways. But a grammar does none of this. Indeed, it is logically possible that there be a person whose linguistic intuitions matched up near enough with our own, but who could neither speak nor understand English. Such a person would serve almost as well as an English speaker as an informant for constructing a grammar of English, provided only that we shared a metalanguage in which we could question him about the sequences of sounds he did not understand. What is important about this bit of fiction is that it is *only* fiction. It is an empirical fact that comprehension and intuition run in tandem. And this fact provides the beginning of the answer to a question that will likely have begun to trouble the reader: Of what interest is a grammar? If a grammar is not, in any exciting sense, a theory of a language, why bother constructing it?

The answer is twofold. First, there is substantial correspondence between the grammatical sentences and the sentences we do in fact use for thought and communication; grammatically related sentences are understood in similar ways[21] (though in our present state of ignorance we have no serious understanding of what it is to "understand sentences in similar ways"); the ability to speak and understand a language is an empirically necessary condition for the possession of linguistic intuitions about the expressions of the language. So one reason for studying grammar is the hope that these overlaps and correlations can be exploited to yield deeper insight into the exciting phenomena of comprehension and communication. Once we have the sort of description of acceptability

---

20. "What Every Speaker Knows," *Philosophical Review*, LXXX, 4 (October 1971): 476–496, and "What Every Grammar Does," *Philosophia*, 3, 1, (January 1973) 85–96.

21. Cf. Chomsky *Syntactic Structures* (The Hague: Mouton, 1957), p. 86: "the sentences (i) *John played tennis* [and] (ii) *my friend likes music* are quite distinct on phonemic and morphemic levels. But on the level of phrase structure they are both represented as *NP-Verb-NP*; correspondingly, *it is evident that in some sense they are similarly understood.*" (Last emphasis added.)

and linguistic intuition provided by a grammar we can begin to seek an explanation of these facts. We can ask what psychological mechanisms underlie the speaker's ability to judge and relate sentences as he does. The parallels between linguistic intuition and other language-related phenomena make it reasonable to hope that insight into the mechanisms underlying intuition will explain much else about language as well. But hope is not to be confused with accomplishment. If we fail to recognize how modest a theory a grammar is, we can expect only to obscure the extent of our ignorance about language, communication, and understanding.

A second reason for doing grammar is that it is something to do. In grammar, at least, we have a coherent set of data that we know how to study, intelligible questions to ask, and some clear indication as to how we can go about answering them. Acceptability and grammatical intuitions are language-related phenomena about which we have the beginnings of an empirical theory. Few other approaches to the phenomena of natural language fare as well. Thus grammar is a natural focus of attention for the investigator concerned with language. It is an entering wedge to a theory of a language, and, for the present at least, there are few competitors.

2

THE IDEA OF INNATENESS

PHILOSOPHICAL CONTROVERSIES ARE notoriously long-lived. And in point of venerability the controversy around innate ideas and innate knowledge is equal to any. It differs, however, from many of its cousins of comparable ancestry. For in the last decade it has emerged anew as a lively debate whose participants include some of the most important philosophers in the English-speaking world. The debate is unique, too, in having been rekindled not by philosophers but by linguists who based their arguments on the findings of modern generative grammar.

It is not surprising that in a controversy extending over two millennia the strands of the argument have become knotted and intertwined. My aim in this essay is to untangle a few of the strands of the argument, with the hope of making it a little easier for readers new to the debate to find their bearings.

The controversy is easy enough to summarize: Some philosophers, as well as linguists, psychologists, and others, allege that human beings have innate knowledge or innate ideas. Others deny it. But what is it to have innate knowledge or an innate idea? There is a pattern running through much of the debate in this area. Advocates of the doctrines of innate ideas and innate knowledge commonly take the notion of innateness itself to be unproblematic. They explain it with a few near synonyms, "inborn" or "unlearned," or with a metaphor or an allegory, and leave it at that. The doctrine's opponents often begin by puzzling over just what the doctrine could possibly mean. They go on to construct a variety of accounts, arguing against each in turn. The advocate's rejoinder, as often as not, is that he has been misunderstood. Thus, in approaching the debate over the innateness doctrine, we would do well to ponder what we are saying of someone when we say that he knows something or has an idea innately.

In working toward an analysis of innateness there are two pitfalls we must avoid. First, we should unpack the concepts in such a way that there *might* be innate ideas or innate knowledge. An account of these notions which makes the claim that a person has innate ideas or knowledge either straightforwardly logically impossible or patently empirically false holds little promise as an explication of what those who advance the claim have in mind. Their view may be false but, if we are to interpret them sympathetically, it will not be trivially false. Second, our account should portray the innateness doctrine as an interesting view about human cognitive mechanisms. An analysis would be suspect in this quarter if it entailed that all knowledge or ideas are innate. Advocates of innateness usually took themselves to be advancing an exciting thesis about a special sort of knowledge or idea. But if, on a given analysis, all knowledge or ideas are innate, there is reason to be suspicious that this exciting thesis has been exchanged for the humdrum claim that, on a special sense of "innate," all knowledge or ideas count as innate.

While counting all knowledge as innate is a symptom that an account is philosophically uninteresting, it is not a sufficient condition. In particular, we should note two historical caveats. In some of his writings Plato seems to endorse the view that all knowledge is innate. But on Plato's view, only part of what we commonly think we know is known innately. The rest isn't worthy of being called knowledge at all. Plato's move is not to bloat the concept of innateness to encompass all knowledge, but rather to shrink the concept of knowledge until it coincides with what we know innately. Descartes, too, sometimes maintains that all ideas are innate. However, as Robert Adams has noted, there is both a narrow and a broad sense in which an idea might be innate for Descartes.[1] When Descartes claims that all ideas are innate he is using the broad sense. But the interesting hypothesis about our cognitive mechanisms is the claim that we have innate ideas in the narrow sense. While Descartes advocates this latter hypothesis, he abjures the stronger one that all ideas are innate in the narrow sense.

Innate Diseases

> I observed . . . that there were in myself certain thoughts that did not proceed from external objects, nor from a determination of my will, but only from the thinking faculty that is in me; and therefore, in order to distinguish the ideas or notions that are the content of these thoughts from other ideas which are adventitious or manufactured, I called them innate. It is in the same sense of the word that we say generosity is innate in certain families; or again that in others certain diseases, e.g. gout and the stone, are innate; not that infants of these families suffer from these diseases in their mother's womb, but because they are born with a certain disposition or liability to contract them. (Descartes, *Notes on a Certain Programme*)

1. Robert Merrihew Adams, "Where Do Our Ideas Come From? Descartes *vs.* Locke," in S. P. Stich (ed.), *Innate Ideas* (Berkeley: University of California Press, 1975), pp. 71–87.

In calling ideas *innate*, Descartes tells us, he is using the same sense of the word we use when we say certain diseases are innate. So let us launch our analysis of innateness by pursuing Descartes' hint and asking what it is to be afflicted with an innate disease. Our strategy then will be to seek an analysis of the notion of an innate disease. Armed with our analysis we will return to tackle the thornier problem of innate knowledge.

To begin let us imagine a disease that at a certain stage, is always characterized by a unique and easily observable set of symptoms. (The lurid details are left to the reader.) In imagining a disease *always* characterized by a unique set of symptoms, we are making a simplifying assumption about the relation between a disease and its symptoms. But the prey we are stalking is *innateness*, not *disease*. A more realistic assumption would complicate the discussion while shedding no further light on the concept that interests us.

Now, under what conditions would we be willing to say that someone having such a disease has it innately? A natural first move is suggested by the parsing of "innate" as "congenital" or "inborn." Perhaps to have the disease innately is just to have the symptoms of the disease from birth. But, as Descartes notes, this will not do. For a person may well have an innate disease though none of its symptoms are evident at birth. It may be that the symptoms appear only at some specific stage later in life—during a certain age span, say, or accompanying some normal bodily change like puberty or menopause. In such a case we are prepared to say that the person has the disease even before the appearance of the symptoms. Of course, unless there is some way to predict the future occurrence of the symptoms, we may not know the person has the disease until he begins to exhibit the symptoms. Still, there is nothing unusual about the claim that he had the disease all along, though we didn't know it until the symptoms appeared. The parallel to the notion of innate knowledge is clear. Those who advocate the doctrine of innate knowledge are often willing to attribute such knowledge to a person even though he has not yet come to believe the proposition he is alleged to know. But here we are getting ahead of ourselves.

We have, then, what appear to be two sorts of innate infirmities, those whose symptoms are present at birth and those whose symptoms appear only later. Let us focus for a while on the second sort. Under what conditions can we properly say that a person is afflicted with such an innate malady? We have seen that the symptoms themselves need not yet have appeared. So perhaps what is called for is an analysis in the form of a conditional: To say that a person has a disease of this second sort innately is to say that if he is of the appropriate age (or at the appropriate stage of life) then he has the symptoms.

To be at all plausible, this proposal demands at least one modification. If the "if . . . then" locution it uses is understood as a material conditional, true if the consequent is true or the antecedent false, then the account as it stands has the consequence that everyone who has yet to attain the appropriate age has the disease innately. What is wanted, rather, is a subjunctive locution forming not a material conditional but a counterfactual conditional. With this modification, our analysis becomes: To say that a person has a disease of the second sort innately is to say that if he were of the appropriate age (or at the appropriate stage of life) then he would have the symptoms.

I think it could be argued that similar moves will be needed in the analysis of the first sort of innate disease, the cases where the symptoms are present at birth. This would, for example, enable us to make sense of talk of a fetus having an innate disease before showing any detectable abnormalities. But rather than pursue this line, let us keep our attention restricted to the second type of case. For ultimately the subjunctive analysis will prove inadequate.

Returning, then, to cases of the second sort, let us attend to a pair of further problems with the analysis as it stands. First, consider the case of an infectious disease caused, say, by a bacterial infection. Let us suppose that, while the disease can be acquired at any age, the symptoms appear during or after puberty. So a child may contract the infection while still an infant. This, it would seem, is a clear case of a person having a disease that is not innate. Yet our analysis, as it stands, implies that the child has the disease innately. From the time he contracts the infection onward, it is true of him that if he were at puberty then he would have the symptoms. Second, our analysis focuses on the period of latency when the symptoms have yet to appear. Thus it does not enable us to segregate innate from noninnate diseases once the symptoms are present. Both these difficulties can be patched if we swap a counterfactual locution for an "independent-of-factual" conditional which is true of the victim from the beginning of his life. We have, then: A person has a disease innately if and only if, from the beginning of his life it is true of him that if he is or were of the appropriate age (or at the appropriate stage of life) then he has or would have the disease's symptoms.

This leaves us with the nice problem of saying just when a life begins. On the answer turns the distinction between innate diseases and diseases caused by abnormal pregnancy. Here I have no solutions to suggest. My suspicion is that the distinction is a fuzzy one, and that on this score the notion of innate disease is fuzzy. My only proposal is that for purposes of our investigation we take life to begin sometime before birth. This will collapse the distinction between the two sorts of innateness, leaving our analysis applicable equally to each.

Unhappily, our analysis is still not adequate. Its fault is excessive pessimism. In defining the notion of innate disease we have left no room for possible cures. Imagine an innate disease whose symptoms, in the normal course of events, appear at age ten. Imagine further that a cure has been developed and administered to one of the disease's victims at age five. Intuitively, we want to say the young patient had the disease until he was five. But this is blocked by our account. For it is not true of him during his first five years that if he were ten years old then he would have the symptoms. Rather what is true of him during these years is a watered-down subjunctive that we might render: If he were ten years old, then, in the normal course of events, he would have the symptoms. So our account, full-blown at last, becomes:

A person has a disease innately at time t if, and only if, from the beginning of his life to t it has been true of him that if he is or were of the appropriate age (or at the appropriate stage of life) then he has or in the normal course of events would have the disease's symptoms.

Timid conditionals, hedged with "in the normal course of events" and the like, are familiar to philosophers who have reflected on the relation between counterfactual and dispositional locutions. Dispositionals, like "x is soluble" or "x is flexible," are commonly weaker than unhedged counterfactuals.[2] For to attribute a dispositional property to an object is not to say what the object would do under certain conditions, but rather to say what it would do under these conditions if surrounding circumstances were normal or natural. So we can, with some justice, dub our final analysis the "dispositional account" of innateness. Descartes it seems had much the same idea. Those who suffer innate diseases, on his account, "are born with a certain disposition or liability to acquire them."

The notion of innate disease, if our dispositional account is correct, is tied essentially to concepts of naturalness or normalcy. The job of unpacking these concepts, of saying what is natural or normal (or when "other things are equal") is notoriously difficult. While clear cases of normal situations and of abnormal ones can be found, there is substantial vagueness in the middle. Our analysis would lead us to expect that this vagueness is reflected in the concept of innateness. The reflection is not hard to find.

Consider the distinction between an innate disease and a susceptibility. To suffer from an innate disease is to be disposed to acquire its symptoms at the characteristic time in the normal course of events. To be susceptible to a (noninnate) disease is to be disposed to acquire its symptoms under certain *special* circumstances. Certain toxic diseases, for example, can be acquired only by certain people. A susceptible person, when exposed to the toxic substance, will come down with the symptoms. At the extremes, the distinction seems clear enough. But notice how the two shade into each other. Suppose a person becomes ill after ingesting a certain amount of a particular chemical. (We can imagine the effects to be cumulative.) Suppose also that the chemical occurs naturally in the drinking water of the person's community. Is this a case of an illness caused by the substance, or of an innate disease whose onset can be prevented by avoiding the substance? Vary the example, now, so that the substance is nitrogen in the air, and ask the same question.

These examples illustrate a central feature of the notion of an innate disease. There are commonly a host of necessary environmental conditions for the appearance of the symptoms of a disease. If these conditions all occur naturally or in the normal course of events, the symptoms will be counted as those of an innate disease. But it is often unclear whether the occurrence of a certain necessary condition is in the normal course of events. So it will often be unclear whether a person is afflicted with an innate disease or is, rather, susceptible to a (noninnate) disease. There is much more that might be said on the topic of

2. Cf. Nelson Goodman, *Fact, Fiction and Forecast* (2d ed.), chap. II, sect. 2 (Indianapolis: Bobbs-Merrill, 1965).

innate infirmities. But it is time to take such conclusions as we have reached and see if they can be applied in our study of innate knowledge.

Innate Diseases, Innate Knowledge, and Innate Belief

Let us begin by trading one problem for another. Questions about the nature and varieties of knowledge are as controversial as any philosophers are wont to consider. But on one point, at least, there is fair agreement: At least one sort of knowledge is a species of belief. This is so-called propositional knowledge or knowledge that, commonly attributed by locutions like "Christopher knows that the earth is round." Not every belief, of course, is an instance of knowledge. False beliefs are counted out; and even among true beliefs further discrimination is needed. Specifying the principles of discrimination is a problem of celebrated difficulty. Happily, it is a problem we can conveniently avoid. For innate knowledge, on the view of most of those who hold there is any, is innate propositional knowledge. And if there is innate propositional knowledge, there are innate beliefs. Let us see what sense we can make of the doctrine that people have innate beliefs. This will prove problem enough so that we need not feel guilty about leaving to others the question of whether innate beliefs are instances of innate knowledge.[3]

By taking innate belief in exchange for innate knowledge we have traded up to a more manageable problem. The notion of belief is not without its puzzles, of course. Still, every analysis must take something as clear. So let us presume that our workaday grasp of the concept of belief is sufficient for the task at hand. Before attending to innate belief, it is worth reminding ourselves that beliefs need not be objects of current reflection. We all now believe many propositions we are not presently thinking about, and some we have never consciously entertained. Thus, in all likelihood, you have long believed that your left thumb is smaller than the pyramid of Cheops, though you have never reflected on the belief until now. Following familiar terminology, we will call those of our beliefs that are currently being entertained "occurrent beliefs" and those we are not currently entertaining "dispositional beliefs."

Enough said on the topic of belief. Let us ponder, now, what might be meant by "innate belief." According to Descartes, "innate" in "innate idea" has the same sense it has in "innate disease." Pursuing our strategy of following up this hint, let us see how well our analysis of "innate disease" can be adapted to "innate belief." Making appropriate changes, our account emerges as follows:

---

3. For some discussion see R. Edgely, "Innate Ideas," in *Knowledge and Necessity*, Royal Institute of Philosophy Lectures, vol. 3 (London: Macmillan, 1970) and the debate between W. D. Hart ("Innate Ideas and A Priori Knowledge") and Alvin Goldman ("Innate Knowledge") in S. P. Stich (ed.), *Innate Ideas* (Berkeley: University of California Press, 1975).

A person has a belief innately at time t if, and only if, from the beginning of his life to t it has been true of him that if he is or were of the appropriate age (or at the appropriate stage of life) then he has, or in the normal course of events would have, the belief occurrently or dispositionally.

This account is not without its virtues. As our introductory quote from Descartes suggests, we can use it to wind our way through some of the more obvious moves in the debate over the doctrine of innate knowledge. Infants, the doctrine's detractors argue, believe nothing; or if they have some beliefs they surely do not include the sophisticated propositions proposed by the doctrine's advocates. But what sense is there to the claim that one of a man's beliefs is innate if he did not have the belief at birth? Here our account has a ready answer. One can have a belief innately without believing it (occurrently or dispositionally) at birth much as one can have a disease innately without showing its symptoms at birth.

There are, however, other problems that our Cartesian (or dispositional) account dodges less successfully. Most critical are problems with the interpretation of the qualification "in the normal course of events." While on the topic of innate diseases we took note that the phrase was uncomfortably vague. Still, we had a passable intuitive feel for cases that were to be clearly counted in or clearly counted out. The trouble with the dispositional account when warped into an analysis of innate belief is that the *same* intuitions seem to swell the ranks of innate beliefs beyond all tolerable limits. For they seem to count in just about all banal truths about commonplace objects. In the normal course of events children are disposed to develop the belief that night follows day and day follows night, that things fall when dropped and that drinking water quenches thirst. Yet surely a notion of innateness distended enough to count these beliefs as innate is bereft of philosophical interest.

In the face of this difficulty we might consider a more liberal construal of "the normal course of events," allowing in those intuitively abnormal cases of children raised in a world of total darkness, without gravity or water.[4] Following this strategy we would read "the normal course of events" as "any physically possible course of events." But this tack is in danger of running aground on the opposite shore. If we allow as "normal" circumstances that are sufficiently bizarre, it seems likely that our account will count no beliefs as innate. Although the issue is an empirical one, it would be surprising if it were shown that there are some beliefs people acquire no matter how bizarre their experiences may be. Beliefs, after all, involve concepts. One cannot believe that armadillos are animals without having the concept of armadillo. Nor can one believe that everything is identical with itself if one is without the concept of identity. And, I suspect, for any concept there

---

4. Note that each of these circumstances must be counted as abnormal by the account of normalcy required for innate diseases. Symptoms that appear in the absence of gravity are not symptoms of an innate disease.

is *some* course of (physically possible) experience which would leave a child without the concept.

Is there, perhaps, some middle course, some way to construe "the normal course of events" which will leave the dispositional concept of innate belief neither empty nor cluttered with unwelcome occupants? One possibility is suggested by our recent observation on the interdependence of beliefs and concepts. Let us allow that having sufficiently exotic experiences a person may find himself lacking any given concept. Still, there may be beliefs that innately accompany concepts; given that a person has had experience sufficient to acquire the concept, he will be disposed to develop the beliefs in the natural course of events. The beliefs, then, are conditionally innate. Here, of course, we must interpret the residual reference to the natural course of events liberally, allowing in any experience compatible with the person having the concept. A more restricted construal would have us again class many banal beliefs as innate.

There is also a new danger. Having a particular concept may *entail* having certain beliefs involving the concept. To take an extreme case, it would be absurd to say a person had the concept of an armadillo but held no true beliefs about armadillos.[5] If it is the case that having a certain concept entails having certain specific beliefs, then the claim that these beliefs are conditionally innate is vacuous. A belief is conditionally innate if a person is disposed to acquire the belief on acquiring a given concept. But if acquiring a concept consists, in part, in acquiring the belief, then the claim that the belief is conditionally innate amounts to the tautology that if someone has a belief then he has it.

Despite this danger, the concept of conditional innateness remains a plausible candidate in our quest for a philosophically interesting unpacking of the dispositional notion of innate belief. While some beliefs may be conditionally innate only in the vacuous way lately considered, others may be conditionally innate for nontrivial reasons. These will be those conditionally innate beliefs the holding of which is not entailed by having the concept they embody. Whether there be such beliefs is open to dispute. But I see no straightforward argument that there are none.

Still, it would be nice to have some examples. Perhaps one of Kant's examples of synthetic a priori knowledge can be bent into an illustration. Kant held that the truths of elementary arithmetic, like $7 + 5 = 12$, were known a priori. He also contended that the judgments these truths express are nowhere contained within the concepts they employ. They are synthetic not analytic truths. Now if we construe a priority as conditional innateness and if we take the claim that "$7 + 5 = 12$" is synthetic to entail that having each of the concepts involved does not entail having the belief that $7 + 5 = 12$, then the belief that $7 + 5 = 12$ is a nonvacuous example of conditional innateness. But the example is not entirely a happy one. Quite apart from its dubious Kant scholarship, the claim that "$7 + 5 = 12$" is synthetic is at best a matter of controversy. Frege and the logicists who followed

---

5. This is, of course, not sufficient to establish the stronger claim that there is some specific belief the holding of which is necessary for the possession of the concept.

him undertook to show that it was analytic. While in more recent times Quine and others have denied that there is any distinction to draw between analytic and synthetic truths. Here the course of our investigation into the dispositional notion of innate belief merges with the dispute over the nature and existence of the analytic-synthetic distinction. To pursue Descartes' suggestion any further along the path we have come would take us too far from the central concerns of this essay.

Our interest in conditional innateness was provoked by the quest for some plausible way to construe "the normal course of events" which would be more liberal than the construal invoked in our concept of innate disease but more restrictive than mere physical possibility. The proposal was that we relativize innate beliefs to specific concepts, and allow as normal any course of events sufficient for the person to have the concept. This move suggests a still more permissive account of normalcy within the boundaries we have staked out. Rather than demand normal experiences be sufficient for the acquisition of some specific concept, we can relax our requirement and demand of normal experience only that it be sufficient for the acquisition of some concept or other. Or better, we can drop the reference to concepts altogether and take as normal any course of experience that is sufficient for the acquisition of some belief or other. A belief is innate for a person, then, if he is disposed to acquire it under any circumstances sufficient for the acquisition of any belief. Here we have a second proposal on how the notion of dispositional innateness might be employed in an account of innate belief. As in the case of conditional innateness, it is not obvious that there are beliefs innate in this sense. Nor, so far as I can see, are there straightforward arguments that there could be none.

Before leaving the topic of dispositional innateness, let us pause to explore one proposal of considerable interest which is not directly in the line of our current reflections. We have lately observed that having a concept, in one plausible sense of this nebulous notion, may involve having certain beliefs. But there is another sense of this notion which is quite independent of belief. To illustrate, suppose an animal or an infant can discriminate red from nonred things; it can be conditioned to respond to red stimuli and can be taught simple tasks that presuppose the ability to discriminate between red and nonred things. We might, under these circumstances, say that the animal or the child has the concept of red even though it has *no* beliefs about red things. Concepts in this sense are prime candidates for *innate* concepts in the sense of innateness modeled after innate diseases. For if simple conditioned learning is to take place, the organism that does the learning must be able to discriminate stimuli that are being reinforced from those not reinforced. And since most organisms can, in fact, be conditioned to some stimuli from birth, some concepts must be innate.[6]

---

6. This theme has been developed by W. V. Quine in a number of places, including his essay, "Linguistics and Philosophy" in S. Hook (ed.), *Language and Philosophy* (New York: New York University Press, 1969), pp. 95–98. Though the argument seems straightforward enough, there is a problem buried here. Let me indicate it briefly. We have contended that conditionability requires a preexisting concept or, as Quine would have it,

It is time to take stock of our progress so far. Our strategy was to follow up Descartes' suggestion by seeking an account of innate belief on the analogy of our analysis of innate disease. We discovered that the analogy is not so straightforward as Descartes may have thought. For buried in the notion of innate disease is an appeal to the normal or natural course of events. And while our intuitions about what is normal or natural serve passably well when we attend to innate disease, the same intuitions yield an intolerably broad notion of innate belief. In casting about for a more restrictive account of what is to be allowed as "normal," we have come upon two possibilities. The first led to the concept of conditional innateness; the second counted a course of experience as "normal" if it led to the acquisition of any belief at all. These alternatives are at best tentative proposals. There is much work yet to be done on the dispositional account of innateness. But in this essay we must abandon the topic here and turn our attention to a quite different attempt at explicating the notion of innate belief.

The Input-Output Model: Another Approach to Innate Belief

The dispositional account of innateness was suggested by Descartes' analogy between innate ideas and innate diseases. The alternative account that is our current topic can be coaxed from the exchange between Socrates and the slave boy in Plato's *Meno*. Though Socrates succeeds in eliciting from the boy the solution to the problem he has posed, Socrates nonetheless insists that he has not *taught* the boy anything. Rather, he tells Meno, he has uncovered something that was in the boy all along. Thus Socrates claims that the boy has some sort of innate belief. But it is clear that it is not a dispositionally innate belief. For at the beginning of the interrogation the boy does not believe what he later "recollects," nor need he ever have come to believe it. The questioning played a crucial role. There is no suggestion that the belief would have arisen without the questioning as part of the normal course of events. Moreover, the questioning did not serve to supply the boy with new concepts. He seems to have all the requisite conceptual apparatus before the questioning begins. So the beliefs he comes to hold are not conditionally

---

a "quality space" or "qualitative spacing of stimulations." Now in the case of colors, tones, and other relatively elementary sensory qualities, our contention seems to have some rudimentary explanatory value. We would like to know much more about quality spaces. But still, to say an organism prior to conditioning must have a qualitative spacing of stimulations seems to add something to the bare observation that the organism is conditionable. Now contrast these cases with other instances of conditionability. Some organisms (some people, for example) can be conditioned to respond differently to paintings in the style of Rubens, as contrasted with paintings in the style of Monet. Other organisms (I presume) cannot be so conditioned. The case seems, for all we have said, quite analogous to the case of colors and tones. But here it seems perverse to postulate that the conditionable organisms have a preexisting quality space. Such a move appears explanatorily vacuous. It adds nothing to the bare observation that the organisms are conditionable. All this is impressionistic. But if my impressions are correct we are left with a problem: Why is the postulation of a preexisting quality space plausible in one sort of case and perverse in the other?

innate. How are we to understand this nondispositional sense of innateness Plato seems to be using?

One idea that takes its cue from Plato's remarks is to view the role of the Socratic interrogation as akin to the role of a trigger or a catalyst. It sets off a process that results in the acquisition of the belief. But, as a catalyst is not part of the end product of a chemical reaction, so the questioning process does not supply the content of the belief. The content of the belief was contained within the boy much as the content of a tape recorded message was contained upon the tape. The questioning experience, like the throwing of the tape recorder's switch, serves only to set off the appropriate mechanism. On this model we can begin to make sense of the claim that the beliefs contained within the boy are innate even though they require certain sorts of experiences to bring them out.

There is at best scant textual evidence for the hypothesis that Plato would have expanded his doctrine along the lines that we have taken. With later authors, however, it is quite clear that they flirted with the model we are considering. Leibniz, for example, contends "the mind has a disposition (as much active as passive) to draw [necessary truths] from its depths; although the senses are necessary to give it the occasion and attention for this and to carry it to some rather than others."[7] He makes much the same point with his favorite metaphor. "It is a disposition, an aptitude, a preformation which determines our soul, and which brings it about that [necessary truths] may be derived from it. Just as there is a difference between the figures which are given to the stone or marble indifferently, and those which its veins already mark out, or are disposed to mark out, if the workman profits by them."[8] A natural reading of the metaphor is that in acquiring knowledge of necessary truths the mind uses experience only as a catalyst providing the occasion or cause for the knowledge being uncovered, but providing little or none of the content of the knowledge, just as when an appropriately grained block of marble is transformed into a statue the workman need only tap and chip a bit to uncover the figure. In *Cartesian Linguistics*, Noam Chomsky finds evidence of this view of experience as a trigger for innate cognitive mechanisms in thinkers as diverse as Schlegel and Herbert of Cherbury.[9]

In several of his discussions of the catalyst or trigger metaphor, Chomsky suggests a variant on the figure. He proposes that we look on belief acquisition as an input-output process, with sensory experience as input and belief as output. If the beliefs that result from a particular pattern of sensory experience are richer or contain more information than the experience, then this added information must be the mind's contribution. If the total sensory input up to a given moment in time is poorer in information than the beliefs acquired to that moment, the excess information is innate. Where the disparity is

7. Leibniz, *New Essays* (1703–1705), I, i, 5.

8. *Ibid.*, 11.

9. N. Chomsky, *Cartesian Linguistics* (New York & London: Harper and Row, 1966), pp. 59–72.

particularly great, the sensory input contributes little or nothing to the belief acquired. It acts merely as a trigger, setting off the innate cognitive mechanisms.

It is important to see that though Chomsky's suggestion is couched in terms rather more modern than those used by Leibniz, it is nonetheless little more than a metaphor. Chomsky is proposing that belief acquisition be viewed as an input-output process and that the mind is interestingly similar to an input-output device. If we are to pursue this proposal seriously, trying to turn it into more than a suggestive metaphor, we should have to give some account of how we measure the comparative richness—or information content—of experiences and beliefs. Existing accounts of information content will not do. They treat of the information in a proposition or sentence, not the information in a belief or stretch of experience. Also, familiar accounts of information content count logical truths as containing minimal information. So adopting such an account for our present purposes would lead us to exclude belief in logical truths as innate beliefs, though such beliefs have often been taken as paradigms of what is known innately.

Even without any developed account of the appropriate notion of information content, we may note one quite fundamental difference between the input-output model of innateness and the pair of dispositional concepts developed previously. On either dispositional account the hypothesis that there are innate beliefs is moot. On the input-output model, however, there can hardly be any doubt that many beliefs are in part innate. Most any empirical belief, for example, will be richer in information content than the experience that led to its acquisition—and this on any plausible account of the appropriate information measures. This is a consequence of the philosophical commonplace that the evidence a person has for an empirical belief rarely entails the belief. While we may come to believe that all armadillos are omnivorous by observing the eating habits of a fair sample of armadillos, the generalization is not implied by any number of propositions attributing varied tastes to particular armadillos.[10] In the case of mathematical or logical beliefs it is rather harder to specify the relevant experiential input. But again it seems that on any appropriate measure of information content the information contained within our mathematical and logical beliefs outruns that contained in our total sensory history.

The upshot of these observations is that when pursuing the input-output model of innate belief, the interesting question is no longer whether there are beliefs that are (in part) innate. Rather what is interesting is *to what degree* our various beliefs are innate. Also of interest is the detailed story about the cognitive mechanisms that lead from

---

10. As this observation indicates, the notion of innateness built on the input-output model is not inimical to empiricism. Hume's doctrine of "natural belief" required an inborn faculty or mental mechanism by which we acquire our beliefs about matters of fact. The beliefs acquired are not entailed by the sensory evidence we have for them. Thus, in the sense of innateness under consideration, they are in part innate. For more on this theme, see G. Harman, "Psychological Aspects of the Theory of Syntax," *Journal of Philosophy*, LXIV, 1967, pp. 75–87.

sensory input to belief. In developing his theory of the acquisition of language, Chomsky is making a tentative effort at sketching in some of these details.

A Priori Knowledge and Innate Ideas: Two More Threads to Untangle

The project with which we began this essay was to untangle some of the strands that run through the long history of the argument over innate ideas and innate knowledge. So far we have succeeded in separating out two basic concepts which historically have often been run together. The several related notions of innateness which flow from Descartes' analogy between innate ideas and innate diseases contrast sharply with innateness conceived on the input-output model. It would be tempting to see much of the historical debate over the innateness doctrine as a consequence of the failure to distinguish these two sorts of innateness. But, though tempting, it would be inaccurate. For, though some of the historical (and modern!) debates can no doubt be traced to the failure to distinguish these two concepts, problems were multiplied by still other confusions. In particular there is a pair of notions whose history is wound together with the history of the idea of innateness. One of them is the concept of a priori knowledge.

In the preceding two sections we retreated from tackling the notion of innate *knowledge*, and focused instead on innate belief. In so doing we avoided need to talk of *warrant* or *justification*—a property a true belief must have to be an instance of knowledge. We thus avoided confronting the issue of a priori knowledge, which is tied to the concept of justification.

For some of the propositions we know our justification is (at least in part) to be traced to sensory experience. But, on the view of many philosophers, we know some propositions whose justification is entirely independent of experience. These are the propositions we know a priori. Our belief in these propositions may have been (in part) *caused* by experience. But the *justification* we have that makes instances of a priori knowledge more than mere belief is not to be found in the experience that caused the beliefs, nor in any other experience. To say that a bit of knowledge is a priori, then, is to say something about its justification, while to say that a belief is innate is to say something about its cause or genesis.[11]

Though the distinction between innateness and a priority seems passably clear, the two have not always been distinguished. Thus Leibniz writes: ". . . very often the consideration of the nature of things is nothing else than the knowledge of the nature of our mind and of those innate ideas which we do not need to seek outside. Thus I call innate those truths which need only this consideration *in order to be verified.*"[12] And

---

11. There is some precedent for a rather narrower notion of a priority. Kant, for example, made it a "criterion" for a "judgment" being a priori that it be "thought as necessary." Following Kant's lead we might say that a person has a priori knowledge of a proposition (in this narrower sense) when he knows the proposition and his justification is independent of experience and the proposition is necessarily true.

12. Leibniz, *New Essays*, I, i, 21; emphasis added.

elsewhere: ". . . it is always clear in all the states of the soul that necessary truths are innate and are proved by *what is internal.*"[13] Here there is maddening tangle. If the truths are verified from within, proved by what is internal, then it is their justification that is independent of experience. So it is a priority, not innateness, that is at issue. Perhaps Leibniz thought that all and only innate knowledge was known a priori. But once the two have been distinguished the claim that they coincide in extension is itself in need of justification.

The second of the pair of concepts whose history is bound up with the history of the doctrine of innate knowledge is the notion of an innate *idea*. Talk of belief or knowledge slips easily into talk about ideas. Indeed, in previous pages I have occasionally slid back and forth from one to the other with a studied equivocation. But though sometimes talk about ideas is but a colloquial variant on talk about knowledge, it is not always so. For the Classical Rationalists, who have loomed large in our discussion of innateness, had quite a unique use for the term "innate idea." Their doctrine of innate ideas is to be understood against the background of the Aristotelian scholasticism that flourished in the late Middle Ages, and it admits of no tidy summary. Happily we need not here attempt an explication of their views, since the job is done with great clarity by Robert Adams.[14]

While the controversy between Classical Rationalists and Classical Empiricists on the topic of innateness was focused as often on innate ideas as on innate knowledge, the modern "rationalists," who defend their innateness doctrine by invoking modern theories of grammar, talk mostly of innate knowledge. So in the remaining section of this essay, I will attempt a brief sketch of the nature of modern grammar. I can then indicate where questions of knowledge—innate or otherwise—are likely to arise.

Grammar and Knowledge[15]

A grammar is a theory. The grammarian's principal data are the judgments speakers make about expressions—judgments, for example, that expressions are or are not grammatical sentences, that sentences are ambiguous, that pairs of sentences are related as active and passive or as simple declarative and yes–no (or wh-) questions,[16] and a host of others. Roughly speaking, the grammarian tries to build a theory which will entail that expressions have the properties speakers judge them to have. If a grammar is to be an adequate

---

13. *Ibid.*, p, 5; emphasis added.

14. Adams, op. cit.

15. This section is adapted from my essay, "What Every Speaker Knows," *Philosophical Review*, Vol. LXXX, no. 4 (October, 1971).

16. E.g., "Max went to the store" and "Did Max go to the store?" are related as simple declarative and yes–no question; "Max went to the store" and "Who went to the store?" are related as simple declarative and wh-question, as are "Max went to the store" and "Where did Max go?"

theory of the language of a speaker, it must entail that an expression has a given grammatical property if the speaker would judge the expression to have the property.

This brief account must be modified in several directions. First, speakers' judgments are not the only data a grammarian may use. Data about what a speaker does and does not say in unreflective speech, data about pronunciation peculiarities and a host of other phenomena may also be taken into account. Also, a grammar is an *idealized* theory. The grammarian will systematically ignore certain discrepancies between what his theory says of some expressions and what the speaker says of the same expressions much as, in the theory of ideal gases, we systematically ignore deviations between predicted correlations of temperature, pressure and volume and observed correlations. In both cases the motive is much the same—the expectation that construction of a complete theory that *accurately* describes all the phenomena is best approached by breaking the job into several parts, first giving the idealized theory, then explaining the deviations.

Commonly a grammar will consist of a set of *rules* (phrase structure rules, transformational rules, and perhaps some others) and a set of *definitions*.[17] The definitions and rules entail a variety of statements. They entail many of the form:

S is a grammatical sentence

where 'S' is replaced by the name of an expression; many of the form:

e is the subject of sentence S

many of the form:

Sentences S and S' are related as active and passive

etc. It is these consequences of the rules and definitions which must agree with speakers' judgments. The rules and definitions form an integrated empirical theory, and both rules and definitions may be modified in the face of recalcitrant data.

The grammarian's theory construction does not stop with a grammar. Having made some progress at grammars for several languages, he turns his attention to *linguistic theory* or the *theory of grammars*. Here the goal is to discover linguistic universals, general features of the grammars of human languages. These universals may be general constraints on the form of grammars—that all are divided into phrase structure and transformational components, say, or that all use rules only of a specified sort. The universals may also include particular rules or definitions which are the same in the grammar of every

---

17. The literature on modern or generative grammars is vast and growing. A good starting place for the reader new to the subject would be N. Chomsky, *Aspects of the Theory of Syntax* (Cambridge, Mass.: MIT Press, 1965).

natural language. If any rules or definitions are universal, they need no longer be specified along with the more idiosyncratic details of individual grammars.

The linguistic theory is also concerned with the acquisition of grammar—how a person comes to have the grammar he does. Here the strategy is to find a function ranking humanly possible grammars. The goal is to find a function that ranks highest among humanly possible grammars that grammar which the child actually acquires, when we first exclude from the class of humanly possible grammars all those that are incompatible with the observed utterances and other data available to the child. Specification of linguistic universals and a measure function of the sort described would provide a (low level) explanation of how the speakers of a language come to have the grammar they do.

These are the two sorts of theories the grammarian constructs. If the theories are correct, they will describe certain facts about speakers' linguistic intuitions (for grammars) and certain facts about all human grammars (for linguistic theory). About what aspects of these theories might speakers be thought to have knowledge? In the recent literature there are, I think, three distinct proposals. First, it might be thought that speakers know the linguistic universals, that they know (perhaps innately) that all human languages have phrase structure and transformational rules, or that the grammar of every language contains some specific rule or that in every natural language an expression is a noun phrase if and only if ____. In short, this first suggestion is that speakers know that p, where 'p' may be replaced by any statement belonging to linguistic theory. Next it might be held speakers know that the particular rules of the grammar of their language are rules of the grammar of their language, or that they know the definitions that, along with the rules, constitute the grammar of their language. Third, and most plausibly, it might be thought that speakers have knowledge of the consequence of the rules and definitions of their grammar. If this suggestion is correct then speakers of English will know that "Mary had a little lamb" is grammatical, that "Mary" is its subject, and that it is several ways ambiguous.[18]

---

18. For some debate about the plausibility of these views, see Chomsky, op. cit, Harman, op. cit., H. Putnam, "The 'Innateness Hypothesis' and Explanatory Models in Linguistics," *Synthese*, 17, 1967, pp. 12–2, and J. Katz, *The Philosophy of Language* (New York & London: Harper and Row, 1966).

3

BELIEFS AND SUBDOXASTIC STATES

THIS IS A paper about a distinction, one which is deeply imbedded in our everyday, pre-theoretic thinking about human psychology. It is a distinction which separates beliefs from a heterogeneous collection of psychological states that play a role in the proximate causal history of beliefs, though they are not beliefs themselves, I will call the states in this latter collection *subdoxastic* states. The distinction is an intuitive one, in the sense that when confronted with descriptions of various imaginable states it is intuitively clear that some are to be counted as beliefs while others are not. Part of my project in this paper is to explain these intuitive decisions by noting some of the characteristics that we ordinarily take beliefs to have which are lacking in subdoxastic states. Since these intuitive judgements mark part of the boundary of our pre-theoretic concept of belief, an explanation of the principles underlying the intuitions may also be viewed as part of an analysis of our ordinary concept of belief. It is this analytic project that occupies the early sections of the paper.

The intuitive distinction between beliefs and subdoxastic states is of interest quite apart from the insight it promises into our ordinary notion of belief. For much of the best recent work in cognitive psychology has ignored it. The implication, albeit a tacit one, of this neglect is that the distinction entrenched in intuition does not mark a psychologically interesting boundary. Now there is surely no *a priori* argument for rejecting this view. There is no reason to expect that every distinction embedded in our intuitive, pre-scientific psychological concepts reflects a distinction worth preserving in an empirically motivated

I am indebted to Clayton Lewis and Robert F. Cummins for helpful criticism of the views set forth in this paper.

psychological theory. What is unsettling about the neglect of the distinction in recent psychology is that it seems to be largely undefended. The fact that pre-theoretically we recognize the distinction as readily and consistently as we do is surely evidence that there is some basis to the distinction, some property or cluster of properties that we tacitly take account of when we classify a given example as a belief or as a subdoxastic state. The properties which we exploit in drawing the distinction may be psychologically uninteresting. But to be confident of this one would like to know what these properties are and why they can be safely ignored in psychological theorizing. The psychologists who ignore the distinction do not inspire confidence in this way. Such limited philosophical discussion as there has been of the topic is not reassuring. Gilbert Harman, in his recent book [7], sketches an argument that might be construed as an attack on the psychological significance of the distinction. So construed, the argument is singularly unconvincing. The latter sections of my paper will be devoted to a critique of Harman's view. I will also try to defend the view that the boundary between beliefs and subdoxastic states marks an important psychological distinction which serious cognitive psychology neglects to its peril.

1

Our first job is to focus in on the particular intuitive distinction I have in mind. Let me begin a bit obliquely by noting the shadow the distinction casts in traditional epistemology. It is obvious that many of our beliefs are inferred from other beliefs. But, as epistemologists were quick to note, there must be some beliefs which are not inferred from others, on pain of circularity or infinite regress. Since Descartes, the orthodox position has been to take as non-inferential those beliefs that concern the believer's own cognitive states—beliefs about what she believes, what she seems to be perceiving, what she seems to remember, etc. In recent years, the orthodoxy has been challenged by philosophers who advocate a much more expansive account of non-inferential belief. The expansionists urge that most perceptually-based beliefs about our immediate surroundings are non-inferential. Thus, while agreeing that our beliefs about our current cognitive states are non-inferential, the expansionists would also include among the non-inferential beliefs the belief that there is a pig nearby, if acquired under unexceptional circumstances as the result of a pig coming into view a few meters away. (cf., for example, [2], pp. 115 ff. and [4], p. 159.) We need not pause here to trace the moves in the debate between the expansionist and the advocate of orthodoxy. For our purposes it is important only to note that, despite their differences, both sides in the dispute recognize that some beliefs must be non-inferential. These non-inferential beliefs may serve as the premises for inferences but not as the conclusion. The class of non-inferential beliefs marks the boundary between two different sorts of psychological states. On one side of the boundary are beliefs, both inferred and non-inferential. On the other side are the psychological states which, though not beliefs, are part of the causal process leading to belief formation. Typically, epistemologists have been silent on the nature and workings of the mechanisms which underlie belief formation. Their silence, no doubt, was rooted in the sensible suspicion that the study of subdoxastic mechanisms is more properly the province of psychology.

2

To sharpen our intuitive feel for the distinction between beliefs and subdoxastic states, let us look at a few examples of the sort of states that fall in the latter category. Consider first the offering of grammatical intuitions. Given a few well-chosen examples of grammatical sentences and a few well-chosen examples of ungrammatical ones, speakers are able to go on to classify new examples as either grammatical or ungrammatical with impressive consistency. This ability seems to be largely independent of previous formal grammatical training. Naive subjects (particularly bright ones) quickly get the point. On the other hand, the ability plainly does depend on some elaborate and little-understood system of psychological states and processes which is gradually built up in the process of language acquisition. Moreover, it seems plausible to speculate that the psychological mechanisms which underlie the offering of grammatical intuitions also play a central role in the much more important business of speech production and comprehension. (For a general discussion of grammatical intuitions see my [14] and [15]; for some critical reaction, see [3] and [5].)

Now suppose that a grammatically naive subject has just been taught by example to apply the labels "grammatical" and "ungrammatical." We give the subject a new sentence and ask whether or not it is grammatical. The subject replies—and presumably believes— that it is grammatical. But if we ask him how he made the judgement and came to hold that belief, he will be at a loss to say. On hearing the sentence, he simply comes to believe that it is grammatical. The belief is non-inferential. There is, of course, a mechanism of some complexity mediating between the subject's hearing the sentence and the formation of the belief that it is grammatical. And, while we know little in detail about the workings of this mechanism, it is plausible to speculate that the mechanism exploits a system of psychological states which serve to store information about the grammar of the subject's language.[1] If this speculation proves accurate, then these states which store grammatical information are a prime example of subdoxastic states. They play a role in the proximate causal history of beliefs, though they are not beliefs themselves. I have, of course, given no

---

1. Speakers might, for example, have a system of states which serves to store or internally represent each of the rules of the grammar. In judging whether a sentence is grammatical, the relevant psychological mechanism might try to produce a derivation of the sentence at hand, aided by some efficient derivation finding heuristic. If it succeeds, it sets in motion a process which ordinarily leads to an affirmative answer. I think this sort of "analysis by synthesis" strategy, though surely logically possible, is wildly implausible as an empirical hypothesis. It does, however, have the advantage of being a particularly straightforward example of the way internally represented grammatical information might be exploited. For a much more subtle illustration of how grammatical information might be represented and utilized, cf. [17].

argument that these states are not beliefs. My claim, rather, is that this is intuitively obvious. After we have seen a few more examples of subdoxastic states, I will try to dissect out those aspects of our concept of belief which are responsible for the intuitions.

3

For a second example of subdoxastic states, let us attend to the complicated matter of depth perception. Our ability to judge the relative distances of objects in our visual field rests on a bewilderingly complex set of factors. Perspective, size, surface texture, the perception of edges and corners, occlusion, illumination gradients and stereopsis all play a role. (For a survey of this topic, see [6], chapter 13.) Some of the information available to our depth perception mechanisms would appear to be redundant. We can, for example, make depth judgements with one eye closed, or about the objects in a painting. In both cases stereopsis is irrelevant. Julesz, in an interesting series of experiments, has shown that binocular disparity alone is enough to bring about perception of depth. [10]. The experiment employed random patterns of black and white dots in a 100 × 100 cell matrix. The randomness of the patterns served to guarantee that no depth information was conveyed by the patterns themselves. When two identical copies of a random dot pattern are presented to a subject, one to each eye, no depth is perceived. However, if a section of one copy of the pattern is displaced laterally, there is a clear perception of depth, with the moved section appearing either in front of or behind the rest of the pattern, depending on whether it was moved toward the nose or toward the ears. When a subject in Julesz's experiment is presented with a pair of dot patterns one of which has a laterally displaced section, he will report—and presumably believe—that some of the dots seem to be in front of or behind the rest. Asked why he believes this, he will be unable to say. Some dots just do look to be in front of the others, and the belief that they do is non-inferential. Underlying the belief there is, no doubt, a complex psychological mechanism which serves to measure the degree of binocular disparity and to use this information in the production of an appropriate belief about apparent relative depth. If, as seems inevitable, the process leading from retinal stimulation to belief involves various psychological states which represent features of the retinal images, then these states are subdoxastic. Though they are causal antecedents of belief, there is a strong intuitive inclination to insist that they are not beliefs themselves.

4

Let us look now at a final example of subdoxastic states. In a series of experiments, E. H. Hess ([8]; see also [9]) presented male subjects with a pair of almost identical photos of a girl. One of the photos had been retouched by enlarging the size of the girl's pupils. The subjects regularly reported (and presumably believed) that the girl in the retouched photo appeared more attractive. However, subjects were quite unable to say why the girl in the retouched photo was more attractive; indeed, they were generally unable to identify any specific differences between the original and retouched photos. Their belief that the girl is more attractive in one photo than in the other is non-inferential. Plainly, there is some cognitive mechanism which detects the enlarged pupil size and which gives rise to the belief that one photo is more attractive than the other. As in the previous examples, we know little about the detailed functioning of this mechanism. However, it is plausible to suppose that there are psychological states which serve to record information about pupil size, and that these states play a role in the process that leads to belief formation. If so, these states are another example of subdoxastic states. They play a role in the proximate causal history of beliefs, but there is a strong intuitive inclination to deny that they are beliefs themselves.

5

Having surveyed some examples of states that fall on the subdoxastic side of the belief-subdoxastic state distinction, let us now consider what the basis may be for our strong intuitive inclination to insist that the sorts of states we have been describing are not beliefs. I think there are two rather different properties that we ordinarily take to be characteristic of belief and which are lacking in the examples of subdoxastic states. The first of these is actually a cluster of properties that revolves around the sort of *access* we ordinarily have to the contents of our beliefs; the second might be characterized as the *inferential integration* of beliefs. I will consider them in turn.

It is ordinarily the case, for typical or paradigmatic examples of belief, that adult subjects can report the contents of their belief. Thus, if a subject is psychologically (and physiologically) normal, inclined to be cooperative and has no motivation to deceive us, then if she believes that p and is asked whether p is the case, she will generally say that it is. (The subject must, of course, be asked in a language she understands and she must be paying attention. Hereafter I will take this to be built into the notion of asking.) Normal cooperative adult subjects can also tell us whether they *believe* that p, if we ask them. The two abilities are distinct. Toddlers, for example, are able to assent to p if they believe it, but are often not able to answer the question: "Do you believe that?" Nonetheless, the two abilities run in tandem in normal adults, and it is hard to believe that they are not intimately connected.

Both of these abilities are themselves associated with an ability to become aware of or to be conscious of the contents of one's beliefs. Suppose, for example, that a subject believes that p but fails to satisfy one or another of the additional conditions which, conjoined with belief, generally guarantee that a subject will assent to p if asked. The subject may be temporarily paralyzed and thus unable to assent to anything. Or he may have a strong desire to mislead his questioner, or simply wish to say nothing. Still, under these circumstances, if we ask a subject whether p is the case, he will generally have a certain sort of characteristic experience which, as best I can discover, has no standard description in English. Some philosophers have labelled the experience "having the occurrent belief that *p*." One might also describe the experience as being aware that *p* or being conscious that *p*. Often, but perhaps not always, the experience of having an occurent belief is accompanied by (consists in?) a perceived inclination to respond to the inquirer's question, or perhaps a response which is thought but not spoken. I do not propose to attempt any thoroughgoing phenomenological account of the experience of having an occurrent belief. Nor, in fact, am I much concerned whether it is a single sort of experience or a group of related ones. My point is the (I hope) uncontroversial one that in typical cases of belief a subject will have a certain sort of characteristic conscious experience when his attention is suitably directed to the content of the belief. While little is known about the psychological mechanisms responsible for the experience of having an occurrent belief, it is certainly plausible to speculate that the processes underlying this conscious experience and the processes underlying a subject's assent to a proposition he believes (under normal circumstances) are in important ways interconnected.

I have been claiming that access to the contents of our beliefs is a general characteristic of beliefs. However, there is a *prima facie* exception to this generalization viz. the unconscious beliefs that figure prominently in psychoanalytic theory. While I admit to some qualms about how seriously psychoanalytic theory ought to be taken, I do not think I need take on all of psychoanalytic theory to defend the claims I want to make about a subject's access to the contents of her beliefs. For all of my claims can be construed as subjunctive conditionals about what would happen (or would be likely to happen) if a subject were normal and otherwise suitably situated. And psychoanalytic theory can be viewed as postulating a psychological mechanism capable of interfering with the ordinary process leading from belief to assent or to conscious awareness. So to protect our generalizations about access, we will have to add to the conditions in the antecedent of our subjunctive conditional a clause specifying that there are no psychological mechanisms at work blocking the ordinary process leading from belief to assent or conscious awareness.

Now one of the ways in which our first two examples of subdoxastic states differ from beliefs is just that subjects have no access to them. People do not assent to a statement of a rule of their grammar as they do to a statement of the contents of a belief. Nor do they have any conscious awareness of the rules of their grammar. Indeed, if they did writing a grammar for a language would be a far less arduous business. Similarly, we cannot report, nor are we consciously aware of any information about binocular disparity. Awareness stops at the level of apparent comparative depth. Of course, it might be the case that these seemingly subdoxastic states are actually analogous to subconscious beliefs in that subjects would have access to them but for the intervention of some presently unsuspected psychological mechanism which blocks the ordinary processes that facilitate access. This possibility reflects something important about our pre-theoretic concept of belief. We might be willing to classify an apparent subdoxistic state as a belief if there were evidence that a subject's access is actively blocked by some mechanism. But we would, I think, be much more reluctant to countenance a special category of beliefs which are by nature not open to conscious awareness or reporting. It is quite central to our concept of belief that subjects under ordinary circumstances have access to their beliefs.

Our third example of a subdoxastic state poses some special problems. In Hess' experiments, subjects were not consciously aware that the pupils in one photo were larger than those in the other. However, at least some of the subjects might have become aware of it if their attention were suitably directed by, say, asking them. In this respect, the state which serves to represent the information that one pupil is larger than another is analogous to quite unexceptional cases of belief. For we are ordinarily quite unaware of most of our beliefs, and the experience of having the belief occurrently is provoked when our attention is directed to the content of the belief. I think this similarity between unproblematic cases of belief and the state that we have hypothesized in the Hess example is reflected in our intuition. For of our three examples, our intuitive inclination to rule that a state is not a belief is weakest in this case. But still, I think there is a strong inclination to resist calling the supposed state a belief. An attractive alternative is to say that, though not a belief itself, the state can give rise to a belief under certain circumstances. And thus the role of drawing a subject's attention to the relative size of the pupils is *not* analogous to what goes on when, for example, we ask a subject (who has been thinking about other things) what her mother's maiden name is. In the latter case, the question serves to make occurrent or bring to consciousness a belief which the subject has had all along. In the former case, however, questioning the subject about relative pupil size serves rather to instigate a process of belief formation in which, perhaps, the pre-existing subdoxastic state plays a role. If I am right that this alternative account of what is going on sits better with our intuition than the account which assimilates the Hess case to standard examples of belief, then we are left with the question of why this should be so. What is it about the state in the Hess example that makes us reluctant to treat it as a belief? I think the answer is that this state shares with our other two examples of subdoxastic states a sort of inferential isolation from the body of our accessible beliefs. This is the topic to which I now will turn.

6

It is characteristic of beliefs that they generate further beliefs via inference. What is more, beliefs are inferentially promiscuous. Provided with a suitable set of supplementary beliefs, almost any belief can play a role in the inference to any other. Thus, for example, if a subject believes that p and comes to believe that if p then q, he may well come to believe that q—and do so as the result of an inferential process. In addition to the well-integrated network of potential deductive inferences, beliefs also generate other beliefs via inductive inference. So there is generally a huge number of inferential paths via which a given belief can lead to most any other. It is in this sense that a person's beliefs are *inferentially integrated*.

Of course, the patterns of valid inference specified in deductive logic and those that would be specified by a theory of inductive logic, if there were such a theory, correspond in no simple way to the inference pattern exhibited among a person's beliefs. We do not, for example, draw all logically possible inferences from our beliefs. Nor are all our inferences logically valid. What is more, there is no reason to suppose a priori that each logically permissible inference is in fact psychologically possible. And it is at least possible there are some beliefs that cannot be acquired by inference at all. The non-inferential beliefs of traditional epistemology would be an example, if indeed there are any such beliefs. However, none of these caveats detracts from our principal point about the inferential integration of beliefs: a person's body of beliefs forms an elaborate and interconnected network with a vast number of potential inference patterns leading from every belief to almost any other.

Now it is my contention that part of the reason we are intuitively inclined to say subdoxastic states are not beliefs is that subdoxastic states, as contrasted with beliefs, *are largely inferentially isolated from the large body of inferentially integrated beliefs to which a subject has access.* This is not to say that subdoxastic states do not play any role in inference to and from accessible beliefs, but merely that they are inferentially impoverished, with a comparatively limited range of potential inferential patterns via which they can give rise to beliefs, and a comparatively limited range of potential inferential patterns via which beliefs can give rise to them. This last remark may strike some as paradoxical. For, it might be protested, inference is a relation *among* beliefs. It is (one of) the ways beliefs generate other beliefs. And if subdoxastic states are not beliefs, then they cannot be *inferentially* related to anything. The objection is an important one, and its central claim—that inference is a relation exclusively among beliefs—is one that will play a prominent role in the following section. For the moment, however, let us grant that at least some of the routes by which subdoxastic states give rise to beliefs or other subdoxastic states can sensibly be taken to be instances of inference. Granting this assumption, the picture I am urging is this. Consciously accessible beliefs are embedded in an elaborate network of potential inferential connections with each other. Each belief is a potential premise in inferences to a vast array of further beliefs. By contrast, the inferential contact between subdoxastic states and beliefs is specialized and limited. When a subdoxastic state can serve as a premise in an inference to beliefs, there is only a narrow range of beliefs to which it may potentially lead. Similarly, when a subdoxastic state can result from an inference with beliefs among the premises, the range of beliefs that can serve in this capacity is restricted and specialized. If we think in terms of a cognitive simulation model, the view I am urging is that beliefs form a consciously accessible, inferentially integrated cognitive subsystem. Subdoxastic states occur in a variety of separate, special purpose cognitive subsystems. And even when the subdoxastic states within a specialized subsystem generate one another via a process of inference, their inferential interactions with the integrated body of accessible beliefs is severely limited. Similarly, in all likelihood, the potential inferential connections among subdoxastic states in different specialized subsystems are extremely limited or non-existent. To get a clearer view of my thesis about the inferential integration of beliefs, let us see how it applies to our examples.

Even on the most generous assumptions about the inferential potential of the states which store grammatical information, these states are largely isolated from the body of a subject's beliefs. These grammar storing states can plausibly be assumed to play a role in the formation of beliefs about what has been said to a person (that is, in the process leading from auditory stimulation to comprehension). They can also, as we have seen, be presumed to play a role in the process leading to formation of beliefs about grammatical properties and relations—the sorts of beliefs expressed when an informant is offering grammatical intuitions. And let us suppose that the processes involved are properly viewed as inferential. Then the states storing grammatical information do have some limited inferential links with beliefs. But let us compare the state storing a grammatical rule with the explicit belief in that rule, say on the part of the linguist.[2] The linguist's explicit belief can enter into an almost endless number of inferences in which the competent speaker's subdoxastic state cannot participate. For example, if a linguist believes a certain generalization to the effect that no transformational rule exhibits a certain characteristic, and if he comes to believe a given transformation which violates the generalization, he may well infer that the generalization is false. But merely having the rule stored (in the way that we are assuming all speakers of the language do) does not enable the linguist to draw the inference. As another example, suppose that, for some putative rule r, you have come to believe that if r then Chomsky is seriously mistaken. Suppose further that, as it happens, r is in fact among the rules stored by your language processing mechanism. That belief along with the subdoxastic state will not lead to the belief that Chomsky is seriously mistaken. By contrast, if you believe (perhaps even mistakenly) that r, then the belief that Chomsky is seriously mistaken is likely to be inferred. It would be easy enough to marshall many more illustrations of the fact that the subdoxistic states which store grammatical information are largely inferentially isolated from beliefs.

The situation is, if anything, clearer for the states which process and store information about binocular disparity. Let us suppose that at a given stage in the process leading to the formation of judgements about apparent comparative depth in Julesz's experiments, a certain subdoxastic state represents the information that a dot on a certain part of the left retina is displaced five seconds further toward the nose then the similarly situated dot on the right retina. It may well be that a fairly complicated process of computation and inference is required for the formation of this subdoxastic state. The process might, for example, utilize and compare information about the distribution of

---

2. There are a pair of assumptions being made here. First, I assume that the grammatical information stored by a competent speaker consists (in part) of rules of the speaker's grammar. As noted in fn. 1, I suspect this is a counterfactual assumption. Second, I assume that grammatical rules can be formulated in such a way that it makes sense to talk of believing a rule. More specifically, I am assuming that appending a formulation of a rule to 'S believes that——' produces a well-formed sentence.

dots on each separate retina in order to locate "corresponding" dots. It may also be the case that the process leading from our hypothesized subdoxastic state to the belief that the displaced dot appears in front of the others is itself inferential. On this assumption, the subdoxastic state does have a potential inferential path to an accessible belief. However, it is a vastly more restrictive path than beliefs have to each other. Contrast, for example, the *subdoxastic state* representing the information that a dot on a certain part of the left retina is displaced five seconds further toward the nose than the similarly situated dot on the right retina, with the *belief* that the dot in that part of the retina is displaced five seconds further toward the nose than the similarly situated dot on the right retina. The subdoxastic state can lead directly only to a restricted class of beliefs about apparent relative depth (and perhaps some other aspects of the visual field). By contrast, the belief, if supplemented by suitable additional beliefs, can lead to just about any belief. There is also a striking contrast in the ways other beliefs can *lead to* either the subdoxastic state or the belief. A subject might inferentially acquire the belief (that a dot on a certain part of the left retina . . . etc.) in numerous and diverse ways. He may be told that the dot is thus displaced by a person he takes to be trustworthy, and infer that it is on the basis of his belief about what his informant believes. Or he may infer it from beliefs formed by observing the readings on certain test instruments. Indeed, most any other belief, say the belief that *p*, can inferentially give rise to the belief about the relative positions of the retinal dots, provided that the subject also believes a proposition of the form *if p then d*, where *d* is the proposition that a dot on a certain part of the left retina . . . etc. On the other hand, it is most likely the case that there are *no beliefs at all* which can lead inferentially to the subdoxastic state that represents the fact that *d*.

This example illustrates with particular clarity a feature also exhibited by our other examples of subdoxastic states. Part of the reason we are inclined to insist that a subdoxastic state is not a belief is that if it were, we would be unable to say *what* belief it was. That is, if a subdoxastic state were taken to be a belief, there would be no sentence *p* such that inserting *p* in "*S* believes that——" would express the fact that the subject was in the state. The problem is most noticeable when, as in our current examples, we contrast the belief that *p* with the subdoxastic state which stores or represents the information that *p*. Since the subdoxastic state differs so markedly from the belief both in its potential inferential connections and in the subject's potential access to it, we are disinclined to identify the subdoxastic state with the belief. But surely if a state representing the information that *p* is a belief at all, then it is the belief that *p*.

These reflections bring us perilously close to a cluster of questions I have been doing my utmost to sidestep. All this glib talk about a state representing information may get one wondering just what it might *mean* to say that a state "represents (the information (or fact) that) *p*." I do not think it would be unreasonable to duck the issue entirely in this paper. For though this talk of states representing facts is difficult to explicate in a philosophically tolerable way, it is surprisingly easy to master intuitively. Even the barest introduction to work in artificial intelligence and cognitive simulation quickly leaves one comfortable with attributions of content or representational status to the states of an information processing theory. And nothing I want to say here presupposes anything more than the ability to use these locutions as they are customarily used. Still, a hint of how I think such talk is to be analyzed may be welcome. On my view, saying that a state in an information processing system represents (the information (or fact) that) *p* is to say that the state bears some interesting resemblances to the belief that *p*. Generally the resemblances are with respect to the ordinary causes of the state, or some part of the inferential pattern of the state, or some other (non-inferential) effect the state may have (or some combination of the three). On this account, of course, the belief that *p* represents (the information (or fact) that) *p*; indeed, it is the prototype of such representation. Also, on my account, many different states can represent *p*, and can do so to varying degrees. There is no minimum degree of resemblance required for us to say that a state represents *p*. Rather, the appropriateness of the content attribution depends on the particular needs and interests of the project at hand. For more on all this, along with a theory about what we are saying when we say a belief is the belief that *p*, see my *From Folk Psychology to Cognitive Science* [16].

Our third example of a subdoxastic state, the Hess example, is quite parallel to the second. The subdoxastic state which serves to represent the information that the pupils in one photo are larger than those in the other is significantly less inferentially integrated with the body of a subject's beliefs than is the *belief* that the pupils in one photo are larger. As in the previous case, the paths leading to formation of the subdoxastic state are relatively few and involve only a restricted range of beliefs (if any), while almost any belief can play a direct role in an inference to the *belief* that the pupils in one photo are enlarged. Also, the subdoxastic state has a significantly more restricted set of possible inferences in which it may play a role. The belief that the pupils in the retouched photo are larger, along with the belief that, say, the earlobes in that photo are much enlarged, may lead to the belief that several facial features are enlarged. But one of Hess' subjects who has the *second* belief is unlikely to infer the belief that several facial features are enlarged (unless, of course, the subdoxastic state gives rise to the conscious *belief* that the pupils are enlarged). I think it is the inferential isolation of the state Hess' subjects are in that incline us to insist these are not to be counted as beliefs.

It is time to take stock of our discussion so far. I began by noting the distinction between beliefs and subdoxastic states, which is quite fundamental to our ordinary, pre-theoretic thinking about beliefs. With some examples of subdoxastic states on hand, we began to look for the basis of our intuitive distinction. My thesis has been that the distinction is drawn on the basis of two characteristics which beliefs exhibit and subdoxastic states do not: access to consciousness and inferential integration. In the course of our discussion we also noted, if only to then ignore, a further principle embedded in our pre-theoretic notion of belief, which ties together the concepts of belief and inference. The principle holds that inference (at least when viewed as a relation among psychological states) is a relation exclusively among beliefs. This principle, along with the features which divide beliefs from subdoxastic states, accounts for the location in traditional epistemology of non-inferential beliefs. For if the psychological states causally underlying a belief are not themselves beliefs, then, according to the principle, the process leading to the belief cannot be inference.

7

This principle that inference is a relation among beliefs deserves a less cavalier look than has been accorded it so far. For the principle plays a central role in an argument advanced by Gilbert Harman aimed at undermining the belief-subdoxastic distinction. Harman notes that "a person determines how far away a perceived object is by means of cues involving overlapping of surfaces and texture gradients." It is natural, he continues, "to describe this as a matter of inference: given these cues the perceiver infers that objects are in those places. The relevant cues make it reasonable to suppose the objects are where the perceiver infers they are" ([7], p. 175). Harman anticipates the objection that talk of perceptual inference uses the word "inference" in a peculiar or special sense. He replies as follows:

> Contemporary psychologists tend to view a perceiver as an information processing mechanism, a kind of analogue computer. . . . Now it is natural to describe mechanical information-processing machines—like computers—as if they could calculate, figure something out, and infer conclusions. When the perceiver is conceived as an information processing device, it becomes natural to describe him in the same way. Having extended the application of 'inference' so that computers can be said to infer, it is natural to extend it so that perceivers are also said to infer. ([7], pp. 176–177)

The view that inference is involved in the formation of beliefs about our perceived environment is hardly novel. Descartes would have had no objection. But Descartes would have balked at Harman's view of the premises for such inferences. In the Cartesian tradition, the premises are beliefs about experience, about how things look to the subject. Harman rejects this position. "One problem is that some aspects of the way things appear is determined by inference. For example, reasoning involving overlap, texture gradients, and perspective figures in the apparent location of objects. Inference gets into the story before it is determined how things look" ([7], p. 180). Nor, on Harman's view, is there any more basic level of visual experience to serve as data. ". . . there does not seem to be any more basic level of visual experience not itself the product of inference, and used itself as data for inference to how things look" ([7], p. 181). Instead, Harman traces the path of inference all the way back to retinal stimulations, which, he holds, are the basic data for perceptual knowledge.

I suggested that the data are the sensory stimulations that provide the input to the complex information processing system composed of brain and nervous system. Perceptual knowledge is based on inference from sensory stimulations. ([7], p. 185)

Finally, Harman claims that retinal stimulations and other sensory stimulations which serve as the basic data for perceptual knowledge are themselves *beliefs*.

Does he [the perceiver] believe the data? He uses them in the way one uses beliefs in inference. So there is some reason to say that he believes them. ([7], p. 186)

Now note that if we go along with Harman, then the distinction between beliefs and subdoxastic states seems to vanish. For on Harman's view, both retinal stimulations and all of the various psychological states that may be inferred from them count as *beliefs*. If Harman is right, then our intuitive psychological theory has led us seriously astray; many states which intuition insists are not beliefs turn out to be beliefs nonetheless. Let us take a more careful look at just how Harman reaches this surprising conclusion.

I think the argument is best viewed as proceeding in two stages, the first defending the view that retinal stimulations and various other intuitively subdoxastic states are inferentially related to beliefs and to each other, and the second marshalling the principle that inference is a relation among beliefs. The claim of the first stage, in turn, follows from a pair of contentions: first, that it is appropriate to use the word "inference" in describing the processes leading to beliefs about our perceived surroundings; and second, that it is suitable to describe these processes as inferential "all the way down," to the level of retinal stimulations.

I am largely in agreement with the claim that there are inferential relations among (intuitively) subdoxastic states, and among subdoxastic states and beliefs. However, I think that Harman's defense of this view deflects attention from the important issue involved. In arguing that inference is involved in the process leading to the formation of beliefs about our perceptual environment, Harman stresses the "naturalness" of this use of the word "inference," a naturalness which is allegedly enhanced by the analogous use in talk of computers. It seems to me, however, that the intuitive naturalness of this use of "inference" is largely beside the point. What is important is not whether perceptual psychologists are using "inference" in some natural extension of its ordinary sense, but rather whether the phenomena they are describing are in important ways similar to more standard cases of inference. Similarly, the conjecture that inferential processes extend all the way down the causal chain to the level of retinal stimulations does not turn on the intuitive naturalness of calling these processes "inferential." What is at stake is whether these processes are in fact in fundamental ways similar to the process of inference in standard cases. These are empirical questions, not to be settled by appeal to ordinary usage. What we need to know are the similarities and differences between the process leading from sensory stimulation to belief, and the process (ordinarily called "inference") leading from pre-existing beliefs to the formation of new beliefs. If the processes are sufficiently similar, the proposed extension of "inference" to cover the former is a reasonable one. At present neither perception nor more standard cases of inference are sufficiently well understood in detail to settle the question definitively. But recent efforts at modeling perception and at modeling inference and problem solving make it plausible that the two processes may be essentially congruent.[3] If this speculation proves true, it will be an empirical result of enormous importance.

The discovery that inference is involved in perception down to the level of sensory stimulation is not, of course, enough to show that intuitively subdoxastic states are beliefs. To get this conclusion we need the additional premise that inference is a relation among beliefs. Harman, as we saw in the last displayed quote above, endorses the premise and draws the conclusion. It is just here that my dissent comes in. Harman and I are agreed that inference likely relates states far removed from anything we would pre-theoretically call a belief. This fact, if it is a fact, puts considerable strain on our pre-theoretic views about beliefs. Harman would accommodate the strain by rejecting our intuitions on what sorts of states to count as beliefs. By contrast, I would accommodate the strain by simply rejecting the principle that inference is a relation exclusively among beliefs. By my lights, what the supposed discovery of inference in deep perceptual processes shows is not that intuitively subdoxastic states are actually beliefs, but rather that the domain of the inference relation includes other states in addition to beliefs.

There is something misleading in the account I have just given of the difference between Harman and myself. For it sounds as though the dispute is largely terminological. He wants to call subdoxastic states "beliefs" and preserve the principle that inference relates only beliefs; I want to renounce the principle and abjure the expanded extension of "belief." The issue, however, is not simply a terminological one. What is at stake is not whether we bloat the extension of "belief" to preserve a principle, but rather whether the old intuitive boundary between beliefs and subdoxastic states divides states which are in fact psychologically different. If it does, then following Harman's terminological proposal would simply make it necessary to coin some new term to denote the class of states we are now intuitively inclined to call "beliefs."

Harman nowhere addresses himself to the issue of the psychological importance of the belief-subdoxastic state distinction. However, in light of his proposed extension of "belief" to cover subdoxastic states and his failure to propose some other way of marking the boundary, I think we might plausibly attribute to him the view that the distinction is of small importance. Yet, as some of Harman's further remarks illustrate, this is not an easy position to espouse consistently. Thus consider the following dilemma. After defending the view that various (intuitively subdoxastic) states, including retinal stimulations,

---

3. For problem solving see [12]; for some interesting work in inference, c.f. [1], ch. 13; for an account of perception which stresses the parallels between perceptual representation and inference on the one hand, and the representation an inference among beliefs on the other hand, see [1], ch. 8; also [11] and [13].

are beliefs because they are used "the way one uses beliefs in inference," Harman is in something of a quandary about just *what* beliefs they are. Just what belief are we to attribute to a perceiver, for example, when his retinal nerve is stimulated in a certain way? An obvious answer: the perceiver believes that his retinal nerve is being stimulated in that way. But, sensibly enough, Harman is unwilling to buy that answer. For he conjures the following objection:

> The typical perceiver knows little psychology and nothing about stimulations of his retinal nerve. So if the data needed for his inference includes claims about his sensory stimulation, he does not believe the data. ([7], p. 185)

Harman is plainly troubled by the objection, and his efforts to parry are a bit bizarre. The perceiver, he concedes, does not have any beliefs *about* sensory stimulations. Rather, the sensory stimulations themselves are the beliefs; it is they which serve as data for perceptual inference

> The data are not about sensory stimulations, they *are* sensory stimulations. . . .
> Does [the perceiver] believe the data? He uses them in the way one uses beliefs in inference. So there is some reason to say that he believes them. ([7], p. 186)

Well and good. The stimulations are beliefs. But beliefs that *what*?

> Sensory stimulations serve the perceiver as non-linguistic representations which cannot be easily put into words. . . .
> In order to be able to express in words the input data, we would have to know much more about the system of representation and its functioning than we now know. Even then it might be impossible to find linguistic representations equivalent to the non-linguistic representations constituted by sensory stimulation. ([7], p. 186)

Now it is pretty clear that part of this reply is simply a bluff. Harman suggests that we might be able to express the content of sensory stimulations if only we knew more about the workings of the system. But it seems pretty plain that there is no sentence which will serve to express the content of retinal stimulations *any better* than a sentence asserting that the retina is being stimulated in a certain way. Indeed, any sentence S which might be proposed as a candidate for expressing the content of retinal stimulations would face just the same difficulties as a sentence specifying how the retina is being stimulated. To see this, consider for a moment why we are unwilling to say of a perceiver whose retina is being stimulated in a certain way that he *believes* it is being stimulated in that way. Harman's reply is that the typical perceiver knows little psychology and nothing about the stimulation of his retinal nerve. But why are we so sure of this? The answer, I think, is that if we were to attribute beliefs about retinal stimulations to a naive perceiver, they would be a most peculiar species of belief, for they would be beliefs to which the perceiver had no access and which were largely inferentially isolated from the remainder of his beliefs. The same would be true if we instead attributed to the perceiver the belief that *p*, where *p* is an arbitrary candidate for expressing the content of a retinal stimulation.

Harman's other strategy for parrying the problem that we cannot find suitable content sentences for retinal stimulations is to retreat into mysticism. Even after we have a decent understanding of the functioning of the perceptual system, "it might be impossible to find linguistic representations equivalent to the non-linguistic representations constituted by sensory stimulations" ([7], p. 186). Their content is so mysterious that it is not expressible by words. It is tempting here to ponder whether it could make any sense to say that a state represents something, but there is no saying what it represents. I shall, however, resist the temptation. For it seems to me that by retreating to this doctrine of the unspeakable, Harman has conceded the principal point that I have been arguing. The states for whose contents it is impossible "to find linguistic representation" are just those that we have been calling subdoxastic, So Harman has conceded, however obliquely, that there is an important difference between beliefs and subdoxastic states. But if Harman and I agree on this central point, serious differences remain in how to characterize the difference. For Harman, the difference turns on the linguistic expressibility of the contents of subdoxastic states. On my view, however, there is no particular problem in expressing the contents of subdoxastic states. Harman sees a problem because he insists that subdoxastic states are beliefs. But it is more than his intuition will tolerate to attribute to a subject the belief that *p*, where *p* expresses the content of the state. Thus he must postulate some mysterious unspeakable content. As I see it, the problem is not in finding a content sentence, but in failing to distinguish subdoxastic states from beliefs. Once the distinction has been recognized, we can assign quite ordinary contents to subdoxastic states without worrying that the subject fails to believe the content sentence.

We began this section with the concern that Harman's arguments appeared to show the distinction between beliefs and subdoxastic states is untenable. I think it fair to conclude that we have found the fault to lie not with the distinction but with the argument trying to undermine it.

8

Where does all this leave us? I believe we have a plausible case for the claim that the intuitive distinction between beliefs and subdoxastic states marks a real and psychologically interesting boundary. Moreover, it is a boundary that has been largely overlooked by contemporary work in cognitive simulation. The reasons for this neglect are not obvious. It would be my guess that, like Harman, many of those concerned with cognitive simulation have been so captivated with the promise of inferential accounts of the mechanisms underlying perception and thought that they have failed to note the rather special and largely isolated nature of the inferential processes between beliefs and subdoxastic states. Failure to take seriously the matter of access to consciousness likely has a less creditable explanation. Since the heyday of behaviorism, conscious awareness has had a bad name among many psychologists. And the attitude seems to persist even among those who have come to see behaviorism as a dead end.

If it is granted that the belief-subdoxastic state distinction is (at least *prima facie*) an important one, then we are left with an intriguing question. Why do inferential integration and access to consciousness run in tandem? Is this just an accident, or is there some underlying mechanism that accounts for both phenomena? My hunch is that it is more than an accident. But if I have inferred that view, the premises I have used are well hidden from conscious access.

REFERENCES

1. Anderson, J. and Bower, G. *Human Associative Memory*. Washington: John Wiley and Sons, 1974.
2. Austin, J. L. *Sense and Sensibilia*. New York: Oxford University Press, 1964.
3. Chomsky, N. and Katz, J. "What the Linguist Is Talking About." *Journal of Philosophy* 71 (1974): 347–367.
4. Dretske, F. *Seeing and Knowing*. Chicago: University of Chicago Press, 1969.
5. Graves, C., Katz, J., et. al. "Tacit Knowledge." *Journal of Philosophy* 70 (1973): 318–330.
6. Haber, R. N. and Hershenson, M. *The Psychology of Visual Perception*. New York: Holt, Rinehart, and Winston, 1973.
7. Harman, G. *Thought*. Princeton: Princeton University Press, 1973.
8. Hess, E. H. "Attitude and Pupil Size." *Scientific American* 212 (1965).
9. Hess, E. H. "The Role of Pupil Size in Communication." *Scientific American* 233 (1975).
10. Julesz, J. *The Cyclopean Eye*. New York: Academic Press, 1970.
11. Moran, T. P. *The Symbolic Imagery Hypothesis: A Production System Model*. Ph.D. Dissertation, Carnegie-Mellon University, 1973.
12. Newell, A. and Simon, H. *Human Problem Solving*. Englewood Cliffs: Prentice Hall, 1973.
13. Pylyshyn, Z. "What The Mind's Eye Tells The Mind's Brain: A Critique on Mental Imagery." *Psychological Bulletin* 80 (1973).
14. Stich, S. P. "What Every Speaker Knows." Philosophical Review 80 (1971): 476–496.
15. Stich, S. P. "Competence and Indeterminacy." In *Testing Linguistic Hypotheses*, Cohen, D. and Wirth, J. R., eds. Washington: John Wiley, 1975.
16. Stich, S. (1983) From *Folk Psychology to Cognitive Science: The Case Against Belief,* Bradford Books/MIT Press.
17. Winograd, T. "Understanding Natural Language." *Cognitive Psychology* 3 (1972): 1–191.

4

AUTONOMOUS PSYCHOLOGY AND THE BELIEF–DESIRE THESIS

A VENERABLE VIEW, still very much alive, holds that human action is to be explained at least in part in terms of beliefs and desires. Those who advocate the view expect that the psychological theory which explains human behavior will invoke the concepts of belief and desire in a substantive way. I will call this expectation *the belief–desire thesis*. Though there would surely be a quibble or a caveat here and there, the thesis would be endorsed by an exceptionally heterogeneous collection of psychologists and philosophers ranging from Freud and Hume, to Thomas Szasz and Richard Brandt. Indeed, a number of philosophers have contended that the thesis, or something like it, is embedded in our ordinary, workaday concept of action.[1] If they are right, and I think they are, then in so far as we use the concept of action we are *all* committed to the belief–desire thesis. My purpose in this paper is to explore the tension between the belief–desire thesis and a widely held assumption about the nature of explanatory psychological theories, an assumption that serves as a fundamental regulative principle for much of contemporary pscyhological theorizing. This assumption, which for want of a better term I will call the *principle of psychological autonomy*, will be the focus of the first of the sections below. In the second section I will elaborate a bit on how the belief–desire thesis is to be interpreted, and try to extract from it a principle that will serve as a premise in the argument to follow. In the

---

1. The clearest and most detailed elaboration of this view that I know of is to be found in Goldman 1970. The view is also argued in Brandt and Kim 1963, and in Davidson 1963. However, Davidson does not advocate the belief–desire thesis as it will be construed below (cf. n. 11).

third section I will set out an argument to the effect that large numbers of belief–desire explanations of action, indeed perhaps the bulk of such explanations, are incompatible with the principle of autonomy. Finally, in the last section, I will fend off a possible objection to my argument. In the process, I will try to make clear just why the argument works and what price we should have to pay if we were resolved to avoid its consequences.

I The Principle of Psychological Autonomy

Perhaps the most vivid way of explaining the principle I have in mind is by invoking a type of science fiction example that has cropped up with some frequency in recent philosophical literature. Imagine that technology were available which would enable us to duplicate people. That is, we can build living human beings who are atom for atom and molecule for molecule replicas of some given human being.[2] Now suppose that we have before us a human being (or, for that matter, any sort of animal) and his exact replica. What the principle of autonomy claims is that these two humans will be psychologically identical, that any psychological property instantiated by one of these subjects will also be instantiated by the other.

Actually, a bit of hedging is needed to mark the boundaries of this claim to psychological identity. First, let me note that the organisms claimed to be psychologically identical include any pair of organisms, existing at the same time or at different times, who happen to be atom for atom replicas of each other. Moreover, it is inessential that one organism should have been built to be a replica of the other. Even if the replication is entirely accidental, the two organisms will still be psychologically identical.

A caveat of another sort is needed to clarify just what I mean by calling two organisms "psychologically identical." For consider the following objection: "The original organism and his replica do not share *all* of their psychological properties. The original may, for example, remember seeing the Watergate hearings on television, but the replica remembers no such thing. He may think he remembers it, or have an identical "memory trace," but if he was not created until long after the Watergate hearings, then he did not see the hearings on television, and thus he could not remember seeing them." The point being urged by my imagined critic is a reasonable one. There are many sorts of properties plausibly labeled "psychological" that might be instantiated by a person and not by his replica. Remembering that p is one example, knowing that p and seeing that p are others. These properties have a sort of "hybrid" character. They seem to be analyzable into a "purely psychological" property (like seeming to remember that p, or believing that p) along with one or more non-psychological properties and relations (like p being true, or the memory trace being caused in a certain way by the fact that p). But to insist that "hybrid" psychological properties are

2. Cf. Putnam 1973 and 1975.

not psychological properties at all would be at best a rather high handed attempt at stipulative definition. Still, there is something a bit odd about these hybrid psychological properties, a fact which reflects itself in the intuitive distinction between "hybrids" and their underlying "purely pscyhological" components. What is odd about the hybrids, I think, is that we do not expect them to play any role in an explanatory psychological theory. Rather, we expect a psychological theory which aims at explaining behavior to invoke only the "purely psychological" properties which are shared by a subject and its replicas. Thus, for example, we are inclined to insist it is Jones's *belief* that there is no greatest prime number that plays a role in the explanation of his answering the exam question. He may, in fact, have *known* that there is no greatest prime number. But even if he did not know it, if, for example, the source of his information had himself only been guessing, Jones's behavior would have been unaffected. What knowledge adds to belief is psychologically irrelevant. Similarly the difference between really remembering that p and merely seeming to remember that p makes no difference to the subject's behavior. In claiming that physical replicas are psychologically identical, the principle of psychological autonomy is to be understood as restricting itself to the properties that can play a role in explanatory psychological theory. Indeed, the principle is best viewed as a claim about what sorts of properties and relations may play a role in explanatory psychological theory. If the principle is to be observed, then the only properties and relations that may legitimately play a role in explanatory psychological theories are the properties and relations that a subject and its replica will share.

There is another way to explain the principle of psychological autonomy that does not appeal to the fanciful idea of a replica. Jaegwon Kim has explicated and explored the notion of one class of properties *supervening* upon another class of properties.[3] Suppose S and W are two classes of properties, and that S and W are the sets of all properties constructible from the properties in S and W respectively. Then, following Kim, we will say that the family S of properties supervenes on the family W of properties (with respect to a domain D of objects) just in case, necessarily, any two objects in D which share all properties in W will also share all properties in S. A bit less formally, one class of properties supervenes on another if the presence or absence of properties in the former class is completely determined by the presence or absence of properties in the latter.[4] Now the principle of psychological autonomy states that the properties and relations to be invoked in an explanatory psychological theory must be supervenient upon the *current, internal physical* properties and relations of organisms (i.e., just those properties that an organism shares with all of its replicas).

---

3. Kim 1978.

4. Kim's account of supervenience is intentionally non-committal on the sort of necessity invoked in the definition. Different notions of necessity will yield different, though parallel, concepts of supervenience.

Perhaps the best way to focus more sharply on what the autonomy principle states is to look at what it rules out. First, of course, if explanatory psychological properties and relations must supervene on *physical* properties, then at least some forms of dualism are false. The dualist who claims that there are psychological (or mental) properties which are not nomologically correlated with physical properties, but which nonetheless must be invoked in an explanation of the organism's behavior, is denying that explanatory psychological states supervene upon physical states. However, the autonomy principle is not inimical to all forms of dualism. Those dualists, for example, who hold that mental and physical properties are nomologically correlated need have no quarrel with the doctrine of autonomy. However, the principle of autonomy is significantly stronger than the mere insistence that psychological states supervene on physical states.[5] For autonomy requires in addition that certain physical properties and relations are psychologically irrelevant in the sense that organisms which differ *only* with respect to those properties and relations are psychologically identical.[6] In specifying that only "current" physical properties are psychologically relevant, the autonomy principle decrees irrelevant all those properties that deal with the history of the organism, both past and future. It is entirely possible, for example, for two organisms to have quite different physical histories and yet, at a specific pair of moments, to be replicas of one another. But this sort of difference, according to the autonomy principle, can make no difference from the point of view of explanatory psychology. Thus remembering that p (as contrasted with having a memory trace that p) cannot be an explanatory psychological state. For the difference between a person who remembers that p and a person who only seems to remember that p is not dependent on their current physical state, but only on the history of these states. Similarly, in specifying that only *internal* properties and relations are relevant to explanatory psychological properties, the autonomy principle decrees that relations between an organism and its external environment are irrelevant to its current (explanatory) psychological state. The restriction also entails that properties and relations of external objects cannot be relevant to the organism's current (explanatory) psychological state. Thus neither my seeing that Jones is falling nor my knowing that Ouagadougou is the capital of Upper Volta can play a role in an explanatory psychological theory, since the former depends in part on my relation to Jones, and the latter depends in part on the relation between Ouagadougou and Upper Volta.

Before we leave our discussion of the principle of psychological autonomy, let us reflect briefly on the status of the principle. On Kim's view, the belief that one set of properties supervenes on another "is largely, and often, a combination of metaphysical convictions

---

5. This weaker principle is discussed at some length in Kim 1977.

6. Note, however, that physical properties that are irrelevant in this sense may nonetheless be *causally* related to those physical properties upon which psychological properties supervene. Thus they may be "psychologically relevant" in the sense that they may play a role in the explanation of how the organism comes to have some psychological property.

and methodological considerations."[7] The description seems particularly apt for the principle of psychological autonomy. The autonomy principle serves a sort of regulative role in modern psychology, directing us to restrict the concepts we invoke in our explanatory theories in a very special way. When we act in accordance with the regulative stipulation of the principle we are giving witness to the tacit conviction that the best explanation of behavior will include a theory invoking properties supervenient upon the organism's current, internal physical state.[8] As Kim urges, this conviction is supported in part by the past success of theories which cleave to the principle's restrictions, and in part by some very fundamental metaphysical convictions. I think there is much to be learned in trying to pick apart the various metaphysical views that support the autonomy principle, for some of them have implications in areas quite removed from psychology. But that is a project for a different paper.

II The Belief–Desire Thesis

The belief–desire thesis maintains that human action is to be explained, at least in part, in terms of beliefs and desires. To sharpen the thesis we need to say more about the intended sense of *explain*, and more about what it would be to explain action *in terms of beliefs and desires*. But before trying to pin down either of these notions, it will be useful to set out an example of the sort of informal belief–desire explanations that we commonly offer for our own actions and the actions of others.

> Jones is watching television; from time to time he looks nervously at a lottery ticket grasped firmly in his hand. Suddenly he jumps up and rushes toward the phone. Why? It was because the TV announcer has just announced the winning lottery number, and it is the number on Jones's ticket. Jones believes that he has won the lottery. He also believes that to collect his winnings he must contact the lottery commission promptly. And, needless to say, he very much wants to collect his winnings.

Many theorists acknowledge that explanations like the one offered of Jones rushing toward the phone are often true (albeit incomplete) explanations of action. But this concession alone does not commit the theorist to the belief–desire thesis as I will interpret it here. There is considerable controversy over how we are to understand the

---

7. Kim 1978.

8. It has been my experience that psychologists who agree on little else readily endorse the autonomy principle. Indeed, I have yet to find a psychologist who did not take the principle to be obviously true. Some of these same psychologists also favored the sort of belief–desire explanations of action that I will later argue are at odds with the autonomy principle. None, however, was aware of the incompatibility, and a number of them vigorously resisted the contention that the incompatibility is there.

'because' in "Jones rushed for the phone because he believed he had won the lottery and he wanted . . ." Some writers are inclined to read the 'because' literally, as claiming that Jones's belief and his desire were the *causes* (or among the causes) of his action. Others offer a variety of non-causal accounts of the relation between beliefs and desires on the one hand and actions on the other.[9] However, it is the former, "literal," reading that is required by the belief–desire thesis as I am construing it.

To say that Jones's belief that he had won the lottery was among the causes of his rushing toward the phone is to say of one specific event that it had among its causes one specific state. There is much debate over how such "singular causal statements" are to be analyzed. Some philosophers hold that for a state or event S to be among the causes of an event E, there must be a law which somehow relates S and E. Other philosophers propose other accounts. Even among those who agree that singular causal statements must be subsumed by a law, there is debate over how this notion of subsumption is to be understood. At the heart of this controversy is the issue of how much difference there can be between the properties invoked in the law and those invoked in the description of the event if the event is to be an instance of the law.[10] Given our current purposes, there is no need to take a stand on this quite general metaphysical issue. But we will have to take a stand on a special case of the relation between beliefs, desires, and the psychological laws that subsume them. The belief–desire thesis, as I am viewing it, takes seriously the idea of developing a psychological theory couched in terms of beliefs and desires. Thus, in addition to holding that Jones's action was caused by his belief that he had won the lottery and his desire to collect his winnings, it also holds that this singular causal statement is true in virtue of being subsumed by laws which specify nomological relations among beliefs, desires and action.[11]

There is one further point that needs to be made about my construal of the belief–desire thesis. If the thesis is right, then action is to be expained at least in part by appeal

9. For a critique of these views, cf. Goldman 1970, chapter 3; Alston 1967b.

10. For discussion of these matters, see Kim 1973. Kim defends the view that the property invoked in the description must be identical with the one invoked in the law. For a much more liberal view see Davidson 1967.

11. Thus Davidson is not an advocate of the belief–desire thesis as I am construing it. For on his view, though beliefs and desires may be among the causes of actions, the general laws supporting the causal claims are not themselves couched in terms of beliefs and desires (cf. Davidson 1970). But Davidson's view, though not without interest, is plainly idiosyncratic. Generally, philosophers who hold that beliefs and desires are among the causes of behavior also think that there are psychological laws to be found (most likely probabilistic ones) which are stated in terms of beliefs and desires. Cf., for example, Hempel 1965, pp. 463–87; Alston 1967a and 1967b; Goldman 1970, chapters 3 and 4.

We should also note that much of recent psychology can be viewed as a quest for psychological laws couched in terms of beliefs and/or desires. There is, for example, an enormous and varied literature on problem solving (cf. Newell and Simon 1972) and on informal inference (cf. Nisbett and Ross 1980) which explores the mechanisms and environmental determinants of belief formation. Also, much of the literature on motivation is concerned with uncovering the laws governing the formation and strength of desires (cf. Atkinson 1964).

to laws detailing how beliefs, desires and other psychological states effect action. But how are we to recognize such laws? It is, after all, plainly not enough for a theory simply to invoke the terms 'belief' and 'desire' in its laws. If it were, then it would be possible to convert any theory into a belief–desire theory by the simple expedient of replacing a pair of its theoretical terms with the terms 'belief' and 'desire.' The point I am laboring is that the belief–desire thesis must be construed as the claim that psychological theory will be couched in terms of beliefs and desires *as we ordinarily conceive of them.* Thus to spell out the belief–desire thesis in detail would require that we explicate our intuitive concepts of belief and desire. Fortunately, we need not embark on that project here.[12] To fuel the arguments I will develop in the following section, I will need only a single, intuitively plausible, premise about beliefs.

As a backdrop for the premise that I need, let me introduce some handy terminology. I believe that Ouagadougou is the capital of Upper Volta, and if you share my interest in atlases then it is likely that you have the same belief. Of course, there is also a perfectly coherent sense in which your belief is not the same a mine, since you could come to believe that Bobo Dioulasso is the capital of Upper Volta, while my belief remains unchanged. The point here is the obvious one that beliefs, like sentences, admit of a type-token distinction. I am inclined to view belief tokens as states of a person. And I take a state to be the instantiation of a property by an object during a time interval. Two belief states (or belief tokens) are of the same type if they are instantiations of the same property and they are of different types if they are instantiations of different properties.[13] In the example at hand, the property that both you and I instantiate is *believing that Ouagadougou is the capital of Upper Volta.*

Now the premise I need for my argument concerns the identity conditions for belief properties. Cast in its most intuitive form, the premise is simply that if a particular belief of yours is true and a particular belief of mine is false, then they are not the same belief. A bit more precisely: If a belief token of one subject differs in truth value from a belief token of another subject, then the tokens are not of the same type. Given our recent account of belief states, this is equivalent to a sufficient condition for the non-identity of belief properties: If an instantiation of belief property p_1 differs in truth value from an instantiation of belief property p_2 then p_1 and p_2 are different properties. This premise hardly constitutes an analysis of our notion of sameness of belief, since we surely do not hold belief tokens to be of the same type if they merely have the same truth value. But no matter. There is no need here to explicate our intuitive notion of belief identity in any detail. What the premise does provide is a necessary condition on any state counting as a belief. If a pair of states can be type identical (i.e., can be instantiations of the same property)

12. For an attempt to explicate our informal concepts of belief and desire in some detail, see Stich (1983).

13. For more on this way of viewing states and events, cf. Kim 1969 and 1976. I think that most everything I say in this paper can be said as well, though not as briefly, without presupposing this account of states and events.

while differing in truth value, then the states are not beliefs as we ordinarily conceive of them.

Before putting my premise to work, it might be helpful to note how the premise can be derived from a quite traditional philosophical account of the nature of beliefs. According to this account, belief is a relation between a person and a proposition. Two persons have the same belief (instantiate the same belief property) if they are belief-related to the same proposition. And, finally, propositions are taken to be the vehicles of truth, so propositions with different truth values cannot be identical. Given this account of belief, it follows straightforwardly that belief tokens differing in truth value differ in type. But the entailment is not mutual, so those who, like me, have some suspicions about the account of belief as a relation between a person and a proposition are free to explore other acounts of belief without abandoning the intuitively sanctioned premise that differences in truth value entail difference in belief.

III The Tension between Autonomy and the Belief–Desire Thesis

In this section I want to argue that a certain tension exists between the principle of psychological autonomy and the belief–desire thesis. The tension is not, strictly speaking a logical incompatibility. Rather, there is an incompatibility between the autonomy principle and some assumptions that are naturally and all but universally shared by advocates of the belief–desire thesis. The additional assumptions are that singular causal statements like the ones extractable from our little story about Jones and the lottery ticket are often true. Moreover, they are true because they are subsumed by laws which invoke the very properties which are invoked in the characterization of the beliefs and desires. A bit less abstractly, what I am assuming is that statements like "Jones's belief that he had won the lottery was among the causes of his rushing toward the phone" are often true; and that they true in virtue of being subsumed by laws invoking properties like *believing that he had just won the lottery*. The burden of my argument is that if we accept the principle of autonomy, then these assumptions must be rejected. More specifically, I will argue that if the autonomy principle is accepted then there are large numbers of belief properties that cannot play a role in an explanatory psychological theory. My strategy will be to examine four different cases, each representative of a large class. In each case we will consider a pair of subjects who, according to the autonomy principle, instantiate all the same explanatory psychological properties, but who have different beliefs. So if we accept the principle of psychological autonomy, then it follows that the belief properties our subjects instantiate cannot be explanatory psychological properties. After running through the examples, I will reflect briefly on the implications of the argument for the belief–desire thesis.

CASE 1: SELF-REFERENTIAL BELIEFS[14]

Suppose, as we did earlier, that we have the technology for creating atom for atom replicas of people. Suppose, further, that a replica for me has just been created. I believe that I have tasted a bottle of Chateau d'Yquem, 1962. Were you to ask me whether I had ever tasted a d'Yquem, 1962, I would likely reply, "Yes, I have." An advocate of the belief–desire thesis would urge, plausibly enough, that my belief is among the causes of my utterance. Now if you were to ask my replica whether he had ever tasted a d'Yquem, 1962, he would likely also reply, "Yes, I have." And surely a belief–desire theorist will also count my replica's belief among the causes of *his* utterance. But the belief which is a cause of my replica's utterance must be of a different type from the one which is a cause of my utterance. For his belief is false; he has just been created and has never tasted a d'Yquem, nor any other wine. So by the premise we set out in section II, the belief property he instantiates is different from the one I instantiate. Yet since we are replicas, the autonomy principle entails that we share all our explanatory psychological properties. It follows that the property of believing that I have tasted a Chateau d'Yquem, 1962, cannot be one which plays a role in an explanatory psychological theory. In an obvious way, the example can be generalized to almost all beliefs about oneself. If we adhere to the principle of autonomy, then beliefs about ourselves can play no role in the explanation of our behavior.

CASE 2: BELIEFS ABOUT ONE'S SPATIAL AND TEMPORAL LOCATION

Imagine, to vary the science fiction example, that cryogenics, the art of freezing people, has been perfected to the point at which a person can be frozen, stored, then defrosted, and at the end of the ordeal be atom for atom identical with the way he was at the beginning of the freezing process. Now suppose that I submit myself to cryogenic preservation this afternoon, and, after being frozen, I am transported to Iceland where I am stored for a century or two, then defrosted. I now believe that it is the twentieth century and that there are many strawberry farms nearby. It would be easy enough to tell stories which would incline the belief–desire theorists to say that each of these beliefs is serving as a cause of my actions. I will leave the details to the reader's imagination. On being defrosted, however, I would presumably still believe that it is the twentieth century and that there are many strawberry farms nearby. Since my current beliefs are both true and my future beliefs both false, they are not belief tokens of the same type, and do not instantiate the same belief property. But by hypothesis, I am, on defrosting, a replica of my current self. Thus the explanatory psychological properties that I instantiate cannot have changed. So the belief property I instantiate when I now believe that it is the twentieth century cannot play any

---

14. The examples in Case 1 and Case 2, along with my thinking on these matters, have been influenced by a pair of important papers by Castañeda 1966 and 1967.

role in an explanatory psychological theory. As in the previous case, the example generalizes to a large number of other beliefs involving a subject's temporal and spatial location.

CASE 3: BELIEFS ABOUT OTHER PEOPLE

In several papers Hilary Putnam has made interesting use of the following fanciful hypothesis.[15] Suppose that in some distant corner of the universe there is a planet very much like our own. Indeed, it is so much like our own that there is a person there who is my doppelganger. He is atom for atom identical with me and has led an entirely parallel life history. Like me, my doppelganger teaches in a philosopy department, and like me has heard a number of lectures on the subject of proper names delivered by a man called 'Saul Kripke.' However, his planet is not a complete physical replica of mine. For the philosopher called 'Saul Kripke' on that planet, though strikingly similar to the one called by the same name on our planet, was actually born in a state they call 'South Dakota,' which is to the north of a state they call 'Nebraska.' By contrast, our Saul Kripke was born in Nebraska—our Nebraska, of course, not theirs. But for reaons which need not be gone into here, many people on this distant planet, including my doppelganger, hold a belief which they express by saying 'Saul Kripke was born in Nebraska.' Now I also hold a belief which I express by saying 'Saul Kripke was born in Nebraska.' However, the belief I express with those words is very different from the belief my doppelganger expresses using the same words, so different, in fact, that his belief is false while mine is true. Yet since we are doppelgangers the autonomy principle dictates that we instantiate all the same explanatory psychological properties. Thus the belief property I instantiate in virtue of believing that Saul Kripke was born in Nebraska cannot be a property invoked in an explanatory psychological theory.

CASE 4: NATURAL KIND PREDICATES

In Putnam's doppelganger planet stories, a crucial difference between our planet and the distant one is that on our planet the substance which we call 'water,' which fills our lakes, etc. is in fact H_2O, while on the other planet the substance they call 'water' which fills their lakes, etc. is in fact some complex chemical whose chemical formula we may abbreviate XYZ. Now imagine that we are in the year 1700, and that some ancestor of mine hears a story from a source he takes to be beyond reproach to the effect that when lizards are dipped in water, they dissolve. The story, let us further suppose, is false, a fact which my ancestor might discover to his dismay when attempting to dissolve a lizard. For the belief–desire theorist, the unsuccessful attempt has as one of its causes the belief that lizards dissolve in water. Now suppose that my ancestor has a doppelganger on the far off

---

15. Putnam 1973 and 1975.

planet who is told an identical sounding story by an equally trustworthy raconteur. However, as it happens that story is true, for there are lizards that do dissolve in XYZ, though none will dissolve in H_2O. The pattern should by now be familiar. My ancestor's belief is false, his doppelganger's is true. Thus the belief tokens instantiate different belief properties. But since *ex hypothesi* the people holding the beliefs are physically identical, the belief properties they instantiate cannot function in an explanatory psychological theory.[16]

This completes my presentation of cases. Obviously, the sorts of examples we have looked at are not the only ones susceptible to the sort of arguments I have been using. But let us now relfect for a moment on just what these arguments show. To begin, we should note that they do *not* show the belief–desire thesis is false. The thesis, as I have construed it here, holds that there are psychological laws which invoke various belief and desire properties and which have a substantive role to play in the explanation of behavior. Nothing we have said here would suffice to show that there are no such laws. At best, what we have shown is that, if we accept the principle of psychological autonomy, then a large class of belief properties cannot be invoked in an explanatory psychological theory. This, in turn, entails that many intuitively sanctioned singular causal statements which specify a belief as a cause of an action cannot be straightforwardly subsumed by a law. And it is just here, I think, that our argument may serve to undermine the belief–desire thesis. For the plausibility of the thesis rests, in large measure, on the plausibility of these singular causal statements. Indeed, I think the belief–desire thesis can be profitably viewed as the speculation that these intuitively sanctioned singular causal statements can be cashed out in a serious psychological theory couched in terms of beliefs and desires. In showing that large numbers of these singular causal statements cannot be cashed out in this way, we make the speculation embodied in the belief–desire thesis appear idle and unmotivated. In the section that follows, I will consider a way in which an advocate of the belief–desire thesis might try to deflect the impact of our arguments, and indicate the burden that this escape route imposes on the belief–desire theorist.

IV A Way Out and Its Costs

Perhaps the most tempting way to contain the damage done by the arguments of the previous section is to grant the conclusions while denying their relevance to the

16. We should note that this example and others invoking natural kind words work only if the extension of my ancestor's word 'water' is different from the extension of the word 'water' as used by my ancestor's doppelganger. I am inclined to agree with Putnam that the extensions are different. But the matter is controversial. For some support of Putnam's view, see Kripke 1972 and Teller 1977; for an opposing view cf. Zemach 1976. Incidentally, one critic has expressed doubt that my doppelganger and I could be physically identical if the stuff called 'water' on the far off planet is actually XYZ. Those who find the point troubling are urged to construct a parallel example using kinds of material not generally occurring within people.

belief–desire thesis. I imagine a critic's objection going something like this: "Granted, if we accept the autonomy principle, then certain belief properties cannot be used in explanatory theories. But this does nothing to diminish the plausibility of the belief–desire thesis, because the properties you have shown incompatible with autonomy are the *wrong kind* of belief properties. All of the examples you consider are cases of *de re* beliefs, none of them are *de dicto* beliefs. But those theorists who take seriously the idea of constructing a belief–desire psychological theory have in mind a theory invoking *de dicto* beliefs and desires. *De re* beliefs are a sort of hybrid; a person has a *de re* belief if he has a suitable underlying *de dicto* belief, *and* if he is related to specific objects in a certain way. But it is only the underlying *de dicto* belief that will play a role in psychological explanation. Thus your arguments do not cast any serious doubt on the belief–desire thesis."[17]

Before assessing this attempt to protect the belief–desire thesis, a few remarks on the *de dicto/de re* distinction are in order. In the recent philosophical discussion of *de re* and *de dicto* beliefs, the focus has been on the logical relations among various sorts of belief attributions. Writers concerned with the issue have generally invoked a substitution criterion to mark the boundary between *de dicto* and *de re* belief attributions. Roughly, a belief attribution of the form.

S believes that *p*

is *de re* if any name or other referring expression within *p* can be replaced with a co-designating term without risk of change of truth value; otherwise the attribution is *de dicto*.[18]

---

17. The idea that *de dicto* beliefs are psychologically more basic is widespread. For a particularly clear example, see Armstrong 1973, pp. 25–31. Of the various attempts to analyze *de re* beliefs in terms of *de dicto* beliefs, perhaps the best known are to be found in Kaplan 1968 and Chisholm 1976.

18. The substitutional account of the *de re/de dicto* distinction has a curious consequence that has been little noted. Though most belief sentences of the form

S believes that Fa

can be used to make either *de re or de dicto* attributions, the substitutional account entails that some can only be used to make *de re* attributions. Consider, for example.

(i) Quine believes that the Queen of England is a turtle.

The claim of course, is false. Indeed, it is *so* false that it could not be used to make a *de dicto* belief attribution. For in all likelihood, there is *no* name or definite description ϕ denoting Elizabeth II such that

Quine believes that ϕ is a turtle

is true. Thus 'Quine believes that the Queen of England is a turtle' is false and cannot be turned into a truth by the replacement of 'the Queen of England' by a codesignating expression. So on the substitutional account, this sentence can be used to make only *de re* attributions. A parallel problem besets Quine's well known substitutional account of *a purely referential position* (Quine 1960, pp. 142 ff.). In (i), the position occupied by 'the Queen of England' can only be regarded as purely referential.

But now given this way of drawing the *de re/de dicto* distinction, my imagined critic is simply wrong in suggesting that all of the examples used in my arguments are cases of *de re* belief. Indeed, just the opposite is true; I intend all of the belief attribution in my examples to be understood in the *de dicto* sense, and all my arguments work quite as well when they are read in this way. Thus, for example, in Case 3 I attribute to myself the belief that Saul Kripke was born in Nebraska. But I intend this to be understood in such a way that

Stich believes 'ϕ' was born in Nebraska

might well be false if 'ϕ' were replaced by a term which, quite unbeknownst to me, in fact denotes Saul Kripke.

There is, however, another way the critic could press his attack that sidesteps my rejoinder. Recently, a number of writers have challenged the substitutional account of the *de dicto/de re* distinction. The basic idea underlying their challenge is that the term '*de re*' should be used for all belief attributions which intend to ascribe a "real" relation of some sort between the believer and the object of his belief. The notion of a real relation is contrasted with the sort of relation that obtains between a person and an object when the object happens to satisfy some description that the person has in mind.[19] Burge, for example, holds that "a *de dicto* belief is a belief in which the believer is related only to a completely expressed proposition (*dictum*)," in contrast to a *de re* belief which is "a belief whose correct ascription places the believer in an appropriate, *nonconceptual, contextual* relation to the objects the belief is about."[20] Thus, if Brown believes that the most prosperous Oriental rug dealer in Los Angeles is an Armenian, and if he believes it simply because he believes all prosperous Oriental rug dealers are Armenian, but has no idea who the man may be, then his belief is *de dicto*. By contrast, if Brown is an intimate of the gentleman, he may have the *de re* belief that the most prosperous Oriental rug dealer in Los Angeles is an Armenian. The sentence

Brown believes that the most prosperous Oriental rug dealer in Los Angeles is an Armenian.

is thus ambiguous, since it may be used either in the *de re* sense to assert that Brown and the rug dealer stand in some "appropriate, nonconceptual, contextual relation" or in the *de dicto* sense which asserts merely that Brown endorses the proposition that the most prosperous rug dealer in Los Angeles (whoever he may be) is an Armenian.

The problem with the substitutional account of the *de dicto/de re* distinction is that it classifies as *de dicto* many belief attributions which impute a "real" relation between

---

19. For more on the distinction between "real" relations and mere "satisfaction" relations, cf. Kim 1977.

20. Burge 1977, pp. 345 and 346; last emphasis added.

the believer and the object of his belief. In many belief attributions the names or definite descriptions that occur in the content sentence do a sort of double duty. First, they serve the function commonly served by names and descriptions; they indicate (or refer to) an object, in this case the object to which the believer is said to be related. The names or descriptions in the content sentence *also* may serve to indicate how the believer conceives of the object, or how he might characterize it. When a name or description serving both roles is replaced by a codesignating expression which does *not* indicate how the believer conceives of the object, then the altered attribution (interpreted in the "double duty" sense) will be false. Thus the substitutional account classifies the original attribution as *de dicto*, despite its imputation of a "real" relation between believer and object.[21]

Now if the *de dicto/de re* distinction is drawn by classifying as *de re* all those belief attributions which impute a "real" relation between believer and object, then the critic conjured in the first paragraph of this section is likely right in his contention that all of my arguments invoke examples of *de re* beliefs. Indeed, the strategy of my arguments is to cite an example of a *de re* (i.e., "real relation") belief, then construct a second example in which the second believer is a physical replica of the first, but has no "real relation" to the object of the first believer's belief. However, to grant this much is not to grant that the critic has succeeded in blunting the point of my arguments.

Let me begin my rejoinder with a fussy point. The critic's contentions were two: first, that my examples all invoked *de re* belief properties; second, that *de re* belief properties are hybrids and are analyzable into *de dicto* belief properties. The fussy point is that even if both the critic's contentions are granted, the critic would not quite have met my arguments head on. The missing premise is that *de dicto* belief properties (construed now according to the "real relation" criterion) are in fact compatible with the principle of psychological autonomy. This premise may be true, but the notion of a "real" relation, on which the current account of *de dicto* belief properties depends, is sufficiently obscure that it is hard to tell. Fortunately, there is a simple way to finesse the problem. Let us introduce the term *autonomous beliefs* for those beliefs that a subject must share with all his replicas; and let us use the term *non-autonomous* for those beliefs which a subject need not share with his replica.[22] More generally, we can call any property which an organism must share with its replicas an *autonomous property*. We can now reconstrue the critic's claims as follows:

1 All the examples considered in section III invoke non-autonomous belief properties.
2 Non-autonomous belief properties are hybrids, analyzable into an underlying autonomous belief property (which can play a role in psychological

---

21. For more on this "double duty" view of the role of names and descriptions in content sentences, see Loar 1972.
22. Of course when the notion of a "real relation" has been suitably sharpened it might well turn out that the autonomous/non-autonomous distinction coincides with the "real relation" version of the *de dicto/de re* distinction.

explanation) plus some further relation(s) between the believer and the object of his belief.

On the first point I naturally have no quarrel, since a principal purpose of this paper is to show that a large class of belief properties are non-autonomous. On the second claim, however, I would balk, for I am skeptical that the proposed analysis can in fact be carried off. I must hasten to add that I know of *no argument* sufficient to show that the analysis is impossible. But, of course, my critic has no argument either. Behind my skepticism is the fact that no such analysis has ever been carried off. Moreover, the required analysis is considerably more demanding than the analysis of *de re* belief in terms of *de dicto* belief, when the distinction between the two is drawn by the substitutional criterion. For the class of autonomous beliefs is significantly smaller than the class of *de dicto* beliefs (characterized substitionally).[23] And the most impressive attempts to reduce *de re* beliefs to *de dicto* plainly will not be of much help for the analysis my critic proposes.[24] But enough, I have already conceded that I cannot prove my critic's project is impossible. What I do hope to have established is that the critic's burden is the burden of the belief–desire theorist. If the reduction of non-autonomous beliefs to autonomous beliefs cannot be carried off, then there is small prospect that a psychological theory couched in terms of beliefs and desires will succeed in explaining any substantial part of human behavior.

A final point. It might be argued that, however difficult the analysis of non-autonomous beliefs to autonomous ones may be, it must be possible to carry it off. For, the argument continues, a subject's non-autonomous beliefs are determined in part by the autonomous psychological properties he instantiates and in part by his various relations to the objects of the world. Were either of these components suitably altered, the subject's non-autonomous beliefs would be altered as well. And since non-autonomous beliefs are jointly determined by autonomous psychological properties and by other relations, there must be some analysis, however complex, which specifies how this joint determination works. Now this last claim is not one I would want to challenge. I am quite prepared to grant that non-autonomous beliefs admit of some analysis in terms of autonomous psychological properties plus other relations. But what seems much more doubtful to me is that the autonomous properties invoked in the analysis would be *belief properties*. To see the reasons for my doubt, let us reflect on the picture suggested by the examples in section III. In each case we had a pair of subjects who shared all their autonomous properties though their non-autonomous beliefs differed in truth value. The difference in truth value, in turn, was rooted in a difference in reference; the beliefs were simply about different persons, places or times. In short, the beliefs represented different states of

---

23. For example, when I say, "I believe that Kripke was born in Nebraska," I am attributing to myself a belief which is substitutionally *de dicto*, but not autonomous.

24. Kaplan's strategy, for example, will be of no help, since his analysans are, for the most part, non-autonomous substitutionally *de dicto* belief sentences. Cf. Kaplan 1968 and Burge 1977, pp. 350 ff.

affairs. If the non-autonomous belief properties of these examples are to be analyzed into autonomous psychological properties plus various historical or external relations, then it is plausible to suppose that the autonomous psychological properties do not determine a truth value, an appropriate reference or a represented state of affairs. So the state of exhibiting one (or more) of these autonomous properties itself has no truth value, is not referential, and does not represent anything. And this, I would urge, is more than enough reason to say that it is not a belief at all. None of this amounts to an *argument* that non-autonomous beliefs are not analyzable into autonomous ones. Those who seek such an analyis are still free to maintain that there will be at least one autonomous belief among the autonomous properties in the analysans of each non-autonomous belief property. But in the absence of an argument for this claim, I think few will find it particularly plausible. The ball is in the belief–desire theorist's court.[25,26]

Appendix

A bit more needs to be said about the premise urged at the end of section II. The premise, it will be recalled, was this:

> If a belief token of one subject differs in truth value from a belief token of another subject, then the tokens are not of the same type.

A number of helpful critics have pointed out to me that we actually have a variety of intuitively sanctioned ways to decide when two belief tokens are of the same type. More-over, some of these patently violate my premise. Thus, for example, if Jones and Smith each believes that he will win the next presidential election, there would be no intuitive oddness to the claim that Jones and Smith have the same belief. Though, of course, if Jones's belief is true, Smith's belief is false. It would be equally natural in this case to say that Jones and Smith have different beliefs. So I cannot rest my premise on our intuitive judgments; the intuitions will not bear the weight.

I think the best way of defending the premise is to make clear how it is related to a certain view (actually a category of views) about what beliefs are. The views I have in mind all share two features in common:

(i)   they take belief to be a relation between a believer and a type of abstract object;

(ii)   they take the abstract objects to be representational—that is, the abstract objects are taken to picture the world as being a certain way, or to claim that

---

25. I am indebted to Robert Cummins, Jaegwon Kim, William Alston and John Bennett for their helpful comments on the topics discussed in this paper.

26. After completing this paper, I was delighted to discover a very similar view in Perry 1979. Fodor 1980 defends a version of the principle of psychological autonomy.

some state of affairs obtains. Thus the object, along with the actual state of the believer's world, determines a truth value.

For example, certain theorists take belief to be a relation between a person and a proposition; a proposition, in turn, determines a truth value for every possible world—truth for those worlds in which it is true and falsity for those worlds in which it is false. A person's belief is true if the proposition is true in his or her world. Rather more old fashioned is the theory which holds belief to be a relation between a person and an image or a mental picture. The belief is true if and only if the mental picture correctly depicts the believer's world.

Now on views such as these which take belief to be a relation between a person and an abstract object, the most natural way of determining when a pair of belief tokens are of the same type is by appeal to the abstract objects. A pair of subjects' belief tokens are of the same type when the subjects are related to the same abstract object. Thus when subjects are in the same possible world, their belief tokens are of the same type only if they are identical in truth value. And this, in effect, was the premise advanced in section II. The thesis of this paper is best taken to be that the principle of psychological autonomy is in conflict with the belief–desire thesis, *when beliefs are construed as in (i) and (ii)*. Let me add a final observation. A number of theorists have taken belief to be a relation between a person and a sentence or sentence-like object. For example, in *The Language of Thought* (Crowell, 1975) Jerry Fodor holds that belief is a relation between a person and a sentence in "the language of thought." It is interesting to ask whether a theory like Fodor's is at odds with the principle of psychological autonomy. The answer, I think, turns on whether the sentences in the language of thought are taken to have truth values, and whether their referring expressions are taken to determine a referent in a given world, independent of the head in which they happen to be inscribed. If sentences in the language of thought are taken to be analogous to Quine's eternal sentences, true or false in a given world regardless of who utters them or where they may be inscribed, then Fodor's view will satisfy (i) and (ii) and will run head on into the principle of psychological autonomy. For Fodor, I suspect, this would be argument enough to show that the sentences in the language of thought are not eternal.

REFERENCES

Alston, W. P. (1967a) "Motives and motivation," *The Encyclopedia of Philosophy*, New York.
Alston, W. P. (1967b) "Wants, actions and causal explanations," in H. N. Castañeda (ed.) *Intentionally, Minds and Perception*, Detroit.
Armstrong, D. M. (1973) *Belief, Truth and Knowledge*, Cambridge.
Atkinson, J. W. (1964) *An Introduction to Motivation*, New York.
Brandt, R. B. and Kim, Jaegwon (1963) "Wants as explanations of actions," *Journal of Philosophy* LX 425–35.

Burge, T. (1977) "Belief de re," *Journal of Philosophy* LXXIV, 338–62.

Castañeda, H. N. (1966) "'He': A study in the logic of self-consciousness," *Ratio*, 8, 130–57.

Castañeda, H. N. (1967) "Indicators and quasi-indicators," *American Philosophical Quarterly* 4, 85–100.

Chisholm, R. (1976) *Person and Object*, LaSalle, IL.

Davidson, D. (1963) "Actions, reasons and causes," *Journal of Philosophy* LX, 685–700.

Davidson, D. (1967) "Causal relations," *Journal of Philosophy* LXIV, 691–703.

Davidson, D. (1970) "Mental events," in L. Foster and J. W. Swanson (eds), *Experience and Theory* Amherst, 1970.

Fodor, J. (1980) "Methodological solipsism considered as a research strategy in cognitive psychology," *Behavioral and Brain Sciences* 3, 63–73.

Goldman, A. (1970) *A Theory of Human Action*, Englewood Cliffs.

Hempel, C. G. (1965) *Aspects of Scientific Explanation*, New York.

Kaplan, D. (1968) "Quantifying in," *Synthese*, 19, 178–214.

Kim, J. (1969) "Events and their descriptions: Some considerations," in N. Rescher et al, (eds), *Essays in Honor of C. G. Hempel*, Dordrecht, Holland.

Kim, J. (1973) "Causation, nomic subsumption and the concept of event," *Journal of Philosophy*, LXX, 217–36.

Kim, J. (1976) "Events as property-exemplifications," in M. Brand and D. Walton (eds), *Action Theory*. Dordrecht, Holland.

Kim, J. (1977) "Perception and reference without causality," *Journal of Philosophy*, 74, 606–20.

Kim, J. (1978) "Supervenience and numological incommensurables," *American Philosophical Quarterly* 15, 2, 149–56.

Kripke, S. (1972) "Naming and necessity," in D. Davidson and G. Harman (eds), *Semantics and Natural Language*. Dordrecht, Holland.

Loar, B. (1972) "Reference and propositional attitudes," *Philosophical Review*, LXXX, 43–62.

Newell, A. and Simon, H. A. (1972) *Human Problem Solving*, Englewood Cliffs.

Nisbett, R. and Ross, L. (1980) *Human Inference: Strategies and Shortcomings of Social Judgment*, Prentice-Hall.

Perry, J. (1979) "The problem of the essential indexical," *Noûs*, 13, 3–21.

Putnam, H. (1973) "Meaning and reference," *Journal of Philosophy* LXX, 699–711.

Putnam, H. (1975) "The meaning of 'meaning,'" in K. Gunderson (ed.), *Language, Mind and Knowledge*, Minneapolis.

Quine, W. V. O. (1960) *Word and Object*, Cambridge.

Stich, S. (1983) *From Folk Psychology to Cognitive Science*, Bradford Books/MIT Press.

Teller, P. (1977) "Indicative introduction," *Philosophical Studies* 31, 173–95.

Zemach, E. (1976) "Putnam's theory on the reference of substance terms," *Journal of Philosophy* LXXXIII, 116–27.

DENNETT ON INTENTIONAL SYSTEMS

DURING THE LAST dozen years, Daniel Dennett has been elaborating an interconnected—and increasingly influential—set of views in the philosophy of mind, the philosophy of psychology, and those parts of moral philosophy that deal with the notions of freedom, responsibility and personhood. The central unifying theme running through Dennett's writings on each of these topics is his concept of an *intentional system*. He invokes the concept to "legitimize" mentalistic predicates (*Brainstorms*, p. xvii),[1] to explain the theoretical strategy of cognitive psychology and artificial intelligence, and, ultimately, to attempt a reconciliation between "our vision of ourselves as responsible, free, rational agents, and our vision of ourselves as complex parts of the physical world of science" (*BS*, p. x). My goal in this paper is to raise some doubts about the "intentional coin" (*BS*, p. xviii) with which Dennett proposes to purchase his moral and "mental treasures." Since I aim to offer a critique of Dennett's views, it is inevitable that much of what I say will be negative in tone. But this tone should not be misconstrued. It is my view that Dennett's

---

1. References to Dennett's writings will be identified in parentheses in the text. I will use the following abbreviations:

BS = Daniel Dennett, *Brainstorms* (Montgomery, VT: Bradford Books, 1978).
TK = Daniel Dennett, "Three kinds of intentional psychology," in *Reduction, Time, and Reality* (ed. R. A. Healey), Cambridge University Press, 1981.
R = Daniel Dennett, "Reply to Professor Stich," *Philosophical Books*, 21, 2 (April, 1980).
TB = Daniel Dennett, "True believers: The intentional strategy and why it works," reprinted in this volume above.

theories are of great importance and will shape discussion in the philosophy of mind for decades to come. Moreover, I think that much of what Dennett says is close to being true. If we reconstruct his notion of an intentional system to eliminate its instrumentalism and its unfortunate infatuation with idealized rationality, we can use the result to give a better account of commonsense mentalistic notions, and also to give a clearer and more tenable account of the strategy of cognitive science. Toward the end of this paper I will sketch the outlines of such a "derationalized" cousin to Dennett's idea of an intentional system.

I

In explaining the idea of an intentional system, Dennett's recurrent illustration is the chess-playing computer. There are, he urges, three quite different stances we might "adopt in trying to predict and explain its behavior" (*BS*, p. 237).

> First there is the *design stance*. If one knows exactly how the computer's program has been designed . . . one can predict the computer's designed response to any move one makes. One's prediction will come true provided only that the computer performs as designed, that is, without breakdown. . . . The essential feature of the design stance is that we make predictions solely from knowledge or assumptions about the system's design, often without making any examination of the innards of the particular object.
>
> Second, there is what we may call the *physical stance*. From this stance our predictions are based on the actual state of the particular system, and are worked out by applying whatever knowledge we have of the laws of nature. . . . One seldom adopts the physical stance in dealing with a computer just because the number of critical variables in the physical constitution of a computer would overwhelm the most prodigious human calculator. . . . Attempting to give a physical account or prediction of the chess playing computer would be a pointless and herculean labor, but it would work in principle. One could predict the response it would make in a chess game by tracing out the effects of the input energies all the way through the computer until once more type was pressed against paper and a response was printed.
>
> There is a third stance one can adopt toward a system, and that is the *intentional stance*. This tends to be the most appropriate when the system one is dealing with is too complex to be dealt with effectively from the other stances. In the case of a chess playing computer one adopts this stance when one tries to predict its response to one's move by figuring out what a good or reasonable response would be, given the information the computer has about the situation. Here one assumes not just the absence of malfunction but the rationality of the design or programming as well.
>
> Whenever one can successfully adopt the intentional stance toward an object, I call that object an *intentional* system. The success of the stance is of course a matter

settled pragmatically, without reference to whether the object *really* has beliefs, intentions, and so forth; so whether or not any computer can be conscious, or have thoughts or desires, some computers undeniably *are* intentional systems, for they are systems whose behavior can be predicted, and most efficiently predicted, by adopting the intentional stance towards them. (*BS*, pp. 237–8; for a largely identical passage, cf. *BS*, pp, 4–7.)

So *any* object will count as an intentional system if we can usefully predict its behavior by assuming that it will behave *rationally*. And what is it to behave rationally? Here, Dennett suggests, the full answer must ultimately be provided by a new sort of theory, *intentional-system theory*, which will provide us with a *normative* account of rationality. This new theory "is envisaged as a close kin of—and overlapping with—such already existing disciplines as epistemic logic, decision theory and game theory, which are all similarly abstract, normative and couched in intentional language" (*TK*, p. 19). Of course, we already have some "rough and ready principles" of rationality which we can and do press into service pending a more detailed normative theory:

1   A system's beliefs are those it *ought to have*, given its perceptual capacities, its epistemic needs, and its biography. Thus in general, its beliefs are both true and relevant to its life. . . .
2   A system's desires are those it ought to have, given its biological needs and the most practicable means of satisfying them. Thus [naturally evolved] intentional systems desire survival and procreation, and hence desire food, security, health, sex, wealth, power, influence, and so forth, and also whatever local arrangements tend (in their eyes—given their beliefs) to further these ends in appropriate measure. . . .
3   A system's behavior will consist of those acts that *it would be rational* for an agent with those beliefs and desires to perform. (*TK*, pp. 8–9)

Obviously these three principles are very rough and ready indeed. However, we also have a wealth of more detailed common-sense principles that anchor our intuitive notion of rationality. Some of these, in turn, are systematized and improved upon by existing theories in logic, evolutionary biology and decision theory. But though the intentional-system theorist can count on some help from these more developed disciplines, he still has a great deal of work to do. Neither singly nor severally do these disciplines tell us what beliefs a given organism or system ought to have, what desires it ought to have, or how it should act, given the beliefs and desires it has. Dennett has no illusions on the point. He portrays intentional-system theory—the general normative theory of rationality—as a discipline in its infancy. When the course of our argument requires some substantive premises about what it would be rational for a system to believe or do, we can follow Dennett's lead and let our common-sense intuitions be our guide.

I have been stressing the role of a normative theory of rationality in Dennett's account of the intentional stance. But there is a second, equally important, component in his view. According to Dennett, when we describe an organism or an artifact as an intentional system, we are making no commitments about the internal physical workings of the system. *Nor are we saying anything about the design or program of the system.* Just as a single program or design description is compatible with indefinitely many physical realizations, so too a single intentional description is compatible with indefinitely many different programs or design descriptions. To view an object as an intentional system we must attribute to it a substantial range of beliefs and desires— the beliefs and desires it would be rational for such an object to have, given its nature and history. However, we need not assume that the beliefs and desires attributed correspond in any systematic way to internal states characterized either physically or functionally. Dennett makes the point vividly with the example of two robots each designed to be identical to a given person, Mary, when viewed from the intentional stance. The first robot, Ruth, "has internal processes which 'model' Mary's as closely as you like" (*BS*, p. 105). It is functionally identical to Mary, though the two may be quite different physically. Since Mary and Ruth share a common design or program, they will behave identically. Thus any beliefs and desires we attribute to Mary we may attribute also to Ruth, and the attributions will be equally useful in predicting their behavior. The second robot, Sally, has a program which is input–output equivalent to Ruth's, though it uses a quite different computational strategy. "Sally may not be a very good psychological model of Mary," since "Sally's response delays, errors and the like may not match Mary's." But at the level of common-sense descriptions of actions, all three will behave alike. ". . . the ascription of all Mary's beliefs and desires (etc.) to Sally will be just as predictive as their ascription to Ruth so far as prediction of action goes" (*BS*, p. 105). So when we adopt the intentional stance, Mary, Ruth and Sally are indistinguishable.

Dennett, then, is a self-professed instrumentalist about the beliefs and desires we ascribe to an object when we adopt the intentional stance toward it. ". . . the beliefs and other intentions of an intentional systems need [not] be *represented* 'within' the system in any way for us to get a purchase on predicting its behavior by ascribing such intentions to it" (*BS*, p. 277). Rather, these "putative . . . states" can be relegated "to the role of idealized fictions in an action-predicting, action-explaining calculus" (*BS*, p. 30). For Dennett, the belief and desire states of an intentional system are not what Reichenbach calls "illata— posited theoretical entities." Rather they are "abstracta—calculation bound entities or logical constructs" (*TK*, p. 20). Of course, it is conceivable that some objects which are usefully treated as intentional systems really do have internal states that correspond to the beliefs and desires ascribed to them in an intentional characterization. As some writers have suggested, there might be functionally distinct neural belief and desire stores where each belief and desire is inscribed in an appropriate neural code. Dennett, however, thinks this is not likely to be true for people, animals and other familiar intentional systems.[2] Be this as it may, the important point in the present context is that when we describe an object in intentional-system terms, we are quite explicitly *not* making any commitment about its workings, beyond the minimal claim that whatever the mechanism causally responsible for the behavior may be, it must be the sort of mechanism which will produce behavior generally predictable by assuming the intentional stance.

This completes my sketch of Dennett's notion of intentional systems. Let us now consider what Dennett wants to do with the notion. The principal project Dennett has in mind for intentional systems is "legitimizing" (*BS*, p. xvii), or providing a sort of "conceptual reduction" (*TK*, p. 30) of various notions in common-sense or folk psycology. The sort of legitimizing Dennett has in mind is explained by analogy with Church's Thesis. Church proposed that the informal, intuitive mathematical concept of an "effective" procedure be identified with the formal notion of a recursive (or Turing-machine computable) function. The proposal "is not provable, since it hinges on the intuitive and unformalizable notion of an effective procedure, but it is generally accepted, and it provides a very useful reduction of a fuzzy-but-useful mathematical notion to a crisply defined notion of apparently equal scope and greater power" (*BS*, p. xviii; cf. also *TK*, p. 30). It is Dennett's hope to provide the same sort of legitimization of the notions of folk psychology by showing how these notions can be characterized in terms of the notions of intentional-system theory. ". . . the claim that every mental phenomenon alluded to in folk psychology is *intentional-system-characterizable* would, if true, provide a reduction of the mental as ordinarily understood—a domain whose boundaries are at best fixed by mutual acknowledgement and shared intuition—to a clearly defined domain of entities, whose principles of organization are familiar, relatively formal and systematic, and entirely general" (*TK*, pp. 30–1).

All this sounds reasonable enough—an exicting project, if Dennett can pull it off. The effort looks even more intriguing when we note how broadly Dennett intends to cast his net. It is his aim to show not only that such "program receptive" (*BS*, p. 29) features of mentality as belief and desire are intentional-system-characterizable, but also that "program resistant features of mentality" like pain, dreams, mental images, and even free will are "captured in the net of intentional systems" (*BS*, p. xviii). But a dark cloud looms on the horizon, one that will continue to plague us. In much of his work Dennett exhibits an exasperating tendency to make bold, flamboyant, fascinating claims in one breath, only to take them back, or seem to, in the next. Thus, scarcely a page after proclaiming his intention to show that a broad range of common-sense mental phenomena are intentional-system-characterizable and thus legitimized, Dennett proclaims himself to be an eliminative materialist concerning these very same phenomena. Beliefs, desires, pains, mental images, experiences—as these are ordinarily understood—"are not good

2. For his arguments on this point, cf. "Brain writing and mind reading," (*BS*, pp. 39–50) and "A cure for the common code," (*BS*, pp. 90–108).

theoretical entities, however well entrenched" (*BS*, p. xx) the terms 'belief,' 'pain,' etc. may be in the habits of thought of our society. So "we legislate the putative items right out of existence" (*BS*, p. xx). How are we to make sense of this apparent contradiction?

There is, I think, a plausible—and uncontradictory—interpretation of what Dennett is up to. The problem he is grappling with is that the fit between our intuitive folk-psychological notions and the intentional-system characterizations he provides for them is just not as comfortable as the fit between the intuitive notion of effective mathematical procedure and the formal notion of Turing computability. Our folk-psychological concepts, "like folk productions generally," are complex, messy, variegated and in danger of incoherence (*TK*, p. 16). By contrast, notions characterized in terms of intentional-system theory are—it is to be hoped—coherent, sharply drawn and constructed with a self-conscious eye for their subsequent incorporation into science (*TK*, p. 6). The intentional-system analysans are intended to be improvements on their analysanda. What they give us is not an "anthropological" (*TK*, p. 6) portrait of our folk notions (warts and all), but rather an improved version of "the parts of folk psychology worth caring about" (*TK*, p. 30). So Dennett is an eliminative materialist about mental phenomena alluded to in warts-and-all folk psychology; what are intentional-system-characterizable are not the notions of folk psychology, but rather related successor concepts which capture all that's worth caring about.

But now what are we to make of the claim that the intentional system *Ersätze* capture all that's worth caring about in folk psychology: What *is* worth caring about? Dennett concedes that an "anthropological" study of unreconstructed folk notions which includes "whatever folk actually include in their theory, however misguided, incoherent, gratuitous some of it may be," (*TK*, p. 6) would be a perfectly legitimate endeavor. Folk theory may be myth, "but it is a myth we live in, so it is an 'important' phenomenon in nature" (*TK*, p. 6).[3] However, Dennett does not share the anthropologist's (or the cognitive simulator's) interest in the idiosyncrasies and contradictions embedded in our folk notions. What is of interest to him, he strongly suggests, is "the proto-scientific quest": "an attempt to prepare folk theory for subsequent incorporation into or reduction to the rest of science," eliminating "all that is false or ill-founded" (*TK*, p. 6). If matters stopped there, we could parse Dennett's "all that's worth caring about" as "all that's worth caring about for the purposes of science." But matters do not stop there. To see why, we will have to take a detour to survey another central theme in Dennett's thinking.

As we have noted, a basic goal of Dennett's theory is to reconcile "our vision of ourselves as responsible, free, rational agents, and our vision of ourselves as complex parts

---

3. This "anthropological quest," when pursued systematically is the business of the cognitive simulator. Cf., for example, Roger Shank and Robert Abelson, *Scripts, Plans, Goals and Understanding* (Hillsdale, NJ: Lawrence Erlbaum Associates, 1977); also Aaron Slomon, *The Computer Revolution in Philosophy* (Atlantic Highlands, NJ: Humanities Press, 1978), ch. 4.

of the physical world of science" (*BS*, p. x). The conflict that threatens between these two visions is a perennial philosophical preoccupation:

> the validity of our conceptual scheme of moral agents having dignity, freedom and responsibility stands or falls on the question: can men ever be truly said to have beliefs, desires, intentions? If they can, there is at least some hope of retaining a notion of the dignity of man; if they cannot, if men never can be said truly to want or believe, then surely they never can be said truly to act responsibly, or to have a conception of justice, or to know the difference between right and wrong. (*BS*, pp. 63–4)

Yet many psychologists, most notoriously Skinner, have denied that people have beliefs, desires and other mental states.[4] This threat to our view of ourselves as moral agents does not arise only from rabid behaviorism. Dennett sees it lurking also in certain recently fashionable philosophical theories about the nature of mental states. Consider, for example, the type-type identity theory which holds that every mental-state type is to be identified with a physical-state type—a brain state characterized in physico-chemical terms. What if it should turn out that there simply is *no* physical-state type that is shared by all beings to whom we commonly attribute the belief that snow is white? If we hang on to the type-type identity theory, then this very plausible empirical finding would seem to entail that there is no such mental state as believing that snow is white. Much the same result threatens from those versions of functionalism which hold that "each mental type is identifiable as a functional type in the language of Turing machine description" (*BS*, p. xvi). For "there is really no more reason to believe you and I 'have the same program' in *any* relaxed and abstract sense, considering the differences in our nature and nurture, than that our brains have identical physico-chemical descriptions" (*BS*, p. xvi). So if we adhere to functionalism, a plausible result in cognitive psychology—the discovery that people do not have the same programs—threatens to establish that people do not have beliefs at all.[5]

We can now see one of the principal virtues of Dennett's instrumentalism about intentional systems. Since describing an object as an intentional system entails nothing whatever about either the physico-chemical nature or the functional design of the mechanism that causes the object's behavior, neither neurophysiology nor "sub-personal cognitive psychology" (which studies the functional organization or program of the organism) could possibly show that the object was not an intentional system. Thus if beliefs and

---

4. Skinner often muddies the waters by claiming to offer "translations" of common-sense mentalistic terms into the language of behaviorism. But, as Dennett and others have noted, (*BS*, pp. 53–70) these "translations" generally utterly fail to capture the meaning or even the extension of the common-sense term being "translated."

5. For an elaboration of the point, cf. Thomas Nagel, "Armstrong on the mind," *Philosophical Review*, 79 (1970), pp. 394–403.

desires (or some respectable *Ersätze*) can be characterized in terms of intentional-system theory, we need have no fear that advances in psychology or brain science might establish that people do not really have beliefs and desires. So the viability of our "conceptual scheme of moral agents" is sustained, in this quarter at least.[6]

Now, finally, it is clear how Dennett's preoccupation with moral themes bears on his eliminative materialism. Recall that Dennett proposes to trade our ungainly folk-psychological notions for concepts characterized in terms of intentional systems. The claim is not that the new concepts are identical with the old, but that they are *better*. They are clearer, more systematic, free from the incoherence lurking in folk notions, *and they capture everything in folk psychology that is worth caring about*. One of the things worth caring about, for Dennett, is the suitability of the clarified notions for incorporation into science. However, if he is to succeed in insulating our moral world-view from the threat posed by scientific psychology, then there is obviously something else Dennett must count as worth caring about. The new concepts built from intentional-system notions must be as serviceable as the older folk notions in sustaining our vision of ourselves as persons.

II

In this section I want to examine just how well Dennett's intentional system *Ersätze* mirror the notions of folk psychology. My focus will be on the "program receptive" notions of belief and desire, concepts which should be easiest to purchase "with intentional coin," and my claim will be that the fit between our common-sense notions and Dennett's proffered replacements is a very poor one.[7] Of course, Dennett does not maintain that the fit is perfect, only that intentional-system theory preserves "the parts of folk psychology worth caring about" (*TK*, p. 30). This is the doctrine I am concerned to challenge. On my view, the move to an intentional-system-characterized notion of belief would leave us unable to say a great deal that we wish to say about ourselves and our fellows. Moreover, the losses will be important ones. If we accept Dennett's trade, we will have no coherent way to describe our cognitive shortcomings nor the process by which we may learn to overcome them. Equally unwelcome, the thriving scientific study of the strengths and weaknesses of human reasoning would wither and die, its hypotheses ruled literally incoherent. What is more, the instrumentalism of Dennett's intentional-system notions seems to fly in the face of some deeply rooted intuitions about responsibility and

---

6. An entirely parallel strategy works for those other common-sense mental phenomena which Dennett takes to be essential to our concept of ourselves as persons—e.g., consciousness (*BS*, p. 269). If we can give an acceptable intentional system *Ersätz* for the folk-psychological notion of consciousness, we need have no fear that advances in science will threaten our personhood by showing that the notion of consciousness is otiose in the causal explanation of our behavior.

7. For some qualms about Dennett's treatment of "program resistant" features of mentality like pains, see my "Headaches," *Philosophical Books*, April 1980.

moral agency. Throughout most of what follows, I will cleave to the fiction that we already have a tolerably well worked out normative theory of rationality, or could readily build one, though in the closing pages I will offer some skeptical thoughts about how likely this fiction is.

I begin with the problems posed by irrationality. An intentional system, recall, is an ideally rational system; it believes, wants and does just what it ought to, as stipulated by a normative theory of rationality. People, by contrast, are not ideally rational, and therein lies a devastating problem for Dennett. If we were to adopt his suggestion and trade up to the intentional-system notions of belief and desire (hereafter IS belief and IS desire), then we simply would not be able to say all those things we need to say about ourselves and our fellows when we deal with each other's idiosyncrasies, shortcomings, and cognitive growth.

Consider belief. Presumably no system *ought* to hold contradictory beliefs, and all systems *ought* to believe all the logical truths, along with all the logical consequences of what they believe (cf. *BS*, pp. 11, 20, 44; *TK*, p. 11). But people depart from this ideal in a variety of ways. We generally fail to believe *all* logical consequences of our beliefs—sometimes because the reasoning required would be difficult, and sometimes because we simply fail to take account of one or more of our beliefs. Suppose, for example, that an astronaut set the controls incorrectly and has sent his craft into a perilous spin. One possible explanation of his mistake would be that the on-board computer was down, and he had to hand-calculate the setting for the controls. He made a mistake in the calculation, and thus came to have a mistaken belief about what the setting should be. Another possibility is that, although he knew the craft was in the gravitational field of a nearby asteroid—indeed he could see it through the window—he simply forgot to take this into account in figuring out where the control should be set. There is nothing in the least paradoxical about these explanations. We offer similar explanations all the time in explaining our own actions and those of other people. Indeed, since these explanations are so intimately bound up with our notions of excuse and blame, quick-wittedness, absent-mindedness and a host of others, it boggles the mind to try imagining how we would get on with each other if we resolved to renounce them. But if, following Dennett, we agree to swap the folk notion of belief for the intentional-system notion, then renounce them we must. It simply makes no sense to attribute inferential failings or inconsistent beliefs to an ideally rational system.

Our intuitive grasp on the notion of rational desire is rather more tenuous than our grasp on the analogous notion for belief. Still, there seem to be many cases in which we want to ascribe desires to people which are not rational on any plausible reading of that term. Jones is a successful writer, in good health, with many friends and admirers. But he says he wants to die, and ultimately takes his own life. Smith has a dreadful allergy to chocolate, and he knows it. One taste and he is condemned to a week of painful, debilitating hives. But he *really* wants that chocolate bar at the checkout counter. After staring at it for a minute, he buys it and gobbles it down. Brown collects spiders. They are of no economic value, and he doesn't even think they are very pretty. But it is his hobby. He wants to add to his collection a specimen of a species found only in the desert. So, despite his dislike of hot weather, he arranges to spend his vacation spider hunting in Nevada. By my lights, both Jones's desire and Smith's are simply irrational. As for Brown, "irrational" seems much too strong. Yet it is certainly implausible to say that he *ought* to want that spider. So, on Dennett's account, it is not a rational desire. But idealized intentional systems have all and only the desires they ought to have: Thus if we trade the common-sense notion of want for Dennett's IS want, we simply will not be able to say that Brown wants the spider or that Jones wants to die.

The existence of examples like the ones I have been sketching is not news to Dennett. From his earliest paper on intentional systems to his most recent, he has struggled with analogous cases. Unfortunately, however, he is far from clear on what he proposes to do about them. As I read him, there are two quite different lines that he proposes; I will call them the *hard line* and the *soft line*. Neither is carefully spelled out in Dennett's writings, and he often seems to endorse both within a single paper. Once they have been sharply stated, I think it will be clear that neither line is tenable.

THE HARD LINE

The hard line sticks firmly with the idealized notion of an intentional system and tries to minimize the importance of the gap between IS beliefs and IS desires and their folk-psychological namesakes. The basic ploy here is to suggest that when folk psychology ascribes contradictory beliefs to people or when it insists that a person does not believe some of the consequences of his beliefs, folk psychology undermines its own usefulness and threatens to lapse into incoherence. When this happens, we are forced back to the design stance or the physical stance:

> The presumption of rationality is so strongly entrenched in our inference habits that when our predictions [based on the assumption] prove false, we at first cast about for adjustments in the information possession conditions (he must not have heard, he must not know English, he must not have seen *x*, . . .) or goal weightings, before questioning the rationality of the system as a whole. In extreme cases personalities may prove to be so unpredictable from the intentional stance that we abandon it, and if we have accumulated a lot of evidence in the meanwhile about the nature of response patterns in the individual, we may find that a species of design stance can be effectively adopted. This is the fundamentally different attitude we occasionally adopt toward the insane. (*BS*, pp. 9–10)

Here, surely, Dennett is *just wrong* about what we do when predictions based on idealized rationality prove false. When a neighborhood boy gives me the wrong change from my purchase at his lemonade stand, I do not assume that he believes quarters are only worth

23 cents, nor that he wants to cheat me out of the 2 cents I am due. My *first* assumption is that he is not yet very good at doing sums in his head. Similarly, when a subject working on one of Wason and Johnson-Laird's deceptively difficult reasoning tasks gets the wrong answer, we are not likely to assume that he didn't understand the instructions, nor that he didn't want to get the right answer. Our *first* assumption is that he blew it; he made a mistake in reasoning.[8] What misleads Dennett here is that he is focusing on cases of counter-intuitive or unfamiliar cognitive failings. When someone seems to have made a mistake we can't readily imagine ourselves ever making, we do indeed begin to wonder whether he might perhaps have some unanticipated beliefs and desires. Or if a person seems to be making enormous numbers of mistakes and ending up with a substantial hoard of bizarre beliefs, we grow increasingly reluctant to ascribe beliefs and desires to him at all. Perhaps we count him among the insane. These facts will assume some importance later one. But they are of little use to the hard-line defense of intentional systems. For it is in the diverse domain of more or less familiar inferential shortcomings that common sense most readily and usefully portrays people as departing from an idealized standard of rationality.

Dennett frequently suggests that we cannot coherently describe a person whose beliefs depart from the idealized standard:

> Conflict arises . . . when a person falls short of perfect rationality, and avows beliefs that either are strongly disconfirmed by the available empirical evidence or are self-contradictory or contradict other avowals he has made. If we lean on the myth that a man is perfectly rational, we must find his avowals less than authoritative: "You *can't* mean—understand—what you're saying!"; if we lean on his right as a speaking intentional system to have his word accepted, we grant him an irrational set of beliefs. Neither position provides a stable resting place, for, as we saw earlier, *intentional explanation and prediction cannot be accommodated either to breakdown or to less than optimal design, so there is no coherent intentional description of such an impasse.* (*BS*, 20; last emphasis added)[9]

In the paper from which the quote is taken, Dennett uses 'intentional description,' 'intentional explanation' and the like for both common-sense belief–desire accounts and idealized intentional system accounts. The ambiguity this engenders is crucial in evaluating his claim. On the idealized intentional systems reading it is a tautology that "there is no coherent intentional description of such an impasse." But on the common-sense reading it is simply false. There is nothing at all incoherent about a (common-sense) intentional description of a man who has miscalculated the balance in his checking account!

---

8. Cf. P. C. Wason and P. N. Johnson-Laird, *The Psychology of Human Reasoning: Structure and Content* (London: Batsford, 1972).

9. For parallel passages, cf. *TB*, p. 19; *R*, p. 74; *BS*, p. 22.

The fact that folk psychology often comfortably and unproblematically views people as departing from the standard of full rationality often looms large in cases where questions of morality and responsibility are salient. Consider the case of Oscar, the engineer. It is his job to review planned operations at the factory and halt those that might lead to explosion. But one day there is an explosion and, bureaucracy being what it is, three years later Oscar is called before a board of inquiry. Why didn't he halt the hazardous operation? It looks bad for Oscar, since an independent expert has testified that the data Oscar had logically entail a certain equation, and it is a commonplace amongst competent safety engineers that the equation is a sure sign of trouble. But Oscar has an impressive defense. Granted the data he had entails the equation, and granted any competent engineer would know that the equation is a sign of trouble. But at the time of the accident neither Oscar nor anyone else knew that the data logically entailed the equation. It was only six months after the accident that Professor Brain at Cambridge proved a fundamental theorem needed to show that the data entail the equation. Without knowledge of the theorem, neither Oscar nor anyone else could be expected to believe that the data entail the equation.

At several places Dennett cites Quine as a fellow defender of the view that the ascription of inconsistent beliefs is problematic.

> To echo a theme I have long cherished in Quine's work, all the evidence—behavioral *and internal*—we acquire for the correctness of one of these ascriptions is not only evidence against the other, but the best sort of evidence. (*R*, p. 74)

However, Dennett misconstrues Quine's point. What Quine urges is not that *any* inconsistency is evidence of bad translation (or bad belief ascription), but rather that *obvious* inconsistency is a sign that something has gone wrong. For Quine, unlike Dennett, sees translation (and belief ascription) as a matter of putting ourselves in our subject's shoes. And the self we put in those shoes, we are too well aware, departs in many ways from the standard of optimal rationality. The point can be made vividly by contrasting Oscar, our safety engineer, with Otto, a lesser functionary. Otto is charged with the responsibility of memorizing a list of contingency plans: if the red light flashes, order the building evacuated; if the warning light goes on, turn the big blue valve; if the buzzer sounds, alert the manager. Now suppose that while he is on duty the red light flashes but Otto fails to order an evacuation. There is a strong prima-facie case that Otto is to be held responsible for the consequences. Either he failed to see the light (he was asleep or not paying due attention), or he did not memorize the contingency plans as he was obligated to, or he has some sinister motive. But, and this is the crucial point, it will be no excuse for Otto to claim that he had memorized the plan, saw the light, and was paying attention, but it just never occurred to him to order the evacuation. It is in these cases of apparently blatant or "incomprehensible" irrationality that we hunt first for hidden motives or beliefs. For, absent these, the subject must be judged irrational in a way we cannot imagine ourselves being irrational; and it is this sort of irrationality that threatens the application of our common-sense notions of belief and desire.

In Dennett's writings there are frequent hints of a second strategy for defending the hard line, a strategy which relies on an evolutionary argument. He cheerfully concedes that he has "left [his] claim about the relation between rationality and evolutionary considerations so open-ended that it is hard to argue against efficiently" (*R*, p. 73). Still, I think it is important to try wringing some arguments out of Dennett's vague meditations on this topic. As I read him, Dennett is exploring a pair of ideas for showing that the gap between IS notions and folk notions is much smaller than some have feared. If he can show this, the hard line will have been vindicated.

The first idea is suggested by a passage (*BS*, pp. 8–9) in which Dennett asks whether we could adopt the intentional stance toward exotic creatures encountered on an alien planet. His answer is that we could, provided "we have reason to suppose that a process of natural selection has been in effect . . ." (*BS*, p. 8). The argument seems to be that natural selection favors true beliefs, and thus will favor cognitive processes which generally yield true beliefs in the organism's natural environment. So if an organism is the product of natural selection, we can safely assume that most of its beliefs will be true, and most of its belief-forming strategies will be rational. Departures from the normative standard required by the intentional stance will be few and far between.

For two quite different reasons, this argument is untenable. First, it is simply not the case that natural selection favors true beliefs over false ones. What natural selection does favor is beliefs which yield selective advantage. And there are many environmental circumstances in which false beliefs will be more useful than true ones. In these circumstances, natural selection ought to favor cognitive processes which yield suitable false beliefs and disfavor processes which yield true beliefs. Moreover, even when having true beliefs is optimal, natural selection may often favor a process that yields false beliefs most of the time, but which has a high probability of yielding true beliefs when it counts. Thus, for example, in an environment with a wide variety of suitable foods, an organism may do very well if it radically overgeneralizes about what is inedible. If eating a certain food caused illness on a single occasion, the organism would immediately come to believe (falsely, let us assume) that all passingly similar foods are poisonous as well. When it comes to food poisoning, *better safe than sorry* is a policy that recommends itself to natural selection.[10]

The second fault in the argument I am attributing to Dennett is a subtle but enormously important one. As stated, the argument slips almost unnoticeably from the claim that natural selection favors cognitive processes which yield true beliefs in the natural environment to the claim that natural selection favors *rational* belief-forming strategies.

10. For a detailed discussion of some examples and further references, cf. H. A. Lewis, "The Argument From Evolution," *Proceedings of the Aristotelian Society*, Supplementary vol. LIII, 1979; also my "Could man be an irrational animal?" *Synthese* 64 (1985), 115–35.

But, even if the first claim were true, the second would not follow. There are many circumstances in which inferential strategies which from a normative standpoint are patently invalid will nonetheless generally yield the right answer. The social-psychology literature is rich with illustrations of inferential strategies which stand subjects in good stead ordinarily but which subjects readily overextend, with unhappy results.[11]

So long as we recognize a distinction between a normative theory of inference or decision making and a set of inferential practices which (in the right environment) generally get the right (or selectively useful) answer, it will be clear that the two need not, and generally do not, coincide. However, in a number of places Dennett seems to be suggesting that there really *is* no distinction here, that by "normative theory of inference and decision" he simply *means* "practices favored by natural selection." This move is at the core of the second idea I see in Dennett for using evolutionary notions to buttress the hard line (Cf. *R*, pp. 73–4). And buttress it would! For it would then become *tautologous* that naturally evolved creatures are intentional systems, believing, wanting and doing what they ought, save when they are malfunctioning. Yet Dennett will have to pay a heavy price for turning the hard line into a tautology. For if *this* is what he means by "normative theory of belief and decision," then such established theories as deductive and inductive logic, decision theory and game theory are of no help in assessing what an organism "ought to believe." Natural selection, as we have already noted, sometimes smiles upon cognitive processes that depart substantially from the canons of logic and decision theory. So these established theories and our guesses about how to extend them will be of no help in assessing what an intentional system should believe, desire or do. Instead, to predict from the intentional stance we should need a detailed study of the organism's physiology, its ecological environment and its history. But predicting from the intentional stance, characterized in *this* way, is surely not to be recommended when we "doubt the practicality of prediction from the design or physical stance" (*BS*, p. 8). Nor, obviously, does *this* intentional stance promise to yield belief and desire attributions that are all but co-extensive with those made in common sense.

This is all I shall have to say by way of meeting the hard line head on, I think it is fair to conclude that the hard line simply cannot be maintained. The differences separating the IS notions of belief and desire from their common-sense counterparts is anything but insubstantial. Before turning to Dennett's soft line, we should note a further unwelcome consequence of rejecting folk psychology in favor of intentional-system theory. During the last decade, cognitive psychologists have become increasingly interested in studying the strengths and foibles of human reasoning. There is a substantial and growing literature aimed at uncovering predictable departures from normative standards of reasoning and decision making, almost all of it implicitly or explicitly cast in the idiom of folk

---

11. Cf. Richard Nisbett and Lee Ross, *Human Inference* (Englewood Cliffs, NJ: Prentice-Hall, 1980).

psychology.[12] Were we to replace folk notions with their intentional-system analogs, we should have to conclude that all of this work limning the boundaries of human rationality is simply incoherent. For, as Dennett notes, "the presuppositions of intentional explanation . . . put prediction of *lapses* in principle beyond its scope . . ." (*BS*, p. 246).[13]

THE SOFT LINE

In contrast with the hard line, which tries to minimize the size or importance of the difference between folk and IS notions, the soft line acknowledges a substantial and significant divergence. To deal with the problems this gap creates, the soft line proposes some fiddling with the idealized notion of an intentional system. The basic idea is that once we have an idealized theory of intentional systems in hand, we can study an array of variations on the idealized theme. We can construct theories about "imperfect intentional systems" (the term is mine, not Dennett's) which have specified deficiences in memory, reasoning power, etc. And we can attempt to determine empirically which imperfect intentional system best predicts the behavior of a particular subject or species. Rather than assuming the intentional stance toward an organism or person, we may assume one of a range of "imperfect intentional stances," from which it will make sense to ascribe a less than fully rational set of beliefs and desires. From these various stances we can give intentional descriptions of our cognitive shortcomings and elaborate an empirical science which maps the inferential strengths and weaknesses of humans and other creatures. We can also legitimize our folk-psychological descriptions of ourselves— protecting "personhood from the march of science" (*R*, p. 75)—by appeal to the imperfect-intentional-system theory which best predicts our actual behavior. But *genuine* intentional-system theory (*sans phrase*) would have a definite pride of place among these theories of imperfect intentional systems. For all of the latter would be variations on the basic IS framework.

Dennett, with his disconcerting penchant for working both sides of the street, never flatly endorses the soft line, though it is clear that he has pondered something like it:

Consider a set *T* of transformations that take beliefs into beliefs. The problem is to determine the set *T*, for each intentional system *S*, so that if we know that *S* believes

---

12. E.g., Nisbett and Ross, ibid., and Wason and Johnson-Laird, ibid., along with the many studies cited in these books.

13. Dennett appends the following footnote to the quoted sentence: "In practice we predict lapses at the intentional level ('You watch! He'll forget all about your knight after you move the queen') on the basis of loose-jointed inductive hypotheses about individual or widespread human frailties. These hypotheses are expressed in intentional terms, but if they were given rigorous support, they would in the process be recast as predictions from the design or physical stance" (*BS*, p. 246). So the scientific study of intentionally described inferential shortcomings can aspire to no more than "loose-jointed hypotheses" in need of recasting. But cf. *TK*, pp. 11–12, where Dennett pulls in his horns a bit.

p, we will be able to determine other things that *S* believes by seeing what the transformations of *p* are for T_s. If *S* were ideally rational, every valid transformation would be in T_s; *S* would believe every logical consequence of every belief (and, ideally, *S* would have no false beliefs). Now we know that no actual intentional system will be ideally rational; so we must suppose any actual system will have a *T* with less in it. But we also know that, to qualify as an intentional system at all, *S* must have a *T* with some integrity; *T* cannot be empty. (*BS*, p. 21)

In the next few sentences, however, Dennett expresses qualms about the soft line:

What rationale could we have, however, for fixing some set between the extremes and calling it *the* set for belief (for *S*, for earthlings, for ten-year-old girls)? This is another way of asking whether we could replace Hintikka's normative theory of belief with an empirical theory of belief, and, if so, what evidence we would use. "Actually," one is tempted to say, "people do believe contradictions on occasion, as their utterances demonstrate; so any adequate logic of belief or analysis of the concept of belief must accommodate this fact." But any attempt to *legitimize* human fallibility in a theory of belief by fixing a permissible level of error would be like adding one more rule to chess: an Official Tolerance Rule to the effect any game of chess containing no more than *k* moves that are illegal relative to the other rules of the game is a legal game of chess. (*BS*, p. 21)

In a more recent paper, Dennett sounds more enthusiastic about the soft line:

Of course we don't all sit in the dark in our studies like mad Leibnizians rationalistically excogitating behavioral predictions from pure, idealized concepts of our neighbors, nor do we derive all our readiness to attribute desires to careful generation of them from the ultimate goal of survival. . . . Rationalistic generation of attributions is augmented and even corrected on occasion by empirical generalizations about belief and desire that guide our attributions and are learned more or less inductively. . . . I grant the existence of all this naturalistic generalization, and its role in the normal calculation of folk psychologist—i.e., all of us. . . . *I would insist, however, that all this empirically obtained lore is laid over a fundamental generative and normative framework that has features I have described.* (*TK*, pp. 14–15, last emphasis added)

Whatever Dennett's considered view may be, I think the soft line is clearly preferable to the hard line. Indeed, the soft line is similar to a view that I have myself defended.[14] As

---

14. In "On the ascription of content," in A. Woodfield (ed.), *Thought and Object* (Oxford University Press, 1982).

a way of focusing in on my misgivings about the soft line, let me quickly sketch my own view and note how it differs from the view I am trying to foist on Dennett. Mine is an effort squarely situated in what Dennett calls "the anthropological quest" (*TK*, p. 6). I want to describe as accurately as possible just what we are up to when we engage in the "folk practice" of ascribing beliefs to one another and dealing with one another partly on the basis of these ascriptions. My theory is an elaboration on Quine's observation that in ascribing beliefs to others "we project ourselves into what, from his remarks and other indications, we imagine the speaker's state of mind to have been, and then we say what, in our language, is natural and relevant for us in the state thus feigned" (*World and Object*, p. 219). As I see it, when we say *S believes that p* we are saying that *S* is in a certain sort of functionally characterized psychological state, viz., a "belief state." The role of the "content sentence," *p*, is to specify *which* belief state it is. If we imagine that we ourselves were not to utter *p* in earnest, the belief we are attributing to *S* is one *similar* (along specified dimensions) to the belief which would cause our own imagined assertion. One of the dimensions of similarity that figures in belief ascription is the pattern of inference that the belief states in question enter into. When the network of potential inferences surrounding a subject's belief state differs substantially from the network surrounding our own belief that *p*, we are reluctant to count the subject's belief as a belief *that p*. Thus we will not have any comfortable way of ascribing content to the belief states of a subject whose inferential network is markedly different from ours. Since we take ourselves to approximate rationality, this explains the fact, noted by Dennett, that intentional description falters in the face of egregious irrationality. It also explains the fact, missed by Dennett, that familiar irrationality—the sort we know ourselves to be guilty of—poses no problem for folk psychology.

A full elaboration of my theory would be a long story, out of place here. What is important for our present purposes is to note the differences between my account and what I have been calling Dennett's soft line. These differences are two. First, my story does not portray folk psychology as an *instrumentalist* theory. Belief states are *functional* states which can and do play a role in the causation of behavior. Thus folk psychology is not immune from the advance of science. If it turns out that the human brain does not have the sort of functional organization assumed in our folk theory, then there are no such things as beliefs and desires. Second, the notion of idealized rationality plays *no role at all* in my account. In ascribing content to belief states, we measure others not against an idealized standard but against ourselves. It is in virtue of this Protagorean parochialism that the exotic and the insane fall outside the reach of intentional explanation.

So much for the difference between my view and Dennett's. Why should mine be preferred? There are two answers. First, I think it is simply wrong that we ordinarily conceive of beliefs and desires in instrumentalist terms—as abstracta rather than illata. It is, however, no easy task to take aim at Dennett's instrumentalism, since the target refuses to stay still. Consider:

Folk psychology is *instrumentalistic* ... Beliefs and desires of folk psychology ... are abstracta. (*TK*, p. 13)

It is not particularly to the point to argue against me that folk psychology is *in fact* committed to beliefs and desires as distinguishable, causally interacting *illata*; what must be shown is that it ought to be. The latter claim I will deal with in due course. The former claim I *could* concede without embarrassment to my overall project, but I do not concede it, for it seems to me that the evidence is quite strong that our ordinary notion of belief has next to nothing of the concrete in it. (*TK*, p. 15)

The *ordinary* notion of belief no doubt does place beliefs somewhere midway between being *illata* and being *abstracta*. (*TK, p.* 16)

In arguing for his sometimes instrumentalism Dennett conjures the sad tale of Pierre, shot dead by Jacques in Trafalgar Square. Jacques

is apprehended on the spot by Sherlock; Tom reads about it in the *Times* and Boris learns of it in *Pravda*. Now Jacques, Sherlock, Tom and Boris have had re-markably different experiences—to say nothing of their earlier biographies and future prospects—but there is one thing they share: they all believe that a French-man has committed a murder in Trafalgar Square. They did not all *say* this, not even "to themselves"; *that proposition* did not, we can suppose, "occur to" any of them, and even if it had, it would have had entirely different import for Jacques, Sherlock, Tom and Boris. (*TK*, p. 15)

Dennett's point is that while all four men believe that a Frenchman committed a murder in Trafalgar Square, their histories, interests and relations to the deed are so different that they could hardly be thought to share a single, functionally characterizable state. This is quite right, but it does not force us to view beliefs as abstracta. For if, as my theory insists, there is a *similarity* claim embedded in belief ascriptions, then we should expect these ascriptions to be both vague and sensitive to pragmatic context. For Jacques and Boris both to believe that a Frenchman committed a murder in Trafalgar Square, they need not be in the very same functional state, but only in states that are sufficiently similar for the communicative purposes at hand.

As Dennett notes, one need not be crucially concerned with what "folk psychology is in fact committed to." Since he aims to replace folk psychology with intentional-system notions, it would suffice to show that the instrumentalism of these latter no-tions is no disadvantage. But here again I am skeptical. It is my hunch that our concept of ourselves as moral agents simply will not sit comfortably with the view that beliefs and desires are mere computational conveniences that correspond in no interesting way to what goes on inside the head. I cannot offer much of an argument for my hunch, though I am encouraged by the fact that Dennett seems to share the intuition lying behind it:

> Stich accurately diagnoses and describes the strategic role I envisage for the concept of an intentional system, permitting the claim that human beings are genuine believers and desirers to survive almost any imaginable discoveries in cognitive and physiological psychology, thus making our status as moral agents well nigh invulnerable to scientific discontinuation. Not 'in principle' invulnerable, for in a science-fiction on mood we can imagine startling discoveries (e.g., some 'people' are organic puppets remotely controlled by Martians) that would upset any particular home truths about believers and moral agenthood you like. . . . (*R*, p. 73)

Now if our concept of moral agenthood were really compatible with the intentional-system construal of beliefs and desires, it is hard to see why the imagined discovery about Martians should be in the least unsettling. For, controlled by Martians or not, organic puppets are still intentional systems in perfectly good standing. So long as their behavior is usefully predictable from the intentional stance, the transceivers inside their heads sanction no skepticism about whether they really have IS beliefs and IS desires. But Dennett is right, of course. We would not count his organic puppets as believers or moral agents. The reason, I submit, is that the morally relevant concept of belief is not an instrumentalistic concept.

The second reason for preferring my line to Dennett's soft line is that the idea of a *normative* theory of beliefs and desires, which is central to Dennett's view, plays no role in mine. And this notion, I would urge, is one we are best rid of. Recall that from the outset we have been relying on rough and ready intuitions about what an organism ought to believe, desire and do, and assuming that these intuitions could be elaborated and systematized into a theory. But I am inclined to think that this assumption is mistaken. Rather, it would appear that the intuitions Dennett exploits are underlain by a variety of different ideas about what an organism ought to believe or desire, ideas which as often as not pull in quite different directions. Sometimes it is an evolutionary story which motivates the intuition that a belief or desire is the one a well-designed intentional system should have. At other times intuitions are guided by appeal to logic or decision theory. But as we have seen, the evolutionary account of what an organism ought to believe and desire just will not do for Dennett, since it presupposes an abundance of information about the ecological niche and physiological workings of the organism. Nor is there any serious prospect of elaborating logic and decision theory into a suitably general account of what an organism ought to believe and desire. Indeed, apart from a few special cases, I think our intuitions about what an organism ought to believe and desire are simply nonexistent. The problem is not merely that we lack a worked-out normative theory of belief and desire; it runs much deeper. For in general we have no idea what such a normative theory would be telling us. We do not really know what it *means* to say that an organism *ought to have* a given belief or desire. Consider some examples:

> Ought Descartes to have believed his theory of vortices?
> Ought Nixon to have believed that he would not be impeached?
> Ought William James to have believed in the existence of a personal God?
> Should all people have perfect memories, retaining for life all beliefs save those for which they later acquire negative evidence?

In each of these cases our grasp of what the question is supposed to *mean* is at best tenuous. The prospects of a *general theory* capable of answering all of them in a motivated way are surely very dim. Worse still, the general theory of intentional systems that Dennett would have us work toward must tell us not only what *people* in various situations ought to believe, but also what other animals ought to believe. Ought the frog to believe that there is an insect flying off to the right? Or merely that there is some food there? Or perhaps should it only have a conditional belief: if it flicks its tongue in a certain way, something yummy will end up in its mouth? Suppose the fly is of a species that causes frogs acute indigestion. Ought the frog to believe this? Does it make a difference how many fellow frogs he has seen come to grief after munching on similar bugs? A normative theory of desire is, if anything, more problematic. Should I want to father as many offspring as possible? Should the frog?

To the extent that these questions are obscure, the notion of a normative theory of belief and desire is obscure. And that obscurity in turn infects much of what Dennett says about intentional systems and the intentional stance. Perhaps Dennett can dispel some of the mystery. But in the interim I am inclined to think that the normatively appropriate attitude is the skepticism I urged in my opening paragraph.[15]

---

15. I have learned a good deal from the helpful comments of Bo Dahlbom, Robert Cummins, Philip Pettit and Robert Richardson.

CONNECTIONISM, ELIMINATIVISM, AND THE FUTURE OF

FOLK PSYCHOLOGY[1]

William Ramsey, Stephen Stich, and Joseph Garon

1 Introduction

In the years since the publication of Thomas Kuhn's *Structure of Scientific Revolutions*, the term "scientific revolution" has been used with increasing frequency in discussions of scientific change, and the magnitude required of an innovation before someone or other is tempted to call it a revolution has diminished alarmingly. Our thesis in this paper is that if a certain family of connectionist hypotheses turn out to be right, they will surely count as revolutionary, even on stringent pre-Kuhnian standards. There is no question that connectionism has already brought about major changes in the way many cognitive scientists conceive of cognition. However, as we see it, what makes certain kinds of connectionist models genuinely revolutionary is the support they lend to a thoroughgoing eliminativism about some of the central posits of common sense (or "folk") psychology. Our focus in this paper will be on beliefs or propositional memories, though the argument generalizes straightforwardly to all the other propositional attitudes. If we are right, the consequences of this kind of connectionism extend well beyond the confines of

1. Thanks are due to Ned Block, Paul Churchland, Gary Cottrell, Adrian Cussins, Jerry Fodor, John Heil, Frank Jackson, David Kirsh, Patricia Kitcher and Philip Kitcher for useful feedback on earlier versions of this paper. Talks based on the paper have been presented at the UCSD Cognitive Science Seminar and at conferences sponsored by the Howard Hughes Medical Foundation and the University of North Carolina at Greensboro. Comments and questions from these audiences have proved helpful in many ways.

cognitive science, since these models, if successful, will require a radical reorientation in the way we think about ourselves.

Here is a quick preview of what is to come. Section 2 gives a brief account of what eliminativism claims, and sketches a pair of premises that eliminativist arguments typically require. Section 3 says a bit about how we conceive of common sense psychology, and the propositional attitudes that it posits. It also illustrates one sort of psychological model that exploits and builds upon the posits of folk psychology. Section 4 is devoted to connectionism. Models that have been called "connectionist" form a fuzzy and heterogeneous set whose members often share little more than a vague family resemblance. However, our argument linking connectionism to eliminativism will work only for a restricted domain of connectionist models, interpreted in a particular way; the main job of Section 4 is to say what that domain is and how the models in the domain are to be interpreted. In Section 5 we will illustrate what a connectionist model of belief that comports with our strictures might look like, and go on to argue that if models of this sort are correct, then things look bad for common sense psychology. Section 6 assembles some objections and replies. The final section is a brief conclusion.

Before plunging in we should emphasize that the thesis we propose to defend is a *conditional* claim: *If* connectionist hypotheses of the sort we will sketch turn out to be right, so too will eliminativism about propositional attitudes. Since our goal is only to show how connectionism and eliminativism are related, we will make no effort to argue for the truth or falsity of either doctrine. In particular, we will offer no argument in favor of the version of connectionism required in the antecedent of our conditional. Indeed our view is that it is early days yet—too early to tell with any assurance how well this family of connectionist hypotheses will fare. Those who are more confident of connectionism may, of course, invoke our conditional as part of a larger argument for doing away with the propositional attitudes.[2] But, as John Haugeland once remarked, one man's ponens is another man's tollens. And those who take eliminativism about prepositional attitudes to be preposterous or unthinkable may well view our arguments as part of a larger case against connectionism. Thus, we'd not be at all surprised if trenchant critics of connectionism, like Fodor and Pylyshyn, found both our conditional and the argument for it to be quite congenial.[3]

2 Eliminativism and Folk Psychology

'Eliminativism,' as we shall use the term, is a fancy name for a simple thesis. It is the claim that some category of entities, processes or properties exploited in a common sense or scientific account of the world do not exist. So construed, we are all eliminativists about

---

2. See, for example, Churchland (1981) & (1986), where explicitly eliminativist conclusions are drawn on the basis of speculations about the success of cognitive models similar to those we shall discuss.

3. Fodor, J. & Pylyshyn, Z. (1988).

many sorts of things. In the domain of folk theory, witches are the standard example. Once upon a time witches were widely believed to be responsible for various local calamities. But people gradually became convinced that there are better explanations for most of the events in which witches had been implicated. There being no explanatory work for witches to do, sensible people concluded that there were no such things. In the scientific domain, phlogiston, caloric fluid and the luminiferous ether are the parade cases for eliminativism. Each was invoked by serious scientists pursuing sophisticated research programs. But in each case the program ran aground in a major way, and the theories in which the entities were invoked were replaced by successor theories in which the entities played no role. The scientific community gradually came to recognize that phlogiston and the rest do not exist.

As these examples suggest, a central step in an eliminativist argument will typically be the demonstration that the theory in which certain putative entities or processes are invoked should be rejected and replaced by a better theory. And that raises the question of how we go about showing that one theory is better than another. Notoriously, this question is easier to ask than to answer. However, it would be pretty widely agreed that if a new theory provides more accurate predictions and better explanations than an old one, and does so over a broader range of phenomena, and if the new theory comports as well or better with well established theories in neighboring domains, then there is good reason to think that the old theory is inferior, and that the new one is to be preferred. This is hardly a complete account of the conditions under which one theory is to be preferred to another, though for our purposes it will suffice.

But merely showing that a theory in which a class of entities plays a role is inferior to a successor theory plainly is not sufficient to show that the entities do not exist. Often a more appropriate conclusion is that the rejected theory was wrong, perhaps seriously wrong, about some of the properties of the entities in its domain, or about the laws governing those entities, and that the new theory gives us a more accurate account *of those very same entities*. Thus, for example, pre-Copernican astronomy was very wrong about the nature of the planets and the laws governing their movement. But it would be something of a joke to suggest that Copernicus and Galileo showed that the planets Ptolemy spoke of do not exist.[4]

In other cases the right thing to conclude is that the posits of the old theory are reducible to those of the new. Standard examples here include the reduction of temperature to mean molecular kinetic energy, the reduction of sound to wave motion in the medium,

---

4. We are aware that certain philosophers and historians of science have actually entertained ideas similar to the suggestion that the planets spoken of by pre-Copernican astronomers do not exist. See, for example, Kuhn (1970), Ch. 10, and Feyerabend (1981), Ch. 4. However, we take this suggestion to be singularly implausible. Eliminativist arguments can't be that easy. Just what has gone wrong with the accounts of meaning and reference that lead to such claims is less clear. For further discussion on these matters see Kuhn (1983), and Kitcher (1978) & (1983).

and the reduction of genes to sequences of polynucleotide bases.[5] Given our current concerns, the lesson to be learned from these cases is that even if the common sense theory in which propositional attitudes find their home is replaced by a better theory, that would not be enough to show that the posits of the common sense theory do not exist.

What more would be needed? What is it that distinguishes cases like phlogiston and caloric, on the one hand, from cases like genes or the planets on the other? Or, to ask the question in a rather different way, what made phlogiston and caloric candidates for elimination? Why wasn't it concluded that phlogiston is oxygen, that caloric is kinetic energy, and that the earlier theories had just been rather badly mistaken about some of the properties of phlogiston and caloric?

Let us introduce a bit of terminology. We will call theory changes in which the entities and processes of the old theory are retained or reduced to those of the new one *ontologically conservative* theory changes. Theory changes that are not ontologically conservative we will call *ontologically radical*. Given this terminology, the question we are asking is how to distinguish ontologically conservative theory changes from ontologically radical ones.

Once again, this is a question that is easier to ask than to answer. There is, in the philosophy of science literature, nothing that even comes close to a plausible and fully general account of when theory change sustains an eliminativist conclusion and when it does not. In the absence of a principled way of deciding when ontological elimination is in order, the best we can do is to look at the posits of the old theory—the ones that are at risk of elimination—and ask whether there is anything in the new theory that they might be identified with or reduced to. If the posits of the new theory strike us as deeply and fundamentally different from those of the old theory, in the way that molecular motion seems deeply and fundamentally different from the "exquisitely elastic" fluid posited by caloric theory, then it will be plausible to conclude that the theory change has been a radical one, and that an eliminativist conclusion is in order. But since there is no easy measure of how "deeply and fundamentally different" a pair of posits are, the conclusion we reach is bound to be a judgment call.[6]

---

5. For some detailed discussion of scientific reduction, see Nagel (1961); Schaffner (1967); Hooker (1981); and Kitcher (1984). The genetics case is not without controversy. See Kitcher (1982) & (1984).

6. It's worth noting that judgments on this matter can differ quite substantially. At one end of the spectrum are writers like Feyerabend (1981), and perhaps Kuhn (1962), for whom relatively small differences in theory are enough to justify the suspicion that there has been an ontologically radical change. Toward the other end are writers like Lycan, who writes:

I am at pains to advocate a very liberal view ... I am entirely willing to give up fairly large chunks of our commonsensical or platitudinous theory of belief or of desire (or of almost anything else) and decide that we were just wrong about a lot of things, without drawing the inference that we are no longer talking about belief or desire .... I think the ordinary word "belief" (qua theoretical term of folk psychology) points dimly toward a natural kind that we have not fully grasped and that only mature psychology will reveal. I expect that "belief" will turn out to refer to some kind of information bearing inner state of a

To argue that certain sorts of connectionist models support eliminativism about the prepositional attitudes, we must make it plausible that these models are not ontologically conservative. Our strategy will be to contrast these connectionist models, models like those set out in Section 5, with ontologically conservative models like the one sketched at the end of Section 3, in an effort to underscore just how ontologically radical the connectionist models are. But here we are getting ahead of ourselves. Before trying to persuade you that connectionist models are ontologically radical, we need to take a look at the folk psychological theory that the connectionist models threaten to replace.

3 Propositional Attitudes and Common Sense Psychology

For present purposes we will assume that common sense psychology can plausibly be regarded as a theory, and that beliefs, desires and the rest of the propositional attitudes are plausibly viewed as posits of that theory. Though this is not an uncontroversial assumption, the case for it has been well argued by others.[7] Once it is granted that common sense psychology is indeed a theory, we expect it will be conceded by almost everyone that the theory is a likely candidate for replacement. In saying this, we do not intend to disparage folk psychology, or to beg any questions about the status of the entities it posits. Our point is simply that folk wisdom on matters psychological is not likely to tell us all there is to know. Common sense psychology, like other folk theories, is bound to be incomplete in many ways, and very likely to be inaccurate in more than a few. If this were not the case, there would be no need for a careful, quantitative, experimental science of psychology. With the possible exception of a few die hard Wittgensteinians, just about everyone is prepared to grant that there are many psychological facts and principles beyond those embedded in common sense. If this is right, then we have the first premise needed in an eliminativist argument aimed at beliefs, propositional memories and the rest of the propositional attitudes. The theory that posits the attitudes is indeed a prime candidate for replacement.

Though common sense psychology contains a wealth of lore about beliefs, memories, desires, hopes, fears and the other propositional attitudes, the crucial folk psychological tenets in forging the link between connectionism and eliminativism are the claims that

---

sentient being. . ., but the kind of state it refers to, may have only a few of the properties usually attributed to beliefs by common sense. (Lycan (1988), pp. 31–2.)

On our view, both extreme positions are implausible. As we noted earlier, the Copernican revolution did not show that the planets studied by Ptolemy do not exist. But Lavoisier's chemical revolution *did* show that phlogiston does not exist. Yet on Lycan's "very liberal view" it is hard to see why we should not conclude that phlogiston really does exist after all—it's really oxygen, and prior to Lavoisier "we were just very wrong about a lot of things."

7. For an early and influential statement of the view that common sense psychology is a theory, see Sellars (1956). More recently the view has been defended by Churchland (1970) & (1979), Chs. 1 & 4; and by Fodor (1988), Ch. 1. For the opposite view, see Wilkes (1978); Madell (1986); Sharpe (1987).

propositional attitudes are *functionally discrete, semantically interpretable*, states that play a *causal role* in the production of other propositional attitudes, and ultimately in the production of behavior. Following the suggestion in Stich (1983), we'll call this cluster of claims *propositional modularity*.[8] (The reader is cautioned not to confuse this notion of propositional modularity with the very different notion of modularity defended in Fodor (1983).)

There is a great deal of evidence that might be cited in support of the thesis that folk psychology is committed to the tenets of propositional modularity. The fact that common sense psychology takes beliefs and other propositional attitudes to have semantic properties deserves special emphasis. According to common sense:

   i) when people see a dog nearby they typically come to believe *that there is a dog nearby*;
   ii) when people believe *that the train will be late if there is snow in the mountains*, and come to believe *that there is snow in the mountains*, they will typically come to believe *that the train will be late*;
   iii) when people who speak English say 'There is a cat in the yard,' they typically believe *that there is a cat in the yard*.

And so on, for indefinitely many further examples. Note that these generalizations of common sense psychology are couched in terms of the *semantic* properties of the attitudes. It is in virtue of being the belief *that p* that a given belief has a given effect or cause. Thus common sense psychology treats the predicates expressing these semantic properties, predicates like 'believes *that the train is late*,' as *projectable* predicates—the sort of predicates that are appropriately used in nomological or law-like generalizations.

Perhaps the most obvious way to bring out folk psychology's commitment to the thesis that propositional attitudes are *functionally discrete* states is to note that it typically makes perfectly good sense to claim that a person has acquired (or lost) a single memory or belief. Thus, for example, on a given occasion it might plausibly be claimed that when Henry awoke from his nap he had completely forgotten that the car keys were hidden in the refrigerator, though he had forgotten nothing else. In saying that folk psychology views beliefs as the sorts of things that can be acquired or lost one at a time, we do not mean to be denying that having any particular belief may presuppose a substantial network of related beliefs. The belief that the car keys are in the refrigerator is not one that could be acquired by a primitive tribesman who knew nothing about cars, keys or refrigerators. But once the relevant background is in place, as we may suppose it is for us and for Henry, it seems that folk psychology is entirely comfortable with the possibility that a person may acquire (or lose) the belief that the car keys are in the refrigerator, while the remainder of his beliefs remain unchanged. Propositional modularity does not, of

8. See Stich (1983), pp. 237 ff.

course, deny that acquiring one belief often leads to the acquisition of a cluster of related beliefs. When Henry is told that the keys are in the refrigerator, he may come to believe that they haven't been left in the ignition, or in his jacket pocket. But then again he may not. Indeed, on the folk psychological conception of belief it is perfectly possible for a person to have a long standing belief that the keys are in the refrigerator, and to continue searching for them in the bedroom.[9]

To illustrate the way in which folk psychology takes propositional attitudes to be functionally discrete, *causally active* states let us sketch a pair of more elaborate examples.

i) In common sense psychology, behavior is often explained by appeal to certain of the agent's beliefs and desires. Thus, to explain why Alice went to her office, we might note that she wanted to send some e-mail messages (and, of course, she believed she could do so from her office). However, in some cases an agent will have several sets of beliefs and desires each of which *might* lead to the same behavior. Thus we may suppose that Alice also wanted to talk to her research assistant, and that she believed he would be at the office. In such cases, common sense psychology assumes that Alice's going to her office might have been caused by either one of the belief/desire pairs, or by both, and that determining which of these options obtains is an empirical matter. So it is entirely possible that on *this* occasion Alice's desire to send some e-mail played no role in producing her behavior; it was the desire to talk with her research assistant that actually caused her to go to the office. However, had she not wanted to talk with her research assistant, she might have gone to the office anyhow, because the desire to send some e-mail, which was causally inert in her actual decision making, might then have become actively involved. Note that in this case common sense psychology is prepared to recognize a pair of quite distinct semantically characterized states, one of which may be causally active while the other is not.

ii) Our second illustration is parallel to the first, but focuses on beliefs and inference, rather than desires and action. On the common sense view, it may sometimes happen that a person has a number of belief clusters, any one of which might lead him to infer some further belief. When he actually does draw the inference, folk psychology assumes that it is an empirical question what he inferred it from, and that this question typically has a determinate answer. Suppose, for example, that Inspector Clouseau believes that the butler said he spent the evening at the village hotel, and that he said he arrived back on the morning train. Suppose Clouseau also believes that the village hotel is closed for the season, and that the morning train has been taken out of service. Given these beliefs, along with some widely shared background beliefs, Clouseau might well

---

9. Cherniak (1986), Ch. 3, notes that this sort of absent mindedness is commonplace in literature and in ordinary life, and sometimes leads to disastrous consequences.

infer that the butler is lying. If he does, folk psychology presumes that the inference might be based either on his beliefs about the hotel, or on his beliefs about the train, or both. It is entirely possible, from the perspective of common sense psychology, that although Clouseau has long known that the hotel is closed for the season, this belief played no role in his inference on this particular occasion. Once again we see common sense psychology invoking a pair of distinct propositional attitudes, one of which is causally active on a particular occasion while the other is causally inert.

In the psychological literature there is no shortage of models for human belief or memory which follow the lead of common sense psychology in supposing that propositional modularity is true. Indeed, prior to the emergence of connectionism, just about all psychological models of propositional memory, save for those urged by behaviorists, were comfortably compatible with propositional modularity. Typically, these models view a subject's store of beliefs or memories as an interconnected collection of functionally discrete, semantically interpretable states which interact in systematic ways. Some of these models represent individual beliefs as sentence-like structures—strings of symbols which can be individually activated by transferring them from long term memory to the more limited memory of a central processing unit. Other models represent beliefs as a network of labeled nodes and labeled links through which patterns of activation may spread. Still other models represent beliefs as sets of production rules.[10] In all three sorts of models, it is generally the case that for any given cognitive episode, like performing a particular inference or answering a question, some of the memory states will be actively involved, and others will be dormant.

In Figure 1 we have displayed a fragment of a "semantic network" representation of memory, in the style of Collins & Quillian (1972). In this model, each distinct proposition in memory is represented by an oval node along with its labeled links to various concepts. By adding assumptions about the way in which questions or other sorts of memory probes lead to activation spreading through the network, the model enables us to make predictions about speed and accuracy in various experimental studies of memory. For our purposes there are three facts about this model that are of particular importance. First, since each proposition is encoded in a functionally discrete way, it is a straightforward matter to add or subtract a *single* proposition from memory, while leaving the rest of the network unchanged. Thus, for example, Figure 2 depicts the result of removing one proposition from the network in Figure 1. Second, the model treats predicates expressing the semantic properties of beliefs or memories as *projectable*.[11] They are treated as the

10. For sentential models, see John McCarthy (1968), (1980), & (1986); and Kintsch (1974). For semantic networks, see Quillian (1969); Collins & Quillian (1972); Rumelhart, Lindsay & Norman (1972); Anderson & Bower (1973); and Anderson (1976) & (1980), Ch. 4. For production systems, see Newell & Simon (1972); Newell (1973); Anderson (1983); and Holland, et al. (1986).

11. For the classic discussion of the distinction between projectable and non-projectable predicates, see Goodman (1965).

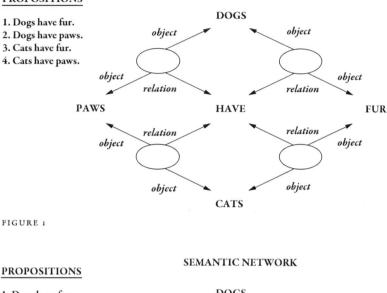

SEMANTIC NETWORK

PROPOSITIONS

1. Dogs have fur.
2. Dogs have paws.
3. Cats have fur.
4. Cats have paws.

FIGURE 1

SEMANTIC NETWORK

PROPOSITIONS

1. Dogs have fur.
2. Dogs have paws.
3. Cats have fur.

FIGURE 2

sorts of predicates that pick out scientifically genuine *kinds*, rather than mere accidental conglomerates, and thus are suitable for inclusion in the statement of lawlike regularities. To see this, we need only consider the way in which such models are tested against empirical data about memory acquisition and forgetting. Typically, it will be assumed that if a subject is told (for example) that the policeman arrested the hippie, then the subject will (with a certain probability) remember *that the policeman arrested the hippie.*[12] And this assumption is taken to express a nomological generalization—it captures something lawlike about the way in which the cognitive system works. So while the class of people who *remember that the policeman arrested the hippie* may differ psychologically in all sorts

12. See, for example, Anderson & Bower (1973).

of ways, the theory treats them as a psychologically natural kind. Third, in any given memory search or inference task exploiting a semantic network model, it makes sense to ask which propositions were activated and which were not. Thus, a search in the network of Figure 1 might terminate without ever activating the proposition that cats have paws.

4 A Family of Connectionist Hypotheses

Our theme, in the previous section, was that common sense psychology is committed to propositional modularity, and that many models of memory proposed in the cognitive psychology literature are comfortably compatible with this assumption. In the present section we want to describe a class of connectionist models which, we will argue, are *not* readily compatible with propositional modularity. The connectionist models we have in mind share three properties:

   i) their encoding of information in the connection weights and in the biases on units is *widely distributed*, rather than being *localist*;
   ii) individual hidden units in the network have no comfortable symbolic interpretation; they are *subsymbolic*, to use a term suggested by Paul Smolensky;
   iii) the models are intended *as cognitive models*, not merely as *implementations* of cognitive models.

A bit later in this section we will elaborate further on each of these three features, and in the next section we will describe a simple example of a connectionist model that meets our three criteria. However, we are under no illusion that what we say will be sufficient to give a sharp-edged characterization of the class of connectionist models we have in mind. Nor is such a sharp-edged characterization essential for our argument. It will suffice if we can convince you that there is a significant class of connectionist models which are incompatible with the propositional modularity of folk psychology.

Before saying more about the three features on our list, we would do well to give a more general characterization of the sort of models we are calling "connectionist," and introduce some of the jargon that comes with the territory. To this end, let us quote at some length from Paul Smolensky's lucid overview.

Connectionist models are large networks of simple, parallel computing elements, each of which carries a numerical *activation value* which it computes from neighboring elements in the network, using some simple numerical formula. The network elements or *units* influence each other's values through connections that carry a numerical strength or *weight* . . .

In a typical . . . model, input to the system is provided by imposing activation values on the *input units* of the network; these numerical values represent some

encoding or *representation* of the input. The activation on the input units propa-
gates along the connections until some set of activation values emerges on the
output units; these activation values encode the output the system has computed
from the input. In between the input and output units there may be other units,
often called *hidden units*, that participate in representing neither the input nor
the output.

The computation performed by the network in transforming the input pattern
of activity to the output pattern depends on the set of connection strengths; *these
weights are usually regarded as encoding the system's knowledge.*[13] In this sense, the
connection strengths play the role of the program in a conventional computer.
Much of the allure of the connectionist approach is that many connectionist
networks *program themselves*, that is, they have autonomous procedures for tuning
their weights to eventually perform some specific computation. Such *learning
procedures* often depend on training in which the network is presented with sample
input/output pairs from the function it is supposed to compute. In learning
networks with hidden units, the network itself "decides" what computations the
hidden units will perform; because these units represent neither inputs nor outputs, they are never "told" what their values should be, even during training…[14]

One point must be added to Smolensky's portrait. In many connectionist models the
hidden units and the output units are assigned a numerical "bias" which is added into the
calculation determining the unit's activation level. The learning procedures for such networks typically set both the connection strengths and the biases. Thus in these networks
the system's knowledge is usually regarded as encoded in *both* the connection strengths
and the biases.

So much for a general overview. Let us now try to explain the three features that
characterize those connectionist models we take to be incompatible with propositional
modularity.

(i) In many non-connectionist cognitive models, like the one illustrated at the end
of Section 3, it is an easy matter to locate a functionally distinct part of the
model encoding each proposition or state of affairs represented in the system.
Indeed, according to Fodor and Pylyshyn, "conventional [computational]
architecture requires that there be distinct symbolic expressions for each state
of affairs that it can represent."[15] In some connectionist models an analogous
sort of functional localization is possible, not only for the input and output

13. Emphasis added.
14. Smolensky (1988), p. 1.
15. Fodor & Pylyshyn (1988), p. 57.

units but for the hidden units as well. Thus, for example, in certain connectionist models, various individual units or small clusters of units are themselves intended to represent specific properties or features of the environment. When the connection strength from one such unit to another is strongly positive, this might be construed as the system's representation of the proposition that if the first feature is present, so too is the second. However, in many connectionist networks it is not possible to localize propositional representation beyond the input layer. That is, there are no particular features or states of the system which lend themselves to a straightforward semantic evaluation. This can sometimes be a real inconvenience to the connectionist model builder when the system as a whole fails to achieve its goal because it has not represented the world the way it should. When this happens, as Smolensky notes,

[I]t is not necessarily possible to localize a failure of veridical representation. Any particular state is part of a large causal system of states, and failures of the system to meet goal conditions cannot in general be localized to any particular state or state component."[16]

It is connectionist networks of this sort, in which it is not possible to isolate the representation of particular propositions or states of affairs within the nodes, connection strengths and biases, that we have in mind when we talk about the encoding of information in the biases, weights and hidden nodes being *widely distributed* rather than *localist*.

(ii) As we've just noted, there are some connectionist models in which some or all of the units are intended to represent specific properties or features of the system's environment. These units may be viewed as the model's symbols for the properties or features in question. However, in models where the weights and biases have been tuned by learning algorithms it is often not the case that any single unit or any small collection of units will end up representing a specific feature of the environment in any straightforward way. As we shall see in the next section, it is often plausible to view such networks as collectively or holistically encoding a set of propositions, although none of the hidden units, weights or biases are comfortably viewed as *symbols*. When this is the case we will call the strategy of representation invoked in the model *subsymbolic*. Typically (perhaps always?) networks exploiting subsymbolic strategies of representation will encode information in a widely distributed way.

(iii) The third item on our list is not a feature of connectionist models themselves, but rather a point about how the models are to be interpreted. In making this point we must presuppose a notion of theoretical or explanatory level which,

16. Smolensky (1988), p. 15.

despite much discussion in the recent literature, is far from being a paradigm of clarity.[17] Perhaps the clearest way to introduce the notion of explanatory level is against the background of the familiar functionalist thesis that psychological theories are analogous to programs which can be implemented on a variety of very different sorts of computers.[18] If one accepts this analogy, then it makes sense to ask whether a particular connectionist model is intended as a model at the psychological level or at the level of underlying neural implementation. Because of their obvious, though in many ways very partial, similarity to real neural architectures, it is tempting to view connectionist models as models of the implementation of psychological processes. And some connectionist model builders endorse this view quite explicitly. So viewed, however, connectionist models are not *psychological* or *cognitive* models at all, any more than a story of how cognitive processes are implemented at the quantum mechanical level is a psychological story. A very different view that connectionist model builders can and often do take is that their models are at the psychological level, not at the level of implementation. So construed, the models are in competition with other psychological models of the same phenomena. Thus a connectionist model of word recognition would be an alternative to—and not simply a possible implementation of—a non-connectionist model of word recognition; a connectionist theory of memory would be a competitor to a semantic network theory, and so on. Connectionists who hold this view of their theories often illustrate the point by drawing analogies with other sciences. Smolensky, for example, suggests that connectionist models stand to traditional cognitive models (like semantic networks) in much the same way that quantum mechanics stands to classical mechanics. In each case the newer theory is deeper, more general and more accurate over a broader range of phenomena. But in each case the new theory and the old are competing at the same explanatory level. If one is right, the other must be wrong.

In light of our concerns in this paper, there is one respect in which the analogy between connectionist models and quantum mechanics may be thought to beg an important question. For while quantum mechanics is conceded to be a *better* theory than classical mechanics, a plausible case could be made that the shift from classical to quantum mechanics was an ontologically *conservative* theory change. In any event, it is not clear that the change was ontologically *radical*. If our central thesis in this paper is correct, then the relation between connectionist models and more traditional cognitive models is

17. Broadbent, D. (1985); Rumelhart & McClelland (1985); Rumelhart & McClelland (1986), Ch. 4; Smolensky (1988); Fodor & Pylyshyn (1988).

18. The notion of program being invoked here is itself open to a pair of quite different interpretations. For the right reading, see Ramsey (1989).

more like the relation between the caloric theory of heat and the kinetic theory. The caloric and kinetic theories are at the same explanatory level, though the shift from one to the other was pretty clearly ontologically radical. In order to make the case that the caloric analogy is the more appropriate one, it will be useful to describe a concrete, though very simple, connectionist model of memory that meets the three criteria we have been trying to explicate.

5 A Connectionist Model of Memory

Our goal in constructing the model was to produce a connectionist network that would do at least some of the tasks done by more traditional cognitive models of memory, and that would perspicuously exhibit the sort of distributed, sub-symbolic encoding described in the previous section. We began by constructing a network, we'll call it Network A, that would judge the truth or falsehood of the sixteen propositions displayed above the line in Figure 3. The network was a typical three tiered feed-forward network consisting of 16 input units, four hidden units and one output unit, as shown in Figure 4. The input coding of each proposition is shown in the center column in Figure 3. Outputs close to 1 were interpreted as 'true' and outputs close to zero were interpreted as 'false.' Back propagation, a familiar connectionist learning algorithm was used to "train up" the network thereby setting the connection weights and biases. Training was terminated when the network consistently gave an output higher than .9 for each true proposition and lower than .1 for each false proposition. Figure 5 shows the connection weights between the

Proposition	Input	Output
1 Dogs have fur.	11000011 00001111	1 true
2 Dogs have paws.	11000011 00110011	1 true
3 Dogs have fleas.	11000011 00111111	1 true
4 Dogs have legs.	11000011 00111100	1 true
5 Cats have fur.	11001100 00001111	1 true
6 Cats have paws.	11001100 00110011	1 true
7 Cats have fleas.	11001100 00111111	1 true
8 Fish have scales.	11110000 00110000	1 true
9 Fish have fins.	11110000 00001100	1 true
10 Fish have gills.	11110000 00000011	1 true
11 Cats have gills.	11001100 00000011	0 false
12 Fish have legs.	11110000 00111100	0 false
13 Fish have fleas.	11110000 00111111	0 false
14 Dogs have scales.	11000011 00110000	0 false
15 Dogs have fins.	11000011 00001100	0 false
16 Cats have fins.	11001100 00001100	0 false

Added Proposition		
17 Fish have eggs.	11110000 11001000	1 true

FIGURE 3

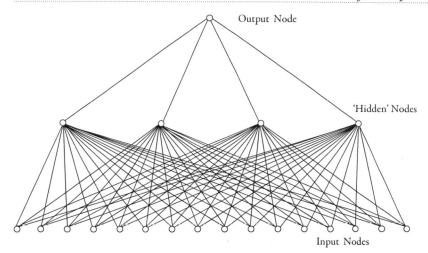

FIGURE 4

Network A

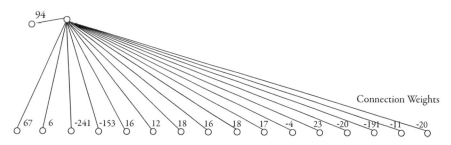

Input weights and bias to first hidden node in network with 16 propositions.

FIGURE 5

input units and the leftmost hidden unit in the trained up network, along with the bias on that unit. Figure 6 indicates the connection weights and biases further upstream. Figure 7 shows the way in which the network computes its response to the proposition *Dogs have fur* when that proposition is encoded in the input units.

There is a clear sense in which the trained up Network A may be said to have stored information about the truth or falsity of propositions (1)–(16), since when any one of these propositions is presented to the network it correctly judges whether the proposition is true or false. In this respect it is similar to various semantic network models which can be constructed to perform much the same task. However, there is a striking difference between Network A and a semantic network model like the one depicted in Figure 1. For, as we noted earlier, in the semantic network there is a functionally distinct sub-part associated with each proposition, and thus it makes perfectly good sense to ask, for any

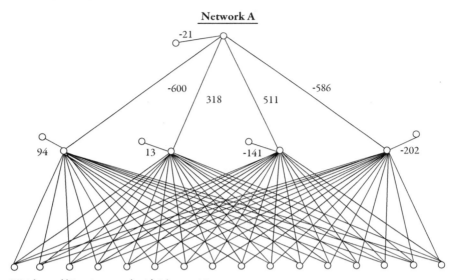

Weights and biases in network with 16 propositions.

FIGURE 6

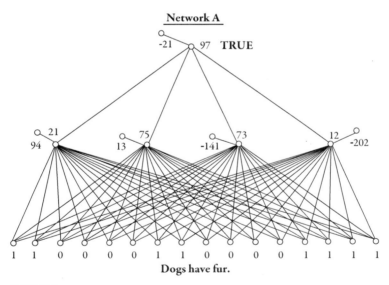

FIGURE 7

probe of the network, whether or not the representation of a specific proposition played a causal role. In the connectionist network, by contrast, there is no distinct state or part of the network that serves to represent any particular proposition. The information encoded in Network A is stored holistically and distributed throughout the network. Whenever information is extracted from Network A, by giving it an input string and seeing whether it computes a high or a low value for the output unit, *many* connection strengths, *many* biases and *many* hidden units play a role in the computation. And any particular weight or unit or bias will help to encode information about *many* different propositions. It simply makes no sense to ask whether or not the representation of a particular proposition plays a causal role in the network's computation. It is in just this respect that our connectionist model of memory seems radically incongruent with the propositional modularity of common sense psychology. For, as we saw in Section 3, common sense psychology seems to presuppose that there is generally some answer to the question of whether a particular belief or memory played a causal role in a specific cognitive episode. But if belief and memory are subserved by a connectionist network like ours, such questions seem to have no clear meaning.

The incompatibility between propositional modularity and connectionist models like ours can be made even more vivid by contrasting Network A with a second network, we'll call it Network B, depicted in Figures 8 and 9. Network B was trained up just as the first one was, except that one additional proposition was added to the training set (coded as indicated below the line in Figure 3). Thus Network B encodes all the same propositions as Network A plus one more. In semantic network models, and other traditional cognitive models, it would be an easy matter to say which states or features of the system encode the added proposition, and it would be a simple task to determine whether or not the representation of the added proposition played a role in a particular episode modeled by the system. But plainly in the connectionist network those questions are quite senseless. The point is not that there are no differences between the two networks. Quite the opposite is the case; the differences are many and widespread. But these differences do not correlate in any systematic way with the functionally discrete, semantically interpretable states posited by folk psychology and by more traditional cognitive models. Since information is encoded in a highly distributed manner, with each connection weight and bias embodying information salient to many propositions, and information regarding any given proposition scattered throughout the network, the system lacks functionally distinct, identifiable sub-structures that are semantically interpretable as representations of individual propositions.

The contrast between Network A and Network B enables us to make our point about the incompatibility between common sense psychology and these sorts of connectionist models in a rather different way. We noted in Section 3 that common sense psychology treats predicates expressing the semantic properties of propositional attitudes as projectable. Thus 'believes that dogs have fur' or 'remembers that dogs have fur' will be projectable predicates in common sense psychology. Now both Network A and Network B might serve as models for a cognitive agent who believes that dogs have fur; both networks store or represent the information that dogs have fur. Nor are these the only two. If we were to train up a network on the 17 propositions in Figure 3 plus a few (or minus a few) we would get yet another system which is as different from Networks A and B as these two are from each other. The moral here is that though there are *indefinitely* many connectionist networks that represent the information that dogs have fur just as well as

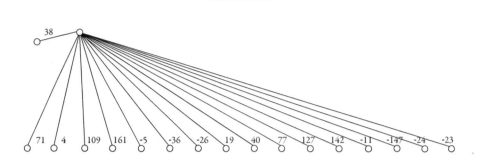

Input weights and bias to first hidden node in network with 17 propositions.

FIGURE 8

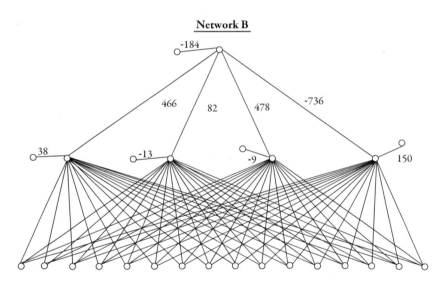

Weights and biases in network with 17 propositions

FIGURE 9

Network A does, these networks have no projectable features in common that are describable in the language of connectionist theory. From the point of view of the connectionist model builder, the class of networks that might model a cognitive agent who believes that dogs have fur is not a genuine kind at all, but simply a chaotically disjunctive set. Common sense psychology treats the class of people who believe that dogs have fur as a psychologically natural kind; connectionist psychology does not.[19]

---

19. This way of making the point about the incompatibility between connectionist models and common sense psychology was suggested to us by Jerry Fodor.

6 Objections and Replies

The argument we've set out in the previous five sections has encountered no shortage of objections. In this section we will try to reconstruct the most interesting of these, and indicate how we would reply.

> Objection (i): Models like A and B are not serious models for human belief or propositional memory.

Of course, the models we've constructed are tiny toys that were built to illustrate the features set out in Section 4 in a perspicuous way. They were never intended to model any substantial part of human propositional memory. But various reasons have been offered for doubting that *anything like* these models could ever be taken seriously as psychological models of propositional memory. Some critics have claimed that the models simply will not scale up—that while teaching a network to recognize fifteen or twenty propositions may be easy enough, it is just not going to be possible to train up a network that can recognize a few thousand propositions, still less a few hundred thousand.[20] Others have objected that while more traditional models of memory, including those based on sentence-like storage, those using semantic networks, and those based on production systems, all provide some strategy for *inference* or *generalization* which enables the system to answer questions about propositions it was not explicitly taught, models like those we have constructed are incapable of inference and generalization. It has also been urged that these models fail as accounts of human memory because they provide no obvious way to account for the fact that suitably prepared humans can easily acquire propositional information one proposition at a time. Under ordinary circumstances, we can just *tell* Henry that the car keys are in the refrigerator, and he can readily record this fact in memory. He doesn't need anything like the sort of massive retraining that would be required to teach one of our connectionist networks a new proposition.

Reply: If this were a paper aimed at defending connectionist models of propositional memory, we would have to take on each of these putative shortcomings in some detail. And in each instance there is at least something to be said on the connectionist side. Thus, for example, it just is not true that networks like A and B don't generalize beyond the propositions on which they've been trained. In Network A, for example, the training set included:

Dogs have fur.	Cats have fur.
Dogs have paws.	Cats have paws.
Dogs have fleas.	Cats have fleas.

20. This point has been urged by Daniel Dennett, among others.

It also included

Dogs have legs.

but not

Cats have legs.

When the network was given an encoding of this last proposition, however, it generalized correctly and responded affirmatively. Similarly, the network responded negatively to an encoding of

Cats have scales.

though it had not previously been exposed to this proposition.

However, it is important to see that this sort of point by point response to the charge that networks like ours are inadequate models for propositional memory is not really required, given the thesis we are defending in this paper. For what we are trying to establish is a *conditional* thesis: *if* connectionist models of memory of the sort we describe in Section 4 are right, *then* propositional attitude psychology is in serious trouble. Since conditionals with false antecedents are true, we win by default if it turns out that the antecedent of our conditional is false.

> Objection (ii): Our models do not really violate the principle of propositional modularity, since the propositions the system has learned are coded in functionally discrete ways, though this may not be obvious.

We've heard this objection elaborated along three quite different lines. The first line— let's call it Objection (iia)—notes that functionally discrete coding may often be *very* hard to notice, and can not be expected to be visible on casual inspection. Consider, for example, the way in which sentences are stored in the memory of a typical von Neuman architecture computer—for concreteness we might suppose that the sentences are part of an English text and are being stored while the computer is running a word processing program. Parts of sentences may be stored at physically scattered memory addresses linked together in complex ways, and given an account of the contents of all relevant memory addresses one would be hard put to say where a particular sentence is stored. But nonetheless each sentence is stored in a *functionally discrete* way. Thus if one knew enough about the system it would be possible to erase any particular sentence it is storing by tampering with the contents of the appropriate memory addresses, while leaving the rest of the sentences the system is storing untouched. Similarly, it has been urged, connectionist networks may in fact encode propositions in functionally discrete ways, though this may not be evident from a casual inspection of the trained up network's biases and connection strengths.

Reply (iia): It is a bit difficult to come to grips with this objection, since what the critic is proposing is that in models like those we have constructed there *might* be some covert functionally discrete system of propositional encoding that has yet to be discovered. In response to this we must concede that indeed there might. We certainly have no argument that even comes close to demonstrating that the discovery of such a covert functionally discrete encoding is impossible. Moreover, we concede that if such a covert system were discovered, then our argument would be seriously undermined. However, we're inclined to think that the burden of argument is on the critic to show that such a system is not merely possible but *likely*; in the absence of any serious reason to think that networks like ours do encode propositions in functionally discrete ways, the mere logical possibility that they might is hardly a serious threat.

The second version of Objection (ii)—we'll call it Objection (iib)—makes a specific proposal about the way in which networks like A and B might be discretely, though covertly, encoding propositions. The encoding, it is urged, is to be found in the pattern of activation of the hidden nodes, when a given proposition is presented to the network. Since there are four hidden nodes in our networks, the activation pattern on presentation of any given input may be represented as an ordered 4-tuple. Thus, for example, when network A is presented with the encoded proposition *Dogs have fur*, the relevant 4-tuple would be (21, 75, 73, 12), as shown in Figure 7. Equivalently, we may think of each activation pattern as a point in a four dimensional hyperspace. Since each proposition corresponds to a unique point in the hyperspace, that point may be viewed as the encoding of the proposition. Moreover, that point represents a functionally discrete state of the system.[21]

Reply (iib): What is being proposed is that the pattern of activation of the system on presentation of an encoding of the proposition p be identified with the belief that p. But this proposal is singularly implausible. Perhaps the best way to see this is to note that in common sense psychology beliefs and propositional memories are typically of substantial duration; and they are the sorts of things that cognitive agents generally have lots of even when they are not using them. Consider an example. Are kangaroos marsupials? Surely you've believed for years that they are, though in all likelihood this is the first time today that your belief has been activated or used.[22] An activation pattern, however, is not an enduring state of a network; indeed, it is not a state of the network at all except when the network has had the relevant proposition as input. Moreover, there is an enormous number of other beliefs that you've had for years. But it makes no sense to suppose that a network could have many activation patterns continuously over a long period of time. At any given time a network exhibits at most one pattern of activation. So activation

---

21. Quite a number of people have suggested this move, including Gary Cottrell, & Adrian Cussins.
22. As Lycan notes, on the common sense notion of belief, people have lots of them "even when they are asleep." (Lycan (1988), p. 57.)

patterns are just not the sorts of things that can plausibly be identified with beliefs or their representations.

Objection (iic): At this juncture, a number of critics have suggested that long standing beliefs might be identified not with activation patterns, which are transient states of networks, but rather with *dispositions to produce activation patterns*. Thus, in network A, the belief that dogs have fur would not be identified with a location in activation hyperspace but with the network's *disposition* to end up at that location when the proposition is presented. This *dispositional state* is an enduring state of the system; it is a state the network can be in no matter what its current state of activation may be, just as a sugar cube may have a disposition to dissolve in water even when there is no water nearby.[23] Some have gone on to suggest that the familiar philosophical distinction between dispositional and occurrent beliefs might be captured, in connectionist models, as the distinction between dispositions to produce activation patterns and activation patterns themselves.

Reply (iic): Our reply to this suggestion is that while dispositions to produce activation patterns are indeed *enduring* states of the system, they are not the right sort of enduring states—they are not the discrete, independently causally active states that folk psychology requires. Recall that on the folk psychological conception of belief and inference, there will often be a variety of quite different underlying causal patterns that may lead to the acquisition and avowal of a given belief. When Clouseau says that the butler did it, he may have just inferred this with the help of his long standing belief that the train is out of service. Or he may have inferred it by using his belief that the hotel is closed. Or both long standing beliefs may have played a role in the inference. Moreover, it is also possible that Clouseau drew this inference some time ago, and is now reporting a relatively long standing belief. But it is hard to see how anything like these distinctions can be captured by the dispositional account in question. In reacting to a given input, say p, a network takes on a specific activation value. It may also have dispositions to take on other activation values on other inputs, say q and r. But there is no obvious way to interpret the claim that these further dispositions play a causal role in the network's reaction to p—or, for that matter, that they do not play a role. Nor can we make any sense of the idea that on one occasion the encoding of q (say, the proposition that the train is out of service) played a role while the encoding of r (say, the proposition that the hotel is closed) did not, and on another occasion, things went the other way around. The propositional modularity presupposed by common sense psychology requires that belief tokens be functionally discrete states capable of causally interacting with one another in some cognitive episodes and of remaining causally inert in other cognitive episodes. However, in a distributed connectionist system like Network A, the dispositional state which produces one activation pattern is functionally inseparable from the dispositional state which produces another. Thus it is impossible to isolate some propositions as causally active in certain cognitive episodes, while others are not. We conclude that reaction

---

23. Something like this objection was suggested to us by Ned Block and by Frank Jackson.

pattern dispositions won't do as belief tokens. Nor, so far as we can see, are there any other states of networks like A and B that will fill the bill.

7 Conclusion

The thesis we have been defending in this paper is that connectionist models of a certain sort are incompatible with the propositional modularity embedded in common sense psychology. The connectionist models in question are those which are offered as models at the *cognitive* level, and in which the encoding of information is widely distributed and subsymbolic. In such models, we have argued, there are no *discrete, semantically interpretable* states that play a *causal role* in some cognitive episodes but not others. Thus there is, in these models, nothing with which the propositional attitudes of common sense psychology can plausibly be identified. If these models turn out to offer the best accounts of human belief and memory, we will be confronting an *ontologically radical* theory change—the sort of theory change that will sustain the conclusion that propositional attitudes, like caloric and phlogiston, do not exist.

REFERENCES

Anderson, J. & Bower, G, (1973). *Human Associative Memory*, Washington, D. C., Winston.
Anderson, J. (1976). *Language, Memory and Thought*, Hillsdale, N.J., Lawrence Erlbaum Associates.
Anderson, J. (1980). *Cognitive Psychology and Its Implications*, San Francisco, W. H. Freeman & Co.
Anderson, J. (1983). *The Architecture of Cognition*, Cambridge, MA, Harvard University Press.
Broadbent, D. (1985). "A Question of Levels: Comments on McClelland and Rumelhart," *Journal of Experimental Psychology: General*, 114.
Cherniak, C. (1986). *Minimal Rationality*, Cambridge, Mass., Bradford Books/MIT Press.
Churchland, P. (1970). "The Logical Character of Action Explanations," *Philosophical Review*, 79.
Churchland, P. (1979). *Scientific Realism and the Plasticity of Mind*, Cambridge, Cambridge University Press.
Churchland, P. (1981). "Eliminative Materialism and Propositional Attitudes," *Journal of Philosophy*, 78, 2.
Churchland, P. (1986). "Some Reductive Strategies in Cognitive Neurobiology," *Mind*, 95.
Collins, A. & Quillian, M. (1972). "Experiments on Semantic Memory and Language Comprehension," in L. Gregg, ed., *Cognition in Learning and Memory*, New York, Wiley.
Feyerabend, P. (1981). *Realism, Rationalism and Scientific Method: Philosophical Papers Vol. 1*, Cambridge, Cambridge University Press.
Fodor, J. & Pylyshyn, Z. (1988). "Connectionism and Cognitive Architecture: A Critical Analysis," *Cognition*, 28.
Fodor, J. (1987). *Psychosemantic: The Problem of Meaning in the Philosophy of Mind*, Cambridge, MA, Bradford Books/MIT Press.
Goodman, N. (1965). *Fact, Fiction and Forecast*, Indianapolis, Bobbs-Merrill.
Holland, J., Holyoak, K., Nisbett, R. & Thagard, P. (1986). *Induction: Processes of Inference, Learning and Discovery*, Cambridge, MA, Bradford Books/MIT Press.
Hooker, C. (1981). "Towards a General Theory of Reduction," Parts I, II & III, *Dialogue*, 20.

Kintsch, W. (1974). *The Representation of Meaning in Memory*, Hillsdale, N.J., Lawrence Erlbaum Associates.

Kitcher, P. (1978). "Theories, Theorists and Theoretical Change," *Philosophical Review*, 87.

Kitcher, P. (1982). "Genes," *British Journal for the Philosophy of Science*, 33.

Kitcher, P. (1983). "Implications of Incommensurability," *PSA 1982*, (Proceedings of the 1982 Biennial Meeting of the Philosophy of Science Association) Vol. 2, ed. by P. Asquith & T. Nickles, East Lansing, Philosophy of Science Association.

Kitcher, P. (1984). "1953 and All That: A Tale of Two Sciences," *Philosophical Review*, 93.

Kuhn, T. (1962). *The Structure of Scientific Revolutions*, Chicago, University of Chicago Press. 2nd Edition (1970).

Kuhn, T. (1983). "Commensurability, Comparability, Communicability," *PSA 1982*, (Proceedings of the 1982 Biennial Meeting of the Philosophy of Science Association) Vol. 2, ed. by P. Asquith & T. Nickles, East Lansing, Philosophy of Science Association.

Lycan, W. (1988). *Judgement and Justification*, Cambridge, Cambridge University Press.

Madell, G. (1986). "Neurophilosophy: A Principled Skeptic's Response," *Inquiry*, 29.

McCarthy, J. (1968). "Programs With Common Sense," in M. Minsky, ed., *Semantic Information Processing*, Cambridge, MA, MIT Press.

McCarthy, J. (1980), "Circumscription: A Form of Non-Monotonic Reasoning," *Artificial Intelligence*, 13.

McCarthy, J. (1986). "Applications of Circumscription to Formalizing Common-Sense Knowledge," *Artificial Intelligence*, 28.

Nagel, E. (1961). *The Structure of Science*, New York, Harcourt, Brace & World.

Newell, A. & Simon, H. (1972). *Human Problem Solving*, Englewood Cliffs, N.J., Prentice Hall.

Newell, A. (1973). "Production Systems: Models of Control Structures," in W. Chase, ed., *Visual Information Processing*, New York, Academic Press.

Quillian, M. (1966). *Semantic Memory*, Cambridge, MA, Bolt, Branak & Newman.

Ramsey, W. (1989). "Parallelism and Functionalism," *Cognitive Science*, 13.

Rumelhart, D. & McClelland, J. (1985). "Level's Indeed! A Response to Broadbent," *Journal of Experimental Psychology: General*, 114.

Rumelhart, D., Lindsay, P. & Norman, D. (1972). "A Process Model for Long Term Memory," in E. Tulving & W. Donaldson, eds., *Organization of Memory*, New York, Academic Press.

Rumelhart, D., McClelland, J. & the PDP Research Group (1986). *Parallel Distributed Processing*, Volumes I & II, Cambridge, MA, Bradford Books/MIT Press.

Sellars, W. (1956). "Empiricism and the Philosophy of Mind," *Minnesota Studies in the Philosophy of Science*, Vol. I, H. Feigl & M. Scriven, eds., Minneapolis, University of Minnesota Press.

Schaffner, K. (1967). "Approaches to Reduction," *Philosophy of Science*, 34.

Sharp, R. (1987). "The Very Idea of Folk Psychology," *Inquiry*, 30.

Smolensky, P. (1988). "On the Proper Treatment of Connectionism," *The Behavioral & Brain Sciences*, 11.

Stich, S. (1983). *From Folk Psychology to Cognitive Science*, Cambridge, Mass., Bradford Books/MIT Press.

Wilkes, K. (1978). *Physicalism*, London, Routledge and Kegan Paul.

7

CONNECTIONISM AND THREE LEVELS OF NATIVISM

William Ramsey and Stephen Stich

1 Introduction

About 25 years ago, Noam Chomsky offered an argument aimed at showing that human beings must have a rich store of innate knowledge, because without such innate knowledge it would be impossible for children to learn a language on the basis of the data available to them. This "argument from the poverty of the stimulus" has had an enormous impact in linguistics, cognitive science, and philosophy. Jerry Fodor has described it as "the existence proof for the possibility of cognitive science . . . [and] quite possibly the only important result to date."[1] Hornstein and Lightfoot have urged that the argument serves as the foundation for most current work in linguistics.[2] And a number of authors, including Chomsky himself, have maintained that the argument from the poverty of the stimulus shows that empiricist theories of the mind are mistaken and that "the only substantive proposal to deal with the problem of acquisition of knowledge of language is the rationalist conception. . . ."[3]

During the last few years, however, a new research program, often called 'Connectionism' or 'Parallel Distributed Processing' (PDP), has attracted considerable attention in cognitive science. Connectionist models of cognitive processes differ in many ways from

1. Fodor (1981), p. 258.
2. Hornstein and Lightfoot (1981b).
3. Chomsky (1972), p. 88.

earlier accounts commonly adopted by Chomskians. What makes them important for our purposes is that they employ powerful new learning techniques that enable systems to acquire complex and subtle skills in a wide variety of domains, without the assistance of large amounts of pre-programmed information. Very early on it was clear that the existence of these strikingly powerful learning strategies was a *prima facie* challenge to Chomsky's nativism. One observer, for example, comments that connectionism "sustains the vision of larger machines that are built on the same principles and that will learn whatever is learnable *with no innate disposition to acquire particular behaviors*" (italics ours).[4] If connectionist models invoking 'back propagation' or other learning algorithms can quickly acquire a large variety of complex skills without the help of 'innate' knowledge, it is natural to wonder whether they might not be able to acquire linguistic skills of the sort Chomsky argued could only be acquired by systems richly endowed with linguistic information at the outset. Motivated in part by just such anti-nativist suspicions, a number of investigators have begun to explore the possibility that connectionist models might acquire natural language syntax, phonology, semantics, and other features of linguistic ability. These efforts to build connectionist networks that learn aspects of natural language are very recent, and the results to date are both fragmentary and controversial. It is too early to venture a prediction on how successful they ultimately will be.

In this paper, our aim will be to explore the relation between connectionism and Chomsky's arguments for the existence of innate knowledge. Along the way, we propose to defend a pair of interrelated conclusions. The first is that there are actually three versions of Chomsky's poverty of the stimulus argument, which make increasingly strong claims about the nature of the cognitive endowments required for learning language. Though the three versions of the argument are often run together in the literature, it is essential to pull them apart if we are to be clear on the bearing that connectionist research might have on nativism. Our second conclusion is that the relation between connectionism and nativism is considerably more complex than many have assumed. There are various connectionist research programs which would, if successful, undermine all three versions of the Chomskian argument. However, the weakest version of the argument, whose conclusion is a doctrine that we will call *minimal nativism*, is easy to reconstruct in a way which will withstand any findings that may be forthcoming from connectionist research. A second version of the argument, aimed at establishing a stronger claim that we will call *anti-empiricism*, can also readily be reconstructed in the face of any foreseeable connectionist successes. However, both Chomsky's formulation of this argument and the reconstruction we will sketch require some sophisticated linguistic data. There has been a fair amount of linguistic research aimed at assembling the sort of data Chomsky's formulation of the argument requires. It is plausible to suppose that if the data needed in Chomsky's formulation are forthcoming, then linguists will be able to find an analogous body of data of the sort required by our reformulation. But, of course, there

---

4. Papert (1987), p. 8.

can be no guarantee on this point until the work is done. The third version of Chomsky's argument seeks to establish the strongest of the three nativist claims, the one we will call *rationalism*. Here there are indeed imaginable connectionist achievements that would show the conclusion of the argument so be false. However, there are also many ongoing connectionist explorations of language learning whose success would be fully compatible with rationalism. The bottom line, then, is that while connectionism challenges Chomskian nativism in a variety of ways, it may well turn out that even the strongest version of nativism is compatible with spectacular connectionist successes in the modeling of language acquisition.

The remainder of the paper will be organized as follows. In Section 2 we will set out the three versions of the poverty of the stimulus argument. In Section 3 we will offer an introductory overview of recent connectionist research and a quick survey of ongoing efforts to get connectionist devices to learn aspects of natural language. In Section 4 we will explore the ways in which the success of these efforts would bear upon the three versions of Chomsky's argument.

2 Three Versions of the Poverty of the Stimulus Argument and Three Levels of Nativism[5]

What changes occur when a child learns a language? The answer, of course, is that there are many changes. The most conspicuous is that the child is able to understand the language, to communicate with it, and to use it for all sorts of purposes. There are also less obvious changes. Once a child has mastered a language, he is capable of making a wide range of judgments about the properties and relations of expressions in the language. Thus, for example, speakers of English are normally capable of judging whether any arbitrary sound sequence constitutes a grammatical sentence of English, and if it does, they are capable of judging whether or not it is ambiguous; they are also capable of judging whether two arbitrary sentences are related as active and passive, whether they are related as declarative and yes-no questions, whether one is a paraphrase of another, whether one entails the other, so on for a number of additional linguistic properties and relations. These sorts of judgments, or 'linguistic intuitions' as they are more typically called, have played a central role in generative linguistics since its inception.

It is, Chomskians maintain, a perfectly astounding fact that ordinary speakers of a language can make a practically infinite number of judgments about the grammatical properties and relations of expressions in their language. The most plausible explanation of this ability, they urge, is that speakers have a generative grammar of their language—an explicit system of rules and definitions—stored somewhere in their mind or brain. On Chomsky's view, "the mature speaker has internalized a grammar with specific properties . . . [and] in understanding speech he makes use of this grammar to assign a precept

5. Parts of this section are borrowed from Stich (1996).

to a signal."[6] "To know a language . . . is to be in a certain mental state . . . consisting of a system of rules and principles."[7] This system of internally represented rules guides the complex and prolific linguistic judgments that the speaker is capable of making. It is also used, in various ways, in the more ordinary processes of language production and comprehension. If there is no internally represented grammar, Chomsky and his followers urge, then it is something of a mystery how speakers are capable of having the linguistic intuitions they have. The mentally stored grammar that is posited is not, of course, accessible to consciousness. Speakers cannot tell us the rules of the grammar represented in their brains any more than they can tell us how they go about recognizing faces or recovering salient information from memory. But if speakers do have an internally represented grammar, then a natural goal for the generative grammarian would be (and has been) to discover that grammar—the grammar that is "psychologically real."

The argument for the thesis that speakers have an internally represented generative grammar of their language has the form of an inference to the best explanation:

> I know of no other account that even attempts to deal with the fact that our judgments and behavior accord with and are in part explained by certain rule systems. . . .[8]

Later, we will explain why many connectionists believe their models call this thesis into question. For now, however, let us assume that Chomsky is right and that speakers do indeed have a mentally stored grammar of their language. We can then develop the three versions of the poverty of the stimulus argument against the background assumption that the mechanisms subserving language acquisition must be able to produce the grammar that the child comes to internally represent.

2.1 THE ARGUMENT FOR MINIMAL NATIVISM

The weakest version of the poverty of the stimulus argument begins with the observation that, during the time span normally required to learn a language, a child is exposed to only a very impoverished sample of often misleading linguistic data. This 'poverty of the stimulus' is due to three important aspects of the 'primary linguistic data':

(1) The set of sentences that a competent speaker of a language can use, comprehend, and offer linguistic intuitions about is vastly larger than the idiosyncratic set of sentences to which children are exposed in the course of learning a language.

---

6. Chomsky (1969). p. 155–56.
7. Chomsky (1980a), p. 48.
8. Chomsky (1980b), p. 12.

(2) While learning their language, the speech children hear does not consist exclusively of complete grammatical sentences. Rather, they are typically exposed to a large assortment of non-sentences, including slips of the tongue and incomplete thoughts, samples of foreign languages, and even intentional nonsense. Thus, the data the child has available for learning to tell sentences from non-sentences are remarkably messy.

(3) Children, unlike linguists, are rarely given any indication that certain queer and complex sentences are ungrammatical, that certain pairs of sentences are paraphrases of one another, and so on. Hence, many sorts of data that linguists rely upon heavily in deciding between competing grammars—such as data derived from speakers' linguistic intuitions—are not available to the child.

That children can acquire a grammar at all on the basis of this sort of data requires that they have a learning mechanism of some sort in place before the acquisition process begins. A video recorder exposed to the primary linguistic data that a child is exposed to does not end up with an internally represented grammar. Nor, for that matter, does a puppy or a young chimpanzee. The cognitive system which the child brings to the task of language learning must be able to go from a limited and messy sample of data to a grammar that generates most of the sentences in the data, and a huge number of additional sentences as well. And any cognitive system capable of projecting beyond the data in this way is going to be reasonably sophisticated. So, given our assumption that children do in fact end up with an internally represented grammar, the 'poverty of the stimulus' seems to require that children come to the language learning task with an innate learning mechanism of some sophistication. Moreover, despite exposure to significantly different samples of data, different children in the same linguistic community end up having essentially the same linguistic intuitions, and thus, it is plausible to suppose, essentially the same internalized grammar. Nor is there any evidence that children have any special predisposition to learn the language of their biological parents. Chinese children raised in an English-speaking environment learn English as easily as English children do. All of this suggests that the innate learning mechanisms that enable children to internalize the grammar of the language spoken around them are much the same in all children.

The crucial step in this first version of the poverty of the stimulus argument is the observation that if the child's innate learning mechanism is to accomplish its task, it must have a strong bias in favor of acquiring certain grammars and against acquiring others. This is because the data that the mechanism has been exposed to by the time grammar acquisition is complete is equally compatible with an indefinitely large class of grammars, many of which will depart in significant ways from the grammar that the child actually attains. The acquisition mechanism must project from the limited data it has available to a correct grammar—one that classifies sentences the way others in the linguistic community classify them. Thus it must somehow reject the indefinitely large class of *in*correct grammars that are equally compatible with the data. The thesis that we will call *minimal* *nativism* is simply the claim that the child approaches the task of language acquisition with an innate learning mechanism that is strongly biased in favor of certain grammars and against others. But, of course, to say that the innate learning mechanism is biased in favor of certain grammars and against others does not commit us to any particular account of the mechanism underlying this bias. It is on just this point that the three levels of nativism differ. Minimal nativism merely insists that the bias must be there. The higher levels of nativism make increasingly strong claims about the mechanism responsible for the bias.[9]

Before moving on to the next version of the argument, it is important to make clear exactly what does and does not follow from minimal nativism. One might think that by establishing the existence of a strongly biased innate learning mechanism, Chomsky has succeeded in undermining the empiricist conception of the mind. But this would be a mistake. For even the staunchest empiricist would readily agree that learning requires sophisticated innate mechanisms and biases. As Quine reminds us, the empiricist "is knowingly and cheerfully up to his neck in innate mechanisms of learning readiness."[10] If Chomsky's argument is supposed to undermine empiricism, then it must say something about the nature of these mechanisms and biases which calls into doubt the empiricist conception of the mind.

2.2 THE ARGUMENT AGAINST EMPIRICISM

At first blush, it might be thought that it would be impossible to argue against *all* empiricist accounts of the mind. For while Chomsky might show that on one or another specific empiricist theory, the mind could not reliably produce the right grammar on the basis of the primary linguistic data, it would always be open to the resourceful empiricist to construct another theory, still adhering to empiricist principles, though diverging in one way or another from the particular empiricist theory that has been refuted. However, there is in Chomsky's writings an ingenious idea for circumventing this problem and refuting all empiricist theories in one fell swoop. We'll call this idea "the Competent Scientist Gambit." The basic idea is to portray a learning mechanism that is at least as powerful as anything dreamt of in the empiricist conception of the mind, and then argue that such a learning mechanism could not do what the child does. If this can be shown,

---

9. It is important to note that the relation between the primary linguistic data and a set of possible grammars is, in many ways, analogous to the abductive relation between evidential data and a set of different explanatory hypotheses. It is a truism in the philosophy of science that abductive inference—the projection from a body of data to an hypothesis that goes beyond the data—cannot be based upon the evidence alone. It requires an appeal to inferential principles or methodological criteria not include in the data. Similarly, since a child's primary linguistic data is compatible with a number of different grammars, his projection must be guided by some antecedent bias or set of constraints. For more on projection and language acquisition, see Gold (1967), Peters (1972), Wexler and Culicover (1980), and Morgan (1986).

10. (1969, p. 95).

then all empiricist theories will fall together. The 'learning mechanism' Chomsky suggests is a competent, rational scientist.

Suppose that we were to pose for such a scientist the task at which the child's mind is so adept. We will give the scientist a typical set of primary linguistic data drawn from some actual human language. Her job will be to discover the grammar of that language—the grammar that children exposed to those data will come to internally represent. In going about the business of constructing and testing hypotheses about the grammar she is trying to discover, the scientist will be able to exploit any inferential strategy that would be permitted by any account of the mind compatible with empiricist strictures. She can record data, do sophisticated data analysis, think up imaginative hypotheses (or mundane ones) and test those hypotheses against the data available to her. Moreover, it is open to her to employ the sorts of methodological principles and intuitions typically employed in empirical theory construction and selection. In discussions of those methodological considerations, simplicity often looms large, and from time to time we will use the term 'simplicity' as a convenient label for the whole package of methodological principles and intuitions that a competent scientist has available.

There is, however, one thing that the competent scientist is not allowed to do. She is not allowed to learn the language from which the primary linguistic data are drawn. There is, of course, no reason to think that the scientist could not learn the language on the basis of that data. She is a normal human, and we are providing her with just the sort of data that generally suffices for normal humans to learn a language. The point of the prohibition is simply that if she were to learn the language, she would then have access to data that the child does not have. She would have her acquired linguistic intuitions about the grammaticality of sentences not presented in the data, as well as her intuitions about ambiguities, about paraphrases, and so on. But if her challenge is to try to do what the child does, then it is obviously unfair for her to use information not available to the child. Clearly it is absurd to suppose that in order to learn his language the child must first learn it, and then generate the data necessary for him to learn it.

We are supposing that after exposure to a decade or so of primary linguistic data from any natural language, the child succeeds in constructing a grammar that projects well beyond his data, and does so correctly, where the standard of correctness is set by the senior members of the child's linguistic community. If the scientist is to match the child's feat, she too must make a monumental projection from the data available to her, and come up with the grammar that has been internalized by those who are producing the data. Chomsky's contention is that given only the information embodied in the primary linguistic data, along with the methodological resources available to her, the competent scientist could not reliably do what the child does. That is, the scientist could not discover the grammar the child comes to internally represent when learning a language.

It is important to understand exactly what is being claimed when Chomsky makes this assertion. Chomsky does not deny that the competent scientist could *think up* the right grammar. Of course she could. *Ex hypothesis* she is intelligent, creative, and resourceful, so if she couldn't think up the right grammar, no one could. However, there is a sense in which this very intelligence and creativity is the scientist's undoing. For just as there is every reason to believe she can think up the *right* grammar—the one the child actually ends up with—so too there is every reason to believe she can think up an endless variety of *wrong* grammars that do not project from the data in the way the child's grammar does. The crucial contention for this version of the poverty of the stimulus argument is that *the methodological resources a scientist has available will not suffice to motivate the proper selection*. Even with the use of criteria such as simplicity, the scientist would still be plagued by an embarrassment of riches. In saying that the scientist would be incapable of 'coming up with' the right grammar, what is meant is that the scientist will have no reliable way of locating the right grammar in the space of possible grammars that are compatible with the limited data she has available.[11]

It now should be clear how the Competent Scientist Gambit is intended to undermine the empiricist conception of learning. It is plausible to view the competent scientist as a strong and generous characterization of the empiricist mind. (Indeed, there will be many things a competent scientist can do that the sort of mind conjured by the Classical Empiricists cannot.) Hence, if the competent scientist is not up to the task, then no learning mechanism compatible with empiricist principles will be adequate for the task of language acquisition. If it can be shown that something at least as resourceful as the empiricist mind would fail at language learning, Chomsky will have succeeded in showing that the empiricist conception of the mind must be mistaken.

Of course for all of this to work, some additional argument is going to be needed. What needs to be shown is that the set of methodological principles and biases available to a competent scientist will not be adequate for successful projection from the primary linguistic data to the grammar of the language from which the data are drawn. One way to show this would be to produce a pair of grammars with the following features:

(i) on all intuitive measures of simplicity the grammars are comparable;
(ii) the grammars make essentially the same judgments about linguistic phenomena that are likely to show up in the primary linguistic data; and
(iii) the grammars make significantly different judgments about linguistic phenomena that are not likely to show up in the primary linguistic data.

If there are examples of this sort, our competent scientist will be unable to choose between the grammars. Since the grammars are both compatible with any plausible body of primary linguistic data, she cannot use the data to rule one out. And since they are both

---

11. Actually, this understates the difficulty that the scientist confronts since, as noted earlier, the primary linguistic data will typically be messy data, containing all sorts of sentences and sentence fragments that the correct grammar will not generate. So the task the scientist confronts is to locate the correct grammar from the enormous class of grammars that are largely (though not necessarily entirely) compatible with the primary linguistic data.

comparably simple, methodological considerations will be of no help. If, in these cases, language learners regularly project in the right way, it follows that the mechanisms responsible for language learning must be more powerful than the empiricist conception of the mind will allow.

In recent years, there has been a fair amount of work in linguistics aimed at compiling examples of just this sort. For example, Hornstein and Lightfoot[12] sketch a case in which the choice between two very different, though comparably simple grammars turns on the paraphrase relations among sentences like (1)–(3):

(1) She told me three funny stories, but I didn't like the one about Max.
(2) She told me three funny stories, but I didn't like the story about Max.
(3) She told me three funny stories, but I didn't like the funny story about Max.

On one of the grammars under consideration, (2) would be considered a paraphrase of (1), though (3) would not. The other grammar correctly entails that both (2) and (3) might be paraphrases of (1). It is, Hornstein and Lightfoot maintain, very unlikely that every child who successfully learns English will have been exposed to primary linguistic data containing evidence about these sorts of relatively abstruse facts concerning paraphrase. If this is right, and if the only sorts of evidence that would suffice to distinguish between the two grammars are comparably abstruse, then our competent scientist is in trouble. Since she is intelligent and resourceful, she will be able to think up both grammars. Since neither grammar is simpler nor superior on other methodological grounds, such considerations will not assist her in making the correct choice. And, unlike the real linguists who actually did worry about the choice between these two grammars, she does not have, and cannot get, the kind of data that would enable her to make the right choice.

The argument just sketched is, of course, very much hostage to the linguistic facts. For the argument to be persuasive there must be a substantial number of examples in which the choice between two equally simple and natural grammars can be made only by appealing to the sort of abstruse evidence that is unlikely to be found in the primary linguistic data. There is by now a substantial collection of plausible cases in the literature.[13] If these cases survive critical scrutiny, Chomsky and his followers will have gone a long way toward making their case against empiricism.

This brings us to the conclusion of the second version of the poverty of the stimulus argument, a doctrine we shall call *anti-empiricism*. This doctrine maintains not only that the innate language learning mechanism must have strong biases, but also that these biases are not compatible with the account of mental mechanisms suggested by even a

---

12. Hornstein and Lightfoot (1981b). See also Hornstein, 1984, Chapter 1.
13. See, for example, Lightfoot (1982) pp. 51–57, and the essays in Horstnein and Lightfoot (1981a).

very generous characterization of the empiricist mind. Anti-empiricism makes a negative claim about the language learning mechanism—a claim about what its biases are not. The third version of the poverty of stimulus argument aims at establishing a positive claim about the way the language learning mechanism does its job.

2.3 THE ARGUMENT FOR RATIONALISM

If the empiricist conception of the mind cannot account for the facts of language learning, what sorts of accounts of the mind can? One way of approaching this question is to focus on exactly why it was that our hypothetical scientist could not do what the child does. The problem was not that she could not think up the right grammar, but rather that she could also think up lots of wrong grammars that were equally simple and equally compatible with the data, and she had no way to decide among them. Confronted with this problem, one strategy that might enable the scientist to duplicate the child's accomplishment would be to narrow the range of grammars she must consider. Suppose it were the case that all the correct grammars of human languages—all the ones that speakers actually have represented in their heads—shared certain properties. If this were so, then the scientist's work would be greatly facilitated if she were informed about these properties at the outset. For then she would never have to consider any of the grammars that do not share the 'universal' features of all human grammars. The richer the collection of universal features, the stronger the constraints they will impose on the class of grammars that the scientist need consider; and the stronger the constraints, the easier her task will become.[14] What does all this suggest about the child's mind? The obvious hypothesis to extract from the analogy between the child's task and the scientist's is that the child's mind comes equipped with information about linguistic universals—biases that are applicable only in the area of language acquisition—that enable it to pick out the right grammar by narrowing the search space. On this hypothesis, the child begins with a rich body of innate information about language which serves to define the class of all human languages. The relatively impoverished environmental stimulus is "viewed as only a trigger; much of the ability eventually attained is determined by genetically encoded principles, which are triggered or activated by environmental stimulus rather than formed by it more or less directly."[15] Clearly this hypothesis goes well beyond the thesis that the biases built into the innate language learning mechanism are non-empiricist. As John Searle notes, "Chomsky is arguing not simply that the child must have 'learning readiness,' 'biases,' and 'dispositions,' but that he must have a *specific* set of linguistic mechanisms at work."[16]

---

14. Actually, what is important here is not that all the correct grammars share certain properties, but only that they are all members of some quite restricted class. Since the distinction makes little difference to our current concerns, we shall ignore it in what follows.

15. Lightfoot (1982), p. 21.

16. Searle (1974), p. 22.

Moreover, this domain specificity of innate mechanisms has been a traditional feature of rationalist conceptions of the mind. For Chomsky and his followers, the central argument for the claim that the child has domain specific language learning biases is, once again, an inference to the best explanation—it is "the only substantive proposal to deal with the problem of acquisition of knowledge of language."[17] And prior to the emergence of connectionism, Chomsky's argument was surely very plausible. Once we realize the difficulties facing the child, it is no easy matter to imagine how he could possibly solve the projection problem and end up with the right grammar, unless he approached the task with a rich set of constraints specifically tailored to the task at hand. The thesis that the innate language learning mechanism embodies such constraints is the conclusion to be drawn from the third version of the poverty of the stimulus argument. We'll call this view *rationalism*.

We've now completed our reconstruction of the three versions of the poverty of the stimulus argument and the conclusions that have been drawn from them. In Section 4 we will explore the ways in which connectionism might be thought to challenge these arguments. Before getting to that, however, we'll need to give a quick sketch of connectionism, and review some recent attempts to study linguistic phenomena in a connectionist framework.

3 An Overview of Connectionist Research on Language

Connectionism is a new style of cognitive modeling that has emerged during the last decade. Connectionist models consist of networks built from large numbers of extremely simple interacting units. Inspired by neuronal architecture, connectionist units are typically linked in such a way that they can excite or inhibit one another by sending activation signals down interconnecting pathways. Networks commonly involve a layer of input units, a layer of output units, and one or more intermediate (or 'hidden') layers, linked by weighted connections through which a wave of activation travels. When the processing proceeds in only one direction, as is the case with 'feed-forward' networks, units modify and transfer the activation signal only to subsequent units and layers. In other, more complicated networks, activation may involve feedback loops and bidirectional communication between nodes, comprising what are often referred to as 'recurrent' networks. The units themselves may have threshold values, which their total input must exceed for activation. Alternatively, they may act in analog fashion, taking an activation values anywhere between 0 and 100%. Connecting links have varying weights or strengths, and the exact nature of the activation signal transferred from one unit to another (that is, its strength and excitatory or inhibitory value) is typically a function of the connection weight and the activation level of the sending unit.

17. Chomsky (1972), p. 88.

This architecture supports a style of computation quite unlike that exploited by earlier cognitive models. For the most part, pre-connectionist model builders have presupposed computational architectures that perform operations best described as 'symbol manipulations.' In such systems, information is generally stored in distinct locations separate from the structures performing computational operations. Information processing in such devices consists of the manipulation of discrete tokens or symbols, which are relocated, copied, and shuffled about, typically in accordance with rules or commands which are themselves encoded in a manner readily discernible by the system.

Connectionist information processing diverges from these earlier models in many ways. Perhaps the most striking aspect of connectionist information processing is that it typically does not involve anything like the manipulation of distinct symbolic tokens. While connectionist modelers sometimes invoke notions of representations to characterize elements of their networks, connectionist representations are generally not at all like the discrete symbolic entities found in classical architectures. This is especially true when the model employs "distributed representations," where the same set of individual units and weights are used to encode divergent bits of information.[18] Another notable difference between connectionist models and earlier cognitive models is that in connectionist models the distinction between structures that store information and structures that process information is virtually non-existent. Information is 'stored' in the connection weights between individual units, which serve as central elements in the processing as well. Hence, familiar notions of stored programs or autonomous command structures which govern computational processing seem to have no place in connectionist architecture.

These differences loom large in the debate over the psychological reality of linguistic rules. As we saw in Section 2.1, Chomsky's formulations of the poverty of the stimulus arguments presupposes that when a child has learned a language he or she ends up with an internally represented generative grammar—typically a set of re-write or production rules each of which consists of a sequence of distinct symbols. Pre-connectionist cognitive models, which view cognition as symbol manipulation, are entirely comfortable with this view. But connectionist models, particularly those exploiting highly distributed representations and non-modular computational strategies, cannot readily accommodate the sorts of symbolic rules posited by generative grammarians. In defense of the claim that linguistic abilities are subserved by an internally represented grammar, Chomsky offered an inference to the best explanation argument. Appeal to internalized grammatical rules was not only the best way to explain linguistic judgments and behavior, Chomsky maintained, it was the *only* explicit, well-developed hypothesis that had ever been suggested. Prior to the emergence of connectionism, that argument had considerable

18. For more on the contrast between discrete and distributed representations, see Ramsey, Stich and Garon (1991).

plausibility.[19] If, however, it turns out that connectionist models can account for much the same range of data about linguistic intuitions and linguistic behavior, it will no longer be possible for Chomsky and his followers to claim that their internalized rule explanations are the "only game in town."

Since connectionist information processing is governed by connection weights between units, the computations can be altered simply by changing the value of these weights. Connectionist researchers realized early on that if weight changes could be executed in a purposeful manner, then these models would manifest a form of learning that seems biologically plausible, and quite revolutionary from a computational perspective. Recent developments have overcome past difficulties in multi-layer weight adjustment, and there are now very powerful learning strategies that enable connectionist networks to, in a sense, program themselves. Perhaps the most widely used learning algorithm is the "generalized delta rule" or "back propagation." developed by Rumelhart, Hinton, and Williams.[20] On this learning strategy, a network undergoes a training period during which it is presented with a series of inputs and allowed to produce an output for each presentation. A comparison is made between the actual output and a target output for each presentation, resulting in an error signal. This signal is subsequently propagated back through the network, adjusting weights in accordance with the learning algorithm. Because the weights are fixed after training, the system is subsequently able to make 'educated' responses to new inputs that were not presented during the learning period. The success of most models is determined by how well they perform such generalizations within a particular task domain.[21]

So much for our general overview. There are many other styles of connectionist processing and learning, but this should suffice to give a sense of the basic elements of the new paradigm. Let's turn now to the growing body of connectionist research devoted to developing models of language processing and language acquisition. Much of this research has been motivated by increasing skepticism about Chomsky's account of language acquisition, and by the suspicion that language processing and acquisition might be more naturally explained by models with connectionist architectures. Prior to the emergence of connectionism, Chomsky often stressed that "it is difficult to imagine how the vague suggestions about conditioning and associative nets that one finds in philosophical and psychological speculations of an empiricist cast might be refined or

---

19. Prior to connectionism there were some dissenting voices. See, for example, Stich (1971), Cummins (1977) and Stabler (1983). However, a common response to the critics was the question: 'What else could it be?' Thus, for example, Berwick writes, "I don't share Stabler's fear that 'we ought to worry about whether we can justify the current emphasis on program-using systems in theories about how people process language.' It's the only game in town" (1983, p. 403).

20. Rumelhart, Hinton, and Williams (1986).

21. For more on connetionist learning techniques, see Rumelhart and McClelland (1986a), Chapters 5, 7, 8, and 11. See also Hinton (1987).

elaborated so as to provide for attested competence. . . ."[22] Many connectionists believe that their new computational tools overcome such failures of the imagination, and have developed impressive models aimed at making the point.

A typical model of this sort is PARSNIP, developed by Hanson and Kegl.[23] This is an auto-associator network[24] that was trained on three sets of syntactically tagged natural language sentences. Beginning with the assumption "that natural language reveals to the hearer a rich set of linguistic constraints . . . that serve to delimit the possible grammars that can be learned" (p. 108), the modelers found that a network trained to produce veridical copies of input could also "induce grammar-like behavior" while performing various linguistic tasks.[25]

> The network learned to produce correct syntactic category labels corresponding to each position of the sentence originally presented to it, and it was able to generalize to another 1000 sentences which were distinct from all three training samples. PARSNIP does sentence completion on sentences, and also recognizes novel sentence patterns absent from the presented corpus. One interesting parallel between PARSNIP and human language users is the fact that PARSNIP correctly reproduces test sentences reflecting deep center-embedded patterns which it has never seen before while failing to reproduce multiply center-embedded patterns.[26]

While Hanson and Kegl concede that their model has certain psychologically implausible features (such as insensitivity to temporal factors), they maintain that

> there are important parallels between the task given to PARSNIP and the task that arises for children as they learn a natural language. Both PARSNIP and the child are only exposed to sentences from natural language, they both must induce general rules and larger constituents from just the regularities to which they are exposed, both on the basis of only positive evidence. PARSNIP's ability to generalize knowledge of constituent structure has been extracted from its experience with natural language sentences.[27]

22. Chomsky (1980c), p. 238.

23. Hanson and Kegl (1987).

24. An auto-associator network is one that attempts to reproduce on the output nodes whatever input it receives on the input nodes. Hence, its input also serves as its teacher and source of the error signal during the training period.

25. It should be noted here that Hanson and Kegl do not feel their model supports anti-nativist conclusions; rather, they believe it helps to delineate those aspects of grammatical structure which can be extracted from the data.

26. Hanson and Kegl (1987), p. 106.

27. Ibid., p. 117.

A number of connectionist models attempt to account for aspects of language that have been difficult to capture in more conventional rule-based systems. It appears that sensitivity to several different sources of information (such as cues from phonetic, semantic, and contextual factors) is much easier to implement in connectionist networks with distributed encodings and parallel processing. One system exploiting this type of architecture was designed by McClelland and Kawamoto (1986) to assign correct case roles to constituents of sentences. The model invokes word order and semantic constraints to determine case assignments and to select contextually appropriate readings of ambiguous words. A similar but more complex model of semantic processing developed by St. John and McClelland (1988) learns mappings between words in particular contexts and concepts, and predicts additional meanings implicit in the sentence.

While these systems focus primarily on semantic aspects of language comprehension, a number of connectionist models have been developed to account for syntactic, phonological, and other non-semantic components of language processing. For example, Fanty (1985) has developed a connectionist parser that incorporates all levels of the parse tree at the same time, producing the surface structure of the sentence as its output. Other efforts at connectionist parsing include models by Cottrell (1985), Waltz and Pollack (1985), Selman and Hirst (1985), and Charniak and Santos (1986). Rumelhart and McClelland (1986b) have produced a network designed to model the acquisition of English past-tense verbs. The most intriguing feature of this model is its ability to replicate putative aspects of human past tense learning such as overgeneralization of regular past-tense forms to irregular forms without incorporating the sort of discrete symbolic rules commonly assumed to account for such phenomena.[28] Elman (1988) has produced a model that learns to divide unbroken stream of input into phonemes, morphemes, and words, a capacity often claimed to be largely innate. The model also produced representations of lexical classes through exposure to word order alone, distinguishing nouns and verbs, for example, and arranging their representations into various semantic hierarchies.

It should be clear from this (by no means exhaustive) survey that connectionist language modeling is a robust and thriving area of research. As we noted at the outset, it is too soon to tell just how successful such work will ultimately be. However, our concern here is not to debate the superiority of connectionist models but to explore how the arguments for nativism will fare if connectionist models prove to be empirically accurate accounts of the mechanisms underlying language acquisition and linguistic competence. That is the issue we'll tackle in the section to follow.

4 Connectionism and Nativism

In Section 2 we detailed three versions of the poverty of the stimulus argument that yield three distinct conclusions making progressively stronger nativist claims. There are two

---

28. For a critical analysis of this network, see Pinker and Prince (1988).

ways in which it might be thought that advances in connectionist language modeling could threaten those arguments. The first focuses on the output of the language acquisition process, the second on the nature of the process itself. We'll begin by sketching both of these challenges, and then go on to ask how much damage they do to each version of the argument from the poverty of the stimulus.

4.1 THE FIRST CONNECTIONIST CHALLENGE: ADULT COMPETENCE IS NOT SUBSERVED BY A GRAMMAR

As set out in Section 2, all three versions of the argument from the poverty of the stimulus begin with the assumption that when a person learns a language he or she ends up with an internally represented grammar of that language, where a grammar is taken to be a system of generative rules built out of an appropriate symbolic vocabulary. The Chomskian defense of this assumption is that "it's the only game in town" for explaining language competence. But, as we saw in Section 3, connectionist models don't readily accommodate the sorts of symbolic rules exploited by generative grammarians. Thus, if it turns out that connectionist models of adult linguistic competence can account for a wide range of linguistic judgments and abilities, Chomskians will no longer be able to claim that a theory positing an internalized grammar is the only option available. And if connectionist models of linguistic competence prove to be empirically *superior* to models invoking internalized grammars, the poverty of the stimulus arguments will have to do without the assumption that the output of the acquisition process includes an internally represented grammar.

4.2 THE SECOND CONNECTIONIST CHALLENGE: CONNECTIONIST LEARNING ALGORITHMS CAN MODEL LANGUAGE ACQUISITION

All three version of the poverty of the stimulus argument conclude that the mechanism responsible for language acquisition must be biased in favor of certain outcomes and against others. On the anti-empiricist version of the argument, the biases are claimed to be incompatible with the account of the mind envisioned in the empiricist tradition. On the rationalist version, the biases are further claimed to be specific to language and applicable only in the domain of language acquisition. But suppose it could be shown that a system using back propagation or another connectionist learning algorithm can do a good job at modeling some impressive part of the child's accomplishment in learning a language. Suppose, for example, that a connectionist acquisition model could mimic the language learner's projection from primary linguistic data to judgments about sentences that he or she has never heard. We might imagine the hypothetical connectionist acquisition model behaving as follows: When provided with a sample of primary linguistic data from any natural language (i.e., a large set of utterances of the sort that a child learning the language might be exposed to, perhaps accompanied by some information about the setting in which the utterance occurs) the model learns to distinguish grammatical sentences in that language from ungrammatical ones with much the same accuracy that a human learner does.

It might well be thought that the existence of such a model would refute all three versions of nativism. For, it might be argued, back propagation and other connectionist learning algorithms, far from being restricted to language, appear to be enormously general in their domain of application. Back propagation has been used successfully in training networks to perform very diverse tasks—from transforming written text into phonemes to distinguishing sonar echoes of rocks from those of undersea mines.[29] Thus the learning model we have imagined appears to pose a direct challenge to the doctrine we have been calling "rationalism." Moreover, connectionist learning algorithms like back propagation seem to be very much in the spirit of the simple, general-purpose learning mechanisms envisioned in the empiricist tradition. Historically, back propagation can be viewed as a variant on a simple learning rule suggested by Hebb.[30] And the (unmodified) 'delta rule' was first proposed by Sutton and Barto as part of their theory of classical conditioning.[31] So if the sort of connectionist acquisition model we have been imagining could actually be built, it would appear to pose a challenge to the doctrine we have been calling 'anti-empiricism.' It might even be urged that the existence of such a model would threaten minimal nativism, since back propagation and other connectionist learning algorithms seem remarkably free from biases of any sort. This may be what Sampson has in mind when he writes: "[T]he knowledge eventually stored in the system, in the pattern of weights, is derived entirely from the input." "The system's only contribution is to react in a passive, mechanical way to individual data items."[32]

These challenges make it sound like connectionism is on a collision course with Chomsky's nativism. On the one hand, if empirically successful connectionist models of adult linguistic competence can be built, a central assumption of the arguments from the poverty of the stimulus will be undermined. On the other hand, if connectionist learning algorithms can project from the primary linguistic data in the way the child does, the conclusions of all three arguments are threatened. However, on our view, even if things turn out well for connectionism, the challenge it will pose to Chomskian nativism will be far from devastating. It is true that in the wake of the connectionist achievements we have been imagining all three versions of the argument from the poverty of the stimulus would come unglued. But this alone would not refute any of Chomsky's nativist conclusions. As we'll see in the section to follow, we can readily formulate a new version of the argument for minimal nativism that sidesteps both

29. Sejnowski and Rosenberg (1987); Gorman and Sejnowski (1988).
30. See Rumelhart, Hinton and McClelland (1986), p. 53.
31. See McClelland, Rumelhart and Hinton (1986), p. 43.
32. Sampson (1987a), p. 877. Sampson (1987b), p. 643.

connectionist challenges. The argument for anti-empiricism can also be reconstructed, as we'll see in Section 4.4, though it will require a sort of empirical evidence rather different from that exploited in Section 2.2. And, as we shall argue in Section 4.5, even Chomskian rationalism may turn out to be compatible with our hypothesized connectionist achievements.

4.3 CONNECTIONISM AND MINIMAL NATIVISM

For argument's sake, let's grant that, despite Chomsky's argument to the contrary, the mechanisms subserving the linguistic skills of a competent speaker do not exploit an internally represented grammar. Rather, we'll suppose that a trained up connectionist network underlies a speaker's ability to judge sentences as grammatical or ungrammatical, etc. On this assumption, the job of the language acquisition mechanism will be to produce an appropriate network, one which judges sentences the way other speakers of the language do. The input available to the acquisition mechanism will be a typically untidy body of primary linguistic data drawn (mostly) from the language being acquired. And, of course, the network that is the output of the acquisition mechanism will have to respond appropriately to a vast class of sentences that the acquisition mechanism was never exposed to.

But now just as there are indefinitely many grammars which are comparably compatible with any given body of primarily linguistic data, though they diverge in the judgments they make about sentences not in that body of data, so too there are indefinitely many connectionist networks that agree, near enough, in their judgments about a given body of primary linguistic data, while diverging in their judgments about sentences not included in the data. Thus the language acquisition mechanism must somehow reject an indefinitely large class of networks all of which are comparably compatible with the data. To do this, obviously the mechanism will have to be strongly biased in favor of acquiring certain networks and against acquiring others. And that is just what minimal nativism maintains. All of this is quite independent of any assumption we might make about the algorithm used by the acquisition mechanism. If a connectionist acquisition mechanism using back propagation can in fact produce a trained up network that makes the right judgments about vast numbers of sentences not included in the primary linguistic data, then the conclusion to be drawn is not that minimal nativism is false, but rather that the learning algorithm being used is strongly biased in favor of certain projections and against others. This should be no surprise. The task of the language acquisition mechanism is an inductive learning task. And as Goodman and others demonstrated long ago, any successful inductive learning strategy must be strongly biased.[33]

---

33. See Goodman (1965). Compare Morgan (1986), p. 15: "It is fairly trivial to demonstrate that no unbiased inductive mechanism can reliably succeed in solving this sort of projection problem."

4.4 CONNECTIONISM AND ANTI-EMPIRICISM

While minimal nativism claims merely that the language learning mechanism must be biased, the Chomskian argument for anti-empiricism maintains that simplicity and other methodological principles of the sort that a scientist might use in deciding among theories will not suffice in explaining the child's success in learning language. Recall that to make this point, the anti-empiricist argument outlined in Section 2.2 needed some sophisticated linguistic evidence. It required us to find cases in which a pair of grammars that are near enough equal with respect to simplicity and other methodological virtues also agree in their judgments about typical bodies of primary linguistic data. If these grammars disagree in their judgments about cases not likely to be found in the primary linguistic data, then the competent scientist trying to duplicate the child's accomplishment would have no way of deciding among them.

This argument for anti-empiricism clearly requires that the mechanism underlying linguistic competence be a grammar, since it rests upon very specific claims about the formal properties of grammars. But as we saw in Section 4.1, the success of connectionism would challenge this assumption. Since connectionist models of competence do not use anything like a grammar, the fact that different *grammars* are compatible with the data and equally simple would not suffice to establish anti-empiricism, if those connectionist models turn out to be right. Hence, the sort of connectionist models of linguistic competence that we have been imagining undermine the standard Chomskian formulation of the argument for anti-empiricism. This hardly constitutes a refutation of anti-empiricism, however, since it is possible to reconstruct an anti-empiricist argument parallel to Chomsky's which assumes that linguistic competence is subserved by a connectionist network.

Since we are assuming that adult linguistic competence is subserved by a connectionist network rather than a grammar, we will have to assemble cases in which a pair of connectionist networks have the following properties:

(i) the networks make much the same judgments about sentences likely to show up in the primary linguistic data;
(ii) the networks make significantly different judgments about sentences that are not likely to show up in the primary linguistic data; and
(iii) on intuitive measures of simplicity (and on other methodological grounds) the networks are much the same.

Since connectionist studies of language are of very recent vintage, and since many researchers in the area are skeptical about nativism, there has been no systematic effort to find such examples. Thus the data needed to secure our reconstructed anti-nativist argument are not available. But there is certainly no *a priori* reason to suppose that the evidence required cannot be found. And in assessing the threat connectionism poses for anti-empiricism, this last point is the crucial one. What it shows is that even if the suppositions in Sections 4.1 and 4.2 are correct, the truth of anti-empiricism will remain an open issue, to be decided by further empirical work. If the appropriate linguistic evidence *can* be found, and if the language acquisition mechanism is indeed a connectionist device exploiting back propagation, then the conclusion to be drawn is not that anti-empiricism is mistaken, but that the connectionist acquisition mechanism embodies biases different from those invoked in the empiricist tradition. More specifically, if the data turn out right, then the connectionist acquisition mechanism must be using something different from simplicity and other intuitive methodological principles. For *ex hypothesi* the acquisition mechanism is preferring one network to another, even though they are comparably simple and equally compatible with the data. Of course, if the data turn out the other way—if the appropriate linguistic examples are not to be found—then we will have no reason to regard anti-empiricism as true.

Before leaving the topic of anti-empiricism, there is one final point that needs attention. As we noted in Section 4.2, back propagation, the most widely used connectionist learning algorithm, was inspired by Hebbian learning rules and by work on classical conditioning. And while back propagation is significantly more sophisticated than Hebb's rule, or the (unmodified) delta rule invoked in the explanation of classical conditioning, it clearly shares a strong family resemblance with them. But, it might be argued, Hebb's rule, and the processes of classical conditioning are surely of a piece with the sort of mental processes that have been posited in the empiricist tradition. So if, as we have been assuming, a connectionist language acquisition device using back propagation could project from the data the way a child does, why should we not conclude that an empiricist acquisition device could succeed to learning language?

As we see it, the issue that is being raised here is how the notion of an 'empiricist' learning mechanism is best understood. Chomsky and his followers have adopted the competent scientist gambit as the acid test for empiricism. Any acquisition mechanism that can reliably do things a competent scientist cannot do does not count as an empiricist mechanism. And on this test it may well turn out that connectionist devices exploiting back propagation are not empiricist mechanisms. The alternative account of the notion of an 'empiricist' learning mechanism rejects the competent scientist standard, with its appeal to intuitive simplicity and other intuitive methodological considerations, and opts instead for the family resemblance criterion. On this account connectionist devices exploiting back propagation probably are empiricist mechanisms. As we see it, the dispute here is largely a verbal one. It will be an interesting and important fact if the competent scientist account of empiricism and the family resemblance account turn out not to coincide. But if this happens, who gets to keep the word 'empiricist' is a matter of very little moment.

4.5 CONNECTIONISM AND RATIONALISM

Rationalism, as we have been using the term, is the thesis that the innate language learning mechanism embodies biases or constraints that are specific to the task of language learning, and of no use in other domains. The Chomskian justification for this thesis relies on the claim that there are no plausible alternatives. Thus in 1980, before the flourishing of connectionism, Wexler and Culicover wrote:

> At the present the constraints we need are quite specifically linguistic. More general theories would be intriguing, as insightful generalization always is, but until we have reason to believe the generalizations (or to formulate them coherently), we must remain skeptical.[34]

Here again, the connectionist achievements we've posited undermine the Chomskian argument. For, as we have noted, connectionist learning algorithms are anything but specifically linguistic. They have been used successfully in a wide variety of domains. So if a connectionist acquisition device could project from the primary linguistic data in the way the child does, Chomskians can no longer claim that rationalist acquisition models are the only game in town.

Undermining Chomsky's version of the argument for rationalism does not, however, show that rationalism is false; nor does it show that connectionism is incompatible with rationalism. For there are a great variety of connectionist learning devices that exploit back propagation. Some of them require idiosyncratic architectures or a great deal of pre-wiring and pre-tuning before they will do an acceptable job of learning in the task domain for which they are designed.[35] And as McClelland and Rumelhart note, such models are "clearly consistent with a rabidly nativist world view."[36] While connectionist research has produced learning strategies that are not domain specific, the extent to which these strategies can succeed in language acquisition without exploiting special architectures is currently unknown. If the only successful connectionist language acquisition devices are of a sort that require language specific architectures and/or language specific pre-tuning, then even the rationalist version of nativism wall have nothing to fear from connectionism. Recently Rumelhart and others have been exploring ways in which connectionist learning algorithms themselves can be modified so as to bias learning in one direction or another.[37] If the best connectionist models of language acquisition exploit a learning algorithm that is particularly adept at language learning and largely useless in other domains, then again rationalism and connectionism will turn out to be comfortably compatible.

Of course, it is also conceivable that connectionist learning models will be able to duplicate significant aspects of the language learner's accomplishment without invoking idiosyncratic architectures, specialized pre-tuning or domain specific learning algorithms,

34. Wexler and Culicover (1980), p. 10.
35. We are indebted to Jeffrey Elman for convincing us of the importance of this point.
36. Rumelhart and McClelland (1986c), p. 140.
37. Rumelhart (personal communication).

and that much the same models will be able to master significant cognitive tasks in domains far removed from language. If such non-domain-specific models were to be developed, they would pose a genuine challenge for Chomskian rationalism.

5 Conclusion

The central claim of this last section has been that the putative incompatibility between connectionism and nativism has been much exaggerated. If adult linguistic competence is subserved by a connectionist network, and connectionist learning devices can duplicate the child's projection from primary linguistic data, all three versions of Chomsky's argument from the poverty of the stimulus will be undermined. However, parallel arguments for minimal nativism and anti-empiricism are easy to reconstruct. On our view, the argument for minimal nativism is entirely conclusive. The argument for anti-empiricism depends on empirical premises whose plausibility requires further investigation. There is no comparable reconstruction of the Chomskian argument for rationalism. However, if the only connectionist language acquisition models capable of projecting the way the child projects invoke language specific algorithms or architectures, then even rationalism will be sustained.

One final point is worth stressing. If it should turn out that non-domain specific models, like those envisioned at the end of Section 4.5, are capable of duplicating significant aspects of the child's accomplishment, and if the argument against empiricism can be successfully reconstructed, then our account of language acquisition would be located in the seldom explored terrain between rationalism and empiricism. It is here, perhaps, that connectionism may hold the most exciting potential for contributing to the nativism debate.

REFERENCES

Berwick, R.: 1983, "Using What You Know: A Computer–Science Perspective," *Behavioral and Brain Sciences* 6, 402–403.

Charniak, E. and E. Santos: 1986, "A Connectionst Context-free Parser which is not Context-free, but then it is not Really Connectionist Either," Department of Computer Science, Brown University.

Chomsky, N.: 1965, *Aspects of the Theory of Syntax*. MIT Press, Cambridge, Massachusetts.

Chomsky, N.: 1966, *Cartesian Linguistics: A Chapter in the History of Rationalistic Thought*, Harper and Row, New York.

Chomsky, N.: 1969, "Comments on Harman's Reply," in S. Hook (ed.), *Language and Philosophy*, New York University Press, New York, pp. 152–159.

Chomsky, N.: 1972, *Language and Mind*, Harcourt Brace Jovanovich, New York.

Chomsky, N.: 1975, *Reflections on Language*, Pantheon Books, New York.

Chomsky, N.: 1980a, *Rules and Representations*, Columbia University Press, New York.

Chomsky, N.: 1980b, "Rules and Representations," *Behavioral and Brain Sciences* 3, 1–61.

Chomsky, N.: 1980c, "Recent Contributions to the Theory of Innate Ideas: Summary of Oral Presentation," in H. Morick (ed.), *Challenges to Empiricism*, Hackett, Indianapolis, pp. 230–40.

Chomsky, N.: 1986, *Knowledge of Language*, Praeger, New York.

Chomsky, N.: 1988, *Language and Problems of Knowledge*, MIT Press, Cambridge, Massachusetts.

Cottrell, G.: 1985, "Connectionist Parsing," in *Proceedings of the Seventh Annual Cognitive Science Society*, pp. 201–11.

Cummins, R.: 1977, "Programs in the Explanation of Behavior," *Philosophy of Science* 44, 269–87.

Elman, J.: 1988, "Finding Structure in Time," CRL Technical Report 8801.

Fanty, M.: 1985, "Context-Free Parsing in Connectionist Networks," Technical Report No. 174, Department of Computer Science, University of Rochester.

Fodor, J.: 1981. *Representations*, MIT Press, Cambridge, Massachusetts.

Gold, E. M.: 1967, "Language Identification in the Limit," *Information and Control* 10, 447–74.

Goodman, N.: 1965, *Fact, Fiction and Forecast*, 2nd ed., Bobbs Merrill, Indianapolis.

Gorman, R. and T. Sejnowski: 1988, "Learned Classification of Sonar Targets Using a Massively Parallel Network," *IEEE Transactions: Acoustics, Speech, and Signal Processing*, 36, 7, pp. 1135–1140.

Hanson, S. and J. Kegl: 1987, "PARSNIP: A Connectionist Network that Learns Natural Language Grammar from Exposure to Natural Language Sentences," in *Proceedings of the Ninth Annual Conference of the Cognitive Science Society*, pp. 106–19.

Hinton, G.: 1987, "Connectionist Learning Procedures," Tech Report No. CMUCS-87–115.

Hornstein, N.: 1984, *Logic as Grammar*, MIT Press, Cambridge, Massachusetts.

Hornstein, N. and D. Lightfoot: 1981, *Explanations in Linguistics*, Longman, London.

Hornstein, N. and D. Lightfoot: 1981b, "Introduction," in Hornstein and Lightfoot (1981a), pp. 9–31.

Lightfoot, D.: 1982, *The Language Lottery*, MIT/Bradford Press, Cambridge, Massachusetts.

McClelland, J., D. Rumelhart, and D. Hinton: 1986, "The Appeal of Parallel Distributed Processing," in Rumelhart and McClelland (1986a), Vol. I.

McClelland, J. L., and A. Kawamoto: 1986, "Mechanisms of Sentence Processing: Assigning Roles to Constituents," in Rumelhart and McClelland (1986a), Vol. II.

Morgan, J: 1986, *From Simple Input to Complex Grammar*, MIT Press, Cambridge, Massachusetts.

Papert, S.: 1988, "One AI or Many?," *Daedalus* 117, 1–14.

Peters, S.: 1972, "The Project Problem: How is a Grammar to be Selected?," in *Goals of Linguistic Theory*, Prentice-Hall, Englewood Cliffs, New Jersey.

Pinker, S., and A. Prince: 1988, "On Language and Connectionism: Analysis of a Parallel Distributed Processing Model of Language Acquisition," *Cognition*, 28, 73–193.

Quine, W. V.: 1969, 'Linguistics and Philosophy,' in S. Hook (ed.), *Language and Philosophy*, New York University Press, pp. 95–98.

Ramsey, W., D. Rumelhart, and S. Stich: 1991, *Philosophy and Connectionist Theory*, Lawrence Erlbaum Associates, Hillsdale, New Jersey.

Ramsey, W., S. Stich and J. Garon: 1991, 'Connectionism, Eliminativism and the Future of Folk Psychology,' in Ramsey, Rumelhart, and Stich, 1991.

Rumelhart, D., G. Hinton and J. McClelland: 1986, 'A General Framework for Parallel Distributed Processing,' in Rumelhart and McClelland (1986a), Vol. I.

Rumelhart, D., G. Hinton and R. Williams: 1986, 'Learning Internal Representations by Error Propagation,' in Rumelhart and McClelland (1986a), Vol. I.

Rumelhart, D. and J. McClelland: 1986a, *Parallel Distributed Processing: Explorations in the Microstructure of Cognition*, Vols. I & II, MIT/Bradford Press, Cambridge, Massachusetts.

Rumelhart, D. and J. McClelland: 1986b, "On Learning the Past Tense of English Verbs," in Rumelhart and McClelland (1986a), Vol. II.

Rumelhart, D. and J. McClelland: 1986c, "PDP Models and General Issues in Cognitive Science," in Rumelhart and McClelland (1986a), Vol. I.

Sampson, G.: 1987a, "Review Article. Parallel Distributed Processing," *Language* 63, 871–86.

Sampson, G.: 1987b, "A Turning Point in Linguistics," *Times Literary Supplement*, June 12, p. 643.

Searle, J.: 1974, "Chomsky's Revolution in Linguistics," in Gilbert Harman (ed.), *On Noam Chomsky: Critical Essays*, Doubleday, New York, pp. 2–33.

Sejnowski, T. and C. Rosenberg 1987, "Parallel Networks that Learn to Pronounce English Text," *Complex Systems*, 1, 145–68.

Selman, B. and G. Hirst: 1985, "A Rule-Based Connectionist Parsing System," *Proceedings of the Seventh Annual Conference of the Cognitive Science Society*.

St. John, M. F. and J. L. McClelland: 1988, "Learning and Applying Contextual Constraints in Sentence Comprehension," in *Proceedings of the 10th Annual Cognitive Science Society Conference*, Lawrence Erlbaum Associates, Hillsdale, New Jersey.

Stabler, E.: 1983, "How Are Grammars Represented?," *Behavioral and Brain Sciences* 6, 391–421.

Stich, S.: 1971, "What Every Speaker Knows," *Philosophical Review* 80, 476–96.

Stich, S.: 1996, "The Dispute Over Innate Ideas," to appear in M. Dascal et al. (ed.), *Sprachphilosophie: Ein Internationales Handbuch Zeitgenossischer Forschung*, Vol. 2. Berlin: Walter de Gruyter, 1041–1050.

Waltz, D. L. and J. B. Pollack: 1985, "Massively Parallel Parsing: A Strongly Interactive Model of Natural Interpretation," *Cognitive Science* 9, 51–74.

Wexler, K. and P. W. Culicover: 1980, *Formal Principles of Language Acquisition*, MIT Press, Cambridge, MA.

SSV: [Still Small Voice—could it be the voice of
conscience?] I do believe you've gone over to Steve Stich.
Have you no conscience?

Answer: There, there; don't fret! What is emerging here is, in a
certain sense, a "no content" account of narrow content; but
it is nevertheless also a fully intentionalist account . . . In effect
I'm prepared to give Stich everything except what he wants.

FODOR, *PSYCHOSEMANTICS*

8

NARROW CONTENT MEETS FAT SYNTAX

1 Introduction

A bit over a decade ago I published a paper in which I argued that Putnam's much discussed Twin Earth thought experiments posed a problem for the view that a psychological theory aimed at explaining human behavior will invoke common-sense intentional concepts like belief and desire.[1] That argument relied on a pair of premises. The first, which I (perhaps infelicitously) called the *principle of psychological autonomy* maintains that any state or property properly invoked in a psychological explanation should supervene on the current, internal, physical state of the organism. Thus, a pair of Putnamian doppelgangers, being molecule for molecule replicas of one another, must share all the same explanatory psychological states and properties. The second premise was that commonsense intentional properties, properties like *believing that Eisenhower played golf* (or *having a belief with the content that Eisenhower played golf*) and *believing that water is wet* (or *having a belief with the content that water is wet*) do not supervene on a person's current, internal, physical state. For want of a better label, I'll call this the *Autonomy* argument.

The first premise of the Autonomy argument was one that I took to be intuitively obvious and widely shared. Thus I offered little by way of support. The second premise seemed to be a straightforward consequence of the usual intuitions about Twin-Earth

---

1. Stich (1978). For The details of Putnam's thought experiment, see Putnam (1975a).

style thought experiments. According to those intuitions, the belief that my doppelganger expresses when he says "Eisenhower played golf" is not *about* Eisenhower, the man whose hand I almost got to shake during the 1956 presidential election; it is about some other statesman in a far off corner of the universe. Thus the truth conditions of my belief and my doppelganger's are different. But it is plausible to suppose that on the conception of content implicit in commonsense psychology, belief tokens that are about different people and that have different truth conditions must have different contents. So my doppelganger and I do not both have beliefs with the content that Eisenhower played golf.

This argument was part of a larger project. Influenced by Quine, I have long been suspicious about the integrity and scientific utility of the commonsense notions of meaning and intentional content. This is not, of course, to deny that the intentional idioms of ordinary discourse have their uses, nor that these uses are important. But, like Quine, I view ordinary intentional locutions as projective, context sensitive, observer relative, and essentially dramatic.[2] They are not the sorts of locutions we should welcome in serious scientific discourse. For those who share this Quinean skepticism, the sudden flourishing of cognitive psychology in the 1970s posed something of a problem. On the account offered by Fodor and other observers, the cognitive psychology of that period was exploiting both the ontology and the explanatory strategy of commonsense psychology. It proposed to explain cognition and certain aspects of behavior by positing beliefs, desires, and other psychological states with intentional content, and by couching generalizations about the interactions among those states in terms of their intentional content.[3] If this was right, then those of us who would banish talk of content in scientific settings would be throwing out the cognitive psychological baby with the intentional bath water. On my view, however, this account of cognitive psychology was seriously mistaken. The cognitive psychology of the 1970s and early 1980s was not positing contentful intentional states, nor was it adverting to content in its generalizations. Rather, I maintained, the cognitive psychology of the day was "really a kind of logical syntax (only psychologized)."[4] Moreover, it seemed to me that there were good reasons why cognitive psychology not only did not but *should* not traffic in intentional states. One of these reasons was provided by the Autonomy argument.

---

2. Quine has urged this view of the propositional attitudes in many places. See, for example Quine (1960:219). For some elaboration on these themes, see Stich (1982); Stich (1983:chs 4–6); Gordon (1986); and Levin (1988).

3. See, for example, Fodor, (1975:ch. 1); Fodor (1980); Fodor (1981: "Introduction"); and Fodor (1987:ch. 1).

4. The quote is from Fodor (1978). For my account of the explanatory strategy of cognitive psychology, *circa* 1980, see Stich (1983:chs 7–9). Perhaps this is the place to say that when I talk of the cognitive psychology of the 1970s and early 1980s, what I have in mind is pre-connectionist cognitive psychology. The qualification is important since, on my view, neither Fodor's account of cognitive theorizing nor my syntactic account will mesh comfortably with the connectionist paradigm. For some elaboration of this point, see Ramsey, Stich, and Garon (1990).

During the last decade, that argument and similar arguments offered by other writers have attracted a fair amount of attention, very little of it favorable.[5] Some critics have focused on the first premise, and have argued that explanatory psychology need not, and does not, restrict itself to states and properties that organisms and their doppelgangers share.[6] Others have focused on the second premise, with some arguing that common-sense psychology does not insist that beliefs with different truth conditions differ in content, or at least that it does not do so consistently, while others challenged the intuition that the beliefs of doppelgangers on Earth and Twin-Earth differ in truth conditions.[7] I think each of these objections raises serious issues, and each merits a detailed reply. But in the present paper I'll say very little about them. My focus here will be on quite a different reaction to the Autonomy argument—a reaction which grants both premises of the argument. This reaction concedes that the *commonsense* notion of intentional content will not play a role in scientific psychology. But it insists that *another* notion of intentional content will be central to psychology. For this second, more technical, and less common-sensical notion of content, it is not the case that if a pair of belief tokens differ in truth conditions, or in what they are about, then they also differ in content. Thus Twin Earth cases and others of their ilk will not show that *this* sort of content does not supervene on the current internal state of the organism. Though my doppelganger and I have beliefs that are about different people (or stuff) and thus have different truth conditions, those beliefs may still have the same content, when content is construed in this new way. Since the ordinary notion of content determines truth conditions—typically conditions in the world beyond the head—while the new technical notion does not, the new notion has been dubbed *narrow content*; the old commonsense notion is often said to be *broad* or *wide*. There are various lines along which the narrow content response to the Autonomy argument can be developed.[8] But, as is appropriate in a volume focused on Fodor, the line I propose to explore is the one that Fodor follows. In section 3.1, I'll give a quick overview of Fodor's account of narrow content.

An objection often urged against the notion of narrow content is that it is not really a species of content at all.[9] One reason for this suspicion is that while it is generally easy to *say* what the (ordinary, broad) content of a belief is, there often seems no way at all to say what the narrow content of a belief is. Narrow content appears to be "radically inexpressible." However, I will argue that this suspicion is mistaken. Indeed, in section 3.2 I will sketch a straightforward way in which readily available resources can be used to construct a vocabulary for attributing narrow content. Of course, this alone is not enough to show that narrow content really is a kind of content, properly so-called. And I must confess

---

5. For similar arguments, see Stack (unpublished); Putnam (1978); and Putnam (1983).

6. See, for example, Burge (1979); Burge (1986); Kitcher (1985); Owens (1987); Baker (1987a).

7. Loar (1987); Lycan (1988: 76–9); Dow (1991).

8. See, for example, Block (1986); Dennett (1982); Devitt (1989); Dow (1991); Loar (1987a).

9. See, for example, Owens (1987) and Baker (1987b).

that I'm not at all sure what it *would* take to show that narrow content is, or isn't, really a kind of content. So I propose to leave that question to be debated by those who think they understand it. As I see it, the major objection to narrow content, as Fodor develops the notion, is that it is very unlikely to be of any more use to psychology than the commonsense notion of broad content. If we taxonomize mental states by their narrow content, there are going to be lots of psychological generalizations that we are not going to be able to state. My argument for this claim is set out in section 3.3.

That argument presupposes a certain conception of the cognitive mind—a conception that portrays the mind as analogous to a kind of computer. Though very familiar, this picture of the mind has never been without its critics, and with the recent flowering of connectionism it has become particularly controversial. However, in the present paper I don't propose to challenge the picture. Since Fodor himself has long been one of its most eloquent advocates, I will simply accept it, if only for argument's sake. In order to launch my argument against narrow content, it will be necessary to sketch in parts of the picture with somewhat more detail than is usually provided. This is the project I'll pursue in section 2.

Before getting on to any of this, however, we would do well to get a bit clearer about the issue that is in dispute. In the article in which I first set out the Autonomy argument, and in various subsequent publications, my "official" thesis was that serious scientific psychology should not invoke commonsense intentional notions like belief and desire. The official thesis certainly does not entail that beliefs, desires, and other propositional attitudes do not exist,[10] nor even that commonsense psychology is not "pretty close to being true"[11]—though it is, of course, consistent with these claims. But it is these claims that are at the heart of Fodor's concern. On his view, "if commonsense intentional psychology really were to collapse, that would be, beyond comparison, the greatest intellectual catastrophe in the history of our species . . . ." (*PS*:xii). This leaves us with a rather delicate question. Just what would it take to show that commonsense intentional psychology had collapsed? Nobody thinks that *all* of commonsense psychology is going to turn out to be correct. Indeed, Fodor cheerfully concedes that "a lot of what common sense believes about the attitudes must surely be false (a lot of what common sense believes about *anything* must surely be false)" (*PS*:15). He also concedes that "you can't make respectable science out of the attitudes as commonsensically individuated" (*PS*:30). The "identity conditions for mental states" that "we need, when doing psychology" are not going to be "those that common sense prefers" (*PS*:30). If all of this is not enough to undermine commonsense psychology and its intentional ontology, one might well wonder how much more it will take. Fortunately, Fodor tells us. He stipulates that a psychological theory will count as "endorsing" commonsense propositional attitudes "just in case it postulates states (entities, events, whatever) satisfying the following conditions:

---

10. On this point see Stich (1983:ch. 11 sec. 1).

11. Fodor (1987:x). Subsequent references to Fodor's *Psychosemantics* will be referred to as *PS* in the text.

(i) They are semantically evaluable.

(ii) They have causal powers.

(iii) The implicit generalizations of commonsense belief/desire psychology are largely true of them.

In effect," Fodor tells us, "I am assuming that (i)–(iii) are the essential properties of the attitudes. This seems to me intuitively plausible; if it doesn't seem intuitively plausible to you, so be it. Squabbling about intuitions strikes me as vulgar" (*PS*: 10).

I am not at all sure whether my intuitions agree with Fodor's here; indeed, I'm not even sure I *have* any intuitions about the essential properties of the attitudes. But no matter. This book is for Fodor; I'll play by his rules. What I propose to argue is that most of the implicit generalizations of commonsense psychology are not likely to turn out to be true of the states posited by psychological theories that cleave to the computational paradigm. So Fodor loses on (iii). Moreover, on at least one plausible reading of what it is to be "semantically evaluable," these states are not semantically evaluable either. Thus Fodor loses on (i) too. Whether or not we accept Fodor's intuitions about what is essential to the attitudes, this should be enough to show that propositional attitude psychology is in trouble.

2 The Computational Paradigm

My goal in this section is to provide a brief sketch of a familiar story about the cognitive mind. Since the basic outline is so well known, I will devote most of my attention to clarifying the ontological underpinnings of this account and the taxonomic strategies it exploits. Much of what I say in this section is based on the rather more detailed account I developed in *From Folk Psychology to Cognitive Science*. Since talk of *states* and the various ways in which they get taxonomized or individuated is going to be of some importance in what follows, I'll begin by making a few proposals about how this talk should be construed. So far as I can see, nothing in the arguments to follow depends on the details. We just need *some* systematic way of talking about states. Most any sensible proposal would do.

As I propose we view them, states are the instantiation of a *property* by an *object* during a *time interval*.[12] There are, of course, venerable disputes about what sorts of things properties are.[13] But for present purposes I propose to be quite permissive. Near enough, I'll count any open sentence with a reasonably clear extension as specifying a property. That raises the notorious question of when two open sentences specify the same property. Fortunately, this is not a question for which we will need any fully general answer. All

---

12. My account of states is modeled on Kim's account of events. See Kim (1969) and Kim (1976).

13. See, for example, Armstrong (1978).

we'll need is the weak principle that open sentences with different extensions specify different properties.

On the view I'm recommending, states count as *particulars* with a more or less definite location in space and time. States also admit of what might be called an *essential* classification into types. A pair of states are of the same *essential type* if and only if they are instantiations of the same property. Although each state has only one essential type, states, like other particulars, can be grouped into nonessential types in an endless variety of ways. A type of state is simply a category of particulars, and we have specified a type when we have set out conditions for membership in the category. Though we are conceiving of states as particulars, it will sometimes be convenient to use the word "state" to talk about a type or category of states, or the property that members of a category have in common. When ambiguity threatens, I'll use "state token" to refer to particulars and "state type" to refer to categories or types.

So much for states. Let me turn, now, to the story about the mind that I have been calling the *computational paradigm*. The central assumption of the story is that the cognitive mind can be viewed as a particular kind of computer—that the mind is, in Fodor's phrase, "a syntax-driven machine" (*PS*: 20). On this view, each cognitive state token is a brain state token—its essential type is determined by some neurophysiological property or other. However, these neurophysiological state tokens can also be viewed as having syntactic structure in something like the same way that sentence tokens in a natural or formal language have a syntactic structure. That is, each cognitive state token can be viewed as belonging to a syntactic type (or having a "syntactic form"), just as each inscription of a sentence in English or in first order predicate calculus can be viewed as having a syntactic form. Cognitive processes consist of temporal sequences of these syntactically structured states. The reason that the cognitive mind can be thought of as a kind of computer is that the mechanism that controls these cognitive processes is "sensitive solely to syntactic properties" (*PS*:19).

This account of the cognitive mind as a computer or a "syntactic engine" has become very familiar in recent years. But, as Michael Devitt notes in a recent article,[14] the account is very easy to misconstrue. Often, when offering quick sketches of the mind-as-computer story, writers will conjure the image of a "belief box" and a "desire box" inside the head in which syntactically structured sentence-like entities are stored. For vividness, it may even be suggested that the sentences be thought of as well formed formulas of some familiar formalized language.[15] But, as Devitt notes, this image invites us to think of the syntactic properties of cognitive state tokens (the properties in virtue of which they fall into one or another syntactic category) as *intrinsic* or "brute physical" properties—properties that we could detect if we looked at the appropriate bits of the brain in isolation, much as we

14. Devitt (1989).

15. For a particularly vivid and influential example of the Belief-Box metaphor, see Schiffer (1981).

could see whether an inscription in a "belief box" had the shape: (x) Fx → Gx. If we think of the syntactic properties of mental states in this way, then it would make perfectly good sense to suppose that in certain brains syntactically structured states might be stored in the "belief box," though the mechanisms which control cognitive processes are *not* sensitive to the syntax. But, along with Devitt, I would urge that this is just the wrong way to conceive of things. Mental state tokens are brain state tokens. But the properties in virtue of which mental state tokens are classified into syntactic categories are not intrinsic features of those brain states; they are not features which depend exclusively on the shape or form or "brute physical" properties of the states. Rather, the syntactic properties of mental states are relational or functional properties—they are properties that certain states of the brain have in virtue of the way in which they causally interact with various other states of the system. To put the point in a slightly different way, we would have no reason to view brain states as syntactically structured unless that structure can be exploited in capturing generalizations about the workings of mind/brain's mechanisms. Attributing syntactic structure to brain state tokens—assigning them to syntactic types—is justified only if some interesting set of causal interactions among those tokens is isomorphic to formal relations among abstract syntactic objects. Here is how I elaborated on this theme in *From Folk Psychology to Cognitive Science*:

> The basic idea . . . is that the cognitive states whose interaction is (in part) responsible for behavior can be systematically mapped to abstract syntactic objects in such a way that causal interactions among cognitive states, as well as causal links with stimuli and behavioral events, can be described in terms of the syntactic properties and relations of the abstract objects to which the cognitive states are mapped. More briefly, the idea is that causal relations among cognitive states mirror formal relations among syntactic objects. If this is right, then it will be natural to view cognitive state tokens as tokens of abstract syntactic objects . . .
>
> The theorist's job in setting out [this sort of] cognitive theory can be viewed as having three parts. First, he must specify a class of [abstract] syntactic objects . . . and do so in a way which assigns a formal or syntactic structure to each of these objects . . .
>
> Second, the theorist hypothesizes that for each organism covered by the theory, there exists a set of state types whose tokens are causally implicated in the production of behavior. He also hypothesizes that there is a mapping from these state types to syntactic objects in the specified class. Several observations about these hypotheses are in order. First, the theorist need say very little about the essential nature of the state tokens which are causally implicated in the production of behavior. Presumably they are physical states of the brain, and thus the properties which constitute their essential types are neurological properties . . . Second, in asserting the existence of the mapping, the order of the quantifiers is of some importance. The theorist is not claiming that the mapping is the same for each subject, but only

that for each subject there is a mapping. So in different subjects, quite different neurological states types may be mapped to a given syntactic object. These . . . two points . . . are in the spirit of functionalism, which stresses the possibility of multiple realizations of mental states . . .

The third part of [this kind of] cognitive theory . . . is a specification of the theory's generalizations. The core idea . . . is that generalizations detailing causal relations among the hypothesized neurological states are to be specified indirectly via the formal relations among the syntactic objects to which the neurological states are mapped. Similarly, generalizations specifying causal relations between stimuli and neurological states will identify the neurological states not by adverting to their essential neurological types but, rather, by adverting to the syntactic objects to which the neurological types are mapped. Ditto for generalizations specifying causal relations between neurological states and behavior.[16]

As Devitt rightly points out, there is a certain tension in this passage that emerges when we ask how we would go about determining whether a pair of brain state tokens in two different people (or in one person at two different times) are tokens of the same syntactic type. One criterion for the syntactic type identity of tokens would require only that the tokens' patterns of causal interactions *with other tokens* be pretty much the same, so both patterns could be captured by the same formal relations among the appropriate system of syntactic objects. A more stringent criterion would require not only that the tokens' patterns of causal interactions with each other be the same, but also that their patterns of causal interaction with *stimuli* and *behavior* be pretty much the same as well. Since the terms "broad" and "narrow" have been appropriated for distinguishing kinds of content, I will call these two standards for determining the syntactic type of a hypothesized brain state token *skinny* and *fat* respectively. Though my writing has sometimes been less than clear on the point, it has always been my intention to invoke *fat syntax* in typing mental state tokens. When Fodor describes the mind as a "syntax-driven machine" it is not clear whether the standard of syntactic type individuation he has in mind is fat or skinny. In what follows, I'll assume that the syntactic types exploited in computational theories of the mind are fat, not skinny, though most of my argument will work either way.

3 Narrow Content

So much for the computational paradigm. Let's now return to the Autonomy argument, and Fodor's strategy for dealing with it. Since the notion of "narrow" content plays a central role in that strategy, I'll start with a sketch of how Fodor proposes to construct the notion. Once that's been done, I'll set out a pair of reasons for doubting that Fodor's

---

16. Stich (1983:149–51).

notion of narrow content will do what he wants. One of these, I'll argue, is pretty easy to handle. The other is not.

3.1

Mental states, we are supposing, are states of the brain. And, while their essential type is neurophysiological, they can also be classified into all sorts of other categories. One such categorization, provided by commonsense psychology, is to type mental state tokens by their content. The problem posed by the Autonomy argument is that the taxonomy imposed by ordinary, "broad" content does not supervene on a person's current, internal, physical properties. So while those states in Fodor's brain which count as beliefs and those in Twin-Fodor's brain which count as beliefs are neurophysiologially the same, they may well differ in content. This difference in content, Fodor notes, must be due to differences in the world around them and their relations to that world.

> Presumably . . . there's something about the relation between Twin-Earth and Twin-Me in virtue of which his "water"-thoughts are about XYZ even though my water-thoughts are not. Call this condition that's satisfied by (Twin-Me, Twin-Earth) condition C (because it determines the *Context* of his "water"-thoughts). (*PS*:48)

Fodor's proposal for constructing a notion of narrow content is to start with the taxonomy provided by the ordinary, broad, truth-condition determining notion of content, and subtract out the contribution of the contextual conditions, like condition C, that "anchor" it.[17] One way of thinking of the narrow content of a thought is that it is what remains of the broad content when we "take away the anchoring conditions" (*PS*: 51). But Fodor cautions against taking this subtraction picture too literally. A better way of thinking of narrow content, he suggests, is to view the narrow content of a thought as a function (in the mathematical sense—a mapping) from contexts to broad contents. Since broad contents determine truth conditions, narrow contents will determine mappings from contexts to truth conditions. "Two [narrow] thought contents are identical only if they effect the same mapping of thoughts and contexts onto truth conditions" (*PS*:48). Thus the thought tokens that lead both Fodor and Twin-Fodor to say "Water is wet" have the same narrow content, since they would have the same broad content if they were embedded in the same context.

> [S]hort of a miracle the following counterfactual must be true: Given the neurological identity between us, in a world where I am in my Twin's context, my

---

17. "I learned 'anchors' at Stanford," Fodor tells us. "[I]t is a very useful term despite—or maybe because of—not being very well defined" (*PS*:49).

"water"-thoughts are about XYZ iff his are. (And, of course, vice versa: in a world in which my Twin is in my context . . . it must be that his water-thoughts are about H$_2$O iff mine are.) (*PS*:48)

3.2

One complaint about this notion of narrow content, the one that Fodor suspects *"really* bugs people" (*PS*:50), is that it seems impossible to say what the narrow content of a thought is. Fodor and Twin-Fodor have thought tokens with the same narrow content. But what is it that they both think? What is the narrow content of those thoughts? It can't be *that water is wet*, since Twin-Fodor doesn't think that. Nor can it be *that XYZ is wet*, since Fodor doesn't think that. It seems that "narrow content is radically inexpressible" (*PC*:50). If this is right, however, it is hard to see how narrow content could serve the purpose for which it is intended. Recall that narrow content was supposed to provide a species of content-based taxonomy that would be useful in scientific psychology. If we insist, as Fodor does, that the states and properties invoked in scientific psychology must supervene on physiological states and properties, then psychological generalizations cannot invoke broad content. An alternative strategy is to couch those generalizations in terms of narrow content. But if narrow content is "radically inexpressible" it would appear that psychology's generalizations could never be stated.[18]

Fodor's response to this problem is to suggest that while we can't *express* the narrow content of the thought that he and his Twin share, we can "sneak up on the shared content by *mentioning*" an appropriate English expression—in this case presumably the sentence: 'Water is wet.' But in offering this response I think Fodor seriously understates the case to be made for his notion of narrow content. We can do more than "sneak up" on the narrow content of a mental state; we can explicitly introduce a way of talking about it. The central idea is very simple. Expressions of the form: "—believes that p" are predicates whose extension in any possible world is the class of people who believe that p in that world. Given these predicates along with the notion of a doppelganger, we can introduce expressions of the form "—believes that [p]" (think of it as "bracketed" belief) whose extensions in any possible world include everyone in that world who believes that p, along with all of their doppelgangers. Similarly, expressions of the form "—has the (broad) content that p" are predicates whose extension in any possible world included the class of brain state tokens whose broad content is p. Here we can introduce expressions of the form "—has the (narrow) content that [p]" whose extension in any possible world includes the class of brain state tokens whose (broad) content is p, along with the

18. I owe this way of making the point to Warren Dow. See Dow (1991). A similar point is made by Baker (1987a).

physically identical tokens in all doppelgangers of people who harbor tokens whose broad content is p.[19] These "bracketed" predicates are no less clear and no less systematic than the broad-content predicates on which they are based.

This strategy for talking about narrow content has what might at first seem to be a curious feature. In some cases the extension of "—has the (narrow) content that [p]" and the extension of "—has the (narrow) content that [q]" are going to be the same even though 'p' and 'q' are replaced by sentences that differ in reference and truth value. Consider, for example, a version of Putnam's aluminum/molybdenum story. In the southern province of a certain English-speaking country, pots are typically made of aluminum, and this fact is known to a southerner, (Southern)Sam, who knows very little else about aluminum. In the northern province, pots are typically made of molybdenum. But in the north, molybdenum is called "aluminum." (Northern)Sam, who is (Southern)Sam's doppelganger, has a belief which he expresses with the words "Pots are typically made of aluminum." Though of course given the standard intuitions in these cases, the belief token he is expressing has the (broad) content that pots are typically made of molybdenum. Now what about the narrow content of the belief (Northern)Sam expresses? Since that belief has the (broad) content that pots are typically made of molybdenum, it has the (narrow) content that [pots are typically made of molybdenum]. But since it is neurophysiologically identical to (Southern)Sam's belief whose (broad) content is that pots are typically made of aluminum, it also has the (narrow) content that [pots are typically made of aluminum]. Similarly, the belief token that (Southern)Sam expresses when he says "Pots are typically made of aluminum" has both narrow (or bracketed) contents. There is nothing particularly surprising about any of this. The device we've introduced for attributing narrow contents exploits the expressions we would use in attributing broad contents and expands their extensions in a systematic way. It is to be expected that in some cases two of these enlarged extensions will coincide.[20]

---

19. Something rather like this was suggested very briefly in Stich (1983:192, fn.). More recently, similar ideas have been developed by Valerie Hardcastle (1990) and Michael Devitt (1989). Perhaps I should add that I do not take my suggestion to be in competition with Fodor's strategy for "sneaking up on" narrow content; mine is just a bit more explicit. Indeed, were I to develop my definition more carefully, and without riding roughshod over the fine distinction between use and mention, it would be obvious that my story, like Fodor's, enables us to talk about narrow content by *mentioning* sentences.

20. This note is for afficionados only. I have argued that (Northern)Sam's belief falls within the extension of both

    (i)   "—has the (narrow) content that [pots are typically made of molybdenum]," and
    (ii) "—has the (narrow) content that [pots are typically made of aluminum]."

But it does not follow that (i) and (ii) are co-extensive. For consider the case of an expert in the North, someone who knows a great deal about how to distinguish aluminum from molybdenum and who also (broadly) believes that pots are typically made of molybdenum. Plainly, his belief is in the extension of (i). Is it also in the extension of (ii)? Not unless he has a doppelganger whose belief has the (broad) content that pots are typically made of aluminum. But if he has a doppelganger in the South, it is not at all clear that his doppelganger

The conclusion I would draw here is that the putative "radical inexpressibility" of narrow content is not a problem that Fodor need worry much about. It is easy enough to devise locutions for attributing narrow content to cognitive states, and these locutions can be used to state psychological generalizations in much the same way that locutions attributing broad content can.

3.3

As I see it, the real problem with narrow content does not derive from our inability to talk about it, and thus state generalizations in terms of it. Rather, the problem is that if the computational paradigm sketched in section 2 is on the right track, then many of the true generalizations—many of those that actually describe mental processes—are not going to be statable in terms of narrow content. The taxonomy of mental states imposed by narrow content is going to be both too coarse and too ill behaved to exploit in a serious scientific psychology. Perhaps the best way to see why a narrow content taxonomy is too coarse is to compare three taxonomic schemes: the one imposed by fat syntax, the one imposed by broad content, and the one imposed by narrow content.

Each mental state token is a brain state token; its "essential" type will be specified neurophysiologically. But a pair of brain state tokens in a pair of people may be very different neurophysiologically, and still count as tokens of the same fat syntactic type, provided that they have basically the same pattern of causal connections with stimuli, with behavior, and with other appropriate brain states. It's also worth noting that if there is a pair of neurophysiologically identical states embedded in a pair of neurophysiologically identical organisms, and if one of these states is in a fat syntactic category, the other will always be in the same fat syntactic category. Fat syntax supervenes on physiology. Our commonsense intuitions about broad content provide another scheme for classifying brain state tokens. The lesson to be learned from Twin-Earth, and from Burge's thought experiments, is that classification by broad content turns on physical, historical and linguistic *context*. Thus broad content does not supervene on physiology, and in this respect its taxonomic categories slice too finely; it sometimes puts an organism and its

---

would (broadly) believe that pots are typically made of aluminum. More likely, the relevant mental state of the expert's Southern doppelganger would be so anomalous that it would have no broad content at all. For unless the story is told in a pretty strange way, you *can't*

(a) be the doppelganger of an expert on aluminum and molybdenum who broadly believes that pots are typically made of molybdenum,
(b) live in a world in which pots are typically made of aluminum,
(c) (broadly) believe that pots are typically made of aluminum.

To see the point, imagine that the Northern expert can distinguish the two metals by touch and sight, and ask what his Southern doppelganger would say when confronting the aluminum pots that are typical in his environment.

doppelganger in different categories. Narrow content provides a third strategy for classifying brain state tokens, one which starts with broad content but ignores context. Thus, despite the terminological oddness, the categories of narrow content are larger than those imposed by a broad content taxonomy. Moreover, like fat syntax, narrow content supervenes on physiology.

All of this might lead one to suppose that the taxonomies imposed by narrow content and fat syntax *coincide*. That is, it might lead one to think that a pair of brain state tokens in a pair of individuals will be of the same fat syntactic type if and only if they have the same narrow content. However, this is all but certain to be a mistake. If we ignore the vagueness of the narrow content taxonomy, a theme to which I'll return shortly, then it may be the case that sameness of fat syntax guarantees sameness of narrow content ("plus or minus a bit," as Fodor might say).[21] But on almost any plausible reading, the categories imposed by a narrow content taxonomy are much larger than those imposed by fat syntax. Thus sameness of narrow content does not guarantee sameness of fat syntax.

The literature is full of examples that illustrate this mismatch. Perhaps the most obvious examples involve people with unusual or defective perceptual systems. To take an extreme case, consider Helen Keller. If Ms Keller were to be told by a trusted informant that there is a fat cat in the room, she would come to believe that there is a fat cat in the room. That is, she would acquire a brain state which functions like a belief and which has the (broad) content that there is a fat cat in the room. Similarly, if I were told by a trusted informant that there is a fat cat in the room, I would acquire a brain state which functions like a belief and which has the (broad) content that there is a fat cat in the room. Thus both Ms Keller's brain state and mine would have the (narrow) content that [there is a fat cat in the room]. But surely those two states differ radically in their fat syntax. There are all sorts of perceptual stimuli (both visual and auditory) that would cause me, but not Ms Keller, to acquire the belief that [there is a fat cat in the room]. And states whose patterns of causal interaction with stimuli differ substantially do not share the same fat syntax. Much the same point could be made, though perhaps less dramatically, with examples of people with other perceptual anomalies, both real, like color blindness, and imagined.[22]

---

21. Fodor (1980:240).

22. For detailed examples along these lines, see Stich (1983:66–8) and Stich (1982:185–8).

Kenneth Taylor has suggested that the objection I am urging against Fodor dissolves if we focus more steadfastly on Fodor's "official" account of narrow content which takes the narrow content of a thought to be *a function* from contexts to broad contents. On my account of narrow content, any two thoughts with the same broad content must have the same narrow content. But, Taylor urges, if we view the narrow content of a thought as a function from contexts to broad contents, then it is entirely possible that Ms Keller's thought and mine do not have the same narrow content. For there might be some contexts in which Ms Keller's thought and mine did not have the same broad content, and if this is possible, then on the function account of narrow content our thoughts do not have the same narrow content.

I am inclined to think that the function account of narrow content is more than a bit obscure. For I am not at all clear about what a *context* is; nor am I sure how we are supposed to play the game of imagining peo-

In the Helen Keller example, differences in fat syntax are due to differences in the way stimuli affect mental states. But there are also cases in which differences in syntactic type are engendered by differences in the way mental states interact with *each other*. Some people are logically acute; it is plausible to suppose that the mechanism underlying their reasoning makes many valid inferences and few invalid ones. Other people are significantly less acute; their mental mechanism makes many fewer valid inferences and many more invalid ones. On a syntactic taxonomy—*even a skinny syntactic taxonomy*—the states being manipulated by these mechanisms are of different syntactic types. But in many such cases the intuitive commonsense taxonomy of broad content classifies the states being manipulated as having the same (broad) content. And, of course, states with the same broad content have the same narrow content. In addition to these normal interpersonal differences in inferential capacities, there are also lots of pathological cases, some real and some imagined, in which people reason in ways very different from the way I reason, but where commonsense psychology is still comfortable in attributing the same broad content.[23] Here too, syntax and narrow content will diverge.

What I have been arguing is that there are major differences between a taxonomy based on narrow content and one based on fat syntax (or skinny syntax, for that matter). In many cases the syntactic taxonomy will be substantially more fine grained, and will draw substantially more distinctions, than the narrow content taxonomy. There are lots of examples in which a pair of belief state tokens will differ in their fat syntax though not in their narrow content. The reason this is important is that, along with Fodor, I have been assuming that the cognitive mind is a "syntactic engine" and that the mechanism controlling cognitive processes is "sensitive solely to syntactic properties." But if this is right, then the generalizations that describe cognitive processes will be statable in syntactic terms, and these will typically be more fine grained than generalizations statable in terms of narrow content. The generalizations of a computational theory will describe different patterns of causal interaction for cognitive states with different fat syntax, even though in many cases those states will have the same narrow content. So if the

---

ple and their thoughts embedded in other contexts. Consider the example in the text. Is Ms Keller's context different from mine? If so, what would it be for me to be in her context? Would I have to have her handicaps? Would I have to have had the same biography? The mind boggles.

But even if we suppose these questions can be answered in some coherent and principled way, I doubt the answers will do Fodor much good. To avoid the objection I am urging, it will have to be the case that the taxonomy generated by the function account of narrow content coincides with the taxonomy generated by fat syntax. And I see no reason to think this will be the case. Certainly, Fodor has offered no argument for this claim. Moreover, if as Taylor suggests, Ms Keller's belief and mine have different narrow contents on the function account, it is hard to see why the same will not be true of the beliefs of other people who broadly believe that there is a fat cat in the room, but who differ from me less radically than Ms Keller does. However, if this is the case, then the function account of narrow content runs the risk of individuating much too finely. Only doppelgangers will have thoughts with the same narrow content.

23. For some examples, see Stich (1983:68–72). For examples of a rather different sort, see Cherniak (1986). For another example, see Dennett (1981b:54–5).

computational paradigm is the right one, then many of the generalizations that describe the mind's workings are simply not going to be statable in terms of narrow content.

Throughout this section I have been writing as though the broad content taxonomy provided by commonsense psychology is reasonably clear and stable, and thus that predicates of the form "—has the (broad) content that p" have a reasonably well defined extension. However, there is good reason to doubt that this is so. Following Quine's lead, a number of writers have assembled cases which seem to show that commonsense intuitions about the extensions of such predicates are highly context sensitive. Whether or not a state can be comfortably classified as having the content that p depends, to a significant degree, on the context in which the question arises.[24] I have developed an account of the tacit principle underlying commonsense content attribution which views them as a sort of similarity judgment. This account explains their context sensitivity, and various other phenomena as well. But whether or not my explanation of the phenomena is correct, I am inclined to think that the data speak for themselves. By varying the context in which the question is asked, we can get competent users of commonsense psychology to judge that a particular cognitive state token clearly has the content that p, or that it clearly does not. If this is right, it provides yet another reason for thinking that the generalizations of a serious scientific psychology will not be statable in the taxonomic categories provided by narrow content. For the categories of a narrow content taxonomy are simply the categories of a broad content taxonomy extended to meet the demands of the principle of autonomy. But the broad content taxonomy of commonsense psychology is too vague, too context-sensitive and too unstable to use in a serious scientific theory. *Narrow* content inherits all of these deficits.

4 Keeping Score

Toward the end of section 1, I quoted the three conditions that, on Fodor's view, would have to be met by the states a psychological theory postulates, if that theory is to count as "endorsing" the propositional attitudes, and thus avoiding the "catastrophe" that would ensue "if commonsense intentional psychology really were to collapse." It's time to ask which of those conditions are likely to be met. Along with Fodor, I'll assume, as I have been all along, that the computational paradigm is correct, and that the mind is "a syntax driven machine" whose operations are "sensitive solely to syntactic properties."

The third condition on Fodor's list is that "the implicit generalizations of commonsense belief/desire psychology" must be "largely true" of the states postulated by the psychological theory in question. Presumably, Fodor's hope went something like this:

---

24. See, for example, Stich (1982:180–203), where I describe the phenomenon as the "pragmatic sensitivity" of belief attributions. See also Stich (1983:90–110). Much the same moral can be drawn from Dennett's examples of the use of intentional notions to describe trees and his example of the young child who asserts that Daddy is a doctor. For the first, see Dennett (1981a:22); for the second, see Dennett (1969:183).

The generalizations of commonsense psychology are couched in terms of (broad) content. But the Twin Earth examples show that "you can't make respectable science out of the attitudes as commonsensically individuated" (*PS*:30). Very well, then, we'll move to narrow content, since, unlike broad content, narrow content supervenes on physiology. Given any commonsense generalization about tokens of the belief that p, there will be a parallel narrow generalization—a generalization about the tokens of the belief that [p]. And that latter generalization will be scientifically respectable.

To satisfy Fodor's third condition, however, it is not sufficient that the narrow analogues of broad content generalizations be scientifically respectable. Most of them must also be true. Now if the mind really is a syntax driven machine, and if syntactic categories can be matched up, near enough, with the categories of narrow content, then it looks like we're home free. But the burden of my argument in 3.3 was that syntactic and narrow content taxonomies will not match up, because the latter is both too coarse and too ill-behaved. If the computational paradigm is correct, I argued, then many of the generalizations that describe the mind's workings are not going to be statable in terms of narrow content. If that's right, then Fodor's third condition will not be satisfied.

Let's turn, now, to Fodor's first condition; that the states a psychological theory postulates must be "semantically evaluable." How well do we fare on this one if the computational paradigm is correct? I am inclined to think that here again the ill behaved context sensitivity of semantic taxonomies poses real problems. If it is indeed the case that by varying the context of the question we can get competent users of commonsense psychology to judge that a particular cognitive state token clearly has the content that p, or that it clearly does not, then it's hard to see how even the tokens, let alone the types posited by a serious, computational, scientific psychology will be "semantically evaluable."

One final point. Suppose I am wrong about the mismatch between syntactic and narrow content taxonomies; suppose that the generalizations of a scientifically solid psychology really can be stated in terms of narrow content. Would it then follow that the states postulated by such a theory are "semantically evaluable"? Fodor himself seems ambivalent. Consider the following:

> [I]f you mean by content what can be semantically evaluated, then what my water-thoughts share with Twin "water"-thoughts *isn't* content . . . We can't say . . . what Twin thoughts have in common. This is because what can be said is ipso facto semantically evaluable; and what Twin-thoughts have in common is ipso facto not. (*PS*:50; the emphasis is Fodor's.)

But, of course, what Fodor's water-thoughts share with Twin 'water'-thoughts, what "Twin-thoughts have in common," *is* narrow content. So in this passage Fodor seems to admit—indeed insist—that narrow content is *not* semantically evaluable. Elsewhere he is even more explicit:

> You can have narrow content without functional-role semantics because *narrow contents aren't semantically evaluable*; only wide contents have conditions of satisfaction. (*PS*:83; the emphasis is Fodor's.)

Still, perhaps this is just a debater's point. For in several other passages Fodor notes that narrow content "is semantically evaluable relative to a context" (*PS*:51). And perhaps this is all that is required to satisfy his first condition. There's no need to decide the point since, as I see it, the real problem with narrow content is not that it fails to be "semantically evaluable" (whatever that might come to) but that it fails to match up with the syntactic taxonomy of a computational psychology.

The remaining item on Fodor's list of conditions is that the states posited by a psychological theory must "have causal powers." On this one Fodor wins easily. If the computational paradigm is on the right track, then the syntactically taxonomized states posited by a correct computational theory are sure to have causal powers.

By my count, the score against Fodor—and against intentional psychology—is two to one.[25]

REFERENCES

Armstrong, D. (1978). *A Theory of Universals*, Cambridge: Cambridge University Press.
Baker. L. (1987a). *Saving Belief: A Critique of Physicalism*, Princeton: Princeton University Press.
Baker, L. (1987b). "Content by courtesy," *Journal of Philosophy*, 84, 197–213.
Block, N. (1986). "Advertisement for a semantics for psychology," in P. French, T. Uehling & H. Wettstein (eds.), *Midwest Studies in Philosophy*, Vol. 10, *Studies in the Philosophy of Mind*, Minneapolis: University of Minnesota Press.
Burge, T. (1979). "Individualism and the mental," *Midwest Studies in Philosophy*, 4, 73–121.
Burge, T. (1986). "Individualism and psychology," *Philosophical Review*, 95, 1, 3–46.
Cherniak, C. (1986). *Minimal Rationality*, Cambridge, MA: MIT Press.
Dennett, D. (1969). *Content and Consciousness*, London: Routledge and Kegan Paul.
Dennett, D. (1981a). "True believers: the intentional stance and why it works," in A. Heath (ed.), *Scientific Explanation*, Oxford: Oxford University Press.
Dennett, D. (1981b). "Three kinds of intentional psychology," in R. Healy (ed.), *Reduction, Time and Reality*, Cambridge: Cambridge University Press.
Dennett, D. (1982). "Beyond belief," in A. Woodfield (ed), *Thought and Object*, Oxford: Oxford University Press.

25. I am indebted to many people for much useful conversation on these matters. Those I can recall are Daniel Dennett, Michael Devitt, Warren Dow, Jerry Fodor, Gary Hardcastle, Patricia Kitcher, Kenneth Taylor and Valerie Hardcastle. I hope the others will accept my thanks anonymously. Special thanks are due to Warren Dow for his helpful comments on an earlier version of this paper.

Devitt, M. (1989). "A narrow representational theory of the mind," in S. Silvers (ed.), *Representations: Readings in the Philosophy of Mental Representation*, Dordrecht: Kluwer.

Dow, W. (1991). *Content and Psychology*, Ph.D. thesis, Department of Philosophy, University of California–San Diego.

Fodor, J. (1975). *The Language of Thought*, Cambridge, MA: Harvard University Press.

Fodor, J. (1978). "Tom Swift and his procedural grandmother," *Cognition*, 6, 229–247.

Fodor, J. (1980). "Methodological solipsism considered as a research strategy in cognitive science," *Behavioral and Brain Sciences*, 3, 1, 63–109.

Fodor, J. (1981). *RePresentations: Philosophical Essays on the Foundations of Cognitive Science*, Cambridge, MA: MIT Press.

Fodor, J. (1987). *Psychosemantics: The Problem of Meaning in the Philosophy of Mind*, Cambridge, MA: MIT Press.

Gordon, R. (1986). "Folk psychology as simulation," *Mind and Language*, 1, 158–171.

Hardcastle, V. (1990). "In defense of a different taxonomy: a reply to Owens," *Philosophical Review*, 99(3), 425, 431.

Kim, J. (1969). "Events and their descriptions: Some considerations," in N, Rescher et al. (eds.), *Essays in Honor of C. G. Hempel*, Dordrecht: Reidel.

Kim, J. (1976). "Events as property exemplifications," in M, Brand & D, Walton (eds.), *Action Theory*, Dordrecht: Reidel.

Kitcher, P. (1985). "Narrow taxonomy and wide functionalism," *Philosophy of Science*, 52, 1, 78–97.

Levin, J. (1988). "Must reasons be rational?" *Philosophy of Science*, 55.

Loar, B. (1987). "Social content and psychological content," in R. Grimm & D. Merrill (eds.), *Contents of Thought: Proceedings of the 1985 Oberlin Colloquium in Philosophy*, Tucson: University of Arizona Press.

Lycan, W. (1988). *Judgment and Justification*, Cambridge: Cambridge University Press.

Owens, J. (1987). "In defense of a different doppelganger," *Philosophical Review*, 96, 521–554.

Putnam, H. (1975a). "The meaning of 'meaning'" in Putnam (1975b).

Putnam, H. (1975b). *Mind, Language and Reality*, Cambridge: Cambridge University Press.

Putnam, H. (1978). *Meaning and the Moral Sciences*, London: Routledge & Kegan Paul.

Putnam, H. (1983). "Computational psychology and interpretation theory," in *Realism and Reason*, Philosophical Papers (Vol. 3), Cambridge: Cambridge University Press.

Quine, W. V. (1960). *Word and Object*, Cambridge, MA: MIT Press.

Ramsey, W., Stich, S. and Garon, J. (1990). "Connectionism, eliminativism and the future of folk psychology," *Philosophical Perspectives*, 4: *Action Theory and Philosophy of Mind*, 499–533.

Schiffer, S. (1981). "Truth and the theory of content," in H. Parrett & P. Bouverese (eds.), *Meaning and Understanding*, Berlin & New York: de Gruyter.

Stack, M. (unpublished). "Why I don't believe in beliefs and you shouldn't either," paper delivered at the annual meeting of the Society for Philosophy and Psychology, 1980.

Stich, S. (1982). "On the ascription of content," in A. Woodfield (ed.), *Thought and Object*, Oxford: Oxford University Press.

Stich, S. (1983). *From Folk Psychology to Cognitive Science: The Case Against Belief*, Cambridge, MA: MIT Press/Bradford Books.

9

FOLK PSYCHOLOGY

Simulation or Tacit Theory?

Stephen Stich and Shaun Nichols

1 Introduction

A central goal of contemporary cognitive science is the explanation of cognitive abilities or capacities (Cummins, 1983). During the last three decades a wide range of cognitive capacities have been subjected to careful empirical scrutiny. The adult's ability to produce and comprehend natural language sentences and the child's capacity to acquire a natural language were among the first to be explored (Chomsky, 1965; Fodor, Bever and Garrett, 1974; Pinker, 1989). There is also a rich literature on the ability to solve mathematical problems (Greeno, 1983), the ability to recognize objects visually (Rock, 1983; Gregory, 1970; Marr, 1982), the ability to manipulate and predict the behavior of middle-sized physical objects (McClosky, 1983; Hayes, 1985), and a host of others.

In all of this work, the dominant explanatory strategy proceeds by positing an internally represented 'knowledge structure'—typically a body of rules or principles or propositions—which serves to guide the execution of the capacity to be explained. These rules or principles or propositions are often described as the agent's 'theory' of the domain in question. In some cases, the theory may be partly accessible to consciousness; the agent can tell us some of the rules or principles he is using. More often, however, the agent has no conscious access to the knowledge guiding his behavior. The theory is 'tacit'

We are grateful to Jerry Fodor for his helpful comments on an earlier version of this paper. Thanks are also due to Joseph Franchi for help in preparing the figures.

(Chomsky, 1965) or 'sub-doxastic' (Stich, 1978). Perhaps the earliest philosophical account of this explanatory strategy is set out in Jerry Fodor's paper, 'The Appeal to Tacit Knowledge in Psychological Explanation' (Fodor, 1968). Since then, the idea has been elaborated by Dennett (1978a), Lycan (1981; 1988), and a host of others.

Among the many cognitive capacities that people manifest, there is one cluster that holds a particular fascination for philosophers. Included in this cluster is the ability to *describe* people and their behavior (including their linguistic behavior) *in intentional terms*—or to 'interpret' them, as philosophers sometimes say. We exercise this ability when we describe John as *believing that the mail has come*, or when we say that Anna *wants to go to the library*. By exploiting these intentional descriptions, people are able to offer explanations of each other's behavior (Susan left the building *because* she believed that it was on fire) and to *predict* each other's behavior, often with impressive accuracy. Since the dominant strategy for explaining any cognitive capacity is to posit an internally represented theory, it is not surprising that in this area, too, it is generally assumed that a theory is being invoked (Churchland, 1981, 1989; Fodor, 1987; Sellars, 1963; see also Olson et al., 1988). The term 'folk psychology' has been widely used as a label for the largely tacit psychological theory that underlies these abilities. During the last decade or so there has been a fair amount of empirical work aimed at describing or modeling folk psychology and tracking its emergence and development in the child (D'Andrade, 1987; Leslie, 1987; Astington et al., 1988).

Recently, however, Robert Gordon, Alvin Goldman and a number of other philosophers have offered a bold challenge to the received view about the cognitive mechanisms underlying our ability to describe, predict and explain people's behavior (Goldman, 1989; Gordon, 1986; unpublished; Montgomery, 1987; Ripstein, 1987; Heal, 1986).[1] Though they differ on the details, these philosophers agree in denying that an internally represented folk-psychological theory plays a central role in the exercise of these abilities. They also agree that a special sort of mental *simulation* in which we use ourselves as a model for the person we are describing or predicting, will play an important role in the correct account of the mechanisms subserving these abilities. In this paper, although we will occasionally mention the view of other advocates of simulation, our principal focus will be on Gordon and Goldman.

If these philosophers are right, two enormously important consequences will follow. First, of course, the dominant explanatory strategy in cognitive science, the strategy that appeals to internally represented knowledge structures, will be shown to be mistaken in at least one crucial corner of our mental lives. And if it is mistaken there, then perhaps theorists exploring other cognitive capacities can no longer simply take the strategy for granted.

---

1. We are grateful to Professor Gordon for providing us with copies of his unpublished papers, and for allowing us to quote from them at some length.

To explain the second consequence we will need a quick review of one of the central debates in recent philosophy of mind. The issue in the debate is the very existence of the intentional mental states that are appealed to in our ordinary explanations of behavior— states like believing, desiring, thinking, hoping, and the rest. *Eliminativists* maintain that there really are no such things. Beliefs and desires are like phlogiston, caloric and witches; they are the mistaken posits of a radically false theory. The theory in question is 'folk psychology'—the collection of psychological principles and generalizations which, according to eliminativists (and most of their opponents) underlies our everyday explanations of behavior. The central premise in the eliminativist's argument is that neuroscience (or connectionism or cognitive science) is on the verge of demonstrating persuasively that folk psychology is false. But if Gordon and Goldman are right, they will have pulled the rug out from under the eliminativists. For if what underlies our ordinary explanatory practice is not a theory at all, then obviously it cannot be a radically false theory. There is a certain delightful irony in the Gordon/Goldman attack on eliminativism. Indeed, one might almost view it as attempting a bit of philosophical ju-jitsu. The eliminativists claim that there are no such things as beliefs and desires because the folk psychology that posits them is a radically false theory. Gordon and Goldman claim that the theory which posits a tacitly known folk psychology is *itself* radically false, since there are much better ways of explaining people's abilities to interpret and predict behavior. Thus, if Gordon and Goldman are right, *there is no such thing as folk psychology!* (Gordon, ch. 2, p. 71; Goldman, ch. 3, p. 93.)

There can be no doubt that if Gordon and Goldman are right, then the impact on both cognitive science and the philosophy of mind will be considerable. But it is a lot easier to doubt that their views about mental simulation are defensible. The remainder of this paper will be devoted to developing these doubts. Here's the game plan for the pages to follow. In sections 2 and 3, we will try to get as clear as we can on what the simulation theorists claim. We'll begin, in section 2, with an account of the special sort of simulation that lies at the heart of the Gordon/Goldman proposal. In that section our focus will be on the way that simulation might be used in the *prediction* of behavior. In section 3, we'll explore the ways in which mental simulation might be used to explain the other two cognitive capacities that have been of special interest to philosophers: *explaining* behavior and producing *intentional descriptions* or *interpretations*. We'll also consider the possibility that simulation might be used in explaining the *meaning* of intentional terms like 'believes,' and 'desires.' Since the accounts of simulation that Gordon and Goldman have offered have been a bit sketchy, there will be a lot of filling in to do in sections 2 and 3. But throughout both sections, our goal will be sympathetic interpretation; we've tried hard not to build straw men. In the following two sections, our stance turns critical. In section 4, we will do our best to assemble all the arguments offered by Gordon and Goldman in support of their simulation theory, and to explain why none of them are convincing. In section 5 we will offer two arguments of our own, aimed at showing why, in light of currently available evidence, the simulation theory is very implausible indeed. Section 6 is a brief conclusion.

2 Predicting Behavior: Theory, Simulation, and Imagination

Suppose that you are an aeronautical engineer and that you want to predict how a newly built plane will behave at a certain speed. There are two rather different ways in which you might proceed. One way is to sit down with pencil and paper, a detailed set of specifications of the plane, and a state of the art textbook on aerodynamic theory, and try to calculate what the theory entails about the behavior of the plane. Alternatively, you could build a model of the plane, put it in a wind tunnel, and observe how it behaves. You have to use a bit of theory in this second strategy, of course, since you have to have some idea which properties of the plane you want to duplicate in your model. But there is a clear sense in which a theory is playing the central role in the first prediction and a model or simulation is playing a central role in the second.[2]

Much the same story could be told if what you want to do is predict the behavior of a person. Suppose, for example, you want to predict what a certain rising young political figure would do if someone in authority tells him to administer painful electric shocks to a person strapped in a chair in the next room. One approach is to gather as much data as you can about the history and personality of the politician and then consult the best theory available on the determinants of behavior under such circumstances. Another approach is to set up a Milgram-style experiment and observe how some other people behave. Naturally, it would be a good idea to find experimental subjects who are psychologically similar to the political figure whose behavior you are trying to predict. Here, as before, theory plays a central role in the first prediction, while a simulation plays a central role in the second.

In both the aeronautical case and the psychological case, we have been supposing that much of the predicting process is carried on outside the predictor. You do your calculations on a piece of paper; your simulations are done in wind tunnels or laboratories. But, of course, it will often be possible to internalize this process. The case is clearest when a theory is being used. Rather than looking in a textbook, you could memorize the theory, and rather than doing the calculations on a piece of paper, you could do them in your head. Moreover, it seems entirely possible that you could learn the theory so well that you are hardly conscious of using it or of doing any explicit calculation or reasoning. Indeed, this, near enough, is the standard story about a wide variety of cognitive capacities.

A parallel story might be told for predictions using simulations. Rather than building a model and putting it in a wind tunnel, you could *imagine* the model in the wind tunnel and see how your imaginary model behaves. Similarly, you could *imagine* putting someone in a Milgram-style laboratory and see how your imaginary subject behaves. But obviously there is a problem lurking here. For while it is certainly possible to imagine a plane

---

2. The wind tunnel analogy is suggested by Ripstein (1987, p. 475ff). Gordon also mentions the analogy in Gordon (1995), but he puts it to a rather different use.

in a wind tunnel, it is not at all clear how you could successfully imagine the behavior of the plane unless you had a fair amount of detailed information about the behavior of planes in situations like this one. When the simulation uses a real model plane, the world tells you how the model will behave. You just have to look and see. But when you are only imagining the simulation, there is no real model for you to look at. So it seems that you must have an internalized knowledge structure to guide your imagination. The theory or knowledge structure that you are exploiting may, of course, be a tacit one, and you may be quite unaware that you are using it. But unless we suppose your imagination is guided by some systematic body of information about the behavior of planes in situations like this one, the success of your prediction would be magic.

When you are imagining the behavior of a person, however, there are various ways in which the underlying system might work. One possibility is that imagining the behavior of a person is entirely parallel to imagining the behavior of a plane. In both cases your imagination is guided by a largely tacit theory or knowledge structure. But there is also a very different mechanism that might be used. In the plane case, you don't have a real plane to observe, so you have to rely on some stored information about planes. You do, however, have a real, human cognitive system to observe—your own. Here's a plausible, though obviously over-simplified, story about how that system normally works:

> At any given time you have a large store of beliefs and desires. Some of the beliefs are derived from perception, others from inference. Some of the desires (like the desire to get a drink) arise from systems monitoring bodily states, others (like the desire to go into the kitchen) are 'sub-goals' generated by the decision-making (or 'practical reasoning') system. The decision-making system, which takes your beliefs and desires as input, does more than generate sub-goals, it also somehow or other comes up with a decision about what to do. That decision is then passed on to the 'action controllers'—the mental mechanisms responsible for sequencing and coordinating the behavior necessary to carry out the decision. (Rendered boxologically, the account just sketched appears in figure 1.)

Now suppose that it is possible to take the decision making system 'off-line' by disengaging the connection between the system and the action controllers. You might then use it to generate decisions that you are not about to act on. Suppose further that in this off-line mode, you can feed the decision-making system some hypothetical or 'pretend' beliefs and desires—beliefs and desires that you do not actually have, but that the person whose behavior you're trying to predict does. If all this were possible, you could then sit back and let the system generate a decision. Moreover, if your decision-making system is similar to the one in the person whose behavior you're trying to predict, and if the hypothetical beliefs and desires you've fed into your system off-line are close to the ones that he has, then the decision that your system generates will often be similar to the one that his system generates. There is no need for a special internalized knowledge structure

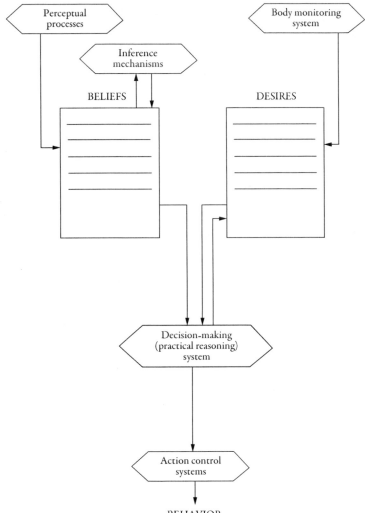

FIGURE I

here; no tacit folk-psychological theory is being used. Rather, you are using (part of) your own cognitive mechanism as a model for (part of) his. Moreover, just as in the case where the prediction exploits a theory, this whole process may be largely unconscious. It may be that all you are aware of is the prediction itself. Alternatively, if you consciously imagine what the target of your prediction will do, it could well be the case that your imagination is guided by this simulation rather than by some internally represented psychological theory.

We now have at least the outline of an account of how mental simulation might be used in predicting another person's behavior. An entirely parallel story can be told about predicting our own behavior under counterfactual circumstances. If, for example, I want to know what I would do if I believed that there was a burglar in the basement, I can simply take my decision-making system off-line and provide it with the pretend belief that there is a burglar in the basement.[3]

In the next section we'll try to get clear on how this process of simulation might be used in explaining various other cognitive capacities. But before attending to that task, we would do well to assemble a few quotes to confirm our claim that the story we've told is very close to the one that those we'll be criticizing have in mind. Gordon is much more explicit than Goldman on the use of simulation in prediction. Here's a passage from his 1986 paper (p. 70):

> [O]ur decision-making or practical reasoning system gets partially disengaged from its 'natural' inputs and fed instead with suppositions and images (or their 'subpersonal' or 'sub-doxastic' counterparts). Given these artificial pretend inputs the system then 'makes up its mind' what to do. Since the system is being run off-line, as it were, disengaged also from its natural output systems, its 'decision' isn't actually executed but rather ends up as an anticipation . . . of the other's behavior.

And another, this time from an unpublished manuscript contrasting his view to Fodor's:

> The Simulation Theory as I present it holds that we explain and predict behavior not by applying a theory but simply by exercising a skill that has two components: the capacity for practical reasoning—roughly, for making decisions on the basis of facts and values—and the capacity to introduce 'pretend' facts and values into one's decision-making typically to adjust for relevant differences in situation and past behavior. One predicts what the other will decide to do by making a decision oneself—a 'pretend' decision, of course, made only in imagination—after making such adjustments. (Gordon, unpublished, p. 3)

Gordon later suggests that the capacity to simulate in this way may be largely innate:

> [Evidence] suggests that the readiness for simulation is a prepackaged 'module' called upon automatically in the perception of other human beings.[4] It suggests also that supporting and complementing the conscious, reportable procedure we call putting ourselves in the other's place, those neural systems that are responsible for the formation of emotions and intentions are, often without our knowledge,

---

3. The burglar in the basement example is borrowed from Gordon (1995, p. 62).

4. The evidence Gordon cites includes the tendency to mimic other people's facial expressions and overt bodily movements, and the tendency in both humans and other animals to direct one's eyes to the target of a conspecific's gaze.

allowed to run off-line: They are partially disengaged from their 'natural' inputs from perception and memory and fed artificial pretend inputs; uncoupled also from their natural output systems, they terminate not as intentions and emotions but as anticipations of, or perhaps just unconscious motor adjustments to, the other's intentions, emotions, behavior. (Gordon, unpublished, p. 5)

3 Other Uses for Simulation: Explanation, Interpretation, and the Meaning of Intentional Terms

Let's turn, now, to people's ability to offer *intentional explanations* of other people's actions. How might mental simulation be used to account for that ability? Consider, for example, a case similar to one proposed by Gordon.[5] We are seated at a restaurant and someone comes up to us and starts speaking to us in a foreign language. How might simulation be exploited in producing an intentional explanation for that behavior?

One proposal, endorsed by both Gordon and Goldman, begins with the fact that simulations can be used in predictions, and goes on to suggest that intentional explanations can be generated by invoking something akin to the strategy of analysis-by-synthesis. In using simulations to predict behavior, hypothetical beliefs and desires are fed into our own decision-making system (being used 'off-line' of course), and we predict that the agent would do what we would decide to do, given those beliefs and desires. A first step in *explaining* a behavioral episode that has already occurred is to see if we can find some hypothetical beliefs and desires which, when fed into our decision mechanism, will produce a decision to perform the behavior we want to explain.

Generally, of course, there will be *lots* of hypothetical beliefs and desires that might lead us to the behavior in question. Here are just a few:

(a) If we believe someone only speaks a certain foreign language and we want to ask him something, then we would decide to speak to him in that language.
(b) If we want to impress someone and we believe that speaking in a foreign language will impress him, then we will decide to speak to him in that language.
(c) If we believe that speaking to someone in a foreign language will make him laugh, and if we want to make him laugh, then we will decide to speak to him in that language.

And so on. Each of these simulation-based predictions provides the kernel for a possible explanation of the behavior we are trying to explain. To decide among these alternative explanations, we must determine which of the input belief/desire pairs is most plausibly attributed to the agent. Some belief/desire pairs will be easy to exclude. Perhaps the

5. Gordon pp. 64 ff.

agent is a dour fellow; he never wants to make anyone laugh. If we believe this to be the case, then (c) won't be very plausible. In other cases we can use information about the agent's perceptual situation to assess the likelihood of various beliefs. If Mary has just made a rude gesture directly in front of the agent, then it is likely the agent will believe that Mary has insulted him. If the rude gesture was made behind the agent's back, then it is not likely he will believe that she has insulted him. In still other cases, we may have some pre-existing knowledge of the agent's beliefs and desires. But, as both Goldman and Gordon note, it will often be the case that there are lots of alternative explanations that can't be excluded on the basis of evidence about the agent's circumstances or his history. In these cases, Goldman maintains, we simply assume that the agent is psychologically similar to us—we attribute beliefs that are 'natural for us' (Goldman, 1989, p. 90) and reject (or perhaps do not even consider) hypotheses attributing beliefs that we consider to be less natural (pp. 90–1). Gordon tells much the same story (1986, p. 65):[6]

> No matter how long I go on testing hypotheses, I will not have tried out *all* candidate explanations of the [agent's] behavior. Perhaps some of the unexamined candidates would have done at least as well as the one I settle for, if I settle: perhaps indefinitely many of them would have. But these would be 'far fetched,' I say intuitively. Therein I exhibit my inertial bias. The less 'fetching' (or 'stretching,' as actors say) I have to do to track the other's behavior, the better. I tend to *feign* only when necessary, only when something in the other's behavior doesn't fit. This inertial bias may be thought of as a 'least effort' principle: the 'principle of least pretending.' It explains why, other things being equal, I will prefer the less radical departure from the 'real' world—i.e. from what I myself take to be the world.[7]

6. Ripstein's account of the role of simulation in intentional exlanation is quite similar.

I wish to defend the claim that imagining what it would be like to be in 'someone else's shoes' can serve to explain that person's actions ... I shall argue that imagining oneself in someone else's situation ... allows actions to be explained without recourse to a theory of human behavior. (Ripstein, 1987, p. 465)

[T]he same sort of modeling [that engineers use when they study bridges in wind tunnels] is important to commonsense psychology: I can use my personality to model yours by 'trying on' various combinations of beliefs, desires and character traits. In following an explanation of what you do, I use my personality to determine that the factors mentioned would produce the result in question ... I do not need to know how you work because I can rely on the fact that I work in a similar way. My model ... underwrites the explanation by demonstrating that particular beliefs and character traits would lead to particular actions under normal circumstances. (Ripstein, 1987, pp. 476–7)

7. As Jerry Fodor has pointed out to us, the logical geography is actually a bit more complex than figure 2 suggests. To see the point, consider the box labeled 'Decision-making (practical reasoning) system' in figure 1. Gordon and Goldman tell us relatively little about the contents of this box. They provide no account of how the practical reasoning system goes about the job of producing decisions from beliefs and desires. However, there are some theorists—Fodor assures us that he is one—who believe that the practical reasoning system goes about its business by exploiting an internally represented decision theory. If this is right, then we exploit a tacit theory each time we make a decision based on our beliefs and desires. But now if we make predictions

Though the views endorsed by Gordon and Goldman are generally very similar, the two writers do differ in their emphasis. For Gordon, prediction and explanation loom large, while for Goldman, the capacity to *interpret* people, or to describe them in intentional terms, is given pride of place. Part of the story Goldman tells about simulation-based intentional description relies on the account of simulation-based explanation that we have just sketched. One of the ways we determine which beliefs and desires to attribute to people is by observing their behavior and then attributing the intentional states that best explain their behavior. A second simulation-based strategy for determining which beliefs and desires to attribute focuses on the agent's perceptual situation and on his or her 'basic likings or cravings' (Goldman, 1989, p. 82):

> From your perceptual situation, I infer that you have certain perceptual experiences or beliefs, the same ones I would have in your situation. I may also assume (pending information to the contrary) that you have the same basic likings that I have: for food, love, warmth, and so on.

As we read them, there is only one important point on which Gordon and Goldman actually *dis*agree. The accounts of simulation-based prediction, explanation

---

about other people's behavior by taking our own practical reasoning system off-line, then we also exploit a tacit theory when we make these predictions. Thus, contrary to the suggestion in figure 2, off-line simulation processes and processes exploiting an internally represented theory are not mutually exclusive, since some off-line simulation processes may also exploit a tacit theory.

In the pages that follow, we propose to be as accommodating as possible to our opponents and to make things as hard as possible for ourselves. It is our contention that prediction, explanation and interpretation of the sorts we have discussed do not use an off-line simulation process, *period*. So if it turns out that Fodor is right (because the practical reasoning system embodies an internally represented theory) *and* that Gordon and Goldman are right (because we predict and explain by taking this system off-line), then we lose, and they win. Also, of course, if Fodor is wrong about how the practical reasoning system works but Gordon and Goldman are right about prediction, explanation and interpretation, again we lose and they win. So as we construe the controversy, it pits those who advocate any version of the off-line simulation account against those who think that prediction, explanation and interpretation are subserved by a tacit theory *stored somewhere other than in the practical reasoning system*. But do keep in mind that we interpret 'theory' broadly. So, for example, if it turns out that there is some non-sentence-like, non-rule-based module which stores the information that is essential to folk-psychological prediction and explanation, and if this module is not used at all in ordinary 'on-line' practical reasoning and decision-making, then we win and they lose.

It might be protested that in drawing the battle lines as we propose to draw them, we are conceding to the opposition a position that they never intended to occupy. As we have already noted, Gordon and Goldman expend a fair amount of effort arguing that a tacit theory is not exploited in folk-psychological prediction and explanation. Since they think that the practical reasoning system *is* exploited in folk-psychological prediction and explanation, presumably they would deny that the practical reasoning system uses an internally represented decision theory. So it is a bit odd to say that *they* win if Fodor is right about the practical reasoning system and they are right about off-line simulation. This is a point we happily concede. It is a bit odd to draw the battle lines in this way. But in doing so, we are only making things more difficult for ourselves. For we must argue that *however the practical reasoning system works* we do not predict and explain other people's behavior by taking the system off-line.

and interpretation that we have sketched all seem to require that the person doing the simulating must already understand intentional notions like belief and desire. A person can't pretend he believes that the cookies are in the cookie jar unless he understands what it is to believe that the cookies are in the cookie jar; nor can a person imagine that she wants to make her friend laugh unless she understands what it is to want to make someone laugh. Moreover, as Goldman notes, when simulation is used to attribute intentional states to agents, it 'assumes a prior understanding of what state it is that the interpreter attributes to [the agent]' (Goldman, 1989, p. 94). Can the process of simulation somehow be used to explain the meaning or truth conditions of locutions like '*S* believes that *p*' and '*S* desires that *q*'? Goldman is skeptical, and tells us that 'the simulation theory looks distinctly unpromising on this score' (1989, p. 93). But Gordon is much more sanguine. Building on earlier suggestions by Quine, Davidson and Stich, he proposes the following account (Gordon, 1986, p. 68):

> My suggestion is that
> (2) [*Smith believes that* Dewey won the election]
> to be read as saying the same thing as
> (1) [Let's do a Smith simulation. Ready? *Dewey won the election*]
> though less explicitly.

We are not at all sure we understand this proposal, and Gordon himself concedes that 'the exposition and defense of this account of belief are much in need of further development' (1986, p. 68). But no matter. We think we do understand the simulation-based accounts of prediction, explanation and interpretation that Gordon and Goldman both endorse. We're also pretty certain that none of these accounts is correct. In the sections that follow, we will try to say why.

4 Arguments in Support of Simulation-based Accounts

In this section we propose to assemble all the arguments we've been able to find in favor of simulation-based accounts and say why we don't think any of them is persuasive. Then, in the following section, we will go on to offer some arguments of our own aimed at showing that there is lots of evidence that simulation-based accounts cannot easily accommodate, though more traditional theory-based accounts can. Before turning to the arguments, however, we would do well to get a bit clearer about the questions that the arguments are (and are not) intended to answer.

The central idea in the accounts offered by Gordon and Goldman is that in predicting, explaining or interpreting other people we simulate them by using part of *our own* cognitive systems 'off-line.' There might, of course, be other kinds of simulation in which we do not exploit our own decision-making system in order to model the person we are simulating. But these other sorts of simulation are not our current concern. To avoid confusion, we will henceforth use the term *off-line simulation* for the sort of simulation that Gordon and Goldman propose. The question in dispute, then, is whether off-line simulation plays a central role in predicting, explaining or interpreting other people. Gordon and Goldman say yes; we say no.

It would appear that the only serious alternatives to the off-line simulation story are various versions of the 'theory-theory' which maintain that prediction, explanation and interpretation exploit an internally represented theory or knowledge structure—a tacitly known 'folk psychology.' So if an advocate of off-line simulation can mount convincing arguments against the theory-theory, then he can reasonably claim to have made his case. The theory-theory is not the only game in town, but it is the only *other* game in town. It is not surprising, then, that in defending off-line simulation Gordon and Goldman spend a fair amount of time raising objections to the theory-theory.

There are, however, some important distinctions to be drawn among different types of theory-theories. Until fairly recently, most models that aimed at explaining cognitive capacities posited internally represented knowledge structures that invoked explicit rules or explicit sentence-like principles. But during the last decade there has been a growing dissatisfaction with sentence-based and rule-based knowledge structures, and a variety of alternatives have been explored. Perhaps the most widely discussed alternatives are connectionist models in which the knowledge used in making predictions is stored in the connection strengths between the nodes of a network. In many of these systems it is difficult or impossible to view the network as encoding a set of sentences or rules (Ramsey, Stich and Garon, 1990). Other theorists have proposed quite different ways in which non-sentential and non-rule-like strategies could be used to encode information. (See, for example, Johnson-Laird, 1983.)

Unfortunately, there is no terminological consensus in this domain. Some writers prefer to reserve the term 'theory' for sentence-like or rule-based systems. For these writers, most connectionist models do not invoke what they would call an internally represented theory. Other writers are more liberal in their use of 'theory,' and are prepared to count just about any internally stored body of information about a given domain as an internally represented theory of that domain. For these writers, connectionist models and other non-sentential models do encode a tacit theory. We don't think there is any substantive issue at stake here. But the terminological disagreements can generate a certain amount of confusion. Thus, for example, someone who used 'theory' in the more restrictive way might well conclude that if a connectionist (or some other non-sentence-based) account of our ability to predict other people's behavior turns out to be the right one, then the theory-theory is mistaken. So far, so good. But it is important to see that the falsity of the theory-theory (narrowly construed) is no comfort at all to the off-line simulation theorist. The choice between off-line simulation theories and theory-theories is plausibly viewed as exhaustive only when 'theory' is used in the *wide* rather than the restrictive way. For the remainder of this paper, we propose to adopt the wide interpretation of 'theory.' Using this terminology, the geography of the options confronting us is

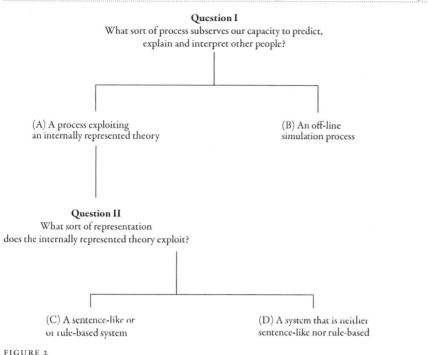

Question I
What sort of process subserves our capacity to predict,
explain and interpret other people?

(A) A process exploiting
an internally represented theory

(B) An off-line
simulation process

Question II
What sort of representation
does the internally represented theory exploit?

(C) A sentence-like or
or rule-based system

(D) A system that is neither
sentence-like nor rule-based

FIGURE 2

represented in figure 2. In the pages that follow, we will be defending option (A) in answer to Question (I). We take no stand at all on Question (II). So much for getting clear on the questions. Now let's turn to the arguments.

Argument 1: No one has been able to state the principles of the internally represented folk-psychological theory posited by the theory-theory.

Both Goldman and Gordon go on at some length about the fact that it has proven very difficult to state the principles or laws of the folk psychological theory that, according to the theory-theorist, guide our interpretations and predictions (Goldman, 1989, p. 167):

> [A]ttempts by philosophers to articulate the putative laws or 'platitudes' that comprise our folk theory have been notably weak. Actual illustrations of such laws are sparse in number; and when examples are adduced, they commonly suffer from one of two defects: vagueness and inaccuracy . . . But why, one wonders, should it be so difficult to articulate laws if we appeal to them all the time in our interpretative practice? (See also Gordon, 1986, p. 67; and unpublished, sec. 3.7.)

Reply: Goldman is certainly right about one thing. It is indeed very difficult to articulate the principles of folk psychology precisely and accurately. But it is hard to see why this fact should be of any comfort to advocates of the off-line simulation theory. For much the same could be said about the knowledge structures underlying all sorts of cognitive capacities. It has proven enormously difficult to state the principles underlying a speaker's capacity to judge the grammaticality of sentences in his language. Indeed, after three decades of sustained effort, we don't have a good grammar for even a single natural language. Nor do we have a good account of the principles underlying people's everyday judgements about the behavior of middle-sized physical objects, or about their ability to solve mathematical problems, or about their ability to play chess, etc. But, of course, in all of these domains, the theory-theory really is the only game in town. The off-line simulation story makes no sense as an account of our ability to judge grammaticality, or of our ability to predict the behavior of projectiles.

The difficulties encountered by those who have sought to describe the rules or principles underlying our grammatical (or mathematical or physical) abilities have convinced a growing number of theorists that our knowledge in these domains is not stored in the form of rules or principles. That conviction has been an important motive for the development of connectionist and other sorts of non-sentential and non-rule-based models. But none of this should encourage an advocate of the off-line simulation theory. The dispute between connectionist models and rule-based models is the dispute between (C) and (D) in figure 2. And that is a dispute *among theory-theorists*. Of course on a narrow interpretation of 'theory,' on which only rule-based and sentence-based models count as theories, the success of connectionism would indeed show that the 'theory-theory' is mistaken. But, as we have taken pains to note, a refutation of the theory-theory will support the off-line simulation account only when 'theory' is interpreted broadly.

Argument 2: Mental simulation models have been used with some success by a number of cognitive scientists.

Here's how Goldman makes the point (1989, p. 86):

> [S]everal cognitive scientists have recently endorsed the idea of mental simulation as one cognitive heuristic, although these researchers stress its use for knowledge in general, not specifically knowledge of others' mental states. Kahneman and Tversky (1982) propose that people often try to answer questions about the world by an operation that resembles the running of a simulation model. The starting condition for a 'run,' they say, can either be left at realistic default values or modified to assume some special contingency. Similarly, Rumelhart [et al.] describe the importance of 'mental models' of the world, in particular, models that simulate how the world would respond to one's hypothetical actions.

Reply: Here, again, it is our suspicion that ambiguity between the two interpretations of 'theory' is lurking in the background and leading to mischief. The 'simulation' models that

Goldman cites are the sort that would be classified under (D) in figure 2. If they are used in the best explanation of a given cognitive capacity, then that capacity is subserved by a tacit theory, and *not* by an off-line simulation. Of course when 'theory' is read narrowly, this sort of simulation will not count as a tacit theory. But, as already noted, on the narrow reading of 'theory' the falsity of internalized theory accounts lends no support at all to the off-line simulation theory.

Argument 3: 'To apply the alleged common-sense theory would demand anomalous precocity.'

What we've just quoted is a section heading in one of Gordon's unpublished papers.[8] He goes on to note that recent studies have shown children as young as two and a half 'already see behavior as dependent on belief and desire.' It is, he suggests, more than a bit implausible that children this young could acquire and use 'a theory as complex and sophisticated' as the one that the theory-theory attributes to them. Goldman elaborates the argument as follows (1985, p. 80):

> [C]hildren seem to display interpretive skills by the age of four, five or six. If interpretation is indeed guided by laws of folk psychology, the latter must be known (or believed) by this age. Are such children sophisticated enough to represent such principles? And how, exactly, would they acquire them? One possible mode of acquisition is cultural transmission (e.g. being taught them explicitly by their elders). This is clearly out of the question, though, since only philosophers have even tried to articulate the laws, and most children have no exposure to philosophers. Another possible mode of acquisition is private construction. Each child constructs the generalizations for herself, perhaps taking clues from verbal explanations of behavior which she hears. But if this construction is supposed to occur along the lines of familiar modes of scientific theory construction, some anomalous things must take place. For one thing, all children miraculously construct the same nomological principles. This is what the (folk-) theory theory ostensibly implies, since it imputes a single folk psychology to everyone. In normal cases of hypothesis construction, however, different scientists come up with different theories.

Reply: There is no doubt that if the theory-theory is right, then the child's feat is indeed an impressive one. Moreover, it is implausible to suppose that the swift acquisition of folk psychology is subserved by the same learning mechanism that the child uses to learn history or chemistry or astronomy. But, once again, we find it hard to see how this can be taken as an argument against the theory-theory and in favor of the off-line simulation

---

8. Gordon (unpublished), sec. 3.5.

theory. For there are other cases in which the child's accomplishment is comparably impressive and comparably swift. If contemporary generative grammar is even *close* to being right, the knowledge structures that underlie a child's linguistic ability are enormously complex. Yet children seem to acquire the relevant knowledge structures even more quickly than they acquire their knowledge of folk psychology. Moreover, children in the same linguistic community all acquire much the same grammar, despite being exposed to significantly different samples of what will become their native language. Less is known about the knowledge structures underlying children's abilities to anticipate the behavior of middle-sized physical objects. But there is every reason to suppose that this 'folk physics' is at least as complex as folk psychology, and that it is acquired with comparable speed. Given the importance of all three knowledge domains, it is plausible to suppose that natural selection has provided the child with lots of help—either in the form of innate knowledge structures or in the form of special-purpose learning mechanisms. But whatever the right story about acquisition turns out to be, it is perfectly clear that in the case of grammar, and in the case of folk physics, what is acquired must be some sort of internally represented theory. Off-line simulation could not possibly account for our skills in those domains. Since the speed of language acquisition and the complexity of the knowledge acquired do not (indeed, could not) support an off-line simulation account of linguistic ability, we fail to see why Gordon and Goldman think that considerations of speed and complexity lend any support at all to the off-line simulation account for our skills in predicting, explaining and interpreting behavior.

Argument 4: The off-line simulation theory is much simpler than the theory-theory.

Other things being equal, we should surely prefer a simple theory to a more complex one. And on Gordon's view (unpublished, sec. 3, p. 7):

> the simulation alternative makes [the theory-theory] strikingly unparsimonious. Insofar as the store of causal generalizations posited by [the theory-theory] mirrors the set of rules *our own* thinking typically conforms to, the Simulation Theory renders it altogether otiose. For whatever rules our own thinking typically conforms to, our thinking continues to conform to them within the context of simulation . . . In the light of this far simpler alternative, the hypothesis that people must be endowed with a special stock of laws corresponding to rules of logic and reasoning is unmotivated and unparsimonious.

Reply: When comparing the simplicity of a pair of theories, it is important to look at the whole theory in both cases, not just at isolated parts. It is our contention that if one takes this broader perspective, the greater parsimony of the simulation theory simply disappears. To see the point, note that for both the theory-theory and the simulation theory the mechanism subserving our predictions of other people's behavior must have two components. One of these may be thought of as a data base that somehow stores or embodies information about how people behave. The other component is a mechanism which applies that information to the case at hand—it extracts the relevant facts from the data base. Now if we look only at the data base, it does indeed seem that the theory-theory is 'strikingly unparsimonious' since it must posit an elaborate system of internally represented generalizations or rules—or perhaps some other format for encoding the regularities of folk psychology. The simulation theory, by contrast, uses the mind's decision-making system as its 'data base,' and that decision-making system would have to be there on any theory, because it explains how we make real, 'on-line' decisions. So the off-line simulation theory gets its data base for free.

But now let's consider the other component of the competing theories. Merely *having* a decision-making system will not enable us to make predictions about other people's behavior. We also need the capacity to take that system 'off-line,' feed it 'pretend' inputs and interpret its outputs as predictions about how someone else would behave. When we add the required cognitive apparatus, the picture of the mind that emerges is sketched in figure 3. Getting this 'control mechanism' to work smoothly is sure to be a *very* non-trivial task. How do things look in the case of the theory-theory? Well, no matter how we go about making predictions about other people, it is clear that in making predictions about physical systems we can't use the off-line simulation strategy; we have to use some sort of internalized theory (though, of course, it need not be a sentence-like or rule-based theory). Thus we know that the mind is going to have to have some mechanism for extracting information from internalized theories and applying it to particular cases. (In figure 1 we have assumed that this mechanism is housed along with the other 'inference mechanisms' that are used to extract information from pre-existing beliefs.) If such a mechanism will work for an internally represented folk physics, it is plausible to suppose that, with minor modifications, it will also work for an internally represented folk psychology. So while the simulation theorist gets the data base for free, it looks like the theory-theorist gets the 'control mechanism' for free. All of this is a bit fast and loose, of course. But we don't think either side of this argument can get much more precise until we are presented with up-and-running models to compare. Until then, neither side can gain much advantage by appealing to simplicity.

Argument 5: When we introspect about our predictions of other people's behavior, it sometimes seems that we proceed by imagining how we would behave in their situation.

Here is how Goldman makes the point (1989, p. 82):

> The simulation idea has obvious initial attractions. Introspectively, it seems as if we often try to predict others' behavior—or predict their (mental) choices—by imagining ourselves in their shoes and determining what we would choose to do.

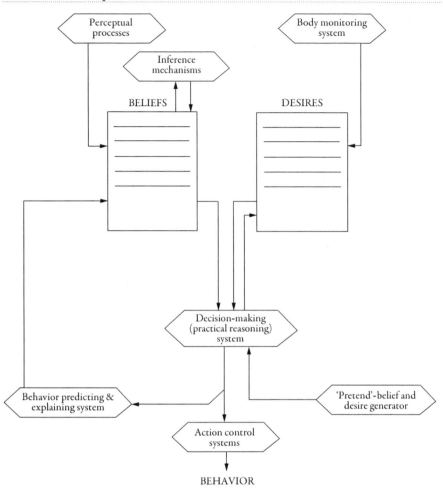

FIGURE 3

And here is Gordon (1986, p. 63):

> [C]hess players report that, playing against a human opponent or even against a computer, they visualize the board from the other side, taking the opposing pieces for their own and vice versa. Further, they pretend that their reasons for action have shifted accordingly ... Thus transported in imagination, they 'make up their mind what to do.'

Both authors are aware that appeal to introspection can be a two-edged sword, since it also often happens that we predict other people's behavior *without* introspecting any imaginary behavior (Goldman, 1989, p. 87):

> [T]here is a straightforward challenge to the psychological plausibility of the simulation approach. It is far from obvious, introspectively, that we regularly place

ourselves in another person's shoes, and vividly envision what we would do in his circumstances.

And (Gordon, 1986, p. 72 n. 4):

Imagery is not always needed in such simulations. For example, I need no imagery to simulate having a million dollars in the bank.

To deal with this 'challenge,' Goldman proposes a pair of replies. First, simulation need not always be introspectively vivid. It can often be 'semi-automatic, with relatively little salient phenomenology.' Second, not all interpretations rely on simulation. In many cases interpreters rely solely on 'inductively acquired information' though the information is 'historically derived from earlier simulations' (1989, pp. 87–8).

Reply: We don't propose to make any fuss at all about the frequent absence of 'salient phenomenology.' For it is our contention that when the issue at hand is the nature of the cognitive mechanism subserving our capacity to interpret and predict other people's behavior, the entire issue of introspective imagination is a red herring. Indeed, it is *two* red herrings. To see the first of them, consider one of the standard examples used to illustrate the role of imagery in thought. Suppose we ask you: 'How many windows are there in your house?' How do you go about answering? Almost everyone reports that they *imagine* themselves walking from room to room, counting the windows as they go. What follows from this about the cognitive mechanism that they are exploiting? Well, one thing that surely *does not* follow is that off-line simulation is involved. The *only* way that people could possibly answer the question accurately is to tap into some internally represented store of knowledge about their house; it simply makes no sense to suppose that off-line simulation is being used here. So even if a cognitive process is *always* accompanied by vivid imagery, that is no reason at all to suppose that the process exploits off-line simulation. From this we draw the obvious conclusion. The fact that prediction and interpretation *sometimes* involve imagining oneself in the other person's shoes is less than no reason at all to suppose that off-line simulation is involved.

It might be suggested that, though imagery provides no support for the off-line simulation hypothesis, it does challenge the theory-theory when 'theory' is interpreted narrowly. For it shows that some of the information we are exploiting in interpretation and prediction is not stored in the form of sentences or rules. But even this is far from obvious. There is a lively debate in the imagery literature in which 'descriptionalists,' like Pylyshyn and Dennett, maintain that the mechanisms underlying mental imagery exploit language-like representations, while 'pictorialists,' like Kosslyn and Fodor, argue that images are subserved by a separate, non-linguistic sort of representation (Pylyshyn, 1981; Dennett 1969, 1978b; Fodor, 1975; Kosslyn, 1981). We don't propose to take sides in this dispute. For present purposes it is sufficient to note that, unless it is supplemented by a persuasive argument in favor of pictorialism and against descriptionism, the introspective evidence does not even challenge the theory-theory *construed narrowly*.

Argument 6: The off-line simulation account is supported by recent experimental studies focusing on children's acquisition of the ability to interpret and predict other people.

On our view, this is far and away the most interesting argument that has been offered in favor of the off-line simulation theory. To see exactly what the experimental studies do, and do not, support, we'll have to look at both the evidence and the argument with considerable care. Gordon does a good job of describing one important set of experiments (1986, pp. 68–9):

> Very young children give verbal expression to predictions and explanations of the behavior of others. Yet up to about the age of four they evidently lack the concept of belief, or at least the capacity to make allowances for false or differing beliefs. Evidence of this can be teased out by presenting children with stories and dramatizations that involve dramatic irony: where we the audience know something important the protagonist doesn't know . . .
>
> In one such story (illustrated with puppets) the puppet-child Maxi puts his chocolate in the box and goes out to play. While he is out, his mother transfers the chocolate to the cupboard. Where will Maxi look for the chocolate when he comes back? In the box, says the five-year-old, pointing to the miniature box on the puppet stage: a good prediction of a sort we ordinarily take for granted . . . But the child of three to four years has a different response: verbally or by pointing, the child indicates the cupboard. (That is, after all, where the chocolate is to be found, isn't it?) Suppose Maxi wants to mislead his gluttonous big brother to the *wrong* place, where will he lead him? The five-year-old indicates the cupboard, where (unbeknownst to Maxi) the chocolate actually is . . . The *younger* child indicates, incorrectly, the box.

These results, Gordon maintains, are hard to square with the theory-theory. For if the theory-theory is correct, then (pp. 69–70):

> before internalizing [the laws and generalizations of folk psychology] the child would simply be unable to predict or explain human action. And *after* internalizing the system, the child could deal indifferently with actions caused by *true* beliefs and actions caused by *false* beliefs. It is hard to see how the semantical question could be relevant.

But, according to Gordon, these data are just what we should expect, if the off-line simulation theory is correct (Gordon, unpublished, sec. 3.6, p. 11):

The Simulation Theory [predicts that] prior to developing the capacity to simulate others for purposes of prediction and explanation, a child will make *egocentric errors* in predicting and explaining the actions of others. She will predict and explain as if whatever she herself counts as 'fact' were also fact to the other; which is to say, she fails to make allowances in her predictions and explanations for false beliefs or for what the other isn't in a position to know.

Reply: According to Gordon, the theory-theory can't easily explain the results of the 'Maxi' experiment, though the off-line simulation theory predicts those results. We're not convinced on either score. Let's look first at just what the off-line simulation story would lead us to expect.

Presumably by the time any of these experiments can be conducted, the child has developed a more or less intact decision-making system like the one depicted in figure 1. That system makes 'on-line' decisions and thus determines the child's actions on the basis of her actual beliefs and desires. But by itself it provides the child with no way of predicting Maxi's behavior or anyone else's. If the off-line simulation theory is right, then in order to make predictions about other people's behavior two things must happen. First, the child must acquire the ability to take the output of the decision-making system off line—treating its decisions as predictions or expectations, rather than simply feeding them into the action controlling system. Second, the child must acquire the ability to provide the system with input other than her own actual beliefs and desires. She must be able to supply the system with 'pretend' input so that she can predict the behavior of someone whose beliefs and desires are different from her own. (These are the two capacities that are represented in figure 3 and absent in figure 1.) There is, of course, no a priori reason to suppose that these two steps happen at different times, nor that the one we've listed first will occur first. But if they do occur in that order, then we might expect there to be a period when the child could predict her own behavior (or the behavior of someone whose beliefs and desires are the same as hers), though she could not predict the behavior of people whose beliefs or desires are different from hers. It is less clear what to expect if the steps occur in the opposite order. Perhaps the result would be some sort of pretending or play-acting— behaving in a way that someone with different beliefs or desires would behave. Though until the child develops the capacity to take the output of the decision-making system off-line, she will not be able to predict other people's behavior or her own. So it looks like the off-line simulation story makes room for three possible developmental scenarios.

(1) The child acquires both abilities at the same time. In this case we would expect to see two developmental stages. In the first the child can make no predictions. In the second she can make a full range of predictions about people whose beliefs and desires are different from her own.

(2) The child first acquires the ability to take the output off-line, and then acquires the ability to provide the system with pretend input. In this case we would expect three developmental stages. In the first, the child can make no predictions. In the second, she can only make predictions about her own behavior or about the behavior of people whose beliefs and desires are identical to hers. In the third, she can make the full range of predictions.

(3) The child first acquires the ability to provide the system with pretend inputs, and then acquires the ability to take the output off-line. In this case, too, we would expect three developmental stages. The first and last stages are the same as those in (2), but in the middle stage the child can play-act but not make predictions.

Now let's return to the Maxi experiment. Which of these developmental scenarios do the children in these experiments exhibit? At first blush, it might be thought that the pattern Gordon reports is much the same as the one set out in scenario (2). But that would be a mistake. The younger children—those who are giving the wrong answers—are not predicting that Maxi would do what someone with their own beliefs and desires would do. For they have no desire to get the chocolate, nor to deceive the gluttonous brother. Those are *Maxi's* desires, not *theirs*. If anything, it would appear that these children are half-way between the second and third stages of scenario (2): they can feed 'pretend' desires into the decision-making system, but not 'pretend' beliefs. Of course none of this shows that the off-line simulation theory is false. It is perfectly compatible with the theory to suppose that development proceeds as in (2), *and* that the transition from the second to the third stage proceeds in two sub-stages—desires first, and then beliefs. (This pattern is sketched in figure 4.) But it is, to say the least, something of an exaggeration to say that the off-line simulation theory 'predicts' the experimental results. The most that can be said is that the theory is compatible with the observed developmental pattern, and with lots of other patterns as well.[9]

For the results that Gordon describes to be at all relevant to the dispute between the off-line simulation theory and the theory-theory, it would have to be the case that the latter theory is *in*compatible with the reported developmental pattern. But that is patently not the case. To see why, we should first note that the theory-theory is not committed to the claim that folk psychology is acquired all in one fell swoop. Indeed, one would expect just the opposite. If children really are acquiring a tacit theory of the mind, they probably acquire it a bit at a time. Thus it might be the case that, at a given

9. Actually, the developmental facts are rather more complicated than Gordon suggests. For, as Leslie (1988) emphasizes, children are typically able to appreciate and engage in pretend play by the time they are two and a half years old—long before they can handle questions about Maxi and his false beliefs. It is not at all clear how the off-line simulation theory can explain both the early appearance of the ability to pretend and the relatively late appearance of the ability to predict the behavior of people whose beliefs and desires differ from one's own.

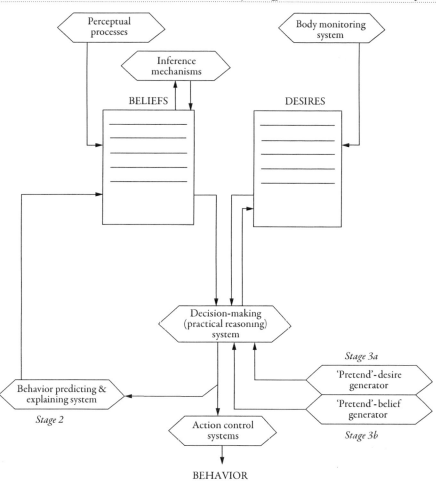

FIGURE 4

stage in development, children have mastered the part of the theory that specifies how beliefs and desires lead to behavior, though they have not mastered the entire story about how beliefs are caused. At this stage, they might simply assume that beliefs are caused by the way the world is; they might adopt the strategy of attributing to everyone the very same beliefs that they have. A child who has acquired this much of folk psychology would (incorrectly) attribute to Maxi the belief that the chocolate is in the cupboard. She would then go on to make just the predictions that Gordon reports. Of course, the theory-theory is also compatible with lots of other hypotheses about which bits of folk psychology are acquired first. Thus, like the off-line simulation theory, it is compatible with (but does not entail) lots of possible developmental patterns. So it looks like the developmental studies that Gordon and Goldman cite can't be used to support one theory over the other.

Argument 7: Autistic children are highly deficient in their ability to engage in pretend play. These children are also frequently unable to impute beliefs to others or to predict other people's behavior correctly.

Here's how Gordon sets out the argument (1986, p. 70):

> Practical simulation involves the capacity for a certain kind of systematic pretending. It is well known that *autistic* children suffer a striking deficit in the capacity for pretend play. In addition, they are often said to 'treat people and objects alike'; they fail to treat others as subjects, as having 'points of view' distinct from their own. This failure is confirmed by their performance in prediction tests like the [Wimmer–Perner 'Maxi' experiment] I have just described. A version of the Wimmer–Perner test was administered to autistic children of ages *six to sixteen* by a team of psychologists . . . *Almost all* these children gave the wrong answer, the 3-year-old's answer. This indicates a highly specific deficit, not one in general intelligence. Although many autistic children are also mentally retarded, those tested were mostly in the average or borderline IQ range. Yet children with Down's syndrome, with IQ levels substantially below that range, suffered no deficit: almost all gave the right answer. My account of belief would predict that only those children who can engage in pretend play can master the concept of belief.

Goldman is rather more tentative. He claims only that the inability of austistic children 'to impute beliefs to others and therefore predict their behavior correctly . . . might . . . be related to their lack of pretend play' (1989, p. 87).

Reply: The fact that autistic children are both incapable of pretend play and unable to predict the behavior of other people in Wimmer–Perner tests is very intriguing. Moreover, Gordon is certainly right in suggesting that the off-line simulation theory provides a possible explanation for these facts. If the off-line simulation theory is right, predicting the behavior of people whose beliefs differ from our own requires an ability to provide our own decision-making system with pretend input. And it is plausible to assume that this ability would also play a central role in pretend play. So if we hypothesize that autistic children lack the ability to provide the decision-making system with pretend input, we could explain both their performance on the Wimmer–Perner test and their failure to engage in pretend play. But, of course, this will not count as an argument for the off-line simulation theory and against the theory-theory if the latter account can offer an equally plausible explanation of the facts. And it will require no creativity on our part to produce such an alternative explanation since one of the investigators who discovered the fact that autistic children do poorly in Wimmer–Perner tests has offered one himself.

Leslie (1988) takes as an assumption 'the hypothesis that human cognition involves *symbolic computations* in the sense discussed . . . by Newell (1980) and particularly by Fodor' (Leslie, 1988, p. 21). He also assumes that an internalized theory of mind underlies the normal adult's ability to predict other people's behavior. An important theme in Leslie's work is that developmental studies with both normal and autistic children can help to illuminate the expressive resources of the 'language of thought' in which our theory of mind is encoded. According to Leslie, the notion of a 'meta-representation' is central in understanding how our theory of mind develops. Roughly speaking, a meta-representation is a mental representation about some other representational state or process. We exploit meta-representations when we think that

Maxi believes that the chocolate is in the box

or that

Maxi's brother wants the chocolate

or that

Mommy is pretending that the banana is a telephone.

On Leslie's view, 'autistic children do not develop a theory of mind normally' (Leslie, 1988, p. 39). And while 'it is far too soon to say with any confidence what *is* wrong' with these children, he speculates that at the root of the problem may be an inability to use meta-representations. If this were true, it would explain both their difficulty with pretend play and their failure on the Wimmer–Perner test.

Though we find Leslie's speculation interesting and important, it is no part of our current project to defend it. To make our case we need only insist that, on currently available evidence, Leslie's hypothesis is no less plausible than Gordon's. Since Leslie's speculation presupposes that normal children acquire and exploit a theory of mind that is encoded in a language of thought, the evidence from studies of autistic children gives us no reason to prefer the off-line simulation account over the theory-theory.[10]

---

10. It's worth noting that both Gordon's account and Leslie's 'predict that only those children who can engage in pretend play can master the concept of belief' (Gordon, 1986, p. 70). This may prove a troublesome implication for both theorists, however. For it is not the case that *all* autistic children do poorly on the Wimmer–Perner test. In the original study reported by Baron-Cohen, Leslie and Frith (1985), only 16 out of 20 autistic subjects failed the Wimmer–Perner test. The other 4 answered correctly. The investigators predicted that these children 'would also show evidence of an ability to pretend play' (p. 43). Unfortunately, no data was reported on the pretend play ability of these subjects. If it should turn out that some autistic children do well on the Wimmer–Perner test *and* lack the ability for pretend play, both Gordon's explanation and Leslie's would be in trouble. If the facts do turn out this way, advocates of the theory-theory will have a variety of other explanations available. But it is much less clear that the off-line simulation account could explain the data, if some autistic children can't pretend but can predict the behavior of people with false beliefs.

Our theme, in this reply and in the previous one, has been that the empirical evidence cited by Gordon and Goldman, while compatible with the off-line simulation theory, is also compatible with the theory-theory, and thus does not support one theory over the other. But there are other studies in the recent literature that *can* be used to support one theory over the other. These studies report results that are comfortably compatible with the theory-theory though not with the off-line simulation account. Before we sketch those results, however, it is time to start a new section. In this section we've tried to show that none of the arguments in favor of the off-line simulation theory is persuasive. In the next one we'll set out a positive case for the theory-theory.

5   In Defense of the Theory-Theory

Argument 1: There are developmental data that are easily accommodated by the theory-theory, but very hard to explain if the off-line simulation account is correct.

Let's start with a description of the experimental setup, and a quick overview of the data.

> The setup of the task in these experiments was rather simple. Two children were placed facing each other on opposite sides of a table. In each trial one child served as subject and had access to the other child's knowledge and his or her own knowledge of the content of a closed box. The box was placed in the middle of the table between the two children. The outside of it was neutral and not suggestive of its content. In each box was a familiar object like a pencil, a comb, a piece of chocolate, and so on. The specific questions were: 'Does (name of other child) know what is in the box or does she not know that?' and 'Do you know what is in the box or do you not know that?' ...
>
> Before the knowledge-questions were asked, either the other or the subject had access to the content of the box. One kind of access was visual perception. In this case either the other child or the subject had a chance to look into the box. The other kind of access was verbal information. Here the experimenter looked into the box and then informed one of the children by whispering the name of the content object into the child's ear. Because the two children were facing each other the subject was fully aware of the information conditions the other child was exposed to, that is, of whether the other child did or did not look into the box and of whether the other was or was not informed. (Wimmer et al., 1988, p. 175)

The results of this experiment were quite striking. The older children (five-year-olds) gave uniformly correct answers. But younger children (three and four-year-olds) did not.

The most frequent error was denial of the other child's knowledge when the other child had looked into the box or was informed by the experimenter.

Most 3-year-olds and some 4-year-olds said that the other did not know what was in the box. This kind of error was nearly absent in children's assessment of their own knowledge. When subjects themselves had looked into the box or were informed, then they claimed to know and they could, of course, tell what was in the box. (Wimmer et al., 1988, pp. 175–6)

In another experiment, designed to be sure that the younger children were aware the other child had looked in the box, the subjects were asked both whether the other child had looked in the box and whether the other child knew what was in the box, 'The children consistently responded affirmatively to the look-question but again quite frequently responded negatively to the knowledge question' (Wimmer et al., 1988, p. 176).

What is going on here? The explanation offered by the experimenters is that younger children are using quite different mental processes in assessing what they know and in assessing what the other child knows. To answer the question, 'Do you know what is in the box?' the children use what the experimenters call the 'answer check procedure.' They simply check to see whether they have an answer to the embedded question in their knowledge base, and if they do they respond affirmatively. To answer the question about the other child's knowledge, the older children used what the experimenters call a 'direct access check procedure.' In effect, they ask themselves whether the other child looked in the box or was told about its contents. If so, they respond affirmatively. If not, they respond negatively. However, the three-year-olds did not use this procedure. They simply checked whether the other child had uttered a correct statement about the box's contents. If she had not, the subject said the other did not know. A very natural way to describe the situation is that while the younger children know that people who say *that p.* typically believe or know *that p*, these children have not yet learned that people will come to know *that p* by seeing or being told *that p*. The younger children have acquired a fragment of folk psychology, while the older children have acquired a more substantial piece of the theory.[11] The older children have not, however, entirely mastered the theory, as indicated by another series of experiments.

These experiments focused on the role of *inference* in the acquisition of knowledge or belief. What they show is that 'four- and five-year olds relied on inference in their own

11. Another experiment reported by Perner et al. (1987) provides some additional evidence for this conclusion. In the first part of the experiment children were shown a box of Smarties (a type of candy), and asked what they thought was in the box. All of them answered that the box contained Smarties. They were then shown that the box contained a pencil, and no Smarties. After this the children were asked three questions:

   (i)   What is in the box?
   (ii) What did you think was in the box when you first saw it?
   (iii) What would a friend, waiting outside, think was in the box if he saw it as it is now?

acquisition of knowledge but denied that the other person might know via inference'
(Wimmer et al., 1988, p. 179):

> Inferential access was realized in these experiments in a very simple and concrete
> way. In a first step the child and the other person together inspected the content of
> a container and agreed that only sweets of a certain kind, for example, black choco-
> late nuts, were in the container. In a second step the other person or the subject was
> prevented from seeing how one choconut was transferred from the container into
> an opaque bag. However, this person was explicitly informed by the experimenter
> about this transfer, for example, 'I've just taken one of the things out of this box and
> put it in the bag.'
>
> The condition where knowledge could be acquired via simple inference was con-
> trasted with a condition where knowledge depended on actually seeing the critical
> object's transfer. In this latter condition two kinds of sweets were in the original
> container, and thus one could only know what the content of the critical bag was by
> having seen the transfer from container to bag.

Once again, the results were quite striking. In most cases the older children (six-year-
olds, in this case) generally gave the right answers both about their own knowledge and
about the other child's knowledge. But although the four-year-olds used inference in
forming their own beliefs, a substantial majority of them exhibited a pattern that the
experimenters called 'inference neglect.'

> The response pattern 'inference neglect' means that the other person was assessed
> according to perceptual access: When the other person saw the object's transfer to
> the bag, 4-year-olds attributed knowledge; when the other did not see this transfer,
> ignorance was attributed even when the other person in fact knew via inference.
> (Wimmer et al., 1988, p. 179)

One plausible way of accounting for these results is to hypothesize that the older children had mastered yet another part of the adult folk psychology. They had learned that
knowledge and beliefs can be caused by inference as well as by direct perceptual access.
And, indeed, this is just the interpretation that the experimenters suggest.

Most of the younger children answered (iii) incorrectly; they failed to predict their friend's false belief. But
more than half of those who got (iii) wrong answered (ii) correctly. They were able to tell the experimenter
that they had thought the box contained Smarties, and that they were wrong. In commenting on this experiment, Leslie notes that

> [d]espite the ability to *report* their false belief, these 3-year-olds could not understand where that false
> belief had come from . . . Despite the fact that they themselves had just undergone the process of getting
> that false belief, the children were quite unable to understand and reconstruct that process, and thus
> unable, minutes later, to predict what would happen to their friend. (Leslie, 1988, pp. 33–4)

In contrast to the 3-year-olds discussed in the previous [experiment], the 4-year-olds and 5-year-olds in the present experiments understood quite well that one has to consider the other person's informational conditions when one is questioned about the other person's knowledge. Their only problem was their limited understanding of informational conditions. They understood only direct visual access as a source of knowledge and this led them to mistaken but systematic ignorance attributions in the case of inferential access. (Wimmer et al., 1988, p. 181)

Let's now ask what conclusions can be drawn from these experiments that will be relevant to the choice between the off-line simulation theory and the theory-theory. A first obvious fact is that the data are all comfortably compatible with the theory-theory. Indeed, the explanation of the data offered by the experimenters is one that presupposes the correctness of the theory-theory. What appears to be happening is that as children get older, they master more and more of the principles of folk psychology. By itself, of course, the theory-theory would not enable us to predict the data, since the theory-theory does not tell us anything about the order in which the principles of folk psychology are acquired. But the pattern of results described certainly poses no problem for the theory-theory.

The same cannot be said for the off-line simulation theory. It is clear that even the younger children in these studies form beliefs as the result of perception, verbally provided information, and inference. So there is nothing about their decision making system, when it is being used on-line, that will help to explain the results. To make predictions about other people, the off-line simulation theory maintains, children must acquire the capacity to take the decision-making system off-line and provide it with some pretend inputs. But there is no obvious way in which this process could produce the pattern of results that has been reported. The difficulty is particularly clear in the case of inference. If the subject has seen that the box contains only chocolate nuts, and if she is told that one of the items in the box has been put in the bag, she comes to believe that there is a chocolate nut in the bag. But if she knows the other child has also seen what is in the box, and that the other child has been told that one of the items in the box has been put in the bag, she insists that the other child does not know what is in the bag. The problem can't be that the subject doesn't realize that the other child knows what is in the box. Children of this age do a good job of attributing belief on the basis of perception. Nor can it be that the subject doesn't believe that the other child believes the transfer has been made. For children of this age are also adept at attributing beliefs on the basis of verbally communicated information. So it looks like the subject has all the information needed for a successful simulation. But the answer she comes up with is *not* the one that she herself would come up with, were she in the subject's place. There are, of course, endlessly many ways in which a resolute defender of the off-line simulation theory might try to accommodate these data. But all the ones we've been able to think of are obviously implausible and *ad hoc*.

Argument 2: Our predictions and explanations of behavior are 'cognitively penetrable.'

One virtue of using a simulation to predict the behavior of a system is that you need have no serious idea about the principles governing the behavior of the target system. You just run the simulation and watch what happens. Sometimes, of course, a simulation will do something that was utterly unexpected. But no matter. If the simulation really was similar to the target system, then the prediction it provides will be a good one. In predictions based on simulations, what you don't know won't hurt you. All of this applies to the off-line simulation theory, of course. If there is some quirk in the human decision-making system, something quite unknown to most people that leads the system to behave in an unexpected way under certain circumstances, the accuracy of predictions based on simulations should not be adversely affected. If you provide the system with the right pretend input, it should simulate (and thus predict) the unexpected output. Adapting a term from Pylyshyn, we might describe this by saying that simulation-based predictions are not 'cognitively penetrable.'[12]

Just the opposite is true for predictions that rely on a theory. If we are making predictions on the basis of a set of laws or principles, and if there are some unexpected aspects of the system's behavior that are not captured by our principles, then our predictions about those aspects of the system's behavior should be less accurate. Theory based predictions are sensitive to what we know and don't know about the laws that govern the system; they *are* cognitively penetrable. This contrast provides a useful way of testing the two theories. If we can find cases in which ignorance about the workings of one's own psychology leads people to make mistakes in predicting what they, or other similarly situated people, would do, it will provide yet another reason to think that the off-line simulation theory is untenable. And, as it happens, cases illustrating cognitive penetrability in the prediction of behavior are not all that hard to find. The literature in cognitive social psychology is full of them. We'll illustrate the point with three examples, but it would be easy to add three dozen more.

First Example

Suppose you are walking through the local shopping mall, and encounter what looks to be yet another consumer product opinion survey. In this one a polite, well-dressed man invites you to examine an array of familiar products—nightgowns, perhaps, or pantyhose—and to rate their quality. A small reward is offered for your participation—you can keep the garment you select. On examining the products, you find no really significant differences among them. (You couldn't, because, unbeknownst to you they are identical.) What would you do? Confronted with this question, most of us think we would report

---

12. Pylyshyn, 1981, 1984. It is perhaps worth noting that we are using the term 'cognitively penetrable' a bit more loosely than Pylyshyn does. But in the present context the difference is not important.

that the garments looked to be very similar, and then choose one randomly. However, when the experiment was actually tried, this turned out to be mistaken. 'There was a pronounced position effect on evaluations, such that the right-most garments were heavily preferred to the left-most garments.' But it was clear that few of the subjects had any awareness at all of the effect of position on their decision. Indeed, 'when questioned about the effect of the garments' position on their choices, virtually all subjects denied such an influence (usually with a tone of annoyance or of concern for the experimenter's sanity)' (Nisbett and Ross, 1980, p. 207).

This sort of case poses real problems for the off-line simulation theory. Most people have no trouble imagining themselves in the situation described. They can supply their decision-making system with vivid 'pretend' input. But few people who have not heard of the experiment predict that they would behave in the way that the subjects behaved. The natural interpretation of the experiment is that people's predictions about their own behavior (and the subjects' explanations of their own choice) are guided by an incomplete or inaccurate theory, one which includes no information about these so-called 'position effects.'

Second Example
Here's another case to run through your own simulator. Suppose someone in the office is selling $1.00 tickets for the office lottery. In some cases, when a person agrees to buy a ticket, he or she is simply handed one. In other cases, after agreeing to buy a ticket, the buyer is allowed to choose a ticket from several that the seller has available. On the morning of the lottery, the seller approaches each purchaser and attempts to buy back the ticket. Now imagine yourself in both roles—first as a person who had been handed the ticket, second as a person who had been given a choice. What price would you ask in each case? Would there be any difference between the two cases? On several occasions one of us (Stich) has asked large undergraduate classes to predict what they would do. Almost no one predicts that they would behave the way that people actually do behave. Almost everyone is surprised to hear the actual results.

Ah, yes, the results; we haven't yet told *you* what they are. When the experiment was actually done, 'no-choice subjects sold their tickets back for an average of $1.96. Choice subjects, who had personally selected their tickets, held out for an average of $8.67!' (Nisbett and Ross, 1980, p. 136). If, like Stich's students, you find this surprising and unexpected, it counts as yet another difficulty for the off-line simulation theory.

Third Example
In the psychology laboratory, and in everyday life, it sometimes happens that people are presented with fairly persuasive evidence that they have some hitherto unexpected trait. In the light of that evidence people form the belief that they have the trait. What will happen to that belief if, shortly after this, people are presented with a convincing case discrediting the first body of evidence? Suppose, for example, they are convinced that the

test results were actually someone else's, or that no real test was conducted at all. Most people expect that the undermined belief will simply be discarded. If until recently I never had reason to think I had a certain trait, and if the evidence I just acquired has been soundly discredited, then surely it would be silly of me to go away thinking that I *do* have the trait. That seems to be what most people think. And the view was shared by a generation of social psychologists who duped subjects into believing all sorts of things about themselves, observed their reactions, and then 'debriefed' the subjects by explaining the ruse. The assumption was that no enduring harm could be done because once the ruse was explained the induced belief would be discarded. But in a widely discussed series of experiments, Ross and his co-workers have demonstrated that this is simply not the case. Once a subject has been convinced that she is very good at telling real from fake suicide notes, for example, showing her that the evidence was completely phony does not succeed in eliminating the belief. Moreover, third-person observers of the experiment exhibit even stronger 'belief perseverance.' If an observer subject watches a participant subject being duped and then debriefed, the observer, too, will continue to believe that the participant is particularly good at detecting real suicide notes (Nisbett and Ross, 1980, pp. 175–9).

Neither of these results should have been at all surprising to anyone if we predict each other's beliefs and behavior in the way that the off-line simulation theory suggests. But clearly the results *were* both surprising and disturbing. We can't simply ask ourselves what we would do in these circumstances and expect to come up with the right answer. For the theory-theorist, this fact poses no particular problem. When our folk psychology is wrong, it is to be expected that our predictions will be wrong too. It is simply another illustration of cognitive penetrability in predicting and explaining behavior. The theory-theory, unlike the off-line simulation theory, predicts that people's predictions and explanations of behavior will be cognitively penetrable through and through. If it is agreed that these experiments confirm cognitive penetrability, the off-line simulation theory is in serious trouble.

6 Conclusion

Our paper has been long but our conclusion will be brief. The off-line simulation theory poses an intriguing challenge to the dominant paradigm in contemporary cognitive science. Moreover, if it were correct the off-line simulation account of psychological prediction and explanation would largely undermine *both* sides in the eliminativism dispute. But it has been our contention that the prospects for the off-line simulation theory are not very bright. None of the arguments that have been offered in defense of the theory are at all persuasive. And there is lots of experimental evidence that would be very hard to explain if the off-line simulation account were correct. We don't claim to have provided a knock-down refutation of the off-line simulation theory. Knock-down arguments are hard to come by in cognitive science. But we do claim to have assembled a pretty serious case against the simulation theory. Pending a detailed response, we don't think the off-line simulation theory is one that cognitive scientists or philosophers should take seriously.

REFERENCES

Astington, J., Harris, P. and Olson, D. (eds) 1988: *Developing Theories of Mind*. Cambridge: Cambridge University Press.

Baron-Cohen, S., Leslie, A. and Frith, U. 1985: Does the autistic child have a 'theory of mind'? *Cognition*, 21, 37–46.

Chomsky, N. 1965: *Aspects of the Theory of Syntax*. Cambridge, MA: MIT Press.

Churchland, P. 1981: Eliminative materialism and the propositional attitudes. *Journal of Philosophy*, 78, 67–90.

Churchland, P. 1989: Folk psychology and the explanation of human behavior. In *A Neurocomputational Perspective*. Cambridge, MA: MIT Press.

Cummins, R. 1983: *The Nature of Psychological Explanation*. Cambridge, MA: MIT Press.

D'Andrade, R. 1987: A folk model of the mind. In D. Holland and N. Quinn (eds), *Cultural Models in Language and Thought*. Cambridge: Cambridge University Press.

Dennett, D. 1969: *Content and Consciousness*. London: Routledge and Kegan Paul.

Dennett, D. 1978a: Artificial intelligence as philosophy and psychology. In *Brainstorms*. Cambridge, MA: MIT Press.

Dennett, D. 1978b: Two approaches to mental images. In *Brainstorms*. Cambridge, MA: MIT Press.

Fodor, J. 1968: The appeal to tacit knowledge in psychological explanation. *Journal of Philosophy*, 65, 627–40.

Fodor, J. 1975: *The Language of Thought*. New York: Thomas Crowell.

Fodor, J. 1981: *Representations*. Cambridge, MA: MIT Press.

Fodor, J. 1987: *Psychosemantics*. Cambridge, MA: MIT Press.

Fodor, J., Bever, T. and Garrett, M. 1974: *The Psychology of Language: An Introduction to Psycholinguistics and Generative Grammar*. New York: McGraw-Hill.

Goldman, A. I. 1989: Interpretation psychologized. *Mind and Language*, 4, 161–85. Reprinted in M. Davies and T. Stone (eds), *Folk Psychology*. Oxford: Blackwell, 1995. Page references are to reprint.

Gordon, R. M. 1986: Folk psychology as simulation. *Mind and Language*, 1, 158–71. Reprinted in M. Davies and T. Stone (eds), *Folk Psychology*. Oxford: Blackwell 1995. Page references are to reprint.

Gordon, R.M. 1995: The simulation theory: Objections and misconceptions. In M. Davies and T. Stone (eds), *Folk Psychology* . Oxford: Blackwell 1995.

Gordon, R. M. Unpublished: Fodor's intentional realism and the simulation theory. MS dated 2/90.

Gregory, R. 1970: *The Intelligent Eye*. New York: McGraw-Hill.

Greeno, J. 1983: Conceptual entities. In D. Gentner and A. Stevens (eds), *Mental Models*. Hillsdale, NJ: Erlbaum.

Hayes, P. 1985: The second naive physics manifesto. In J. Hobbs and R. Moore (eds), *Formal Theories of the Commonsense World*. Norwood, NJ: Ablex, 1–36.

Heal, J. 1986: Replication and functionalism. In J. Butterfield (ed.), *Language, Mind and Logic*. Cambridge: Cambridge University Press.

Johnson-Laird, P. 1983: *Mental Models: Towards a Cognitive Science of Language, Inference and Consciousness*. Cambridge, MA: Harvard University Press.

Kahneman, D. and Tversky, A. 1982: The simulation heuristic. In D. Kahneman, P. Slovic and A. Tversky (eds), *Judgment Under Uncertainty*. Cambridge: Cambridge University Press.

Kosslyn, S. 1981: The medium and the message in mental imagery: A theory. In N. Block (ed.), *Imagery*. Cambridge, MA: MIT Press.

Leslie, A. 1987: Pretense and representation: The origins of 'theory of mind.' *Psychological Review*, 94, 412–26.

Leslie, A. 1988: Some implications of pretense for mechanisms underlying the child's theory of mind. In J. Astington, P. Harris and D. Olson (eds), *Developing Theories of Mind*. Cambridge: Cambridge University Press.

Lycan, W. 1981: Form, function and feel. *Journal of Philosophy*, 78, 24–50.

Lycan, W. 1988: Toward a homuncular theory of believing. In *Judgement and Justification*. Cambridge: Cambridge University Press.

Marr, D. 1982: *Vision*. San Francisco: Freeman.

McCloskey, M. 1983: Naive theories of motion. In D. Gentner and A. Stevens (eds), *Mental Models*. Hillsdale, NJ: Erlbaum.

Montgomery, R. 1987: Psychologism, folk psychology and one's own case. *Journal for the Theory of Social Behavior*, 17, 195–218.

Newell, A. 1980: Physical symbol systems. *Cognitive Science*, 4, 135–83.

Nisbett, R. and Ross, L. 1980: *Human Inference*. Englewood Cliffs, NJ: Prentice-Hall.

Olson, D., Astington, J. and Harris, P. 1988: Introduction. In J. Astington, P. Harris and D. Olson (eds), *Developing Theories of Mind*. Cambridge: Cambridge University Press.

Perner, J., Leekam, S. and Wimmer, H. 1987: Three-year-olds' difficulty with false belief: The case for a conceptual deficit. *British Journal of Developmental Psychology*, 5, 125–37.

Pinker, S. 1989: *Learnability and Cognition*. Cambridge, MA: MIT Press.

Pylyshyn, Z, 1981: The imagery debate: Analog media versus tacit knowledge. In N. Block (ed.), *Imagery*. Cambridge, MA: MIT Press.

Pylyshyn, Z. 1984: *Computation and Cognition*. Cambridge, MA: MIT Press.

Ramsey, W., Stich, S. and Garon, J. 1990: Connectionism, eliminativism and the future of folk psychology. *Philosophical Perspectives*, 4, 499–533.

Ripstein, A. 1987: Explanation and empathy. *Review of Metaphysics*, 40, 465–82.

Rock, I. 1983: *The Logic of Perception*. Cambridge, MA: MIT Press.

Rumelhart, D., Smolensky, P., McClelland, J. and Hinton, G. 1986: Schemata and sequential thought processes in PDP models. In J. McClelland, D. Rumelhart and the PDP Research Group, *Parallel Distributed Processing*, vol. 2. Cambridge, MA: MIT Press.

Sellars, W. 1963: Empiricism and the philosophy of mind. In *Science, Perception and Reality*. London: Routledge and Kegan Paul.

Stich, S. 1978: Beliefs and subdoxastic states. *Philosophy of Science*, 45, 499–518.

Wimmer, H., Hogrefe, J. and Sodian, B. 1988: A second state in children's conception of mental life: Understanding informational access as origins of knowledge and belief. In J. Astington, P. Harris and D. Olson (eds), *Developing Theories of Mind*. Cambridge: Cambridge University Press.

10

INTENTIONALITY AND NATURALISM

Stephen Stich and Stephen Laurence

1 Catastrophe Theory

Intentional irrealism is the doctrine that meaning is a myth. A bit more precisely, it is the claim that nothing in the world instantiates intentional properties—that intentional predicates are true of nothing. If intentional irrealism is correct, then it is not the case that

(1) 'Snow is white' means that snow is white.

or that

(2) George Bush often thinks about winning the next election.

or that

(3) Lincoln wanted to free the slaves.

Nor is it the case that

(4) Thinking about winning the election sometimes causes Bush to smile.

or that

(5) Lincoln's desire to free the slaves caused him to sign the Emancipation Proclamation.

We are grateful to Brian McLaughlin for many hours of helpful discussion. Versions of this essay have been presented at CUNY Graduate Center, Notre Dame University, the University of North Carolina-Greensboro, the Australian National University, and the University of Virginia. Comments and criticisms from those audiences are acknowledged with thanks. After completing work on this essay, early in 1992, we were delighted to discover that Michael Tye (1992 & 1994) had independently arrived at a very similar view.

Obviously, intentional irrealism has some very startling consequences. If it is true, then a very substantial part of what we read in our textbooks, teach our children, and say to each other is mistaken. Indeed, as Fodor has remarked, with only a bit of hyperbole,

> if it isn't literally true that my wanting is causally responsible for my reaching, and my itching is causally responsible for my scratching, and my believing is causally responsible for my saying . . . if none of that is literally true, then practically everything I believe about anything is false and it's the end of the world. (1990c, 156)

Though we rather doubt that the world would come to an end, perhaps Fodor is closer to the mark in claiming that if intentional irrealism is correct and "commonsense intentional psychology really were to collapse, that would be, beyond comparison, the greatest intellectual catastrophe in the history of our species. . . . The collapse of the supernatural didn't compare" (1987, xii).

Very well, then, let's agree that intentional irrealism is a very radical doctrine. But why on earth should anyone *worry* about it? Why does anyone think it is even remotely plausible? In the quotation with which we began this chapter, Fodor maintains that the "deepest motivation for intentional irrealism" is the suspicion "that the intentional can't be naturalized." Viewed as a bit of sociology, it is our guess that Fodor is right. In recent years, many philosophers have put a very high priority on providing a "naturalistic" account of intentional categories.[1] Moreover, there is an unmistakable tone of urgency in much of this literature. Naturalizing the intentional isn't just an interesting project, it is vitally important. *Something dreadful* will follow if it doesn't succeed. And for many writers, we suspect, that dreadful consequence is intentional irrealism.[2] But this sociological fact raises a philosophical puzzle. *Why* would irrealism (or some comparably unsettling conclusion) follow if "the intentional can't be naturalized?" What is the connection between the existence or nonexistence of a naturalistic account of intentional categories and the truth or falsehood of claims like (1)–(5)? These are the questions that motivate this essay.

To answer them, of course, it will be necessary to say just what is involved in "naturalizing" the intentional. And, as we shall see, there is no shortage of answers to choose

---

1. See, for example, Block (1986), Devitt (1990), Dretske (1981; 1988), Field (1978), Fodor (1984; 1987; 1990b; 1990c), Loar (1981), Lycan (1988), Millikan (1984), Papineau (1987), Schiffer (1982), Stalnaker (1984).

2. Schiffer provides a characteristically forthright illustration of this attitude. On his view, the question of how the semantic and the psychological are related to the physical is "an urgent question" since "we should not be prepared to maintain that there *are* semantical or psychological facts unless we are prepared to maintain that such facts are completely determined by, are nothing over and above, physical facts" (1982, 119).

    On Fodor's view, the urgency of the issue reaches to the very core of contemporary academic life. For if the intentional can't be naturalized, then lots of people who work in cognitive science should no longer get government-sponsored research grants: "If it turns out that the physicalization—naturalization—of intentional science . . . is impossible, . . . then it seems to me that what you ought to do is do your science in some other way. . . . If you really can't give an account of the role of the intentional in the physical world . . . [then] by Christ . . . we should stop spending the taxpayer's money" (1990b, 202–3).

from. But not just any answer will do. A satisfactory account of what it is to "naturalize the intentional"—an account that makes sense of what Fodor sees as "the deepest motivation for intentional irrealism"—will have to satisfy a pair of constraints. First, it will have to sustain an argument from the premise that intentional notions can't be naturalized to the conclusion that intentional irrealism or some other deeply troubling doctrine is true. Second, there must be some reason to think that, when "naturalizing" is unpacked along the lines proposed, it is in fact the case that the intentional can't be naturalized. For even if nonnaturalizability entails irrealism, this is surely nothing to worry about if the claim that the intentional can't be naturalized is neither intuitively plausible nor supported by a convincing argument.

It is our contention that, while various accounts will satisfy one or the other of these constraints, there is no account of what it is to naturalize the intentional that will satisfy *both* of them. To support our contention, we will survey a number of proposals on what "naturalization" comes to, and we will go on to argue that none of these candidates will satisfy both of the constraints. Obviously, this strategy won't provide a conclusive case for our conclusion, since there may be some quite different account of naturalizing that does satisfy both constraints. But if so, we haven't a clue about what it might be.

If we are right, if there is no account that satisfies both constraints, then there is something deeply misguided about the urgency that imbues so much of the recent literature in this area. It may, of course, be perfectly reasonable to adopt one or another account of what it would be to naturalize the intentional, and to explore the possibility of bringing it off. A successful naturalization might well be an impressive and valuable accomplishment. But if it should turn out that intentional notions can't be naturalized, *no dire consequences will follow*. We will not have to rewrite history, or renounce intentional psychology, or revise the way we describe and explain people's behavior. It will not be the end of the world. It won't even be the beginning of the end.

Before launching into our survey of accounts of "naturalizing," a few words are in order on some of the other troubling consequences that might be thought to follow if naturalization does not succeed. In Fodor's writing, and elsewhere in the literature, the dominant worry is the one that has been center stage in this section: If the intentional can't be naturalized, then intentional irrealism will have won the day. But often enough, one finds suggestions of other calamities that may ensue if naturalization fails. One of these is that intentional states might turn out to be causally impotent. In the passage quoted earlier, for example, Fodor frets that it's the end of the world if it isn't literally true that his wanting is causally responsible for his reaching and his believing is causally responsible for his saying. In Fred Dretske's writing, the worry that intentional states might turn out to be causally inert is frequently cited as a motive for seeking a naturalized account of these states. Indeed, Dretske sometimes suggests that if intentional states are causally impotent, then perhaps we should not include them in our ontology at all: "If beliefs and desires are not causally relevant to behavior, I, for one, fail to see why it would be worth having them. . . . If reasons aren't causes, one of the chief—indeed (for certain people) the *only*—motive for including them in one's inventory of the mind, vanishes" (1989, 1).[3] Another, rather different concern is that if naturalization fails, then there could be no serious *science* of intentional psychology because there could be no *laws* that invoke intentional terms or intentional properties. We are no more impressed by these worries than we are about the concern over irrealism. For, as we shall argue in the sections that follow, on any reading of the claim that the intentional can't be naturalized which is even remotely likely to be true, neither of these calamitous consequences would follow.

2 Naturalizing and Conceptual Analysis

Once upon a time, something called *conceptual analysis* was all the rage in philosophy. The journals back then were filled with attempts to provide necessary and sufficient conditions for the application of a term or a concept. And, more often than not, when one philosopher published such an "analysis" another philosopher would describe a hypothetical situation in which we would intuitively say that the analysans applied and the analysandum did not, or vice versa. For people who remember those bygone days (only one of us does), much of the literature on naturalizing the intentional provokes a strong sense of deja vu. Consider, for example, the following quotation:

> The worry about representation is above all that the semantic (and/or the intentional) will prove permanently recalcitrant to integration in the natural order. . . . What is required to relieve the worry is therefore, at a minimum, the framing of *naturalistic* conditions for representation. That is, what we want at a minimum is something of the form '*R represents S' is true iff C* where the vocabulary in which condition C is couched contains neither intentional nor semantic expressions. (Fodor 1984, 32)

Of course, an interest in providing necessary and sufficient conditions is not, by itself, enough to convict a philosopher of engaging in conceptual analysis. For typically, a conceptual analyst will not be happy with just any set of conditions that happen to be coextensive with the predicate being analyzed. If a proposed analysis is to be acceptable, it has to be the case that the coextension obtains not only in all actual cases but in imaginary or hypothetical cases as well. The biconditional specifying the analysis must not only be true, it must be *necessary*. Moreover, the alleged coextension in all possible worlds is supposed to be testable by consulting our linguistic intuition and determining what we would say about hypothetical cases. This method would seem to make the most sense if we suppose that the coextension derives from the meaning of the concepts that underlie our predicates—the analysans (the right-hand side of the biconditional) unpacks the meaning of the concept expressed by the analysandum.

---

3. See also Dretske (1988, 80) and Dretske (1990, 6).

Is it the case that Fodor and others who worry about the possibility that the intentional can't be naturalized are actually worried about the possibility that the meaning of intentional predicates or intentional concepts can't be set out as a set of necessary and sufficient conditions which do not themselves invoke intentional terms? We're not at all sure. Indeed, it is our suspicion that these philosophers have *no* clear idea of what "naturalizing" amounts to and that much of their anxiety can be traced to this confusion. But if it is not clear that these philosophers really want a conceptual analysis, it is clear that if "naturalizing" is understood in this way, it will not satisfy the first of our two constraints.

Indeed, it is rather ironic that Fodor often seems to be troubled by the fact that our intentional concepts can't be analyzed in nonintentional terms. For among contemporary philosophers, no one has been more adamant than Fodor in insisting that we should not expect our terms or concepts to be analyzable *at all*. Here is an example of the sorts of things he says when this mood is upon him:

It seems to me to be among the most important findings of philosophical and psychological research over the last several hundred years (say, since Locke first made the reductionist program explicit) that attempts at conceptual analysis practically always fail.

Consider, for example, the failure of the reductionist program within the study of language. . . . What I'll call the *Definition Hypothesis* [is the claim that] (a, weak version) . . . many de facto lexical concepts are definable; and (b, strong version) that they are definable in a vocabulary of sensory-terms-plus-logical-syntax.

It's simply notorious that the stronger version of this claim has proved to be untenable. . . . But what's equally true, and considerably more striking, is that the evidence seems to bear against the definition hypothesis even in the weak version; if there are no plausible cases of definition in a sensory vocabulary, there are also remarkably few plausible examples of definition in a *non*-sensory vocabulary, one indication of which is the striking paucity of working examples in the standard literature. There is 'bachelor,' which is supposed to mean 'unmarried man'; . . . there are jargon terms, which are explicitly and stipulatively defined; . . . there is a handful of terms which belong to real, honest-to-God axiomatic systems; . . . and then there are the other half million or so items that the OED lists. About these last apparently nothing much can be done. (1981, 283–84)

On our view, there can be no serious quarrel with Fodor's assessment of the track record of conceptual analysis. Though lots of very clever people have tried very hard to produce them over the centuries, we still have no plausible definitions for 'knowledge' or 'cause' or 'law' or 'freedom,' or for any of the other terms that loom large in philosophical discussion. Moreover, as Fodor goes on to illustrate, it is no easier to provide definitions for more mundane terms like 'paint' or 'parent' or 'pig.' The more one plays the game of trying to provide exceptionless, intuitively acceptable necessary and sufficient conditions, the more one is inclined to accept Fodor's conclusion: "When it comes to definitions, the examples almost always don't work" (1981, 288).

What are we to make of this situation? Well, of course, it might be that conceptual analysis is just *hard* and that if we keep at it we will ultimately succeed in producing a significant number of intuitively acceptable definitions. However, it is also entirely possible that we will never succeed—that the project of defining most common predicates is simply impossible.

If it *is* impossible, this will have important consequences for those parts of philosophy and psychology that deal with the structure of human concepts. There is a venerable tradition in this area which assumes that the concept or mental structure underlying the use of most predicates is actually a mentally represented definition—a set of necessary and sufficient conditions. In deciding whether or not a term applies to a given case, this "classical view" maintains, we are either consciously or (more typically) unconsciously determining whether the case at hand satisfies the conditions of the definition. If it turns out that there just are no definitions for most terms, then obviously the classical account of the structure and use of concepts will have to go.[4]

In recent years, there has been a growing realization that the classical account of concepts is in deep trouble, and a number of interesting alternatives have been proposed. Perhaps the best known of these are the prototype and exemplar accounts of concepts developed by Eleanor Rosch and her associates. On the prototype theory, concepts are weighted lists of features that are characteristic of the most typical members of the category that the concept picks out. The list will generally include lots of features that are not necessary for category membership. On the exemplar story, concepts are, in effect, detailed mental descriptions of particular members of the category. Thus, for example, the concept underlying your use of the word 'dog' might include detailed descriptions of Lassie and Rin Tin Tin. In determining whether to categorize something as a dog, this theory maintains, you assess the similarity between the target and the various exemplars stored in semantic memory (see Smith and Medin 1981, chaps. 4–6). Fodor has proposed a very different alternative to the classical account of concepts. On his view, the concepts that underlie most of our one-word predicates have no structure at all—or at least none that is relevant to the semantic properties of the concept. Of course, if this is right it is very hard to see how these concepts might be learned. And that's just fine with Fodor, since he thinks they are all innate (see Fodor 1981).

This is not the place to elaborate the details of these various "non–classical" theories of concepts or to debate their virtues and shortcomings. Our reason for mentioning them was simply to make clear that there are lots of interesting theories about concepts on the market which are compatible with (and which might well explain) the finding that most of our concepts appear to have no intuitively acceptable definitions. So, if it is indeed the

---

4. For a useful discussion of the classical view, see Smith and Medin (1981, chap. 3).

case that most concepts have no definitions, there is nothing much to worry about. Rather, the appropriate response is to get busy and try to determine which of the various non-classical theories of concepts is correct. It would, by contrast, be simply *mad* to think that if most of our concepts can't be defined, then the terms that express those concepts are not true of anything. The inference from *The predicate '_____ is a pig' cannot be defined* to *There are no such things as pigs* is simply perverse. Concern about porcine irrealism is not even a remotely appropriate reaction to the collapse of the classical theory of concepts. But, of course, exactly the same can be said about intentional predicates. Perhaps there are good reasons to worry about intentional irrealism being true, but the fact that '*R* represents *C*' can't be defined surely isn't one of them.[5]

What about the other two concerns that we sketched at the end of section 1? If intentional terms can't be defined, does it follow that intentional states are causally impotent or that there are no laws invoking intentional properties? In both cases, we maintain, the answer is clearly *no*. To see why, consider a few analogies. If the classical theory of concepts is wrong, then there will be no way to provide necessary and sufficient conditions for predicates like '*x* shot *y*' or '*z* died.' But from this, surely, it does not even begin to follow that it is not literally true that being shot by John Wilkes Booth caused Lincoln to die. And, of course, if the classical theory is wrong, then terms like 'force,' 'mass,' and 'gravity' won't be definable, either. But it would be at best a bad joke to conclude from

---

5. In the passage from Fodor (1984) quoted at the beginning of this section, he insists that "what we want at a minimum is something of the form '*R represents S' is true iff C*....*" But in later papers Fodor is prepared to accept a lot less. In the following passage, for example, he no longer insists on necessary and sufficient conditions. Rather, he tells us, merely sufficient conditions will do: "I want a *naturalized* theory of meaning; a theory that articulates, in nonsemantic and nonintentional terms, sufficient conditions for one bit of the world to be *about* (to express, represent, or be true of) another bit." (1987, 98; see also Fodor, 1990c, 51–52). As noted by Jones et al. (1991), if we read him literally, this is just too easy. Here are two sufficient conditions that seem to meet Fodor's requirement:

> If R is Fodor's most recent utterance of "meaning holism is a *crazy* doctrine" (or the thought that underlies it), then R is *about* meaning holism, and R is true iff meaning holism is a crazy doctrine.
> If R is Laurence's most recent utterance of "Madonna is daring" (or the thought that underlies it), then R is about Madonna and expresses the proposition that Madonna is daring.

Obviously, it would be an easy task to produce indefinitely many more. But perhaps this reading is uncharitably literal. Perhaps what Fodor requires in a naturalized theory of meaning are sufficient conditions which follow from the meaning of the terms involved. It is easy enough to provide intuitively plausible sufficient conditions of this sort for many nonintentional terms. Here's one: "For all x, if x is a sow, then x is a pig." But, of course, examples like this are cheating. In the spirit of Fodor's requirement that sufficient conditions for representation or aboutness be stated in *nonsemantic* and *nonintentional* terms, we should require that the sufficient conditions for being a pig be stated in *nonporcine* terms. Once *this* requirement is imposed, however, providing meaning-based sufficient conditions for being a pig looks to be just about as intractable as providing a full-blown definition. If it is impossible to provide such sufficient conditions, that will be an interesting result in lexical semantics. But it will *not* entail that there are no pigs. Similarly, if it turns out that meaning-based sufficient conditions cannot be given for intentional locutions, it will not follow that meaning is a myth.

this that there are no laws that invoke these terms. If the classical view of concepts collapses, it will not take all of physics with it. The situation seems entirely parallel for intentional terms. If it turns out that they can't be analyzed or defined, this would provide no reason at all to conclude that intentional states are causally impotent or that there are no laws invoking them. So if "naturalizing the intentional" requires providing a classical analysis of intentional concepts, then if the intentional can't be naturalized, we have found no reason to think that anything at all troublesome will follow.

3 Naturalizing, Natural Kinds, and Essential Properties

To set the stage for our second account of what it might be to naturalize the intentional, we'll begin with a brief reminder of some very influential doctrines in the philosophy of language. Consider so-called natural kind predicates like 'water' or 'gold.' What is it that determines which parts of the world are in the extension of such predicates? According to the widely discussed causal-historical account of reference, the answer to this question must invoke the notion of "essential properties" of natural kinds—properties that everything in the extension of a natural-kind term must have. A bit fancifully, the causal-historical story might be sketched as follows:

> A kind term first acquires its referent when it is used to "baptize" or "dub" some newly noted samples of the stuff to which the term will refer. This process is sometimes described as "grounding" the predicate. Once the predicate has been grounded, it can be transmitted from one speaker to another in appropriate communicative settings. And those to whom the predicate is passed can pass it on again. The speakers who originally ground the predicate need have no deep understanding of the nature of the stuff they are dubbing; indeed, they may have all sorts of wildly mistaken beliefs about it. The speakers who acquire the predicate via reference-preserving transmissions need never have come in contact with anything in the extension of the predicate. They, too, can harbor many false beliefs about the nature of the stuff to which the term refers.

Now obviously, there is something missing in this tale. For a predicate like 'gold' gets grounded on just a few samples of gold. And yet the extension of the predicate must include *all* the gold that ever has or ever will exist in the universe. What is the relation between the dubbed samples and the rest of the gold in the universe, in virtue of which the dubbing succeeds in attaching the term to all gold, wherever it may be? It is here that the doctrine of *essential properties* is typically brought into play. The basic idea is that individual items are grouped into natural kinds in virtue of the possession of certain essential properties, and it is the job of science to discover what these properties are. Thus, for example, science tells us that having atomic number 79 is the essential property of gold, that being H_2O is the essential property of water, and so on. When a natural-kind term gets grounded, the term comes to apply not only to the samples present at the dubbing but also to everything else in the universe that has the same essential properties.

How does all of this relate to the project of naturalizing the intentional? To see the answer, let's go back to the quotation from Fodor near the beginning of the previous section. What was worrying Fodor was that intentional categories might "prove permanently recalcitrant to integration in the natural order." And what was required to relieve the worry was "a framing of naturalistic conditions for representation . . . something of the form '*R represents S' is true iff C* where the vocabulary in which condition C is couched contains neither intentional nor semantic expressions." Our first pass at unpacking this requirement was to view it as a demand for a conceptual analysis. But it could equally well be viewed as asking for a specification of an underlying essential property— the property in virtue of which the predicate '*R* represents *S*' applies to all and only those pairs of things in the universe such that the first represents the second. On this interpretation, the biconditional needed to naturalize the representation relation would have a status akin to the one Putnam and others have attributed to biconditionals like:

(6) (x) x is water iff x is H_2O.

It is a necessary truth, but its necessity has nothing to do with the structure of the concepts that speakers invoke when they use the terms involved. It isn't known a priori, and it can't be discovered by probing intuitions or by doing psycholinguistics. The only way to discover it is to do the appropriate sort of science.

How likely is it that *this* is what philosophers want when they set about trying to naturalize the intentional? Well, there are some practitioners of the craft who offer accounts of representation that rely heavily on notions borrowed from science (typically evolutionary biology). Some of these writers go out of their way to explain that they are not trying to capture our intuitions about representation and thus are not worried by the fact that their analyses have counterintuitive consequences.[6] All of this is compatible with the interpretation that these philosophers are seeking an account of the essential properties of representation. But we don't propose to press the point, since, as we noted earlier, we rather suspect that most of the writers who worry about naturalizing the intentional have no clear idea of what naturalizing amounts to. What is clear is that if 'naturalizing' is interpreted in this way, then once again it will not satisfy our first constraint.

One way of arguing for this claim would be to mount a head-on assault on the whole idea of scientifically discoverable essential properties and on the account of the reference of natural-kind terms that goes along with it. There is already a substantial literature pointing out the shortcomings of this rather trendy package of ideas, and we have

6. See, for example, Millikan (1989, 290–91).

considerable sympathy with the emerging critique.[7] But all that would make a very long argument, and we have a much shorter one to offer.

Suppose it is the case that the doctrine of essential properties and the associated story about reference can survive serious scrutiny. Suppose further that when 'naturalizing' is interpreted in the way we've just sketched, it turns out that 'R represents S' and other intentional predicates cannot be naturalized. Would this be enough to make intentional irrealism plausible? Surely, the answer is *no*. To see the point, we need only note that there are endlessly many predicates for which no one would even dream of seeking scientifically discoverable essential properties. Yet it would be simply perverse to claim that these predicates can't be truly applied to anything. Nobody seriously thinks that anything remotely analogous to (6) would be available for such one-place predicates as 'couch,' 'car,' 'war,' 'famine,' or 'die,' nor for two-place predicates like 'owns,' 'kills,' 'throws,' 'mates with,' 'fixes,' or 'crushes.' But it would be preposterous to suggest that this entails there is no killing or war or famine and that no one ever owns anything or dies. If natural-kind terms are defined as those whose extension is determined by scientifically discoverable essential properties, then one way of putting our point is that there are many, many predicates that are not natural-kind terms, and the fact that they are not natural-kind terms is no reason at all to suppose that they cannot be truly predicated of anything. So, if it turns out that nothing analogous to (6) is forthcoming for intentional predicates, the right conclusion is not that those predicates are true of nothing but simply that, in the sense lately defined, they are not natural-kind terms. And that would hardly be the end of the world.

Could it be that while intentional irrealism doesn't follow from the fact that intentional predicates aren't natural-kind terms, something comparably unsettling does follow? Let's take a brief look at the pair of possibilities suggested at the end of section 1. The first of them focuses on the causal efficacy of intentional states. Might it be the case that if intentional predicates aren't natural-kind terms in the sense we've defined, then they can't be used to make causal claims that are literally true? This strikes us as a singularly implausible suggestion. For, as we noted earlier, it is literally true that being shot by John Wilkes Booth caused Abraham Lincoln to die, though neither 'shoots' nor 'dies' is likely to be the sort of term whose extension is determined by scientifically discoverable essential properties. So, even if it turns out that intentional predicates are not natural-kind terms in the sense we've defined, the causal efficacy of intentional states and processes might still be on a par with the causal efficacy of shooting, crushing, eating, or mating. And that should be efficacy enough for anyone.

A second possibility is that if intentional predicates aren't natural-kind terms, then perhaps there could be no science of intentional psychology. For, it might be argued, such a science would have to include intentional laws, and laws can only be stated with natural-kind terms. No kind terms, no laws; no laws, no science. Now as we see it, the problem here comes with the link between kind terms and laws. *Why* can laws only be stated with

7. Canfield (1983), Donnellan (1983), Leplin (1979;1988), Shapere (1982).

natural-kind terms? One might view it as simply a stipulative definition: natural-kind terms just are the sorts of terms that can occur in law-like statements. But now we have a potential equivocation on our hands. For we have been assuming that natural-kind terms are defined as those whose extension is determined by scientifically discoverable essential properties, and the current argument proposes a very different definition. Of course, it might be claimed that these two definitions pick out the same class of terms—that all and only terms whose extension is determined by scientifically discoverable essential properties can be used in law-like statements. But we find this a singularly implausible proposal. For in sciences far removed from psychology, there appear to be lots of terms invoked in laws for which nothing much like (6) is in the offing. We see no reason at all to suppose there are scientifically discoverable essential properties that fix the reference of terms like 'inflation,' 'fitness,' 'mass,' 'gravity,' or 'electric charge,' for example. If this is right—if there are lots of terms invoked in scientific laws whose extensions are not fixed in the way that the causal-historical theory claims the extensions of terms like 'gold' are fixed—then the putative threat to intentional psychology disappears.

Thus far we have been arguing that an account of naturalizing the intentional which requires producing something akin to (6) will not satisfy the first of our two constraints. Neither intentional irrealism nor any other catastrophic consequence follows if the intentional can't be naturalized, when 'naturalizing' is interpreted in this way. But we are also inclined to think that if we take seriously the story about reference that serves as a backdrop for the current proposal on naturalizing, then our second constraint will not be satisfied, either. For if that story is correct, then the usual arguments aimed at showing that the intentional can't be naturalized just don't go through.

Those arguments typically begin by describing some feature or cluster of features that are important or essential for intentional states, *on the commonsense account of these states.* The arguments then try to show that respectable scientific theories cannot accommodate states with the features in question. The conclusions the arguments draw are just the ones that Fodor feared: that the intentional "will prove permanently recalcitrant to integration in the natural order" and that "there is no place for intentional categories in a physicalistic view of the world." However, if the causal-historical account of reference is correct, then the conclusions of these arguments do not follow from the premises. For on the causal-historical account, the essential properties that determine the extension of natural-kind terms are to be discovered by science, and our commonsense views about the things we are referring to with natural-kind terms may be wildly, hopelessly wrong. Indeed, the fact that ignorance and error do not undermine reference is taken to be a major selling point of the causal-historical theory.[8] But if our commonsense views about the things we are referring to may be seriously mistaken, then the (alleged) fact that common sense imbues intentional states with scientifically unacceptable features entails nothing at all about the scientific respectability of intentional states. For common sense may just be

---

8. See, for example, Devitt and Sterelny (1987, secs. 4.2 and 5.2).

wrong; our intentional terms may actually refer to states that do not have these scientifically unacceptable features. So if the causal-historical theory of reference is correct, there can be no serious argument from premises about the commonsense characterization of intentional states to conclusions about the role that the intentional states referred to by commonsense psychology might play in scientifically acceptable theories. Without some argument along those lines, however, it is hard to see why we would have any reason to believe that the intentional can't be naturalized.[9]

4 Naturalizing and Supervenience

> It's hard to see . . . how one can be a Realist about intentionality without also being, to some extent or other, a Reductionist. If the semantic and the intentional are real properties of things, it must be in virtue of their identity with (or maybe of their supervenience on?) properties that are themselves *neither* intentional *nor* semantic. If aboutness is real, it must be really something else. (Fodor 1987, 98)

4.1 THE GAME PLAN

Thus far we haven't done very well in finding interpretations of 'naturalizing' that satisfy our two constraints. But in the passage just quoted, Fodor seems to be making a pair of suggestions that we haven't yet explored. To avoid irrealism, intentional properties must be *identical with* or *supervene upon* nonintentional properties. So, perhaps naturalization should be explained in terms of property identity or supervenience. In the current section, we'll consider whether either of *these* proposals satisfies our two constraints. Actually, we will focus almost entirely on supervenience, since on all plausible accounts of that notion, it is a weaker relation than identity. Indeed, on most accounts, property identity entails supervenience, and thus nonsupervenience entails non-identity. So, if nothing nasty follows from the fact that the intentional doesn't supervene on the nonintentional, then the fact that intentional properties are not identical with nonintentional ones will be no cause for worry.

In restricting our attention to supervenience, we are not exactly making things easy for ourselves, however. For the literature on supervenience has blossomed profusely during the last few years, and this literature suggests a variety of different ways in which the idea that the intentional supervenes on the nonintentional may be spelled out.[10] These alternatives differ on a pair of dimensions. First, the notion of one class of properties supervening on another can be explicated in two different ways, one of which (so-called *strong supervenience*) entails the other (*weak supervenience*). Second, there are various options that might be proposed as the "supervenience base" for intentional properties—the

---

9. For some elaboration on the argument set out in the last two paragraphs, see Stich (1991a).

10. Haugeland (1982), Horgan (1982), Kim (1978; 1982; 1984; 1987), Lewis (1983), Petrie (1987), Teller (1984).

class of properties on which intentional properties are expected to supervene. In the arguments that follow, we will restrict our attention to weak supervenience. For, since strong supervenience entails weak supervenience, the failure of weak supervenience entails the failure of strong. Thus, if we can show that no untoward consequences follow when weak supervenience does not obtain, the same conclusion will follow if strong supervenience fails.

Here's the game plan. We'll begin with a brief explanation of the two notions of supervenience. We'll then attend to three different candidates that might be proposed as the supervenience base for intentional properties. In each of these three cases, we will argue that the constraints set out in section 1 are not met. In the first two cases, it is the first constraint that isn't satisfied: Neither irrealism nor the other unwelcome consequences follow if supervenience fails. In the third case, it is the second constraint that isn't satisfied. For in this case, it is wildly implausible that supervenience fails. We will follow all of this with a brief discussion of another notion of supervenience, so-called *global supervenience*, whose precise relation to the other two notions is a matter of some dispute. Here again, we will argue, nothing catastrophic follows if intentional properties fail to supervene on the various bases that have been proposed. End of game plan. It's time to get to work.

4.2   TWO NOTIONS OF SUPERVENIENCE

Supervenience is usually construed as a relation between two classes of properties. So to begin, let us adopt the following convention. Let B and S be two classes of properties (think of them as the base class and the supervenient class) whose members are $b_1, b_2, \ldots,$ $b_i, \ldots$ and $s_1, s_2, \ldots s_i, \ldots$ respectively. Now, the basic idea is that one class of properties, S, supervenes on a second, B, if the presence or absence of properties in the first class is completely determined by the presence or absence of properties in the second class. There are various ways in which this basic idea can be made more precise.

Perhaps the most intuitive way to proceed is to exploit the notion of a B- or S-doppelganger. A B-doppelganger of an object is an object that has exactly the same B properties as the original. An S-doppelganger is one which has exactly the same S properties. Thus, for example, if B includes only two sorts of properties, height and weight, then your B-doppelgangers are all and only those things that have the same height and weight that you do. One vivid way to explicate the various versions of the idea that B properties determine S properties is to use the picturesque language of possible worlds. If in all possible worlds, every pair of B-doppelgangers that exist in that world are also S-doppelgangers, then we will say that *S weakly supervenes on B*. So, if S weakly supervenes on B, then in any possible world we select, if we know that a pair of objects in that world share the same B properties, we know they share the same S properties as well. And if a pair of objects in that world do not share the same S properties, we know that there must be at least one B property that one has and the other doesn't. We can build a stronger notion of supervenience if we relax the restriction that the B-doppelgangers are in the same world. We will say that *S strongly supervenes on B* if all B-doppelgangers of an object, no matter what possible world they inhabit, are also S-doppelgangers. Obviously, strong supervenience entails weak supervenience. Plainly, there are lots of other distinctions that might be drawn by restricting attention to one or another special class of possible worlds. But we will leave all of that to the aficionados. Henceforth, when we use 'supervenience' we will mean weak supervenience, as characterized above, unless otherwise specified.

4.3 THE SUPERVENIENCE BASE: THREE PROPOSALS

On what sorts of properties might it be thought (or hoped) that intentional properties should supervene? As we read the literature, there are at least three proposals for the base class on which intentional properties must supervene if nasty consequences are to be avoided. We propose to consider each of these proposals, proceeding from the most restrictive to the least.

4.3.1 Current, Internal, Physical Properties

The first idea is that something untoward will follow if the intentional properties of an organism do not supervene on the *current, internal, physical properties* of the organism. These are the properties that organisms share with their Putnamian doppelgangers—the hypothetical particle for particle replicas that exist in some far corner of space-time.[11] And if intentional properties supervene on current, internal, physical properties, then in any given world, organisms must have the same intentional properties as their Putnamian doppelgangers. What makes this proposal particularly interesting is that it is widely agreed that there are possible worlds in which organisms and their Putnamian doppelgangers *do not* share all of their intentional properties. Indeed, that's the main point that Putnam's famous thought experiment was supposed to establish. George Bush has many beliefs *about* Michail Gorbachev; he has no beliefs at all about Twin Gorbachev, the atom-for-atom replica in some far-off corner of the universe. The situation is just the opposite for George Bush's doppelganger. Twin Bush has lots of beliefs about Twin Gorbachev and none about the Gorbachev who leads his life in our part of the universe. But while there is considerable agreement about the fact that at least some intentional properties don't supervene on current, internal, physical properties, there is much less agreement on what unwelcome consequences this failure of supervenience is supposed to entail. Let's consider the options.

First on our list, as always, must be the specter of intentional irrealism—the thesis that intentional properties aren't "real properties of things." But surely intentional irrealism

---

11. This idea, or something like it, is suggested in Stich (1978a; 1983) and in Fodor (1980; 1987; 1991). For the original account of Putnamian doppelgangers, see Putnam (1975).

would be a preposterous conclusion to draw from the fact that intentional properties don't supervene on current, internal, physical properties. For there are lots of properties of objects that don't supervene on their current, internal, physical properties—often, it would appear, for much the same reason that intentional properties do not. And it would be quite absurd to suggest that nonsupervenience entails irrealism in *all* these cases. To see the point, consider a few examples. There are lots of copies of Picasso paintings in the world. And some of them are astoundingly accurate. Let us imagine that someone produces a "perfect" copy—a canvas that is an atom-for-atom duplicate of the original. Of course, the perfect copy would still be a *copy*, it wouldn't be the original. For to be an original Picasso, a canvas must have the right *history*—it must actually have been painted by Picasso. Much the same point can be made about real $100 bills. A master counterfeiter might produce a bill that is an atom-for-atom replica of one produced by the Bureau of Engraving and Printing. But it would still not be a *real* $100 bill. Indeed, as Fodor has noted, not even *God* can make a real $100 bill. Only a branch of the U.S. Treasury can do that (1987, 45). It follows, then, that neither the property of being an original Picasso nor the property of being a genuine $100 bill supervenes on the current, internal, physical states of an object. So, if a property's failure to supervene on current, internal, physical states were sufficient to show that nothing has the property, then it would follow that there are no genuine Picassos or real $100 bills. But that, of course, is just silly. The idea that intentional irrealism follows from failure to supervene on current, internal, physical states is equally silly.

Before pushing on, it will be useful to mention a rather different sort of example. Both genuine Picassos and real $100 bills are artifacts. And it might be thought that natural properties or categories are not linked to history in this way. But this is almost certainly a mistake. To see the point, consider the classification of organisms into species. Regardless of how similar a pair of organisms are, it is plausible to suppose that they will not count as members of the same species unless they also share the appropriate sort of evolutionary history. If there are creatures in Australia that evolved from birds, then they do not count as members of the same species as Stich's cat, Eggplant, no matter how similar their current, internal, physical states and Eggplant's current, internal, physical states may be. And if scientific explorers on Mars should come upon a macromolecule that is an atom-for-atom replica of an HIV virus isolated on Earth, it would not be an HIV virus unless it shared a common evolutionary ancestry with HIV viruses found on Earth. If this is right, then the property of being a cat and the property of being an HIV virus do not supervene on the current, internal states of the entities that have those properties. But here again, it would be simply absurd to conclude that there are no such things as cats or HIV viruses.

What we have been arguing in the last two paragraphs is that intentional irrealism does not even begin to follow from the fact that intentional properties do not supervene on the current, internal, physical states or organisms. Let's now ask whether one of our other discomforting conclusions follows from the failure of the intentional to supervene on this sort of base. Does it, perhaps, follow that intentional states, though they exist, must be causally impotent—that believings can't cause sayings, that wantings can't cause scratchings—and thus that the end of the world is near? It seems clear that the answer is no. To see why, consider an analogy. Suppose some poor fellow, call him Henry, is crushed to death when an original Picasso sculpture falls on him. Being crushed by an original Picasso caused Henry to die. In some possible world in which Henry exists, we may suppose that he has a twin who is crushed to death by an atom-for-atom identical statue but one which was not made by Picasso. So, being crushed by an original Picasso does *not* cause Twin Henry to die. Nonetheless, it is "literally true" that being crushed by an original Picasso caused Henry to die. Consider now the case of intentional causation. Suppose that both Bush and Twin Bush say, "Gorbachev is bold." Only Bush believes that Gorbachev is bold, however; Twin Bush believes that Twin Gorbachev is bold. Does this difference somehow entail that it could not be "literally true" that Bush's belief caused his utterance? Since it appears that this case is entirely parallel to the previous one, it's hard to see why we should be skeptical about one causal claim and not about the other.

Another worry that one might have at this point focuses on the causal efficacy *of properties* rather than *states*. The concern might be put like this:

> Though it is true enough that Bush's belief state causes his utterance despite its failure to supervene on his current, internal, physical properties, it isn't true that this state causes his utterance *in virtue of being the belief that Gorbachev is bold*. What is worrisome about this sort of failure to "naturalize" the intentional is that it makes intentional properties casually irrelevant.[12]

Now, we are none too clear about how one goes about determining the causal efficacy of properties. But, for argument's sake, let us grant that if intentional properties do not supervene on the current, internal, physical properties of organisms, then intentional properties are not causally efficacious. Would this be a major catastrophe? So far as we can see, it would be no catastrophe at all. For, given any intentional property, it is easy to find a "narrow" surrogate of that property which *does* supervene on the current, internal, physical state of the organisms. Following Stich (1991b), we can take the property of believing that *[p]* to be the narrow surrogate of believing that *p*. The extension of the expression, "_____ believes that *[p]*" is just the class of all possible individuals who believe *that p* along with all of their current-internal-physical-property doppelgangers.[13] Similarly, we could construct a "narrow" surrogate for the property of being an HIV virus. The

---

12. For a vivid illustration of this worry, see Dretske (1988, 79–80).

13. Alternatively, if the reference to possible individuals is problematic, we can take the extension of "_____ believes that *[p]*" in a given possible world to be the class of all individuals in that world who believe that *p*, and all their current-internal-physical-property doppelgangers in that world, and all individuals in that world who are current-internal-physical-property doppelgangers of individuals in other possible worlds who believe that *p*. (The account in Stich 1991b neglects this last conjunct.)

extension of this surrogate property would be the class of all possible entities that have the property of being an HIV virus, along with all their current-internal-physical-property doppelgangers. Here, again, the narrow surrogate *will* supervene on the current, internal, physical states of the entities in question. Thus, even if we grant that intentional properties (and properties like being an HIV virus) are not causally efficacious, there is no reason to fear that the end of the world is near. In both cases, the properties fail to be causally efficacious because they have historical or relational components "built in." But it is easy enough to characterize narrow surrogates that factor out the historical or relational components. And we see no reason at all to suppose that these narrow surrogates are not causally efficacious. It's hard to think that even Fodor's Granny could ask for more.[14]

Let's turn to the worry about laws. Does the fact that intentional properties don't supervene on current, internal, physical states indicate that they cannot play a role in laws? There are, in the literature, a number of arguments aimed at establishing some sort of link between laws and properties that supervene on the current, internal, physical states of systems. But we don't propose to tackle these arguments head-on, for, if the truth be known, we are not at all sure we really understand them.[15] But we are sure that when one starts looking at cases, the proposed link seems very implausible. Consider the HIV virus. Though the details are still to be worked out, it is plausible to assume there is a law-like connection between infection by the HIV virus and the death of certain cells that play an important role in the immune system. Thus, something like the following might well turn out to be a law:

For all x, if x is infected by the HIV virus (and certain further conditions are met), then most of x's T-cells will be destroyed.

But if the current worry were correct, then there could be no such law, because being infected by the HIV virus is not a property that supervenes on an organism's current, internal, physical state. For a rather different example, consider Greshem's law, which claims that bad money drives good money out of circulation. Plainly, neither the property of being money nor the properties of being good and bad money supervene on the current, internal, physical state of coins, banknotes, wampum, and the like. But this is no reason at all to suppose that Greshem's law is mistaken. Analogously, the fact that intentional properties do not supervene on the current, internal, physical states of organisms does not entail that intentional properties cannot play a role in laws. So, the reading of "naturalizing the intentional" which requires showing that the intentional supervenes on the current, internal, physical state of the organism fails to satisfy our first constraint.

14. For more on Fodor's Granny and her views, see Fodor (1987, passim) and Loewer and Rey (1991, ii).

15. One of these arguments is found in Fodor (1987, chap. 2). Another is in Fodor (1991). Fodor himself no longer claims to understand the first of these. For a critique of the second, see Christensen (1992).

If the intentional can't be naturalized (in this sense), nothing on our list of unwelcome consequences will follow.

4.3.2 All Physical Properties

A second proposal for a supervenience base widens the base class by dropping the restriction to *current, internal* states. On this proposal, intentional properties will be naturalized if we can show that they supervene on *physical* properties of the organism. Though it is not entirely clear which properties to count as physical properties, a natural way to construe the current proposal is to take the physical properties to be those that might be invoked in physical laws. When the proposal is construed in this way, however, just about everything we said in the previous section can be repeated with minor modifications. More specifically:

1. Intentional properties do not supervene on physical properties. The crucial difference between Bush and Twin Bush is that the former has had appropriate causal interactions with Gorbachev, while the latter has had completely parallel interactions with Twin Gorby. But having had appropriate causal interactions with Gorby (rather than Twin Gorby) is not the sort of property that is likely to be invoked by a physical law.

2. Being a genuine Picasso or a real $100 bill doesn't supervene on physical properties either.

3. Thus, if the fact that a property, p, does not supervene on physical properties is sufficient to establish that nothing has p, then we would have to be irrealists about genuine Picassos and real $100 bills. And that's absurd.

4. So, the failure of the intentional to supervene on the physical will give no support at all to intentional irrealism.

5. The properties that differentiate people who are crushed by original Picassos from their twins who are crushed by perfect copies are not properties that will be invoked in physical laws. But it may still be literally true that Henry's death was caused by being crushed by an original Picasso. Analogously, the fact that Bush believes that Gorbachev is bold, while Twin Bush believes that Twin Gorbachev is bold, does not entail that Bush's utterance was not caused by his belief.

6. Finally, the properties that distinguish real HIV viruses from their atom-for-atom duplicates on Mars are not properties that physics is likely to invoke. Nonetheless, it may well turn out to be a law that if a person is infected by HIV, then most of his or her T-cells will die. So, the fact that a property does not supervene on physical properties does not preclude it from being invoked in a law. Thus, the failure of the intentional to supervene on the physical would not entail that intentional properties can't be invoked in laws.

We conclude that the second proposed base does no better than the first. If naturalizing the intentional means showing that the intentional supervenes on the physical, then if the intentional can't be naturalized, none of our catastrophic consequences will follow.

4.3.3 All Nonintentional Properties

The final proposal for a supervenience base that we will consider is the one that Fodor seems to be urging in the quotation with which we began this section. If semantic and intentional properties are real properties of things, he urges, they must be identical with or supervene on "properties that are themselves neither intentional nor semantic." So, let's ask whether our constraints are satisfied if we construe naturalizing the intentional to require that intentional properties weakly supervene on the class of all nonintentional and nonsemantic properties. The answer we would urge is no. But in this case, the problem is with the second constraint, not the first. For when naturalizing is understood in this way, the claim that the intentional can't be naturalized is extremely implausible—indeed it may be incoherent. To see the point, we need only remind ourselves of what has to be the case if one class of properties, S, does not supervene on another, B. For supervenience to fail, there must be a possible world in which there are B-doppelgangers that are not S-doppelgangers. That is, there must be objects, x and y, in some world that share all of their B properties but do not share all of their S properties. On the current proposal, the B properties are *all* nonintentional and nonsemantic properties. So the B-doppelgangers, x and y, must share their physical properties, their relational properties, their spatial location, their temporal location, and their history. But surely, if x and y share *all* of these properties, then x and y are *identical*. And if x and y are identical, then they share all their properties, including their intentional properties.

On the current reading of what naturalizing comes to, it would indeed be a catastrophe if the intentional could not be naturalized. For if this happened, then in some possible world there would be a single object which both did and did not have a certain property, and logic itself would crumble.[16] Fortunately, there is not the slightest reason to take this prospect seriously.

4.4 GLOBAL SUPERVENIENCE

Before bringing this chapter to a close, we propose to take a brief look at a third strategy for spelling out the idea of one class of properties supervening on another, the one that goes by the label 'global supervenience.' In defining both weak and strong supervenience, the notion of *objects* that were B- or S-doppelgangers of one another played a central role.

---

16. This argument will not work if naturalizing is unpacked in terms of strong supervenience, since in that case the B-doppelgangers might be in different possible worlds. Our view about the account of naturalizing that requires strong supervenience on all nonintentional properties is much the same as our view—set out at the end of 4.4—about the account that requires global supervenience on those properties.

But, as the name suggests, in global supervenience the central notion is that of *worlds* that are doppelgangers of one another. A pair of possible worlds are doppelgangers of one another with respect to a given property if and only if the total distribution of the property in one of those worlds is the same as the total distribution of the property in the other. So, for example, a possible world which is exactly like our world except for the fact that Stich's cat, Eggplant, has a black nose rather than a pink one would be a shape- and size-doppelganger of the actual world. But that world would not be a color-doppelganger of the actual world. With this notion in hand, we can define global supervenience as follows: A class of properties, S, globally supervenes on a class of properties, B, if and only if all possible worlds that are B-doppelgangers are also S-doppelgangers. So if S globally supervenes on B, then if a pair of worlds are indistinguishable with respect to the properties in B, they will also be indistinguishable with respect to the properties in S.

In the previous section, we considered three proposals for the base class on which it might be thought that intentional properties should supervene. The first of these, the class of current, internal, physical properties of an object, has no obvious application when global supervenience is at issue. But the other two, the class of physical properties and the class of all nonintentional properties, might both be proposed as a global supervenience base for the class of intentional properties. Let's consider each of them in turn.

Recall that, as we proposed to unpack the notion, a physical property is one that might be invoked in a physical law. Do intentional properties globally supervene on physical properties, when physical properties are construed in this way? The answer, we think, is clearly no. For it seems extremely plausible to suppose that there is a possible world, W_1, that is a physical doppelganger of the actual world as it exists right now but which has no history at all. W_1 is one of those worlds that Russell often worried about. It was created just a few seconds ago, fully stocked with phony fossils and light waves racing toward earth just as they would be if they had been emitted by stars millions of years ago. But if W_1 has no history, then, according to many philosophers, the distribution of intentional properties in W_1 must be very different from the distribution of intentional properties in our world. For in our world, Laurence has lots of beliefs about Julius Caesar; he is connected to Caesar in just the right way to have these beliefs, whatever that way is. But in W_1, Laurence has no beliefs about Caesar. There was no Caesar to have beliefs about in W_1, so Laurence couldn't be connected to him in the right way.

Very well, then, intentional properties do not globally supervene on physical properties. What follows? Nothing terribly troublesome, so far as we can see. The arguments here are pretty much the same as those in 4.3.2. There are *lots* of properties that do not globally supervene on physical properties—the property of being a genuine Picasso, for example (there are no genuine Picassos in W_1), and the property of being a real $100 bill. But from the fact that these properties do not globally supervene on the physical, it surely does not follow that there are no real Picassos and $100 bills in our world. Analogously, from the fact that the intentional doesn't globally supervene on the physical, it does not follow that intentional properties are not instantiated in our world. The property of being an HIV virus doesn't globally supervene on the physical, either. But from this we cannot conclude that this property can't be invoked in laws, nor, alas, can we conclude that being infected by HIV doesn't cause people to die. And here, again, the situation for intentional properties looks to be exactly the same.

What about the broader base, the class of all nonintentional properties? Do intentional properties globally supervene on this base? Once again, so far as we can see, the answer is no. For it certainly seems to be logically possible for there to be a world W_2, that is a nonintentional doppelganger of the actual world but in which trees or cars or dead people have beliefs or desires or some other intentional states. And it also seems logically possible for there to be a world, W_3, that is a nonintentional doppelganger of the actual world but in which Dan Quayle has no thoughts at all—he's just a mindless organic robot. The sorts of worlds we are imagining are, near enough, the sorts that some property dualists suppose the actual world might be. And whatever problems one might think this sort of property dualism confronts, it certainly does not seem to be a logically incoherent view. If it is not logically incoherent, if worlds like W_2 and W_3 really are possible, then intentional properties do not globally supervene on nonintentional properties. But it is hard to see why anyone would think that catastrophic consequences follow. Surely the logical possibility of a world like W_2 or W_3 does not entail that intentional properties are not instantiated in the actual world. Nor, so far as we can see, does it even begin to entail that *in our world* intentional states are causally impotent or that they cannot be invoked in laws of nature.

At this point, we fear, a resolute opponent might begin fiddling with the notion of possibility that is embedded in the definition of global supervenience. Such an opponent might suspect that problems will arise if there are pairs of *nomologically possible* worlds or *metaphysically possible* worlds that are nonintentional doppelgangers but not intentional doppelgangers. The path on which our imagined opponent has embarked is not one we're tempted to follow, for we suspect that it leads directly to a metaphysical swamp. Moreover, even if unwelcome consequences really do follow in these cases—and we see no clear reason to suppose that they do—we are inclined to think that both of them violate our second constraint. It is certainly not intuitively plausible that there are pairs of nomologically or metaphysically possible words that *are* nonintentional doppelgangers but *are not* intentional doppelgangers. Most people, including many who seem to have exquisitely subtle metaphysical intuition, have no intuitions at all about matters like this. So, until someone presents a plausible argument that such world pairs are nomologically or metaphysically possible, we see no reason to take the prospect seriously.

5 Conclusion

It's time to sum up. We began with Fodor's observation that "the deepest motivation for intentional irrealism derives . . . from a certain ontological intuition: . . . that the intentional can't be *naturalized.*" But we have had no success at all in making sense of this motivation. If the motivation is to stand up to scrutiny, there must be some account of what naturalizing the intentional comes to which satisfies a pair of constraints. First, the account must sustain an argument from the premise that the intentional can't be naturalized to the conclusion that nothing satisfies intentional properties (or perhaps to the conclusion that intentional states are causally impotent, or to the conclusion that there can be no intentional laws). Second, the claim that the intentional can't be naturalized must not turn out to be utterly implausible. None of the accounts we have been considering satisfy both of these constraints. Of course, it is always possible that there is some other account that will satisfy the constraints. But at this point we think the ball is in the other guy's court. Until some account of naturalizing is given that satisfies both constraints, the most plausible view is that the motivation that Fodor recounts is simply confused. There may be good reasons to take the prospect of intentional irrealism seriously, but the worry that the intentional can't be naturalized is not one of them.

REFERENCES

Baker, L. (1987). *Saving Belief*, Princeton, Princeton University Press.

Block, N. (1986). "Advertisement for a Semantics for Psychology," in P. French et al., eds., *Midwest Studies in Philosophy: Studies in the Philosophy of Mind*, Minneapolis, University of Minnesota Press.

Canfield, J. (1983). "Discovering Essence," in C. Ginet & S. Shoemaker, eds., *Knowledge and Mind*, Oxford, Oxford University Press.

Christensen, D. (1992). "Causal Powers and Conceptual Connections," *Analysis*, 52.

Devitt, M. (1990). "A Narrow Representational Theory of the Mind," in W. Lycan, ed., *Mind and Cognition*, Oxford, Basil Blackwell.

Devitt, M. & Sterelny, K. (1987). *Language and Reality*, Cambridge, MA, Bradford Books/MIT Press.

Donnellan, K. (1983). "Kripke and Putnam on Natural Kind Terms," in C. Ginet & S. Shoemaker, eds., *Knowledge and Mind*, Oxford, Oxford University Press.

Dretske, F. (1981). *Knowledge and the Flow of Information*, Cambridge, MA, Bradford Books/ MIT Press.

Dretske, F. (1988). *Explaining Behavior*, Cambridge, MA, Bradford Books/MIT Press.

Dretske, F. (1989). "Reasons and Causes," *Philosophical Perspectives*, 3.

Dretske, F. (1990). "Does Meaning Matter?" in E. Villanueva, ed., *Information, Semantics and Epistemology*, Oxford, Basil Blackwell.

Field, H. (1978). "Mental Representation," *Erkenntnis*, 13.

Fodor, J. (1980). "Methodological Solipsism Considered as a Research Strategy in Cognitive Psychology," *Behavioral and Brain Sciences*, 3.

Fodor, J. (1981). "The Present Status of the Innateness Controversy," in J. Fodor, *Representations*, Cambridge, MA, Bradford Books/MIT Press.

Fodor, J. (1984). "Semantics, Wisconsin Style," *Synthese*, 59. Reprinted in Fodor (1990). [Page references are to Fodor (1990).]

Fodor, J. (1987). *Psychosemantics*, Cambridge, MA, Bradford Books/MIT Press,

Fodor, J. (1990a). *A Theory of Content and Other Essays*, Cambridge, MA, Bradford Books / MIT Press.

Fodor, J. (1990b). "Psychosemantics, or: Where Do Truth Conditions Come From?" in W. Lycan, ed., *Mind and Cognition*, Oxford, Basil Blackwell.

Fodor, J. (1990c). "Roundtable Discussion," in P. Hanson, ed., *Information, Language and Cognition*, Vancouver, University of British Columbia Press.

Fodor, J. (1991). "A Modal Argument for Narrow Content," *Journal of Philosophy*, 88.

Haugeland, J. (1982). "Weak Supervenience," *American Philosophical Quarterly*, 19.

Horgan, T. (1982). "Supervenience and Microphysics," *Pacific Philosophical Quarterly*, 63.

Jones, T., Mulaire, E. & Stich, S. (1991). "Staving Off Catastrophe: A Critical Notice of Jerry Fodor's *Psychosemantics*," *Mind and Language*, 6, 1.

Kim, J. (1978). "Supervenience and Nomological Incomensurables," *American Philosophical Quarterly*, 15.

Kim, J. (1982). "Psychophysical Supervenience," *Philosophical Studies*, 41.

Kim, J. (1984). "Concepts of Supervenience," *Philosophy and Phenomenological Research*, 45.

Kim, J. (1987). "'Strong' and 'Global' Supervenience Revisited," *Philosophy and Phenomenological Research*, 48.

Leplin, J. (1979). "Reference and Scientific Realism," *Studies in History and Philosophy of Science*, 10.

Leplin, J. (1988). "Is Essentialism Unscientific?" *Philosophy of Science*, 55.

Lewis, D. (1983). "New Work for a Theory of Universals," *Australasian Journal of Philosophy*, 61.

Loar, B. (1981). *Mind and Meaning*, Cambridge, Cambridge University Press.

Loewer, B. & Rey, G., eds., (1991). *Meaning in Mind: Fodor and His Critics*, Oxford, Blackwell.

Lycan, W. (1988). *Judgement and Justification*, Cambridge, Cambridge University Press.

Millikan, R. (1984). *Language, Thought and Other Biological Categories*, Cambridge, MA, Bradford Books / MIT Press.

Millikan, R. (1989). "In Defense of Proper Function," *Philosophy of Science*, 56.

Papineau, D. (1987). *Reality and Representation*, Oxford, Basil Blackwell.

Petrie, B. (1987). "Global Supervenience and Reduction," *Philosophy and Phenomenological Research*, 48.

Putnam, H. (1975). "The Meaning of Meaning," in K. Gunderson, ed., *Language, Mind and Knowledge: Minnesota Studies in the Philosophy of Science*, 7.

Schiffer, S. (1982). "Intention Based Semantics," *Notre Dame Journal of Formal Logic*, 23.

Shapere, D. (1982). "Reason, Reference and the Quest for Knowledge," *Philosophy of Science*, 49, 1.

Smith, E. & Medin, D. (1981). *Categories and Concepts*, Cambridge, MA, Harvard University Press.

Stalnaker, R. (1984). *Inquiry*, Cambridge, MA, Bradford Books / MIT Press.

Stich, S. (1978). "Autonomous Psychology and the Belief-Desire Thesis," *The Monist*, 61.

Stich, S. (1983). *From Folk Psychology to Cognitive Science*, Cambridge, MA, Bradford Books / MIT Press.

Stich, S. (1991a). "Do True Believers Exist?" *The Aristotelian Society*, Supplementary Volume LXV.

Stich, S. (1991b). "Narrow Content Meets Fat Syntax," in B. Loewer & G. Rey, eds., *Meaning in Mind: Fodor and His Critics*, Oxford, Blackwell.

Stich, S. (1996). *Deconstructing the Mind*, New York, Oxford University Press.

Teller, P. (1984). "A Poor Man's Guide to Supervenience and Determination," *Southern Journal of Philosophy*, Supplement to Volume 22.

11

WHAT *IS* FOLK PSYCHOLOGY?

Stephen Stich and Ian Ravenscroft

1 Introduction

For the last two decades a doctrine called "eliminative materialism" (or sometimes just "eliminativism") has been a major focus of discussion in the philosophy of mind. It is easy to understand why eliminativism has attracted so much attention, for it is hard to imagine a more radical and provocative doctrine. What eliminativism claims is that the intentional states and processes that are alluded to in our everyday descriptions and explanations of people's mental lives and their actions are *myths*. Like the gods that Homer invoked to explain the outcome of battles, or the witches that Inquisitors invoked to explain local catastrophes, they *do not exist*. According to eliminativists, there are no such things as beliefs or desires or hopes or fears or thoughts. These putative states and processes are the badly misguided posits of a seriously mistaken theory, just like phlogiston and caloric fluid and the luminiferous ether.[1]

If eliminativism is right, then as Jerry Fodor has suggested, it might well be "the greatest intellectual catastrophe in the history of our species" (1987, p. xii). To see why, we need only consider the consequences of the doctrine in various domains of intellectual activity. Let's start with history: did Lincoln sign the Emancipation Proclamation because he

---

1. Another species of eliminativism claims that the conscious states do not exist. In this paper, however, our focus will be on the version of eliminativism that takes intentional states as its target.

wanted to abolish slavery? Or was it because he thought it would be a strategically useful move, helping to weaken the Confederacy? If eliminativism is right, then neither of these explanations could possibly be correct, since there are no wants and there are no thoughts. Consider epistemology: from Descartes to the present, epistemologists have tried to construct a systematic theory that will tell us which of a person's beliefs are justified, and which are not. But if eliminativism is right, there are no justified beliefs; there are no beliefs at all. Or consider anthropology: some researchers have claimed that a variety of human emotions, like fear, surprise and disgust are cultural universal rooted in biology; others have urged that all emotions are "social constructions." But if eliminativism is right, then there is something profoundly misguided about this dispute. For fear, surprise and disgust are intentional states, and eliminativism claims that there are no such things. Finally, consider psychology: if eliminativism is right, then much of what goes on in clinical psychology is bound to be useless. People's problems can't be remedied by removing irrational beliefs or making them aware of subconscious desires; there are no such things. And, obviously, if eliminativism is right, then as Fodor insists, many cognitive psychologists ought to "do [their] science in some other way . . ." Or at least, they "should stop spending the taxpayer's money" (1990, pp. 202–203).

Although advocates of eliminativism are not always as clear or careful as one might wish, they are typically inclined to make four distinct claims that might be formulated as follows:

(1) "Belief," "desire" and other familiar intentional state expressions are among the theoretical terms of a commonsense theory of the mind. This theory is often called "folk psychology."

(2) Folk psychology is a seriously mistaken theory. Many of the claims it makes about the states and processes that give rise to behavior, and many of the presuppositions of those claims, are false.

(3) A mature science that explains how the mind/brain works and how it produces the behavior we observe will not refer to the commonsense intentional states and processes invoked by folk psychology. Beliefs, desires and the rest will not be part of the ontology of a mature scientific psychology.

(4) The intentional states of commonsense psychology do not exist.

It is clear that the first of these claims is a crucial presupposition of the second. After that, the putative relations among the claims gets a bit murky. It sometimes appears that both friends and foes of eliminativism assume that (2) can be used to establish (4). And, of course, if (4) is right then (3) comes pretty much for free. For if beliefs and desires don't exist then surely a mature science has no business invoking them. In other places it seems that (2) is taken to support (3). If that's the way the argument is supposed to go, then presumably (3) will be taken to support (4), though explicit arguments from one to the other are not easy to find.

Most of the literature debating the plausibility of eliminativism has focused on the second of these claims.[2] In this paper, however, our focus will be on the first. That premise of the eliminativist argument has already provoked a certain amount of debate, with some writers protesting that commonsense psychology cannot be regarded as a causal or explanatory theory because its principles are partly normative or largely analytic. Others maintain that the basic function of folk psychology is not to predict and explain, but to warn, promise, congratulate and to do a thousand and one other jobs that are fundamental to the smooth workings of our interpersonal lives.[3] Eliminativists typically concede most of these points, but argue that it makes little difference. Whatever other uses it may have, they insist, folk psychology is still a causal and explanatory theory, and a seriously mistaken one.[4]

We propose to raise a rather different collection of concerns about the idea that ordinary intentional expressions are theoretical terms in a commonsense theory. Our central contention is that this idea can be unpacked (and, indeed, *has* been unpacked) in a variety of very different ways. Though many writers on both sides of the eliminativism debate take (1) to be unambiguous and unproblematic, there are actually *lots* of things that the label "folk psychology" might be (and *has* been) used to denote. Moreover, on *some* interpretations of (1) the remainder of the eliminativist argument will be in serious trouble. For on some readings, "folk psychology" is not the sort of thing that makes claims or expresses propositions. Thus it is not the sort of thing that *can* be either true or false. And obviously, on those readings the second step in the eliminativist argument couldn't possibly be right. For if folk psychology makes no claims, it makes no false claims. Our goal in this paper is to pull apart these various readings of "folk psychology" and to get as clear as possible on which ones are and which are not compatible with the remainder of the eliminativist's argument.

Before getting on to that, however, it will be useful to consider another issue. The idea that "belief," "desire" and other intentional locutions are terms embedded in a commonsense theory has become commonplace in the philosophy of mind. But though talk of a "folk theory" and its "posits" is all but ubiquitous in the recent literature, it is also rather puzzling. Ordinary folk certainly don't take themselves to be invoking a theory when they use intentional terms to explain other people's behavior. Still less do they think they are using a theory when they report their own beliefs and desires. So why is it that so many philosophers and cognitive scientists are convinced that our everyday predictions and explanations of behavior do involve some sort of theory? Why does this idea seem so plausible to many philosophers and psychologists, and so implausible to almost everyone

---

2. See, for example, P.M. Churchland (1981), P.S. Churchland (1986), Fodor (1987), Horgan and Woodward (1985), Jackson and Pettit (1990), Kitcher (1984), Ramsey, Stich, and Garon (1990), Sterelny (1990), Stich (1983) and Von Eckardt (1993).

3. See, for example, Sharpe (1987) and Wilkes (1981, 1984, 1991).

4. See Stich (1983), Ch. 10; P.M. Churchland (1989).

else? One good way to approach these questions is to track down the history of the idea. That is what we propose to do in the two sections to follow. While we do not pretend to be serious historical scholars, we think it is pretty clear that the view set out in (1) has two major historical roots. One of them is to be found in the work of Wilfrid Sellars, the other in the dominant explanatory strategy of contemporary cognitive science.

2 Folk Psychology's Sellarsian Roots

A major theme in Sellars' philosophy is a sustained attack on "the myth of the given"—the idea that some of our beliefs or claims have a privileged epistemic status because the facts that make them true are "given" to us by experience. One class of claims that has traditionally been accorded this special status are pronouncements about one's own "sense data" or the content of one's perceptual experience. On the traditional view, a person's sincere claim that she is now seeing a blue object might well turn out to be mistaken. But her sincere claim that she is now experiencing blue sense data (or that she is now having experiences "as if" she were seeing a blue object) could not turn out to be mistaken. Another class of claims that are immune from error, according to the traditional view, are claims about one's own apparent memories and beliefs. Stich can't be certain that he has in fact climbed Ayers Rock. But he can be certain that he now seems to remember climbing Ayers Rock. And while his belief itself might be false, his sincere claim that he believes he climbed Ayers Rock on his 42nd birthday can't be mistaken. Sellars was a trenchant critic of these claims to certainty, and of the foundationalist epistemology that typically went along with them. And though his assault on the traditional notion of sense data is not directly relevant to the eliminativist's skepticism about intentional states, his attack on the idea that our claims about our own beliefs and memories could not be mistaken most emphatically is. For, of course, if Stich's sincere claim that he believes he climbed Ayers Rock is enough to guarantee that he *does* believe it then, since we make such sincere claims all the time, beliefs must exist, and eliminativism is a non-starter.

To counter the idea that our claims about our own beliefs and thoughts are underwritten by a special, introspective faculty that guarantees the truth of those claims, Sellars begins by "making a myth . . . or, to give it an air of up-to-date respectability, by writing a piece of science fiction—anthropological science fiction" (1956, p. 309). For our purposes, Sellars' myth can be viewed as having three stages. The first of these is "a stage in pre-history in which humans are limited to what I shall call a Rylean language, a language of which the fundamental descriptive vocabulary speaks of public properties of public objects located in Space and enduring through Time" (p. 309). At this stage in the myth, our "Rylean Ancestors" have no terms in their language for beliefs, thoughts or other "inner mental episodes." The second stage in the myth begins with the appearance in this "Neo-Rylean culture" of "a genius—let us call him Jones" (p. 314).

[I]n the attempt to account for the fact that his fellow men behave intelligently not only when their conduct is threaded on a string of overt verbal episodes—that is to say as we would put it, when they "think out loud"—but also when no detectable verbal output is present, Jones develops a *theory* according to which overt utterances are but the culmination of a process which begins with certain inner episodes. *And let us suppose that his model for these episodes* which initiate the events which culminate in overt verbal behavior *is that of overt verbal behavior itself. In other words, using the language of the model, the theory is to the effect that overt verbal behavior is the culmination of a process which begins with "inner speech."* (pp. 317–318; emphasis is Sellars')

At this stage of Sellars' myth, the theory is only applied to other people. But in the third stage Jones and his compatriots learn to apply the theory to themselves. At first they apply it to themselves in much the same way that they apply it to others. They infer various theoretical claims by attending to their own behavior. A bit later, they discover a new way of applying the language of the theory to themselves. Here is how Sellars tells the tale:

[O]nce our fictitious ancestor, Jones, has developed the theory that overt verbal behavior is the expression of thoughts, and taught his compatriots to make use of the theory in interpreting each other's behavior, it is but a short step to the use of this language in self-description. Thus, when Tom, watching Dick, has behavioral evidence which warrants the use of the sentence (in the language of the theory) "Dick is thinking 'p'." . . . Dick, using the same behavioral evidence, can say, in the language of the theory, "I am thinking 'p'." . . . And it now turns out—need it have?—that Dick can be trained to give reasonably reliable self-descriptions, using the language of the theory, without having to observe his overt behavior. Jones brings this about, roughly, by applauding utterances by Dick of "I am thinking that p" when the behavioral evidence strongly supports the theoretical statement "Dick is thinking that p"; and by frowning on utterances of "I am thinking that p," when the evidence does not support this theoretical statement. Our ancestors begin to speak of the privileged access each of us has to his own thoughts. *What began as a language with a purely theoretical use has gained a reporting role.* (p. 320; emphasis is Sellars')

So, in Sellars' myth, expressions of the form "I am thinking that p" are theoretical expressions which have acquired "a reporting use in which one is not drawing inferences from behavioral evidence" (p. 321).

Now if, like Sellars, one is concerned to rebut the claim that our reports of our own thoughts are beyond challenge, the myth of Jones suggests how the argument might run. For suppose the myth were true. The inner episodes that Jones hypothesizes in stage two are supposed to be real events that are causally linked with behavioral episodes. Positing them to account for certain aspects of the observable behavior of people is, as Sellars stresses, on all fours with positing molecules to account for certain aspects of the observable behavior of gases. Thus, for mental states as for molecules, there will be some occasions on which the inference from the observed behavior to the theoretical claim may be mistaken. Occasionally, an anomalous event may cause the observed behavior in the absence of the hypothesized internal state. Similarly, when we have been trained to give "reasonably reliable self-descriptions, using the language of the theory, without having to observe [our own] overt behavior" it may occasionally happen that this process misfires, and that we describe ourselves as thinking that p, in the absence of the hypothesized internal state. Moreover, though Sellars himself did not stress the point, there is a more pervasive way in which our self-descriptions might turn out to be wrong. For it might turn out that Jones was less of a genius than we had thought—more of a Velikovsky, perhaps, than a Newton. His entire theory might turn out to be a bad idea. Other thinkers might discover better ways to explain the behavior that Jones' theory was designed to explain—ways that don't posit internal states modeled on observable verbal behavior. If that's the way the myth unfolds, then it may not be just the occasional theoretical self-description that turns out to be false. They may *all* be false.

Before we take these possibilities seriously, however, there is a pair of problems that must be confronted. The first of these focuses on the status of the myth itself. The possibilities set out in the previous paragraph were preceded by the *supposition* that the myth is true. But surely that's just silly. There was no historical Jones or anyone much like him, and there is no reason at all to suppose that talk about thoughts and other inner mental events was introduced as an explicit theoretical posit. Presumably what Sellars would say here is that the myth is a bit like Wittgenstein's ladder which we kick away after we have climbed it. The reason for telling the myth about Jones is to loosen the grip of another myth, this one the Cartesian "myth" in which introspection gives rise to infallible knowledge about our own mental states. If the Sellarsian myth were true, then we would talk *just as we now do* about inner mental states. But this talk would be both theoretical and fallible. Once we appreciate the point, the myth is irrelevant. It doesn't much matter what the actual history of our language is. What matters is that people could talk about inner mental states just the way we do, and their sincere self reports could be mistaken.

A second problem in assessing the significance of Sellars' myth focuses not on the truth of the myth but on the nature of the theory that the myth describes. As Sellars tells the story, Jones actually set out a theory and taught it to his compatriots. But nothing much like that seems to go on in our current practice. We don't explicitly teach our children a theory that enables them to apply mental terms to other people. Indeed, unlike Jones and his friends, we are not even able to *state* the theory, let alone teach it. If you ask your neighbor to set out the principles of the theory of the mind that she has taught her children, she won't have the foggiest idea what you're talking about. An essential step in

Sellars' argument is the claim that, if the myth were true, we would talk just as we now do about mental states. But isn't this rather implausible? Surely if each of us had been taught an explicit theory of the mind, and if we invoke this theory in applying mental state terms to others, then both our developmental history and our adult linguistic practice would be rather different from what they actually are. At a minimum, there would be more aware-ness and discussion of the theory, and more explicit appeal to its principles than we find in current linguistic practice. Rather than tackling this problem head on, we think the best strategy, at this point, is to break off our discussion of Sellars, and attend to the other major source of the idea that mental states are the posits of a folk theory. As we noted earlier, that source is to be found in the dominant explanatory strategy of contemporary cognitive science. As our discussion of that strategy proceeds, we will find an obvious way in which a neo-Sellarsian might respond to the objection that none of *us* can even state Jones' theory, let alone teach it.

3 Cognitive Science and the Appeal to Tacit Theory

From its earliest days, a central concern of cognitive science has been the explanation of various cognitive or behavioral capacities. The capacity of speakers to recognize and make various judgments about sentences of their language was among the first to be studied in detail. Other pioneering studies attempted to explain the capacity to solve various sorts of problems including problems in logic, chess problems, cryptarithmetic problems and a variety of others. During the last three decades, many additional capacities have been explored. In all of this work, the most common explanatory strategy is to suppose that people's performance in executing these various capacities is guided by an internalized "knowledge base" or "knowledge structure." Typically a knowledge structure will be a set of principles or rules that constitute a recipe or program enabling people to carry out the activity in question by exploiting more basic capacities in a systematic way. Those more basic capacities can themselves be explained by reiterating the strategy at a lower level. They are decomposed into still more basic ones which are systematically marshalled under the guidance of another recipe or program.

The first philosophical account of this approach to psychological explanation that we know of was provided in Jerry Fodor's paper, "The appeal to tacit knowledge in psycho-logical explanation" (1968). And, though the picture has become a fairly familiar one, we think it is worth quoting Fodor's vivid exposition at some length.

> Here is the way we tie our shoes:
> There is a little man who lives in one's head. The little man keeps a library. When one acts upon the intention to tie one's shoes, the little man fetches down a volume entitled *Tying One's Shoes*. The volume says such things as: "Take the left free end of the shoelace in the left hand. Cross the left free end of the shoelace over the right free end of the shoelace . . .", etc.

When the little man reads the instruction "take the left free end of the shoelace in the left hand," he pushes a button on a control panel. The button is marked "take the left free end of a shoelace in the left hand." When depressed, it activates a series of wheels, cogs, levers, and hydraulic mechanisms. As a causal consequence of the functioning of these mechanisms, one's left hand comes to seize the appropriate end of the shoelace. Similarly, *mutatis mutandis*, for the rest of the instructions.

The instructions end with the word "end." When the little man reads the word "end," he returns the book of instructions to his library.

That is the way we tie our shoes. (pp. 63–64)

Now, as Fodor goes on to note, there are some obvious things wrong with this story. First, of course, the whimsical bit about the cogs and wheels will have to be replaced by a more biological story. Second, and more seriously,

some of the behaviors . . . involved in shoe tying are of considerable complexity. . . . A serious theory of the behavioral integrations involved in tying one's shoes must explicate this complexity. . . . Prima facie . . . grasping a shoelace should be considered complex behavior, because doing so involves motions that also play a role in other actions.

We might thus consider expanding the population in one's head to include subordinate little men who superintend the execution of the "elementary" behaviors involved in complex sequences like grasping a shoelace. When the little man reads "take the left free end of the shoelace in the left hand," we imagine him ringing up the shop foreman in charge of grasping shoelaces. The shop foreman goes about supervising that activity in a way that is, in essence, a microcosm of supervising tying one's shoe. Indeed the shop foreman might be imagined to superintend a detail of wage slaves, whose functions include: searching inputs for traces of shoelace, flexing and contracting fingers on the left hand, etc. (pp. 64–65)

A bit later, Fodor explains how this process ultimately comes to an end:

We refine a psychological theory by replacing global little men by less global little men, each of whom has fewer unanalyzed behaviors to perform than did his predecessors. . . .

A completed psychological theory must provide systems of instructions to account for the forms of behavior available to an organism, and it must do so in a way that makes reference to no unanalyzed psychological processes. One way of clarifying the latter requirement is the following. Assume that there exists a class of *elementary* instructions which the nervous system is specifically wired to execute. Each elementary instruction specifies an *elementary operation*, and an elementary operation is one which the normal nervous system can perform but of which it cannot perform a proper part. Intuitively speaking the elementary operations are those which have no theoretically relevant internal structure. (pp. 65–66)

There are three additional points that need to be made before asking how this explanatory strategy links up with our concerns about folk psychology. The first is that the strategy does not require that bosses have any conscious access to the information their underlings are using. In some cases a person may be able to tell us a great deal about the principles that guide his activity; in other cases he may be able to report some of the principles but not others; and in still other cases he may not have a clue about how he accomplishes the task. In those cases where the person can't recount or even recognize the principles he (or one of his subsystems) is using, it is often said that the principles are "tacit" or "unconscious." The second point is that it is often natural enough to describe the principles being used as a "theory" of the task domain or of how to accomplish the task in question. So, putting this point together with the previous one, it will sometimes be the case that the principles specified in an explanation of the sort Fodor envisions will constitute a "tacit or unconscious theory" of the domain or task in question. Here, of course, we have an obvious way to address the problem that we left unresolved in our discussion of Sellars' myth. If people regularly exploit *tacit* theories of the sort that Fodor describes, then we should not expect them to be aware of the principles of the theory or to appeal to those principles in discussion.

The third point is a bit more subtle. In Fodor's account, the little man inside the head has a single book specifying a set of rules for accomplishing the task at hand. But we might also imagine that in some instances the little man has *two* books for a given ability. One of the books contains declarative sentences rather than rules. These might, for example, be a set of axioms for some branch of mathematics or science. Or they might be a set of principles detailing generalizations and more idiosyncratic facts in some other domain. Now, of course, axioms or generalizations or statements of fact cannot, by themselves, tell us how to do anything. That's the job of the second book, which is much the same as the book imagined in Fodor's shoe-tying example. It provides rules for using the information in the first book to accomplish some task. So, for example, if the first book contains statements of the laws in some branch of physics, the second book might contain rules which specify how to use these laws to solve physics problems. Or perhaps the first book contains an axiomatic specification of all the sentences in a given language, and the second book contains a set of rules for using this specification efficiently in determining whether or not a given sentence is in the language. If one thinks of theories as the sorts of things that make claims, and thus as the sorts of things that can be true or false, then one might be inclined to say that only the books containing declarative sentences count as "theories." The books that contain programs or recipes can do a good job or a bad job at accomplishing their task. But since they don't make any claims, they don't count as theories. We don't think that anything much turns on this terminological issue. What is important is the point about truth. If the little man accomplishes his task using only a recipe or a program, we may, if we wish, choose to describe that program as a theory. But it makes no obvious sense to say that the "theory" he is exploiting is either true or false.

4 Interpreting "Folk Psychology"

The central goal of this paper, it will be recalled, is to explore various possible interpretations of the assumption that beliefs, desires and other commonsense mental states are posits of a folk theory of the mind. We are now in a position to tackle that project head-on.

Cognitive science, as we have just seen, typically attempts to explain cognitive and behavioral capacities by positing an internalized and often tacit theory. Among the various capacities that normal adults display, there is a fascinating cluster in which talk of mental states looms large. It is hardly surprising that many people have been tempted by the idea that this cluster of capacities might be explained by appeal to a tacit theory. Before considering the various ways in which such an explanation might work, we would do well to assemble at least a partial list of the "folk psychological" capacities or abilities that need explaining.

(i) Perhaps the most obvious of these is the one that was center stage in Sellars' myth of Jones. We use terms like "believe," "think," "want" and "desire" to *describe* ourselves and each other. We say things like the following all the time:

> Columbus believed that the earth was round.
> Henry VIII wanted a male heir.
> Anna thinks there is someone knocking at the door.

And, while we occasionally dispute such claims, in the overwhelming majority of cases they are readily accepted and strike us as completely unproblematic. This widespread agreement is a manifestation of a widely shared capacity to describe—or as philosophers sometimes like to say, to *interpret*—people using intentional idioms.[5]

(ii) We not only describe people using these folk psychological idioms, we also use the descriptions to construct *explanations* of people's behavior. We say things like:

> Henry VIII divorced Catherine of Aragon because he wanted a male heir.

---

5. It is often claimed that at least some of those intentional idioms, and the capacity to apply them, vary markedly from culture to culture (see, for example, Hacking, 1982, Needham, 1972, and the essays collected in Harré, 1986). That sort of cultural relativism, if it turns out to be correct, is entirely compatible with the various accounts of folk psychology to be set out in this section. If people in different cultures use different intentional categories, and if their use of these categories is guided by a tacit theory, then the tacit theories will also differ from culture to culture.

and

Anna is looking through the peep-hole because she thinks that there is someone knocking at the door.

And here too, in the vast majority of cases these explanations are widely accepted and strike us as entirely unproblematic. Within our culture a capacity to construct this sort of explanation seems to be universal among normal adults.

(iii) In addition to offering explanations of behavior, we are also quite adept at producing *predictions* of how people will behave. Sometimes these predictions are embedded in a discourse that also mentions the beliefs, desires and other mental states of the person whose behavior is being predicted. But on other occasions we predict someone's behavior without saying anything about her mental states. In one respect, our ability to produce predictions is rather similar to the previous two abilities on our list. For in this case, too, there is remarkably widespread inter-personal agreement. Asked to predict what the motorist will do as she approaches the red light, almost everyone says that she will stop. But there is another respect in which the ability to predict is much more impressive than the ability to offer descriptions and explanations. For in the case of predictions, there is often an independent and readily available check on their accuracy. And as many philosophers have noted, it is a striking fact that in the vast majority of cases our predictions turn out to be *correct*. Though we are certainly not infallible, it is very often the case that people do what we predict they are going to do.

(iv) The ability to produce predictions of people's behavior is one which manifests itself in our *linguistic* behavior. But we also have a capacity to *anticipate* other people's behavior without saying anything at all. In watching a baseball game, our eyes immediately jump to the hot-tempered manager when the umpire throws his star player out of the game. We anticipate that he will come storming out of the dugout. Seeing the furious manager approaching, the umpire may anticipate what is to come and beat a hasty, though silent, retreat. Now it might be thought that these cases are just like the ones in which people make verbal predictions, except that they don't actually utter the prediction. They just say it silently to themselves. But there is also a *prima facie* similarity between our ability to anticipate people's behavior and the ability that animals have to anticipate the behavior of other organisms. The family cat is very good at anticipating which way mice will run, and at anticipating which way the neighbor's dog will run. In both cases he reacts appropriately, though we rather doubt that he is saying anything to himself as he does it.

(v) The final entry on our list is the only one that overtly involves what might be thought of as *principles* or *generalizations* of a folk psychological theory. There is a wide range of generalizations about the interactions among stimuli, mental states and behavior that people in our culture occasionally utter, and are generally quite willing to endorse when asked. To give you a feel for the sort of ability we have in mind consider whether or not you agree with the following claims:

(v-i) When a normal person is looking at a traffic light which changes from red to green she usually comes to believe that it has changed from red to green.

(v-ii) If a person believes that all scorpions are poisonous, and if she comes to believe that Henry's pet is a scorpion, then she will typically come to believe that Henry's pet is poisonous.

(v-iii) If a person sitting at a bar wants to order a beer, and if she has no stronger desire to do something that is incompatible with ordering a beer, then typically she will order a beer.

We trust you agreed with all of them. In so doing you were manifesting the widely shared ability to recognize folk psychological generalizations.

That's the end of our list of capacities. It is, as we noted earlier, only a partial list. Normal adults in our society have lots of other abilities in which talk of mental states plays a central role. In the absence of a theory about the mechanisms underlying these abilities, there is no obvious or natural way of drawing a boundary and saying exactly which capacities do and do not count as "folk psychological capacities." That vagueness will make for problems as we proceed. But for the moment we propose to ignore it and focus on the five capacities we have listed.

Let's begin by assuming that something like Fodor's story provides the correct explanation for those abilities, and let's consider some of the ways in which this story might be developed. To start us off, let's ask how the explicit generalizations mentioned in (v) are related to the underlying knowledge structure—the book that the little man in the head consults. Perhaps the simplest answer is that *these very generalizations* are encoded in the underlying knowledge structure. Indeed, to tell a really simple story we might suppose that the underlying knowledge structure consists of *nothing but* these explicit generalizations. If this simple story were right, then all the principles we use in employing our various folk psychological abilities would be readily recognizable. But, for two very different reasons, we think this is an unlikely option. First, there are just too many generalizations. People who find (v-i)–(v-iii) to be intuitively obvious will find an all but infinite class of similar generalizations to be equally obvious. And it seems absurd to suppose that all of those generalizations are internally represented. A natural suggestion here is that what we have internally represented is a set of more abstract generalizations—we might think of them as "axioms" of folk psychology—which in conjunction with other internalized information entail (v-i)–(v-iii) and all the other more concrete generalizations that we recognize as intuitively obvious. The second problem with our simple story is just the opposite of the first. If we restrict ourselves to the generalizations that people are prepared to endorse, then in all likelihood there are too few of them to do the job required. A serious and fully explicit account of how we accomplish the feats recounted in (i)–(v) will almost certainly require more rules and principles than people can state or recognize as intuitively obvious. It is to be expected that in this area, as in every other area that cognitive scientists have explored, there is a great deal of information being used that is simply not accessible to introspection. If this is right, then at least part of what is written in the little man's book will be "tacit" or "unconscious." Moreover some of the information that is not available to introspection may not even be statable in terms that the agent can understand. Linguistic ability provides a valuable analogy here. If Chomsky and his followers are even close to being right about the "tacit knowledge" that subserves a speaker's ability to judge whether or not a given sentence is grammatical, then most people would require a crash course in generative linguistics before they could begin to understand an explicit statement of what they "tacitly know."

We can now begin to pull apart some of the very different ways in which the label "folk psychology" might be used. In a series of influential papers, David Lewis drew attention to what he called the "platitudes" of commonsense psychology (Lewis, 1970, 1972). These are generalizations that are "common knowledge" amongst ordinary folk. Almost everyone assents to them, and almost everyone knows that almost everyone else assents to them. These platitudes are, near enough, the intuitively obvious generalizations discussed in the previous paragraph. On Lewis' view these platitudes constitute an implicit definition of the terms of commonsense psychology. But suppose that the speculations in the last paragraph are correct, and that platitudes like (v-i)–(v-iii) are the consciously accessible consequences of a substantially richer set of mostly tacit or unconscious psychological rules and generalizations that people in our culture share. Suppose, further, that these tacit rules and generalizations also play a central role in explaining folk psychological capacities like (i)–(iv).[6] If these suppositions are correct, then we might well be tempted to reserve the term "folk psychology" for the *underlying internally represented* rules and generalizations. Moreover, a neo-Lewisian might well propose that it is these internal generalizations that fix the meaning or reference of the terms of commonsense psychology.

---

6. As we noted earlier, there is no obvious way of deciding which capacities to count as "folk psychological capacities." Thus the current supposition is itself a bit vague. It might turn out that the rules and generalizations subserving (i)–(v) are a tightly integrated set, perhaps even a "module" in something like the sense set out in Fodor (1983). If that is the case, then we would do well to let these integrated rules and generalizations determine which capacities to count as "folk psychological"—the folk psychological capacities are the capacities that these rules and generalizations explain. But it might also turn out that the rules and generalizations we use are not modular or even tightly integrated—that different subsets of rules and generalizations explain different capacities. If that's how things work, then the only way to eliminate the vagueness is by stipulation. Folk psychological capacities will not be a psychologically natural kind.

There is, however, nothing mandatory about this terminology. We might equally well elect to use the term "folk psychology" in a way that is more akin to Lewis' usage—as a label for the collection of folk psychological "platitudes" that people in our culture readily recognize and assent to.[7] Or, since the collection of "platitudes" is likely to be large and ungainly, we might reserve the label "folk psychology" for a set of more abstract general-izations—a "theory" if you will—that systematizes the platitudes in a perspicuous way and that (perhaps in conjunction with some other commonly known information) entails them. That systematization might well invoke terms and concepts that are quite unfamiliar to ordinary folk, in the same way that an attempt to systematize our linguistic intuitions probably would. What makes the proposals set out in this paragraph funda-mentally different from the various possibilities considered in the previous paragraph is that on these readings, *"folk psychology" is not claimed to be an internally represented knowledge structure or body of information; it is not part of the mechanism that subserves the abilities recounted in (i)–(v).* On these readings, folk psychology "ain't in the head." To mark this distinction we propose to call these accounts of folk psychology *external* accounts. Accounts on which folk psychology *is* part of the mechanism subserving (i)–(v) we call *internal.*

The distinction between internal and external accounts of folk psychology is at least roughly parallel to a distinction between two different ways of interpreting the sorts of generative grammars produced by linguists. Linguistic intuitions are a principal source of data for generative grammar. These intuitions are spontaneous judgements about the grammaticality and other grammatical features of sentences presented to a speaker. And it is generally agreed that a correct grammar is a theory which entails most of those judgements. On the analogy we are urging, linguistic intuitions are analogous to people's spontaneous judgements about the correctness or incorrectness of proposed folk psycho-logical platitudes. Some theorists (e.g., Stich, 1972, and perhaps Soames, 1984) claim that capturing the intuitions (along with "simplicity") is all that is expected of a grammar; a correct grammar, on this view, is nothing more than a useful systematization or axiomat-ization of linguistic intuitions. Other theorists (e.g., Chomsky & Katz, 1974; Fodor, 1981a) have higher aspirations for grammar. On their view, a grammar should not only capture (or entail) most linguistic intuitions, it should also be part of the mechanism that is causally responsible for the production of those intuitions, and for a variety of other linguistic capacities. On this view, people are assumed to have an internally represented body of linguistic rules or principles that is brought into play in producing linguistic intuitions and in processing and producing speech. A correct grammar is one that spec-ifies the internally represented rules. Understood in this way, grammar is analogous to

---

7. Here, again, the proposal is a bit vague, since there is no obvious well-motivated way to determine which platitudes count as "folk psychological." Nor is it clear how widely accepted a claim must be in order to count as a "platitude."

folk psychology, construed *internally*. On the other view, grammar is analogous to folk psychology construed *externally*.

It has often been noted that when grammars are construed externally they may be seriously underdetermined both by the data of linguistic intuition and by considerations of simplicity. There may be a number of quite different, though comparably simple, ways to construct a theory that entails most of a speaker's linguistic intuitions. So on an external view of grammar, there may be several quite different grammars of a language or a dialect, all of which are equally correct. Much the same is true for external accounts of folk psychology. For even if we find some principled way of saying which "platitudes" or folk psychological intuitions a theory must systematize, there may be very different, though comparably simple, ways in which this can be done. This point is particularly important if, as we speculated earlier, a good systematization of folk psychological intuitions may invoke terms or concepts that are unfamiliar to the people whose intuitions are being systematized. For these concepts might well be viewed as among the deeper "theoretical" notions of folk psychology. They are thus prime candidates for the eliminativist critique. But if there is no unique external systematization of folk psychology, then *the eliminativist who adopts an external account of folk psychology will have no determinate target.*

Let us return, now, to internal accounts of folk psychology. For the remainder of this section we propose to explore various ways in which attempts to construct internal accounts might turn out, and to consider the implications of these various possibilities for the eliminativist's argument.

At the end of section 3, we noted that for any given capacity the little man in the head may have *two* books rather than one. The information guiding the exercise of various cognitive capacities may divide into two parts: one consisting of declarative sentences or some similar notation for encoding propositions about the relevant domain, and the other consisting of rules or procedures which specify what to do with these declarative sentences—how to use them to accomplish the task at hand. Applying this distinction to the case of commonsense psychology, we might conjecture that the knowledge structure underlying the skills in (i)–(v) divides into two parts. One of these is a set of (putative) laws and/or generalizations and/or facts about the ways in which the states of commonsense psychology interact with each other, with environmental stimuli, with behavior and with other relevant aspects of an agent's situation. The other part is a program—a set of rules for extracting predictions, explanations, etc. from these laws, generalizations and facts. If this is how the system works, it suggests two quite distinct ways in which the term "folk psychology" might be employed. It might be used as a label for the entire knowledge structure (the program plus the propositional information), or it might be reserved just for the part that contains the propositional information. On that latter usage, it makes perfectly good sense to ask whether folk psychology is true or false. On the former usage, however, only part of folk psychology is the sort of thing that can be true or false.

There is, however, another possibility to reckon with here, one which is much less congenial to the eliminativist's argument. It might turn out that the system subserving folk psychological skills contains only one book, not two, because the system is all rules and no propositions. If that's how the system works, and if we adopt the internal reading according to which "folk psychology" is used as a label for this system, then it will make no clear sense to say that folk psychology is either true or false. So if, as is entirely possible, folk psychology (construed internally) is all rules and no propositions, then the second step of the eliminativist's argument cannot possibly be correct. The upshot of all of this is that eliminativists who adopt an internal view of folk psychology are committed to an empirical speculation—the speculation that folk psychology *isn't* all rules and no propositions—and this speculation might well turn out to be mistaken.[8]

There is also quite a different way in which it might turn out that folk psychology, construed internally, is not the sort of thing that can possibly be either true or false. Thus far we have been following Fodor in assuming that the "knowledge structure" underlying our folk psychological abilities is encoded in something akin to a language. But during the last decade there has been a growing tendency in cognitive science to propose theories in which the information subserving various abilities is not encoded in anything like linguistic form. Perhaps the most widely discussed theories of this type are those that propose to account for certain cognitive capacities by positing one or another sort of connectionist device. Quite a different idea for the non-linguistic encoding of information is the hypothesis that mental models of various sorts underlie our cognitive capacities (Johnson-Laird, 1983). Both the connectionist approach and the mental models approach are very controversial, of course. Moreover, to draw the conclusions we want to draw from them, we have to proceed rather carefully. It is perfectly possible to view certain sorts of connectionist models and certain sorts of mental model theories as storing information that can be straightforwardly captured by a set of propositions or a set of sentences (McGinn, 1989, Ch. 3). Indeed, in some cases mental models and connectionist networks can actually be used to encode declarative sentences, or something very much like them. Thus it is not the case that connectionist or mental model approaches are inevitably in conflict with prepositional or even linguistic accounts of information storage. However, in other connectionist and mental model theories, there may be no unique and well-motivated way to map or translate the information stored into a set of propositions or declarative sentences. If a theory of this sort should prove to provide the best account of folk psychological skills like those sketched in (i)–(v), then we might well use the label "folk psychology" for the connectionist network or mental model posited by the theory. But since *ex hypothesi* there is no well-motivated mapping from the network or model to a set of declarative sentences or propositions, it would make no obvious sense to say that

---

8. A caveat: even if folk psychology (construed internally) is all rules and no propositions, it may be the case that the rules of this folk psychological program, or the concepts they invoke, presuppose various claims that could turn out to be false. The notion of presupposition being relied on here could do with considerable clarification. But assuming that adequate clarification can be provided, the presuppositions of folk psychology might be a suitable target for the eliminativist's critique.

folk psychology is either true or false. So in this case, too, eliminativists who adopt an internal view of folk psychology are buying into a controversial empirical assumption. They are assuming that folk psychological skills are *not* subserved by connectionist networks or mental models of the sort lately considered. Without this assumption, the eliminativist's argument couldn't get started.

It's time to sum up. A central theme in this section has been that there are various quite different ways in which we might choose to use the term "folk psychology." A first choice turns on the distinction between external and internal readings. External accounts either collect or systematize the intuitively recognizable generalizations of commonsense psychology, while internal accounts focus on the cognitive mechanism that underlies our ability to have those intuitions, to predict behavior, etc. If we opt for an external reading of "folk psychology," then folk psychology is clearly the sort of thing that makes claims, and some of those claims might turn out to be false. So on external readings, the eliminativist is guaranteed a target. But since there may be many quite different, comparably simple ways to systematize the intuitively recognized generalizations, that target may be far from unique. Also, the target may not be all that interesting, since on external accounts the principles of folk psychology may have little or nothing to do with the impressive range of commonsense psychological skills that people possess. They may have nothing to do with the processes by which we actually produce intentional descriptions, predictions and explanations of behavior.

Internal accounts use the label "folk psychology" for the knowledge structures that actually underlie skills like those recounted in (i)–(v). So on internal accounts folk psychology plays a major role in the explanation of our ability to predict and explain each other's behavior. But on internal construals of folk psychology, the eliminativist's argument *may* turn out to be incoherent. For it is entirely possible that the knowledge structure underlying our commonsense psychological skills consists *entirely* of instructions, or it may be a connectionist device or mental model that does not map comfortably on to a set of sentences or propositions. The eliminativist who adopts an internal reading of "folk psychology" must make the risky bet that none of these options will turn out to be correct. For if one of them is correct, then premise (2) in the eliminativist's argument can't be right, since folk psychology is not the sort of thing that can be either true or false.

We're afraid that all of this has turned out to be rather complicated. Perhaps Fig. 1 will be of some help in seeing how the various possible interpretations of "folk psychology" that we have been pulling apart are related to each others.[9] The options that are compatible with step (2) in the eliminativist argument are on the left; those that are not are on the right. There is, however, one increasingly important view of folk psychology that does not fit comfortably anywhere in Fig. 1. To conclude this paper we propose to take a brief look at this view and its implications for eliminativism.

---

9. Thanks are due to Christopher O'Brien for help in preparing Fig. 1.

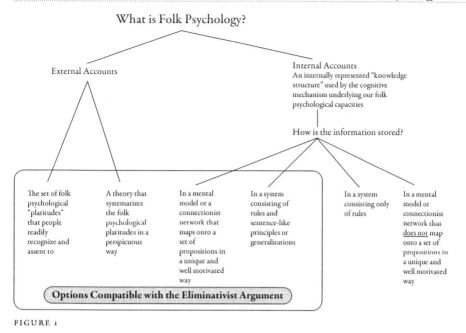

FIGURE 1

5 Eliminativism and Simulation Theory

As we noted in section 3, the most common explanatory strategy in cognitive science posits internalized bodies of information, or "knowledge structures," that are brought into play when people exercise cognitive capacities. Language processing, various sorts of problem solving, visual recognition and a host of other abilities have been studied from within this explanatory paradigm. To many people it seems inevitable that an explanation of folk psychological capacities like those recounted in (i)–(v) will also posit some sort of internally represented information store. But in recent years a number of philosophers and psychologists, most prominently Robert Gordon (1986, 1992), Alvin Goldman (1989, 1992), and Paul Harris (1992), have suggested a way in which some of the capacities on our list might be explained without using anything much like the internalized knowledge structures that are omnipresent in contemporary cognitive science. Their central idea is that we might predict other people's behavior by using our own decision-making system to simulate someone else's decision making. To make this strategy work we must first (consciously or unconsciously) imagine ourselves in the situation of the "target"— the person whose behavior we are trying to predict. We imagine what his beliefs are and what his desires are (to the extent that these are relevantly different from our own). We then feed these imagined (or "pretend") beliefs and desires into our decision-making system and allow it to decide what to do. But rather than acting on that decision, we use it as a basis for predicting what the target person will do. If we have done a good job in imagining the target's beliefs and desires, and if his decision-making system works in much the same way that ours does, then our decision will be the same as his, and our prediction will be correct.[10]

Some critics of this proposal have suggested that it could not possibly work, or that it must *covertly* appeal to internalized rules or knowledge structures. We think both of these contentions are mistaken. The simulation theory provides a real alternative to the prevailing explanatory strategy in cognitive science for explaining our capacity to predict and explain other people's behavior. We are far from being advocates of the simulation theory, however, because we don't think it does a very good job of explaining the experimental data on the acquisition and deployment of folk psychological skills. The details of this critique make for a long story, which one of us has tried to tell elsewhere (Stich & Nichols, 1992, 1995).

Our present concern is not to renew the debate over the correctness of simulation theory, but rather to ask what happens to the eliminativist argument if it should turn out (contrary to our expectations) that simulation theory is correct. A number of authors on both sides of the debate have maintained that if simulation theory is right, eliminativism will be undermined. Here is how Stich and Nichols (1992) argue for this conclusion:

> *Eliminativists* maintain that there really are no . . . [intentional states]. Beliefs and desires are like phlogiston, caloric and witches; they are the mistaken posits of a radically false theory. The theory in question is "folk psychology"—the collection of psychological principles and generalizations which, according to eliminativists (and most of their opponents) underlies our everyday explanations of behavior. The central premise in the eliminativist's argument is that neuroscience (or connectionism or cognitive science) is on the verge of demonstrating persuasively that folk psychology is false. But if Gordon and Goldman are right, they will have pulled the rug out from under the eliminativists. For if what underlies our ordinary explanatory practice is not a theory at all, then obviously it cannot be a radically false theory. There is a certain delightful irony in the Gordon/Goldman attack on eliminativism. Indeed, one might almost view it as attempting a bit of philosophical jujitsu. The eliminativists claim that there are no such things as beliefs and desires because the folk psychology that posits them is a radically false theory. Gordon and Goldman claim that the theory which posits a tacitly known folk psychology is *itself* radically false, since there are much better ways of explaining people's abilities to interpret and predict behavior. Thus, if Gordon and Goldman are right, *there is no such thing as folk psychology*![11]

---

10. Advocates of simulation theory have also proposed ways in which this process might be used to generate intentional descriptions and explanations (see Stich & Nichols, 1992, Sec. 3).

11. For similar arguments, see Gordon (1986, p. 170) and Goldman (1989, p. 182).

Now it's our contention that Stich and Nichols (and Gordon and Goldman) were being much too hasty in concluding that simulation theory puts eliminativism out of business.[12] And, in light of the distinctions we drew in the previous section, the reason should be obvious. Simulation theory suggests an account of the mechanisms underlying our capacity to predict and explain people's behavior, and that explanation makes no appeal to an internalized theory or knowledge structure. So if simulation theory is correct, then *on the internal reading* there is no such thing as folk psychology. But simulation theorists do not deny the obvious fact that people have intuitions about folk psychological platitudes; nor do they deny that it might be possible to systematize those intuitions by constructing a theory that entails them. That theory would be a folk psychology *on the external reading*, and it might well turn out to be a seriously mistaken theory. So the right conclusion to draw from the assumption that simulation theory is correct is not the jazzy claim that eliminativism has been undermined, but only the much more modest claim that eliminativists must opt for an external account of folk psychology.

REFERENCES

Chomsky, N., &. Katz, J. (1974). What the linguist is talking about. *Journal of Philosophy 71*, 347–367.

Churchland, P.M. (1981). Eliminative materialism and the propositional attitudes. *Journal of Philosophy, 78*, 67–90.

Churchland, P.M. (1989). Folk psychology and the explanation of human behavior. In P.M. Churchland (Ed.), *A neurocomputational perspective* (pp. 111–127). Cambridge, MA: MIT Press.

Churchland, P. S. (1986). *Neurophilosophy*. Cambridge, MA: Bradford Books/MIT Press.

Fodor, J. (1968). The appeal to tacit knowledge in psychological explanation. *Journal of Philosophy, 65*. Reprinted in Fodor (1981b). Page references are to Fodor (1981b).

Fodor, J. (1981a). Some notes on what linguistics is about. In N. Block (Ed.), *Readings in philosophy of psychology* (pp. 197–207). Cambridge, MA: Harvard University Press.

Fodor, J. (1981b). *Representations*. Cambridge, MA: Bradford Books/MIT Press.

Fodor, J. (1983). *The modularity of mind*. Cambridge, MA: Bradford Books/MIT Press.

Fodor, J. (1987). *Psychosemantics*. Cambridge, MA: Bradford Books/MIT Press.

Fodor, J. (1990). Roundtable discussion. In P. Hanson (Ed.), *Information, language and cognition*. Vancouver: University of British Columbia Press.

Goldman, A. (1989). Interpretation psychologized. *Mind and Language, 4*, 161–185.

Goldman, A. (1992). In defense of the simulation theory. *Mind and Language, 7*, 104–119.

Gordon, R. (1986). Folk psychology as simulation. *Mind and Language, 1*, 158–171.

12. This constitutes a change in view for one of us (S.S.), prompted, in large measure, by the arguments urged by the other (I.R.). The argument set out in this paragraph was first proposed by Ravenscroft. At about the same time, much the same argument was proposed by Gerard O'Brien (1993) and by Ian Hunt. We've also heard a similar argument from Kenneth Taylor. Stich wishes to thank all of these philosophers for convincing him that his previous view was mistaken.

Gordon, R. (1992). Replies to Stich and Nichols and Perner and Howes. *Mind and Language, 7*. 87–97.

Hacking, I. (1982). Wittgenstein the psychologist. *New York Review of Books, 29*, 5.

Harré, R. (1986). *The social construction of emotions*. Oxford: Basil Blackwell.

Harris, P. (1992). From simulation to folk psychology: The case for development. *Mind and Language, 7*, 120–144.

Horgan, T., & Woodward, J. (1985). Folk psychology is here to stay. *Philosophical Review, 94*, 197–226.

Jackson, F., & Pettit, P. (1990). In defense of folk psychology. *Philosophical Studies. 59*, 31–54.

Johnson-Laird, P. (1983). *Mental models: Towards a cognitive science of language, inference and consciousness*. Cambridge, MA: Harvard University Press.

Kitcher, P. (1984). In defense of intentional psychology. *Journal of Philosophy. 81*, 89–106.

Lewis, D. (1970). How to define theoretical terms. *Journal of Philosophy. 67*, 427–446.

Lewis, D. (1972). Psychophysical and theoretical identifications. *Australasian Journal of Philosophy. 50*, 249–258.

McGinn, C. (1989). *Mental content*. Oxford: Basil Blackwell.

Needham, R. (1972). *Belief, language and experience*. Chicago: University of Chicago Press.

O'Brien, G. (1993). A conflation of folk psychologies. In K. Neander & I. Ravenscroft (Eds.), *Prospects for intentionality*. Working Papers in Philosophy, 3. Canberra: Research School for Social Science, Australian National University.

Ramsey, W., Stich, S., & Garon, J. (1990). Connectionism, eliminativism and the future of folk psychology. *Philosophical Perspectives. 4*, 499–533.

Sellars, W. (1956). Empiricism and the philosophy of mind. In H. Feigl & M. Scriven (Eds.), *Minnesota studies in the philosophy of science* (Vol. 1, pp. 253–329). Minneapolis: University of Minnesota Press.

Sharpe, R. (1987). The very idea of a folk psychology. *Inquiry, 30*, 381–393.

Soames, S. (1984). Linguistics and psychology. *Linguistics and Philosophy. 7*, 155–179.

Sterelny, K. (1990). *The representational theory of mind*. Oxford: Basil Blackwell.

Stich, S. (1972). Grammar, psychology and indeterminacy. *Journal of Philosophy. 69*, 799–818.

Stich, S. (1983). *From folk psychology to cognitive science*. Cambridge, MA: Bradford Books/MIT Press.

Stich. S., & Nichols, S. (1992). Folk psychology: Simulation or tacit theory? *Mind and Language, 7*, 31–75.

Stich, S., & Nichols, S. (1995). Second thoughts on simulation. In M. Davies & T. Stone (Eds.), *Mental simulation: Philosophical and psychological essays*. Oxford: Basil Blackwell.

Von Eckardt, B. (1993). *What is cognitive science?* Cambridge, MA: Bradford Books/MIT Press.

Wilkes, K. (1981). Functionalism, psychology and the philosophy of mind. *Philosophical Topics*, 12, 147–167.

Wilkes, K. (1984). Pragmatics in science and theory in common sense. *Inquiry, 27*, 339–361.

Wilkes, K. (1991). The relationship between scientific psychology and common sense psychology. *Synthese, 89*, 15–39.

12

THE FLIGHT TO REFERENCE, OR HOW *NOT* TO MAKE PROGRESS

IN THE PHILOSOPHY OF SCIENCE

Michael A. Bishop and Stephen Stich

THERE IS A common strategy among contemporary philosophers for resolving issues in the philosophy of science. It involves making philosophical issues turn on questions of reference. We will call this strategy "the flight to reference." The thesis we will defend in this paper can be stated very simply: Whenever the flight to reference strategy is invoked there is a crucial step that is left undefended, and without a defense of this step, the flight to reference is a fatally flawed strategy for resolving philosophical issues. Despite its importance, the undefended move in flight to reference arguments almost always goes unnoticed and, to the best of our knowledge, no one has made a serious attempt to show how the move might be justified.

Those who invoke the flight to reference always rely on one or another version of what we will call a *substantive* account of reference, an account that takes reference to be some sort of complex relationship between referring terms and entities or classes of entities in the world.[1] Their arguments can always be analyzed into three separate stages. In the first

Earlier versions of the arguments developed in this paper were presented to the philosophy of science discussion group at Canterbury University in Christchurch, New Zealand, the Beijing Forum for Philosophy of Science at the Institute of Philosophy of the Chinese Academy of Social Sciences, the Philosophy Colloquium at the Graduate Center of the City University of New York, and at conferences at the University of Utah and Humboldt University in Berlin. We are grateful to all of these audiences for much valuable feedback. Special thanks are due to Philip Catton, Steve Downes, Hartry Field, Heimir Geirsson, Philip Kitcher and an anonymous referee for *Philosophy of Science*.

1. Causal-historical theories of reference like those advocated by Kripke (1972), Putnam (1975) and Devitt (1981) are prime examples of the sort of theory of reference that we will classify as "substantive." So too are

stage, they adopt (and sometimes explain and defend) their favored substantive account of reference; they say what specific relation or relations must obtain between a referring term and an entity or class of entities in order for the former to refer to the latter. In the second stage, they argue that on their account of reference the relation obtains between some term that is important for the debate at hand and some object or class of objects in the world. Or, alternatively, they can argue that the relation fails to obtain between the important term and any object or class in the world. At this stage, assuming all has gone well, the appropriate conclusion to draw is a conclusion about reference. But the philosophical debates in which these appeals to reference are embedded are not themselves debates about the reference of a term. Rather, they are debates about ontology or truth or some other matter. The third stage of the flight to reference strategy is an attempt to close this gap. The theorist uses the conclusion about reference drawn in stage 2 as a premise in an argument whose conclusion is explicitly about truth or ontology or some other matter. But in order to do this the theorist relies (often tacitly) on one of a family of principles about reference. These principles all look to be obvious and trivial. Indeed, they are so obvious that some might think they are analytic or constitutive for reference. No relation could plausibly count as the reference relation unless it satisfied these principles.

It is at exactly this point that the flight to reference comes to grief. Presumably because the principle or principles invoked in stage 3 seem to be constitutive for reference, those who adopt the flight to reference strategy never try to establish that the reference relation adopted in stage 1 satisfies the principle. And this is the fatal gap in all flights to reference. For if the principle really is constitutive for reference, then theorists cannot legitimately claim that their favored substantive relation actually *is* the reference relation unless they give us some reason to suppose that their relation satisfies the principle. On the other hand, if the principle is not constitutive for reference, then before invoking it theorists must give us some reason for supposing that their relation satisfies the principle. Without an argument that the relation endorsed in stage 1 satisfies the principle invoked (or more typically, assumed) in stage 3, the flight to reference can tell us nothing about ontology or truth. And thus it cannot do the philosophical work that those who invoke the strategy want it to do.

It is our belief that this fatal defect in the flight to reference strategy undermines many influential arguments in the philosophy of science and elsewhere in philosophy. In this paper we will focus on arguments in two domains. The first, to be discussed in Section 1, is the debate about eliminative materialism, where the flight to reference is invoked by

---

description theories like those defended by Russell (1919), Searle (1958) and Lewis (1970, 1972), and hybrid theories such those developed by Evans (1983) and Kitcher (1978, 1993). Deflationary accounts of reference of the sort defended by Field (1986, 1994) and Horwich (1990) are the principle examples of theories that do not count as "substantive" on our use of the term. The argument to be developed in this paper does not need a hard and fast distinction between substantive and non-substantive accounts of reference. It requires only that those who employ the flight to reference strategy adopt accounts of reference that are obviously substantive.

writers on both sides of the issue. The second, to be discussed in Section 2, is the debate over scientific realism. There our focus will be on Philip Kitcher's sophisticated attempt to use the flight to reference to defend a version of scientific realism.[2]

1 The Eliminative Materialism Debate: Reference and Ontology

Eliminative materialism is the view that intentional states, like beliefs and desires, do not exist. This is an ontological thesis—a thesis about whether instances of particular kinds of states inhabit our universe. Framed in this way, it is not clear why the truth of eliminativism should be related to theories about how words connect up to the world. To see how the eliminativism issue comes to depend on a semantic issue, consider the following argument for eliminativism:

> (1) Folk psychology is an empirical theory and, like any empirical theory, it consists of various substantive theses. Beliefs and desires are among the theoretical states posited by folk psychology, and terms like 'belief' and 'desire' can be viewed as the central theoretical terms in this theory.
>
> (2) Folk psychology is "a false and radically misleading conception of the causes of human behavior and the nature of cognitive activity" (Churchland 1984, 43).

Both of these claims are very controversial, of course. But let us suppose they are true. It follows that beliefs and desires are posits of a false theory. How is the eliminativist going to get from there to the conclusion that beliefs and desires do not exist? Here is another claim that is often invoked in eliminativist arguments.

> (3) Theoretical terms are like definite descriptions. They refer to (or are satisfied by) those things that have (most of) the properties specified by the theory. Thus,
>
> (3a) The central theoretical terms of false and radically misleading theories do not refer to anything.[3]

At this point, the first stage of the flight to reference is in place. In (3) a substantive theory is proposed about the relation that must obtain between terms and things in the world if the former are to refer to the latter. The second stage of the flight to reference strategy follows from (1), (2) and (3a), which together entail

> (4) '__ is a belief' does not refer to anything.

<hr/>

2. In another paper (Bishop and Stich, in preparation) we examine the role that the flight to reference has played in recent debates about moral realism.

3. Many philosophers on both sides of the eliminativism debate have advocated one or another version of the description theory of reference for theoretical terms. See, for example, Lewis 1970, 1972; Churchland 1984, 56; McGinn 1991, 150: Stich 1983, Ch. 1. For a more detailed discussion of the role that description theories of reference have played in the eliminativism debate, see Stich 1996, §4.

So now we have a conclusion about reference. To get from there to a conclusion about the existence of beliefs, we need some principle linking reference and existence. And for this third stage of the flight to reference, the following principle looks like an ideal candidate:

(5) (x) Fx iff 'F__' refers to x.

What (5) says is that something is an F if and only if 'F__' refers to it.[4] And from (4) and (5) the eliminativist conclusion follows:

(6) -(Ex) x is a belief. Or, less formally, beliefs do not exist.

But now what about (5)? What justification do we have for it? Well, it is hard to think of a more *obvious* claim about reference. Indeed, (5) is one of those apparently trivial principles that looks to many to be *analytic* or *constitutive* for reference. We confess that we have never really understood the notion of a constitutive principle, and for familiar reasons we are deeply skeptical about the notion of analyticity (see White 1950, Quine 1953, Harman 1967). But none of these concerns are relevant here. For we are more than happy to concede that, for whatever reason, (5) is certainly a principle that any account of the reference relation must respect. If a putative reference relation fails to satisfy (5), it couldn't really be the reference relation. And here we confront the crucial gap in the flight to reference strategy. For at the first stage, in (3), the argument offers a substantive account of the reference relation for theoretical terms. But is it the *right* account? Given what we have just conceded about (5), it *can't* be the right account unless it makes (5) true. Does it? Well, perhaps. But we have been offered no argument at all for this. And it is far from *obvious* that the (putative) reference relation sketched in (3) will make (5) come out true. Indeed, advocates of other substantive accounts of reference, which specify relations that are not extensionally equivalent, must think that when reference is understood as in (3), (5) is just plain false.

To see all this a bit more clearly, it will be useful to consider how an anti-eliminativist might concede the first two premises of the eliminativists' argument, but use the flight to reference strategy to come to exactly the opposite conclusion. There is no need to invoke

---

4. (5) should be interpreted as a schema whose instances include:

(5-p) (x) x is a pig iff '__ is a pig' refers to x.

and

(5-b) (x) x is a belief iff '__ is a belief' refers to x.
It might be a bit better to state (5) as follows, invoking satisfaction rather than reference:
(5-s) (x) Fx iff 'F__' is satisfied by x.
But since the difference is of no importance in our arguments, we will stick with (5).
We propose to avoid fussing about technical matters like this whenever possible.

a hypothetical anti-eliminativist here, since there is a very real and very acute one who has adopted just this approach. William Lycan accepts the view that folk psychology is an empirical theory and that terms like 'belief' and 'desire' are among the central theoretical terms of the theory. He also thinks it is entirely possible that folk psychology will turn out to be seriously mistaken because beliefs do not actually have most of the properties that folk psychology attributes to them. But none of this inclines Lycan to accept the eliminativists' ontological conclusion, since he rejects the account of reference urged in (3) and (3a), and adopts a much more "liberal" account.

> I am at pains to advocate a very liberal view. Unlike David Lewis (1972), and unlike Dennett (1978) and Stich (1982, 1983), I am entirely willing to give up fairly large chunks of our commonsensical or platitudinous theory of belief or of desire (or of almost anything else) and decide that we were just wrong about a lot of things, without drawing the inference that we are no longer talking about belief or desire. To put the matter crudely, I incline away from Lewis's Carnapian and/or Rylean cluster theory of reference of theoretical terms, and toward Putnam's (1975) causal-historical theory. As in Putnam's examples of 'water,' 'tiger,' and so on, I think the ordinary word 'belief' (qua theoretical term of folk psychology) points dimly toward a natural kind that we have not fully grasped and that only mature psychology will reveal. I expect that 'belief' will turn out to refer to some kind of information-bearing inner state of a sentient being..., but the kind of state it refers to may have only a few of the properties usually attributed to beliefs by common sense. (Lycan 1988, 31–32)

On the account that Lycan "is at pains to advocate" a theoretical term, T, refers to objects of kind O by virtue of a certain kind of complex causal-historical chain that connects uses of T to O (or to instances of O). The right kind of chain combines *groundings*, in which a term is introduced by a speaker who is in an appropriate causal relation with some instance of the kind, and *transmissions*, in which the term is conveyed from speaker to speaker. For our purposes, the details of the causal-historical account of reference are not essential (see Putnam 1975, Kripke 1972, Devitt 1981). What is important is that in "inclining toward" a Putnam-style theory of reference, Lycan has made the first move in the flight to reference; he has endorsed a substantive account of reference specifying an empirical relation that must obtain for terms of a certain kind to refer to things in the world.

One important fact about causal-historical accounts of reference is that they give no support to (3a). Quite to the contrary. On causal-historical accounts it is entirely possible for a theoretical term to refer even though it is embedded in a radically mistaken theory. This is enough to scuttle the eliminativist version of the flight to reference strategy, since without (3a) the eliminativist cannot get (4), and the argument grinds to a halt. But Lycan is not content to stop there, since he has his own version of the flight to reference. On his view it will probably turn out there is a "kind of information-bearing inner state" that stands in the appropriate causal-historical relation to our current uses of the ordinary word 'belief.' And if this is right, then (4) is not just unsupported, it is false; '__ is a belief' *does* refer to something. This is the second stage in Lycan's version of the flight to reference.

The third stage in Lycan's version is entirely parallel to the third stage in the eliminativists' version. In both cases, the third stage must rely on (5) or something similar. And in both cases the necessary steps seem so obvious that it is hardly necessary to state them. If s is an instance of the appropriate kind of information-bearing inner state, then '__ is a belief' refers to s. From this and (5) it follows that

(7) s is a belief.

And from this it follows that

(8) (Ex) x is a belief. Or, less formally, beliefs do exist.

So Lycan uses the flight to reference not merely to challenge the eliminativists' argument but also to argue that their conclusion is false.

The problem with Lycan's argument comes at exactly the same place as the problem with the eliminativists' argument. Both of them take (5) to be obvious, and so do we. No word-world relation would count as the reference relation if it did not satisfy (5). But Lycan has given us no more reason than the eliminativists did to suppose that if we take reference to be the relation he favors, it will make (5) true.[5] Moreover, there is nothing obvious or trivial about the claim that Lycan's relation will make (5) true. Since the causal-historical relation is not extensionally equivalent to the (putative) reference relation invoked in the eliminativists' version of the flight to reference, they cannot *both* make (5) true, though of course they could both fail to make (5) true. Moreover, these are not the only two games in town. In attempting to give an account of reference, 20th century philosophers have proposed a variety of non-extensionally equivalent relationships between referring terms and things in the world. At most one of these can make (5) true, and there is no guarantee that any of them does.

We think the moral to be drawn here is quite clear. Philosophers who wish to invoke the flight to reference strategy must *defend* the claim that the substantive account of reference they endorse will make (5) (and similar obvious principles about reference) come out true. It is not an assumption anyone who accepts a substantive account of reference

---

5. Actually, it is not the schema (5) but instances of (5), like (5-p) and (5-b) in fn. 4 that can be true or false. Our claims about the truth of (5) on various accounts of reference should be taken as shorthand for claims about the truth of all appropriate substitution instances of (5).

gets for free.[6] However, it is hardly ever recognized that the assumption *needs* to be defended and, to the best of our knowledge, no one has ever tried. We do not claim to have an argument showing that it is impossible to defend assumptions of this sort. But since we have no idea how one would even begin to construct such an argument, and as far as we know no one else has ever tried, we are inclined to be more than a bit skeptical. What we do claim is that without a defense of this essential assumption, attempts to invoke the flight to reference are fatally flawed.

2 The Scientific Realism Debate: Reference and Truth

Scientific realism is defined by a cluster of theses, the most important of which is that successful, mature scientific theories are true or approximately true. Why should we believe this? The standard justification for scientific realism is an abductive argument: Mature scientific theories exhibit great explanatory and predictive success, and they facilitate our effective interventions in the world. The best explanation for this success is that such theories are *true* (or approximately true) representations of reality. Versions of this abductive argument can be found in many places including Smart 1968, Putnam 1978, Boyd 1984, and Kitcher 1993.

---

6. It might well be the case that proponents of deflationary accounts of reference *do* get (5) for free. But deflationary accounts are useless in flight to reference arguments, since they provide no way of arguing for the second stage without begging the question. To see why this is the case, a bit more detail about deflationary theories is needed.

On deflationary accounts, predicates like '___is true' and '___refers to ___' exist "solely for the sake of a certain logical need" (Horwich 1990, 2). Reference "is merely a device for semantic ascent" (Horwich 1990, 8), it "is not a complex relation; a naturalistic or conceptual reduction is not needed and should not be expected" (Horwich 1990, 121). According to deflationists, a schema like (5) specifies what the word 'refers' means. If this is right, then deflationists who do not share our qualms about analyticity might well claim that (5) is analytic. This is half of what we had in mind when we conceded that deflationists might get (5) for free. The other half is that deflationists do not make any other systematic claims about reference. Since they do not think there is any "unified conceptual or naturalistic" (Horwich 1990, 124) reduction of reference, (5) captures all there is to be said about the reference relation in general. Thus there is no need to argue that the deflationists' substantive account of reference makes (5) come out true. They do not offer a substantive account.

If (5) and its instances are all we have to work with, however, there is no way to bring off the second stage of a flight to reference argument. Consider, for example, Lycan's flight to reference argument against eliminativism. He assumes (5-b):

(5-b) (x) x is a belief iff '___ is a belief' refers to x.

and then uses the causal-historical account of reference to argue that there are states which satisfy the right hand side of the bi-conditional. No such move is available to a deflationist. The only way in which a deflationist can establish that '___is a belief' refers to a "kind of information-bearing inner state of sentient beings" is to go through the left hand side of (5-b) and argue that the kind of state in question is a belief. But, of course, that is exactly the claim that the flight to reference argument is supposed to establish. So deflationists cannot invoke the flight to reference without begging the question.

The "pessimistic induction" is perhaps the most serious challenge to scientific realism. Larry Laudan (1984) presents this challenge in dramatic fashion by proposing a long list of theories that had great explanatory, predictive, and pragmatic successes but were false, and not just in detail. The laws and explanations proposed in these theories invoked substances, entities, and processes that do not exist. Among the examples Laudan cites are catastrophist geology, theories of spontaneous generation, the humoral theory of medicine, the effluvial theory of static electricity, the phlogiston theory of chemistry, the vibratory theory of heat, the vital force theories of physiology, and the theory of circular inertia (121). Laudan is very explicit about the lessons to draw from the history of science. "This list, which could be extended ad nauseam, involves in every instance a theory that was once successful and well confirmed, but which contained central terms that (we now believe) were nonreferring" (121). "Since realists would presumably insist that many of the central terms of the theories enumerated above do not genuinely refer, it follows that none of those theories could be approximately true (recalling that the former is a necessary condition for the latter)" (122–123).

In *The Advancement of Science* (1993), Philip Kitcher adduces an ambitious defense of scientific realism. A central part of Kitcher's response to the pessimistic induction is a version of the flight to reference strategy. Before we get to that, however, we will have to back up a bit and explain how Kitcher prepares the ground for his flight to reference. Kitcher begins by considering an example that looms large in Laudan's work, 19th century wave theories of light. These theories held that light consists of waves propagated in a pervasive fluid-like medium, the aether. Laudan notes that "the optical aether functioned centrally in explanations of reflection, refraction, interference, double refraction, diffraction and polarization" as well as in "some very startling predictions" (e.g., Fresnel's spot) "that, when tested, proved correct" (113–114). To prevent historical facts like the undeniable success of wave theories of light from undermining scientific realism, Kitcher's first step is to propose a distinction between a theory's *working posits*, which play an essential role in the theory's success, and its *presuppositional posits*, which do not. According to Kitcher, light waves (also known as "aether waves," "aether vibrations," and "electromagnetic waves") were a working posit of wave theories, while the aether was only a presuppositional posit.

Distinguish two kinds of posits introduced within scientific practice, *working posits* (the putative referents of terms that occur in problem-solving schemata) and *presuppositional posits* (those entities that apparently have to exist if the instances of the schemata are to be true). The ether is a prime example of a presuppositional posit, rarely employed in explanation or prediction, never subjected to empirical measurement (until, late in the century A. A. Michelson devised his famous experiment to measure the velocity of the earth relative to the ether), yet seemingly required to exist if the claims about electromagnetic and light waves were to be true. The moral of Laudan's story is not that theoretical positing in general is untrustworthy, but that presuppositional posits are suspect. (Kitcher 1993, 149)

If Kitcher is right about all of this, then scientific realists need not worry about the fact that historically successful theories posited entities that do not exist, so long as the posits are presuppositional. But what about the *working* posits of theories that were once successful but that have now been abandoned? Kitcher is careful not to make any sweeping ontological claims; he does not say that the working posits of such theories always exist. What he does instead is focus on *reference*. To defend his version of scientific realism from the challenge posed by abandoned theories that were successful in their prime, Kitcher proposes to argue that many tokens or utterances of terms for working posits in such theories *succeed in referring*, and thus that many utterances of sentences containing these terms can be true, and often are. So, for example, Kitcher claims that sometimes a wave theorist's "tokens of 'light wave' . . . genuinely refer to electromagnetic waves of high frequency" (1993, 146), and on some occasions, "Priestley's token of 'dephlogisticated air' refers to . . . oxygen" (1993, 100). Often the statements that Priestley made when he used 'dephlogisticated air' were true, and indeed some of these statements expressed important new discoveries. What we find in the writings of the phlogistonians, Kitcher maintains, are "true doctrines trying to escape from flawed language" (1993, 100).

To support all of this, Kitcher (1978, 1993) sets out an elegant version of the flight to reference. In the first stage he advances a new, context sensitive, hybrid theory of reference in which the distinction between the reference of expression-types and the reference of expression-tokens plays a central role. In Kitcher's theory an expression-type like 'light wave' or 'dephlogisticated air' will have a number of different "modes of reference"—a number of different ways of connecting, or failing to connect, with nature. One token of 'light wave' with a given mode of reference might refer to electromagnetic radiation, while a different token with a different mode of reference might fail to refer to anything.

> Modes of reference . . . fall into three types. A token's mode of reference is of the descriptive type when the speaker has a dominant present intention to pick out something that satisfies a particular description and the referent of the token is whatever satisfies the description. The baptismal type is exemplified when the speaker has a dominant present intention to pick out a particular present object (or a set of objects, one member of which is present). Finally, the conformist type covers those (many) instances in which the speaker intends that her usage be parasitic on those of her fellows (or her own earlier self), and, in this case, the reference of her token is determined through a long causal chain that leads back to an initial usage, a usage in which a token produced by a first user has its reference fixed either in the descriptive or in the baptismal mode. (Kitcher 1993, 77–78)

In the second stage of his flight to reference, Kitcher applies his theory of reference to episodes in the history of science. He describes cases in which different utterances or tokens of obsolete terms refer on some occasions and fail to refer on others. For example, when Priestley used 'dephlogisticated air' with the intention to refer to "the substance obtained when the substance emitted in combustion is removed from the air" that token of the term was empty; it referred to nothing. Its mode of reference is of the descriptive type, and the description is not true of anything—there is no substance (no phlogiston) emitted during combustion that anyone could remove from the air. On another occasion, when Priestley used the term 'dephlogisticated air' with the dominant intention to refer to the substance that he and the mice he was using breathed in a specific experimental setting, the mode of reference of the token was of the baptismal type. And on those occasions "Priestley's token of 'dephlogisticated air' refers to the substance which he and the mice breathed—namely oxygen" (1993, 100). In this example, Kitcher's theory of reference, along with the facts about Priestley's intentions, entails that a token of a term for a working posit succeeds in referring even though contemporary science regards the term as obsolete. This, of course, is just the sort of conclusion needed in the second stage of a flight to reference.

In the third stage of Kitcher's flight to reference, the focus moves from reference to truth. Kitcher concludes, for example, that "Priestley enunciated various true statements which had not previously been accepted" (1993, 99). His general conclusion is that proponents of obsolete but successful theories often succeeded in discovering important new truths, and they also succeeded in stating those truths despite their use of obsolete, theory-laden terms like 'aether waves' and 'dephlogisticated air.' If this is right, then an interesting form of scientific realism survives the pessimistic induction. Laudan's picture of obsolete but successful scientific theories—a picture on which most of their claims are false—is much too simple and very misleading. On Kitcher's alternative picture, many tokens of obsolete theoretical terms succeeded in referring to things that really do exist, and many of the claims made by those who advocated these theories were true. But how, exactly, can Kitcher get from the stage 2 conclusions about reference to the stage 3 conclusions about truth? We very much doubt that he can do it at all.

As usual, our objection will focus on the tension between the first and third stages. For simplicity's sake, let us use a slightly tidied up hypothetical example. On a certain occasion (we will call it "o"), Priestley used 'dephlogisticated air' with a baptismal mode of reference, intending to refer to the substance he had just produced in a particular experimental procedure. The first two stages of Kitcher's flight to reference give us the following three premises:

(9) On occasion o, Priestley uttered, "dephlogisticated air supports combustion better than ordinary air."
(10) On occasion o, "dephlogisticated air" refers to oxygen.
(11) Oxygen supports combustion better than ordinary air.

All three of these premises are entirely unproblematic. (9) is assumed to be a historical fact; (10) follows from Kitcher's theory of reference along with the assumptions we are making about occasion o; and (11) is a fact endorsed by contemporary chemistry. From these three premises, Kitcher wants to draw the following conclusion:

>   (C) On occasion o, Priestley's utterance, "Dephlogisticated air supports combustion better than ordinary air" is true.

But (C) does not follow from the above three premises, at least not directly. The inferential gap becomes evident when we note that the conclusion states that an utterance is true, but the premises say nothing about the conditions under which utterances are true. In order for this argument to succeed, then, we need some principle that connects reference and truth for utterances. An obvious candidate would be something like the following.

>   (12) An utterance of the form 'Fa' is true iff (Ex) (this token of 'a' refers to x and x satisfies this token of 'F__').

Actually, this is not quite enough to get Kitcher's conclusion. To make all the pieces fit together, we need to replace (11) with

>   (11') Oxygen satisfies '__ supports combustion better than ordinary air.'

And one might ask how, exactly, we can justify the replacements.[7] This is not a problem we propose to press, however, since as we see it the real problem with the argument is centered on (12). What justification do we have for (12)? The most natural answer, we think, is that (12) hardly needs justification. Indeed, it is yet another of those claims about reference that some theorists might take to be analytic. And while we are already on record as being skeptical about analyticity, we would happily concede that (12) is *obvious* in much the same way that (5) was. No account of the reference relation that failed to make (12) true could possibly be correct.

So what is the problem? The answer, of course, is entirely parallel to the answer we gave in our critique of the eliminativist and anti-eliminativist versions of the flight to reference. Kitcher has given us a substantive theory of reference. It is a subtle and complex account that differs in various ways from the accounts offered by other theorists. What he has not done, indeed what he has not even begun to do, is argue that the complex relation

---

7. Alternatively, we could use a less general version of (12) like

>   (12') An utterance of the form 'a supports combustion better than ordinary air' is true iff (Ex) (this token of 'a' refers to x and x supports combustion better than ordinary air.)

that he calls "reference" makes all instances of (12) come out true. And it is certainly not *obvious* that Kitcher's relation does this. For as noted earlier, there are lots of substantive accounts of reference to be found in the literature, and most of them specify relations that are not extensionally equivalent to the one Kitcher so carefully describes. Moreover, the relation specified by some of these competing accounts (particularly those that emphasize the "descriptive mode") will make the right hand side of some instances of (12) come out false when Kitcher's account makes it come out true, while the relation specified by other competing accounts (particularly those that emphasize the "baptismal mode") will make the right hand side of some instances of (12) come out true when Kitcher's account makes it come out false. Let $R_{descriptive}$ and $R_{baptismal}$ be two such alternative relations. Then if Kitcher's relation makes all instances of (12) come out true, neither of the others do, while if either $R_{descriptive}$ or $R_{baptismal}$ makes all instances of (12) come out true, then Kitcher's relation does not. Without some *argument* for the claim that *his* relation makes all instances of (12) come out true (and thus that the others do not) Kitcher has no justification for invoking (12). And without (12) or something like it, Kitcher cannot get from (9), (10) and (11) to (C); he cannot get from premises about the complex relation that he calls "reference" to conclusions about truth. The most important element of scientific realism is the claim that successful scientific theories are true (or approximately true), and Kitcher's elaborate flight to reference argument provides no justification at all for this claim.[8]

A defender of Kitcher's flight to reference arguments might protest that similar argumentative strategies are common in science.[9] Consider the classic example of Neptune's discovery. In the early 1800s, astronomers found that the observed orbit of Uranus did not fit the best available predictions. By 1836 "most astronomers had accepted the hypothesis of an exterior planet" to account for the discrepant observations (Grosser 1979, 54). About seven years later, John Couch Adams and Urbain Jean Joseph Leverrier independently calculated approximately where the new planet would be found in the sky. Although Adams assured English astronomers that "the planet would appear no smaller than a star of the ninth magnitude" they "elected to map all stars down to the eleventh magnitude" (Grosser 1979, 108). Across the Channel, Leverrier assured French astronomers that they would not have to map all the stars since the disk of the new planet would

---

8. It might be thought that Kitcher's argument could sustain a somewhat less central element of scientific realism, namely the claim that terms for the working posits of successful theories succeed in referring—or at least that some tokens of such terms succeed in referring. But even this is problematic. For if it is indeed the case that no account of the reference relation that failed to make (12) true could possibly be correct, then without an argument that *his* account of reference makes (12) true, Kitcher has no grounds for claiming that the complex substantive relation he describes really is reference. Though he has established that certain tokens of 'dephlogisticated air' stand in the relation he describes to oxygen, he is not entitled to draw any conclusions about the *reference* of those tokens until he offers an argument that his relation makes (12) and other obvious (or "constitutive") principles about reference true.

9. The line of defense sketched here was suggested to us by Philip Kitcher.

be very distinctive. But no French observatories searched. In frustration, Leverrier wrote to an assistant at the Berlin Observatory, J.G. Galle, asking him to look for Neptune. The letter reached Galle on 23 September 1846. That evening, Galle described what looked to be a star of the eighth magnitude that was not listed in his star charts. He had found Neptune.

Here we have an instance of scientific reasoning from some phenomena (the observed discrepancy in Uranus' orbit) to a theoretical posit (the planet Neptune) and then to a further conclusion (Neptune's apparent magnitude and location). Kitcher's flight to reference seems to employ just this kind of argumentative strategy: from some phenomena (various facts about a scientist's use of a particular expression on a particular occasion) to a theoretical posit (a certain expression successfully refers) and then to a further conclusion (a scientist's utterance on a particular occasion is true). If the former strategy is acceptable (and we certainly agree that it is), then isn't the latter strategy also acceptable? The answer, we maintain, is that it is not because there is a crucial disanalogy between the strategies. In the scientific case, *both inferences were based on extraordinarily well-confirmed empirical theories.* A well-placed confidence in various theories, including Newtonian physics, as well as many careful observations led scientists to conjecture that Neptune exists. And on this assumption, Adams and Leverrier could reasonably infer many things about the undiscovered planet—its mass, its distance from the Earth and Sun, its apparent magnitude and location—once again, all on the basis of extraordinarily well-confirmed theories.

If we take this analogy seriously, we should expect each inferential step in the flight to reference strategy to be supported by well-confirmed empirical theories. But they are not. Indeed, one way to see the point of our argument more clearly is to note how the flight to reference strategy utterly fails to meet the epistemic standards set by Adams and Leverrier. In Kitcher's flight to reference, principle (12) supported the second inference, from reference to truth. What justifies it? Kitcher, like all other proponents of flight to reference arguments, does not offer (12) as a principle that is part of, or implied by, a well-confirmed empirical theory. We suspect that many philosophers assume that principles like (12) are constitutive for reference, which would explain why no one has proposed an empirical theory that would justify these principles. For argument's sake, we are prepared to grant this assumption. But now, those who urge arguments like Kitcher's face a dilemma:

(i) If Kitcher claims that (12) is constitutive for reference, he gets the second inference for free, but he still needs to justify the first one. What reason is there to believe that the word-world relation specified (or defined?) by Kitcher's theory actually satisfies principle (12), which is *by hypothesis* constitutive for reference? As is typical in flight to reference arguments, no well-confirmed empirical theory is in sight. But an argument of some sort is essential. For it cannot simply be *stipulated* that the word-world relation Kitcher specifies has the property of making (12) true, any more than Adams could simply stipulate that Neptune would appear no smaller than a star of the ninth magnitude.

(ii) If Kitcher does not claim that (12) is constitutive for reference (or that (12) is obvious and that any acceptable account of reference must make it come out true), then we will offer no objection to the first inferential step. But what about the second inference? What reason is there to believe that the word-world relation specified by Kitcher's theory actually satisfies principle (12)? After all, *by hypothesis* (12) is not constitutive for reference. Once again, some sort of argument is essential.

If we take the proposed analogy with scientific reasoning seriously, those who invoke the flight to reference owe us full-blown, well-confirmed empirical theories that support the contention that their favored reference-relations satisfy principles like (12). But we are willing to settle for less. Any sort of cogent argument will do.

3 Conclusion

Logical positivists believed that all philosophical questions are really questions about language. While the tenets that lead to this view of philosophy have faded, a remnant of the view has survived and flourished: the temptation to make philosophical issues turn on questions of reference. We have described one common strategy for trying to resolve philosophical issues by appeal to substantive accounts of reference, the strategy we have called the flight to reference. And we have argued that there is a fatal gap in all arguments employing this strategy. In order for a claim about reference to be relevant to claims about existence or truth or some other philosophically important notion, a principle linking reference to that notion is required. However, those who rely on such principles face a dilemma. Either they take the principles to be obvious constraints on any substantive account of reference, or they do not. If they do, then they are simply not entitled to claim that their own favored substantive relation really is the reference relation unless they give us some reason to suppose that their relation will make the relevant principle true. If they do not, then they are free to claim that their favored relation is indeed reference, but they cannot invoke the principle until they argue that when reference is identified with the relation they have specified, it makes the principle come out true. Either way, then, a theorist who invokes the flight to reference must argue that when the substantive reference relation endorsed in the first stage of the flight is plugged into the principle relied upon in the third stage, the relation makes the principle come out true. And that, we suspect, will be no easy task.

REFERENCES

Bishop, M. and S. Stich (in preparation), "Moral Realism and the Flight to Reference."
Boyd, R. (1984), "The Current Status of Scientific Realism," in Jarrett Leplin (ed.), *Scientific Realism*. Berkeley: University of California Press, pp. 41–82.

Churchland, P. M. (1984), *Matter and Consciousness*. Cambridge, MA: MIT Press.

Dennett, D. (1978), *Brainstorms*. Cambridge, MA: MIT Press.

Devitt, M. (1981), *Designation*. New York: Columbia University Press.

Evans, G. (1983), "The Causal Theory of Names," *Proceedings of the Aristotelian Society* 47: 187–208.

Field, H. (1986), "The Deflationary Concept of Truth," in G. MacDonald and C. Wright (eds.), *Fact, Science, and Value*. Oxford: Blackwell, pp. 55–117.

———. (1994), "Deflationist Views of Meaning and Content," *Mind* 103: 249–285.

Grosser, M. (1962/1979), *The Discovery of Neptune*. New York: Dover Publications.

Harman, G. (1967), "Quine on Meaning and Existence I," *Review of Metaphysics* 21: 125–151.

Horwich, P. (1990), *Truth*. Oxford: Blackwell.

Kitcher, P. (1978), "Theories, Theorists and Theoretical Change," *Philosophical Review* 87: 519–547.

———. (1993), *The Advancement of Science*. Oxford: Oxford University Press.

Kripke, S. (1972), *Naming and Necessity*. Cambridge, MA: Harvard University Press.

Laudan, L. (1984), *Science and Values*. Berkeley: University of California Press.

Lewis, D. (1970), "How to Define Theoretical Terms," *Journal of Philosophy* 67: 17–25.

———. (1972), "Psychophysical and Theoretical Identifications," *Australasian Journal of Philosophy* 50: 249–258.

Lycan, W. (1988), *Judgement and Justification*. Cambridge: Cambridge University Press.

McGinn, C. (1991), "Mental States, Natural Kinds and Psychophysical Laws," in *The Problem of Consciousness*. Oxford: Basil Blackwell, pp. 126–152.

Putnam, H. (1975), "The meaning of 'Meaning,'" in *Mind, Language and Reality*. Cambridge: Cambridge University Press, pp. 215–271.

———. (1978), *Meaning and the Moral Sciences*. London: Routledge & Kegan Paul.

Quine, W.V. (1951), "Two Dogmas of Empiricism," *Philosophical Review* 60: 20–43.

Russell, B. (1919), "Descriptions," in *Introduction to Mathematical Philosophy*. London: George Allen & Unwin Ltd., pp. 167–180.

Searle, J. (1958), "Proper Names," *Mind* 67: 166–173.

Stich, S. (1982), "On the Ascription of Content," in A. Woodfield (ed.), *Thought and Object*. Oxford: Oxford University Press, pp. 153–206.

———. (1983), *From Folk Psychology to Cognitive Science*. Cambridge, MA: MIT Press.

———. (1996), "Deconstructing the Mind," in *Deconstructing the Mind*. Oxford: Oxford University Press, pp. 3–90.

Smart, J.J.C. (1968), *Between Science and Philosophy*. New York: Random House.

White, M. (1950), "The Analytic and the Synthetic: An Untenable Dualism," in S. Hook (ed.), *John Dewey: Philosopher of Science and Freedom*. New York; Dial Press, pp. 316–330.

13

THE ODD COUPLE

The Compatibility of Social Construction and Evolutionary Psychology

Ron Mallon and Stephen Stich

1 Introduction

By all appearances there is a battle raging for the soul of the social sciences. On one side, and in some disciplines the prevailing establishment, are social constructionists and other advocates of what John Tooby and Leda Cosmides have dubbed the Standard Social Science Model (SSSM).[1] Social constructionists emphasize the enormous diversity of social and psychological phenomena to be found in cultures around the world and throughout history, and much of the research in this tradition has been devoted to

We would like to thank Peter Carruthers, Paul Griffiths and Catherine Lutz for help and comments on earlier drafts.

1. Throughout we use 'social constructionist' as a label for those who advocate important parts of the Standard Social Science Model. This can be misleading in three different ways. First, social constructionism is sometimes identified (usually pejoratively) with a set of radical metaphysical theses that call into question the mind independence of reality or the possibility of knowing it (e.g., Pinker 1997, 57). We use 'social constructionism' for the more limited and prima facie more plausible view that particular features of human psychology or social life are culturally caused and local in character. A second source of confusion is that 'social constructionist' as we use it includes theorists who do not characterize themselves as social constructionists, but nonetheless endorse the cultural locality of a given phenomenon. Finally, 'social constructionism' thus characterized picks out only one portion of the more extensive doctrine Tooby and Cosmides call the Standard Social Sciences Model (1992, 31–32). Closely enough, then, all SSSM advocates are social constructionists in our sense, though not all social constructionists need endorse every aspect of SSSM as characterized by Tooby and Cosmides. Still, we take it that the examples of social constructionists we discuss and the doctrines they hold are paradigmatic examples of SSSM advocates.

describing that diversity—in emotions, moral and religious beliefs, sexual behavior, kinship systems, theories about nature, and much else besides.[2] Advocates of the SSSM are heirs to the empiricist conception of the mind as a blank tablet which experience writes upon. And while no serious social constructionist would deny that our innate mental endowment imposes *some* constraints on what we can learn and what we can do, they believe that most of these constraints are weak and uninteresting. Thus when it comes to explaining the diversity of psychological phenomena like emotions, beliefs, and preferences, differences in the surrounding culture loom large. Those cultural differences are in turn explained by differences in history and in local conditions.

On the other side are evolutionary psychologists who advocate a distinctly rationalist-inspired conception of the mind.[3] According to evolutionary psychologists, human minds have a rich, species-typical cognitive architecture composed of functionally distinct systems—"mental organs" as Steven Pinker has called them—that have been shaped by natural selection over millions of years. Many of these mental organs embody complex, domain-specific algorithms and theories (or stores of information) which play a major role in shaping and constraining beliefs, preferences, emotional reactions, sexual behavior, and interpersonal relationships. This evolved psychology also plays a major role in shaping and constraining social institutions. In studying social and psychological phenomena, evolutionary psychologists focus on commonalties rather than differences, and in explaining these commonalties they emphasize the contributions of innate, information-rich mental mechanisms that were selected to be adaptive in the sorts of environments in which humans evolved.

Advocates of the SSSM have little sympathy with this quest for cross-cultural patterns and universal features of human psychology. The highly influential anthropologist, Clifford Geertz, apparently doubts that there are any substantive universals to be found. "There is," he writes, "a logical conflict between asserting that, say, 'religion,' 'marriage,' or 'property' are empirical universals and giving them very much in the way of specific content, for to say that they are empirical universals is to say that they have the same content, and to say they have the same content is to fly in the face of the undeniable fact that they do not" (Geertz 1973, 39).

Evolutionary psychologists are not much moved by this sort of skepticism, however. On their view the demand for exceptionless universals sets the standard too high. According to Tooby and Cosmides,

---

2. See, e.g., Lutz 1988, Kessler and McKenna 1977, Oberoi 1994, Shweder 1985.

3. We use the term 'evolutionary psychologist' expansively to include a variety of naturalistic psychological approaches of the sort sketched below. The term has recently been used proprietarily to refer to evolutionary approaches of the sort favored by John Tooby, Leda Cosmides and Steven Pinker (Tooby and Cosmides 1992, Pinker 1997). This latter group is distinguished by its commitment to the thesis of "massive modularity": the claim that a great many (perhaps even all) mental processes, including core cognitive processes, are subserved by domain-specific mechanisms.

Whenever it is suggested that something is "innate" or "biological," the SSSM-oriented anthropologist or sociologist rifles through the ethnographic literature to find a report of a culture where the behavior (or whatever) varies. . . . Upon finding an instance of reported variation, the item is moved from the category of "innate," "biological," "genetically determined," or "hardwired" to the category of "learned," "cultural," or "socially constructed." . . . Because almost everything human is variable in one respect or another, nearly everything has been subtracted from the "biologically determined" column and moved to the "socially determined" column. The leftover residue of "human nature," after this process of subtraction has been completed, is weak tea indeed. (1992, 43)

On the face of it, the dispute between social constructionists and evolutionary psychologists has two major and interrelated components. First, there is an empirical disagreement about the extent to which all normal humans share innate, informationally-rich mental mechanisms that strongly constrain our psychology and our social interactions and institutions. Second, there is a strategic or methodological disagreement—a disagreement about the best way to make progress in understanding psychological and social phenomena. Evolutionary psychologists urge that we focus on what people have in common, while social constructionists think that it is more important to attend to the many ways in which people differ. We do not deny that there are real and important disagreements on both of these points. But it is our contention, and one of the central theses of this paper, that there is a third, much less obvious issue dividing social constructionists and evolutionary psychologists. This disagreement is not an empirical dispute about the nature of the human mind nor is it a methodological dispute about the best way of studying minds and social phenomena. Rather, it is a *semantic* disagreement (or perhaps it is better described as a *philosophical* disagreement—we've never been very clear about how much of semantics counts as philosophy). What is at issue is the *meaning* and *reference* of many ordinary terms for mental states, and for other psychological and social phenomena—terms like 'anger,' 'disgust,' 'gender,' and 'homosexuality.'

We think it is crucially important to bring this covert component of the dispute out into the open. When we have a clear view of the role that this third component of the dispute is playing, it will also become clear that this philosophical dispute can easily be bracketed and set aside. Evolutionary psychologists could easily accept the semantic assumptions made by social constructionists—if only for argument's sake—without changing in the least the claims they want to make about minds, evolution, and social interactions. Moreover, and this is the other central thesis of this paper, once the philosophical dispute has been set aside, the remaining empirical and methodological disagreements between social constructionists and evolutionary psychologists look much less serious. When the fog that the philosophical dispute engenders has been cleared, social constructionists and evolutionary psychologists look less like adversaries and more like natural partners.

In this paper our focus will be on the dispute between evolutionary psychology and social constructionist approaches to the emotions, though we think that much of what we say is more generally applicable. The emotions are a crucial case, both because they play a central role in discussions of other social and psychological phenomena like violence, sexual behavior, religious practices, and moral beliefs, and also because there has been extensive research on the emotions within both an evolutionary psychology paradigm and a social constructionist paradigm. In fact, when reading this literature, it is easy to get the feeling that each side considers the emotions one of its success stories.

Here is how we will proceed. In Section 2, we will give a brief overview of the social constructionist approach by sketching a few details from Catherine Lutz's (1988) widely admired study of the emotions of the Ifaluk, inhabitants of a Micronesian atoll. In Section 3, we will provide a quick review of work on emotions in the evolutionary psychology tradition and set out a model of the psychological mechanisms underlying the emotions drawn from recent work in that tradition. Though there are lots of disagreements over how the details are to be filled in, there is a growing consensus among evolutionary psychologists on the broad outlines of the sort of model we will describe. At the core of this model is an innate, evolved system for triggering and sequencing emotional responses, present in all normal humans. Another important feature of the model is that it allows for quite extensive cross-cultural variation both in the circumstances that provoke various emotions and in the patterns of behavior that the emotions produce. Since this sort of variation is a central theme in social constructionist accounts of the emotions, one might well wonder whether social constructionists and evolutionary psychologists have anything left to disagree about.

The answer, as we will demonstrate in Section 4, is *yes*. For while evolutionary psychologists agree that emotions can be provoked by different situations in different cultures, and that they can give rise to quite different patterns of behavior, they maintain that the emotions themselves are cross-cultural universals. Fear, anger, sadness, and other emotions can be found in all cultures. And this is a claim that many social constructionists vigorously dispute. Must social constructionists then reject the sort of nativistic, evolutionary psychological model of the emotions set out in Section 3? Here, we think, the answer in *no*. For, as we will argue in Section 5, social constructionists can maintain that emotions like fear and anger are not cross-cultural universals and *still* accept the evolutionary psychologists' account of the mechanisms underlying the emotions, provided that they accept what we will call a *thick description* account of the meaning and reference of ordinary language emotion terms. And, it is our contention that, either explicitly or tacitly, most social constructionists do indeed assume that a thick description account is correct. But we will also note that the thick description account of meaning and reference is not the only game in town. There are numerous alternative accounts of meaning and reference to choose from, some of which will not sustain the social constructionists' claim that emotions are culturally-local.

In Section 6, we will begin by asking which account of the meaning and reference of emotion terms is correct, and go on to suggest that no one really knows and that the question itself may not be clear enough to *have* a determinate answer. But we will also argue that *it really doesn't matter* which side is right since it is easy to see how this dispute can be bracketed and set aside. Moreover, and this is the essential point, once we set aside this dispute over the reference of emotion terms, it is far from clear that any deep disagreements between social constructionist and evolutionary psychological accounts remain. The philosophically motivated controversy about universality is little more than a distraction which obscures the fact that the findings and theories produced on both sides of the divide, far from being in competition with one another, are actually complementary. Many people will find our conclusion quite startling since it is widely believed that the battle between social constructionists and evolutionary psychologists is driven by radically different views about the nature of minds, social institutions and human kinds. If we are right, there is relatively little fundamental disagreement about any of these matters. What drives the dispute is a covert philosophical disagreement whose resolution is of little moment to those on either side.

2 The Social Constructionist Approach to the Emotions

When studying the emotions, as when studying other social and psychological phenomena, social constructionists are primarily concerned to describe the rich, multifaceted, culturally-local network in which the phenomena are embedded. Since many social constructionists concerned with the emotions are anthropologists, problems of translation are a major concern. Thus their inquiry often begins by focusing on the *words* for emotions that are used in the culture they are studying and the problem of how those words should be translated. In order to accomplish this task, social constructionists pay careful attention to a number of interrelated aspects of emotion discourse and behavior in the target culture, including:

i) the often very complex circumstances in which people in that culture claim that they or others experience the emotions picked out by various emotion words

ii) the pattern of inferences that are drawn when someone is believed to be experiencing the emotion

iii) the patterns of interaction that exist (and/or that people in the culture *believe* to exist) among the emotions and also among emotions and other mental states and among emotions and various sorts of behavior; some of these interactions will be within a single person while others involve two or more people

iv) the ways in which both emotions and discourse about emotions interact with the moral, political and economic lives of the people in the culture.

When done well, the detailed "ethnopsychological" accounts that result from studies of this sort—"thick descriptions" as Geertz would call them—can be fascinating. Part of what makes them so interesting is that many of the patterns described are wonderfully exotic, differing in surprising and unexpected ways from the patterns of interaction in which our own emotions and emotion language are embedded.

To see how all this works in practice, let us briefly review Lutz's account of the emotion that the Ifaluk people call '*song*.' *Song* is an emotion akin to the one that we call 'anger,' though in contrast with anger, there is a strong moral component to *song*. In order to count as being or feeling *song*, an Ifaluk must be *justifiably* angry at another person who has engaged in morally inappropriate behavior. The Ifaluk have an array of other terms for types of anger that do not involve this moral dimension: '*tipmochmoch*' for the irritability that often accompanies sickness, '*linger-inger*' for anger that builds up slowly when one is confronted with a series of minor annoyances, etc. (1988, 157). But they have no generic term that picks out all and only these various sorts of anger (Lutz, pers. comm.).

There are various sorts of moral transgression that can provoke *song*. Lutz's account of these reasons or triggering conditions for the emotion make it clear how the emotion is woven into the fabric of Ifaluk society, and also how very different that society is from ours. One important category of events that can provoke *song* is the violation of a taboo, and among the Ifaluk taboos are not in short supply. There are taboos that apply only to women (they are forbidden to enter the canoe houses or to work in the taro gardens when they are menstruating) and others that apply only to men (they are not to enter birth houses). Other taboos apply to everyone. Violation of these taboos provokes *song* among the chiefs who may impose fines or other punishments. On a less public level, *song* is often provoked when people fail to live up to their obligation to share (160) or when they are lazy, loud, or disrespectful. (165) From a Western perspective, one of the stranger features of *song* is that it can be provoked by a sort of excited happiness that the Ifaluk call '*ker*.' "Happiness/excitement," Lutz reports, "is an emotion people see as pleasant but amoral. It is often, in fact, *im*moral because someone who is happy/excited is more likely to be unafraid of other people. While this lack of fear may lead them to laugh and talk with other people, it may also make them misbehave or walk around showing off" (167).

Just as the circumstances that can provoke *song* are different from those that can provoke anger in our culture, so too is the pattern of behavior that a *song* person may display. In the West, anger often leads to physical confrontation and sometimes to violence. But among the Ifaluk, according to Lutz, "it is expected that those who are justifiably angry [*song*] will *not* physically aggress against another. And in fact, interpersonal violence is virtually nonexistent on the island." (176) Some of the behavior that the Ifaluk exhibit when they are *song* is familiar enough. They may refuse to speak or eat with the offending party or produce a facial expression indicative of disapproval. But other *song*-induced behavior is rather more exotic. People often react to *song* by gossiping about the offending person so that he or she may learn indirectly that someone claims to be justifiably angry with them (175). In extreme cases they may threaten to burn down the offending person's house (171) or fast or threaten suicide (174).

When people learn that they are the object of another person's *song*, the typical reaction is to experience the emotion that the Ifaluk call '*metagu*' which Lutz characterizes as a sort of fear or anxiety. *Metagu* can be brought on by circumstances other than the *song* of another—strange situations is one that Lutz mentions (186)—but the term is not used for the sort of fear produced by sudden and unexpected events like the falling of a coconut nearby (202), nor is it used for the fearful emotion produced by events like the erratic behavior of a drunk (203). When offenders experience *metagu*, it leads them to behave more calmly and appropriately and it also often leads them to take some corrective action like apologizing, paying a fine levied by the chiefs, or sending some object of value to the aggrieved parties or their families. This causes those experiencing *song* to "forget their justifiable anger" (175). Figure 1 is Lutz's sketch of some of the relationships among *song*, *metagu*, and *ker*.

As noted earlier, the Ifaluk concept of *song*, in contrast with the Western notion of anger, is intrinsically tied to moral concerns. One *cannot* be *song* unless one's anger is justified. And, according to the prevailing moral views, if two people are involved in a dispute, only one can *really* be *song*, regardless of what the other person may think about the emotion he or she is experiencing (173). Not surprisingly, "daily negotiations over who is *song* and over the proper reasons for that anger lie at the heart of the politics of everyday life" (170). It would, of course, be quite bizarre for two people in our culture to assume that only one could be genuinely angry with the other and to argue about which one it was. In this way, our conception of anger seems quite different from the Ifaluk conception of *song*. Nor is it clear that we have *any* notion that corresponds all that closely to *song*, since even our notion of justifiable anger can be and often is applicable to *both* parties to a dispute. *Metagu* also has a role to play in the moral and political life of the Ifaluk community, since people who describe themselves

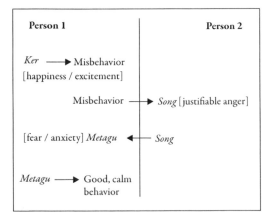

FIGURE 1 Lutz's account of the interrelationships among *song*, *metagu*, and *ker*. (Lutz 1988, 168)

as *metagu* declare themselves to be harmless and in accord with the moral code of the island (201–202).

What we have presented in this section is only a fragment of the complex cultural web into which the emotional life of the Ifaluk is woven. Our goal has been to illustrate the social constructionist approach to the study of emotion and to provide a few examples of the sort of culturally-local facts that play a central role in the ethnopsychological descriptions of those who adopt this approach.

3 The Evolutionary Psychology Account of the Emotions

The account of the emotions on which we believe contemporary evolutionary psychologists are converging had its beginnings in Charles Darwin's *The Expression of the Emotions in Man and Animals* (1872 [1998]). Darwin pioneered a technique in which subjects are shown photographs of emotionally expressive faces and asked to identify the emotion that the person is experiencing. Using this test Darwin demonstrated that people are capable of identifying emotions from facial displays with considerable reliability. However, Darwin used the technique only on English test subjects. To learn about other cultures, he relied on an extensive correspondence with missionaries, traders, and others. Unfortunately, the questionnaires he used included some rather leading questions, rendering his cross-cultural findings suspect.

In part because of these methodological problems, Darwin's work on facial expressions made relatively little impact until, in the late 1960s and early 1970s, a number of researchers, including Paul Ekman, Wallace Friesen, and Carol Izard began using Darwin's experimental strategy with subjects from non-Western cultures. The results of this work have become quite famous and have made a major impact on subsequent research on the emotions. In one series of experiments, members of the preliterate Fore language group in Papua New Guinea, who had rarely if ever seen Western faces before Ekman and his colleagues arrived, succeeded in picking out photos of Western faces that expressed the emotions involved in various emotionally charged stories. The Fore were also asked to show how their own faces would look if the events in the stories happened to them. American university students who were shown video tapes of the faces that the Fore produced were comparably successful matching the faces with the intended emotion (Ekman and Friesen 1971). These results, along with much other cross-cultural work on the facial expression of emotion, have convinced many investigators that there do indeed exist *universal* facial expressions for some emotions including happiness, sadness, anger, fear, and disgust. In later work Ekman and others have also accumulated evidence indicating that some of these emotions are accompanied by characteristic patterns of autonomic nervous system activity (Ekman, Levenson, and Friesen 1983; Levenson 1992).

To explain these findings, Ekman and his colleagues posited the existence of *affect programs* associated with each emotion. Affect programs can be thought of as universal and largely automated or involuntary suites of coordinated emotional responses that are subserved by evolved, innate mental and physiological mechanisms present in all normal members of the species.

While the immediate consequences of the initiation of an affect program are taken to be universal, Ekman and his colleagues recognized early on that behaviors further along in the causal stream may be strongly influenced by culture. One of the most dramatic examples of this was Ekman's demonstration that when Japanese subjects were shown unpleasant films in the presence of an authority figure they would begin the muscle contractions required to produce the facial expressions of negative emotions, but then immediately mask these expressions with a polite smile. American subjects, by contrast, made no attempt to mask the expression of negative emotions, nor did Japanese subjects when they viewed the distressing films alone. Ekman and his colleagues explained these findings by positing the existence of culturally-local "display rules" which can override or radically alter the pattern of emotional expression after an affect program has begun to unfold (Ekman 1972). In subsequent work, other researchers in the evolutionary psychology tradition have expanded and elaborated upon this idea, positing display rules and other sorts of culturally-local mental representations that affect not only facial expressions but also tone of voice, posture, self reports about one's emotional experience, and other cognitive and behavioral patterns that follow after the initiation of an affect program (Hochschild 1979, Mesquita and Frijda 1992, Levenson 1994).

What is it that initiates or "triggers" an affect program? What gets it going? In the mid-1970s Ekman proposed that the system of affect programs was linked to an innate "appraisal mechanism" which selectively attends to those stimuli (external or internal) that are the occasion for one or another emotion. Once it is triggered by appropriate stimuli, the appraisal mechanism operates automatically and initiates the appropriate affect program. It is not clear whether Ekman ever thought that there are some stimuli which the appraisal mechanism is built to respond to directly, without the mediation of other cognitive states and processes. But by the mid-1990s he had come to believe that just about all the activity of the appraisal mechanism was affected by culturally-local factors (Ekman 1994, 16).

Similar proposals have been developed by a number of other researchers. One sophisticated example of these is found in the work of Richard Lazarus who considers the problem of "reconciling biological universals with cultural sources of variability" to be among the most important issues that a theory of emotion must resolve (1994, 163). On Lazarus' theory, each emotion is innately linked to an abstractly characterized set of conditions specifying the circumstances under which it is appropriate to have the emotion. Since these conditions specify relations in which a person may stand to some aspect of the physical or social environment, Lazarus calls them "core relational themes" (1994, 164). Some examples of the core relational themes Lazarus proposes are:

Anger A demeaning offense against me and mine
Fright An immediate, concrete, and overwhelming physical danger
Sadness Having experienced an irrevocable loss (1994, 164)

Lazarus thinks of the link between core relational themes and emotions as a sort of innate "if–then form of reasoning." "[I]f a person appraises his or her relationship to the environment in a particular way, then a specific emotion—which is tied to the appraisal pattern—always follows.... The 'if–then' formula is, in effect, a *psychobiological principle*, which helps us understand universals in the antecedents of emotions" (1994, 165). But, of course, it will typically require *lots* of cognitive activity for a person to determine that a situation specified in one of the core relational themes obtains. And this cognitive activity, which must occur before the appraisal mechanism triggers the emotion, will be very much dependent on culturally-local beliefs, values, and expectations. What counts as a demeaning offense in one culture may be no offense at all in another, and one often must know a great deal about both a culture and its environment to realize that one is in great physical danger.

Putting all of these ideas together, Robert Levenson has offered the "biocultural model" of the emotions, depicted in Figure 2, which "reflects a confluence between innate and learned influences" (Levenson 1994, 125). The "innate hardwired" parts of the

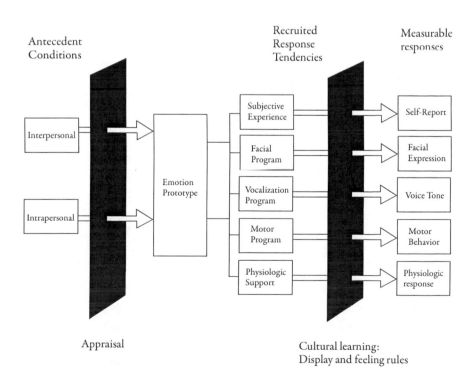

FIGURE 2 Levenson's Biocultural Model (1994, 126).

model—corresponding roughly to Ekman's appraisal and affect program mechanisms—are in the center of the diagram, between the black panels. Those panels are "the primary loci of cultural influences" and can include local knowledge and belief, local values, and display rules of various sorts.

While those who study emotion in the evolutionary psychology tradition disagree, often quite vigorously, about lots of the details, we think that most of them would concede that a model like Levenson's is on the right track—that *something* along those lines will be needed to explain both the innate and universal aspects of the emotions and the enormous cultural variability in the circumstances that elicit emotions and in the behavioral and cognitive consequences that emotions produce.

4 The Debate over Universality

From what we have said so far about social constructionist and evolutionary psychological approaches to the emotions, the reader might well wonder where evolutionary psychologists and social constructionists *disagree*? There is no obvious logical incompatibility in the two accounts that we have presented. Quite the opposite. An evolutionary psychologist might well take on board much of Lutz's detailed ethnopsychology as an illustration of one of the ways in which the black panels in Levenson's model can be filled in. Lutz describes local knowledge, beliefs, and values among the Ifaluk that determine such things as what sorts of behavior is offensive and how one is expected to behave when angered by an offense of that sort, or what sorts of situations are dangerous and how best to deal with that kind danger, and so on. And this is just the sort of information needed for "appraisal" of the situation and for determining a culturally appropriate response. Social constructionists, for their part, could embrace a model like Levenson's as providing a framework for a theory about the psychological mechanisms underlying many of the phenomena that Lutz and other anthropologists have described, a framework that would explain how innate mechanisms interact with culturally-local beliefs and values. But if the two research programs fit together so nicely, why does it often seem that the two sides are at war? What is all the fighting about?

The answer, or at least one important part of the answer, is that evolutionary psychologists and social constructionists are inclined to make very different claims about the *universality* of emotions. For theorists like Ekman and Lazarus, the psychological mechanisms between the black panels in Levenson's diagram are innate adaptations, present in all normal humans. Moreover, when the appraisal system (whose innate components are housed in the box labeled "Emotion prototype" in Levenson's model) determines that the abstract conditions (or the "core relational theme") appropriate to fear or anger or sadness have been satisfied, *fear or anger or sadness ensues*. Since situations that satisfy the abstract conditions are present in all cultures (though these situations may be quite different in different cultures), people in all cultures will experience these emotions. Indeed, since evolutionary psychologists maintain that some of the mechanisms in models like Levenson's are homologous to mechanisms in other species, they are not at all uncomfortable about attributing some emotions to members of other species (Lazarus 1994, 170).

Social constructionists, for the most part, will have none of this. For them, emotions are culturally-local phenomena, and thus people in very different cultures typically have very different emotions. *Song* and *metagu* are Ifaluk emotions which outsiders do not experience, *Amae* is a Japanese emotion that is unknown (or at least unrecognized) in the West.[4] And *accidie* is an emotion that once was widespread in the West but now has disappeared.[5] Moreover, it is not just exotic emotions like *metagu* or *amae* that social constructionists have claimed to be culturally-local. They make much the same claim for emotions that are commonplace in our own culture. So, for example, Jean Briggs (1970) claims that anger is unknown among the Inuit, and Averill agrees that "anger *as a specific emotion*" is not "universal across all cultures" (1994, 143; italics in original). Robert Levy (1984) suggests that sadness is unknown amongst Tahitians. And, perhaps most radically of all, Richard Shweder (1994) maintains not only that there are no universal emotions, but also that there may well be some cultures in which there are no emotions at all!

5 The Philosophical Origin of the Dispute

What is going on here? How could researchers whose theories appear to complement each other so nicely disagree so sharply about the universality of emotions? Since they have no fundamental disagreements about the psychological mechanisms underlying the emotions[6] or about the important role that culturally-local beliefs, preferences, and values play in people's emotional lives, why are they at loggerheads about the cultural locality of emotions? The answer, we maintain, or at least one very important part of the answer, is that social constructionists and evolutionary psychologists have a deep though largely hidden *philosophical* disagreement—a disagreement about the meaning and the reference of the emotion terms that ordinary folk use, words like 'anger,' '*metagu*,' 'fear,' and '*song*.' To make the point, we will begin by sketching one version of what is perhaps the most widely held view, among philosophers, about the meaning and refer-

---

4. Harré maintains that "The Japanese . . . create and sustain an emotion, *amae*, quite distinct from anything found in the adult repertoire of Western cultures" (1986, 10). The Japanese psychiatrist Doi characterizes *amae* as "a sense of helplessness and the desire to be loved." (Quoted in Morsbach and Tyler 1986, 290.)

5. Harré and Finlay-Jones 1986. Harré writes: "I offer accidie as an example of an obsolete emotion, since I think modern people do not associate any specific emotion with laziness or procrastination in the carrying out of tasks that duty demands. . . . The basic idea of accidie was boredom, dejection or even disgust with fulfilling one's religious duty" (221).

6. Indeed, social constructionists rarely say *anything at all* about the psychological and physiological mechanisms that subserve emotions, though they do not deny the existence of such mechanisms (see, e.g., Lutz 1988, 210).

ence of terms about mental states. We will then argue that if one held this view one might agree that Levenson's model (or something very like it) was the correct account of the psychological mechanisms underlying the emotions, *and still insist that emotions are culturally-local.*

The account of the meaning of mental state terms that we will present is a version of what is sometimes called *analytic functionalism*, though for reasons that will soon be obvious, we prefer to call it *the description theory.* Views like it have been endorsed by many philosophers, most notably David Lewis. As we view the description theory, it makes three interrelated claims. The first is that the mental state terms of ordinary language can be treated as *theoretical* terms. The second is that theoretical terms are implicitly defined by the theory in which they are embedded. Building on a strategy first proposed by Ramsey, Lewis showed how the implicit definition that a theory provides for its theoretical terms can be turned into an explicit definition in the form of a *definite description* of the theoretical entities being defined.[7] There is an important sense in which the implicit definitions provided by a theory are *holistic* since the theory implicitly defines *all* its theoretical terms in one fell swoop, and in the definite descriptions that explicitly define each theoretical term, the entire theory plays a role in determining the content of the description. The third claim of the description theory is that the theory which implicitly defines ordinary mental state terms is commonsense (or "folk") psychology, which Lewis characterizes as our "extensive, shared understanding of how we work mentally"—an understanding that "is common knowledge among us" (1994, 416). On Lewis's view, our commonsense psychological theory implicitly defines *all* of our ordinary language mental state terms, including terms for the basic propositional attitudes (like 'belief' and 'desire'), terms for qualitative states (like 'pain'), and terms for the emotions. Thus mental state concepts are, to use David Armstrong's memorable phrase, "package deal concepts" (1968, 253). If Lewis's description theory, or something close to it, is the correct theory about the meaning of ordinary mental state terms, then a culture's folk psychological theory implicitly defines their emotion terms, and to fully understand the meaning of one ordinary language emotion term in a culture requires knowing the meanings of all the others.

The ethnopsychological accounts provided by researchers like Lutz are intended *inter alia* to describe part of the folk psychology of the culture being studied. The beliefs about the causes, effects, and moral implications of emotions that Lutz reports are common knowledge (or at least common *belief*) among the Ifaluk. But how much of this belief structure are we to count as part of the Ifaluk's commonsense *psychology*, and thus as contributing to the meaning of their emotion terms? Lewis offers little guidance here, and opinions may differ. Those who would include within the purview of commonsense psychology only a relatively small part of an ethnopsychology like the one

---

7. For further details, see Lewis 1970, 1972, or Stich 1996, 74ff.

Lutz offers adopt what we propose to call an *austere* account of folk psychology, while those who would include much more of a Lutz-style ethnopsychology within folk psychology advocate what we shall call an *opulent* view of folk psychology.[8] This terminology can be extended, in an obvious way, to apply to description theories of meaning as well. An *opulent description theory* is one that maintains that a great deal of ethnopsychology contributes to the meaning of mental state terms, while an *austere description theory* holds that only a much smaller part of ethnopsychology is relevant to the meaning of these terms.

So much for the *meaning* of mental state terms. Now what about their *reference*? To what things in the world do these terms refer? Since the explicit definitions of mental state terms, on a theory like Lewis's, take the form of definite descriptions, the most obvious proposal is that the terms refer to those things in the world that satisfy the descriptions—the things the descriptions are true of. But, as Lewis noted long ago (1972, 210ff.), this would be a rather extreme doctrine, since if any aspect of a folk psychological theory turned out to be mistaken, then *all* the mental state terms that the theory implicitly defined would end up referring to nothing at all. The remedy, Lewis proposed, is to require that the referents of mental state terms *more or less* satisfy the descriptions provided by folk theory. But how much is that, exactly? The answer, of course, is that Lewis's proposal is vague, and different theorists may wish to diminish the vagueness by insisting on a more or less stringent standard. On what we will call the *high accuracy* end of the spectrum are those who insist that a mental state term refers to a state only if *most* of what folk psychology says about states of that kind is true of the state in question. On the *low accuracy* end of the spectrum are those who will allow much more error in folk psychology before concluding that the terms of folk psychology do not refer. One final bit of terminology: We shall use the term *thick description theory* for accounts that combine an *opulent* description theory of the meaning of mental state terms with a *high accuracy* theory of reference for those terms.

What does all of this have to do with the dispute between social constructionists and evolutionary psychologists? To see the connection, let's assume that a theorist has adopted a thick description theory for the meaning and reference of emotion terms. What might such a theorist conclude about the universality or cultural locality of emotions? Lutz and her fellow ethnopsychologists tell us a great deal about the common knowledge about mental states that people in a culture share. Among the Ifaluk, for example, it is common knowledge that if a man comes into the birthing house, or if a woman works in the taro gardens when she is menstruating, it will provoke *song* in those who know about it. And it is common knowledge that when one realizes one is the object of someone's *song*, one typically experiences *metagu*. On an opulent description theory,

---

8. The terms 'opulent' and 'austere' are borrowed from Horgan and Graham 1990, though the meanings we have assigned them are not quite the ones that Horgan and Graham propose.

these and many other similar claims are part of the folk psychological knowledge of the Ifaluk and thus they contribute to the meaning of '*song*' and '*metagu*.' Moreover, on a thick description account of reference, which requires high accuracy, most of these claims must be true of a mental state if it is to count as an instance of *song* or *metagu*. But, of course, in our culture there is no mental state that satisfies (or comes close to satisfying) the thick description that Lutz provides for *song* and *metagu*. If *we* learn that someone we know has worked in a taro garden while menstruating, it provokes no emotion at all. So there is no mental state in *our* culture that counts as an instance of *song*. *Song* does not exist here.

Much the same applies in the opposite direction. It is common knowledge in our culture that if someone burns the national flag, shouts racial epithets, reaches out and touches a stranger, or gives someone "the finger," it is likely to provoke anger in those around him, and that that anger will often lead to a heated exchange of words and occasionally to physical confrontation and violence. On an opulent account, these and many similar commonly-known facts are part of *our* folk psychological theory and thus part of the meaning of our term 'anger.' For a thick description theorist, most of them must be true of a mental state if that state is to count as an instance of anger. But situations like these would not provoke any emotion among the Ifaluk, and (if Lutz is right) no mental state there is likely to lead to violence. So, if one accepts a thick description account of the reference of emotion terms, it follows that among the Ifaluk, *anger does not exist*.

It is important to note that the argument leading to these conclusions is quite independent of any views one might have about the psychological mechanisms underlying the emotions. All that matters is that emotion terms get their meaning from the relevant folk psychological theory, that folk theories are construed opulently and differ substantially in different cultures, and that most of what the folk theory says about a state must be true if the state is to count as an instance of the emotion in question.

What we have argued so far is that *if* one accepted a thick description account of the meaning and reference of emotion terms, then in light of the facts that Lutz and others report one should conclude that the emotions denoted by commonsense emotion terms are culturally-local. But is this what leads social constructionists to this conclusion? Do *they* accept a thick description theory? Here, we must admit, the answer is less than clear cut. The social constructionist anthropologists and psychologists who study the emotions rarely set out and defend their semantic views in any systematic way, nor do they pay careful attention to the distinctions between meaning and reference or use and mention that are so central to philosophical discussion. Still, we think there is good reason to suspect that something somewhere in the vicinity of the thick description theory is indeed playing an important role in the thinking of many social constructionists. Consider, for example, the following passage from Shweder:

> Across languages, the range of implications, suggestions, and connotations of psychological state terms do not easily map, at least not *lexically*; and to adequately

understand the meaning of the terms in either language is to understand a good deal about different local systems of values and particular ways of life. Under such circumstances of hazardous lexical mapping, any strong claim about the distribution around the world of the "emotions," as we define them, is bound to be controversial. (1994, 33–34; italics and quotation marks in the original)

Since Shweder thinks that understanding the meaning of psychological state terms requires understanding a good deal about local values and ways of life, and since he takes this to be relevant to the distribution of the emotions themselves, we don't think it is too much of a stretch to see something like a thick description theory hovering in the wings. This impression is reinforced by another passage in which Shweder invokes the same "package deal" metaphor that Armstrong used in one of the earliest formulations of the description theory (or "analytic functionalism") (1994, 36).

Similar ideas about meaning can be found in Lutz:

Emotion words are treated here as coalescences of complex ethnotheoretical ideas about the nature of self and social interaction. . . . To understand the meaning of an emotion word is to be able to envisage (and perhaps to find oneself able to participate in) a complicated scene with actors, actions, interpersonal relationships in a particular state of repair, moral points of view, facial expressions, personal and social goals, and sequences of events. (1988, 10)

Here again we think it is plausible to think that if Lutz were to recast these ideas in the vocabulary favored by analytic philosophers, the result would bear more than a passing resemblance to the thick description theory.

Now what about those on the other side—the evolutionary psychologists who champion a "biosocial" model—what account of meaning and reference do they accept? It is impossible to give a positive answer to this question, since the evolutionary psychologists who study emotions say little about semantics. However, it is possible to give a negative answer. Since theorists in this tradition insist that emotions like fear and anger are to be found in *all* human cultures and probably in many other species as well, and since they recognize that there are significant cross-cultural differences in the situations which provoke these emotions and the behaviors they lead to, they *cannot* accept a thick description account of the reference of emotion terms. For 'fear' and 'anger' are terms in English and, as we saw earlier, the thick description theory entails that if a mental state does not share most of the causes and effects of anger that are commonly known among English speakers, then that state does not count as an instance of anger. Also, though the point is less important for our purposes, since evolutionary psychologists sometimes claim that there are terms synonymous with English emotion terms in languages whose speakers have folk psychological theories that are significantly different from ours, they cannot accept an opulent description theory of the meaning of emotion terms. Being unable to accept thick description theories of meaning and reference is hardly a major embarrassment for evolutionary psychologists, since those theories are far from the only games in town. And among the alternatives available, there are some—most notably *causal/historical* theories of reference (Putnam 1975, Devitt and Sterelny 1987)—that would enable evolutionary psychologists to say what they want to say about the universality of emotions while not in the least contesting that Lutz and others have demonstrated that ethnopsychologies differ quite substantially from one culture to another.

6 Who's Right, and Why It Doesn't Matter

What we have argued in the previous section is that the dispute between social construc-tionists and evolutionary psychologists over the universality of the emotions *could be* generated by a philosophical (or semantic) disagreement about the meaning and refer-ence of ordinary language emotion terms. We also suggested, albeit more tentatively, that this philosophical disagreement *is* largely responsible for the dispute, though the point has gone almost entirely unnoticed by partisans on both sides. If we are correct, then the next obvious question to ask is: Who's right? Does the thick description theory give the correct account of the meaning and reference of commonsense mental state terms, or is the correct account to be found among one of the competing theories on which an emo-tion term may refer to a mental state even if much of what the relevant folk psychological theory claims about the state is not true? These are questions that are being hotly debated in the philosophical literature, and we will not even *try* to answer them here.[9] Indeed, one of us has argued at some length that there is an important sense in which the questions *cannot* be answered until those debating them get a lot clearer than they are now on what facts a theory of reference must answer to and thus what counts as getting a theory of reference right (Stich 1996, Ch. 1).

This might sound like bad news, since if we cannot determine who's right about refer-ence we cannot settle the debate about the universality of the emotions. But we are inclined to be rather more optimistic since, for two rather different reasons, *it really doesn't much matter who's right*. The first reason why it really doesn't matter is that if the debate about the universality of the emotions is indeed driven by disagreements about meaning and reference, then the debate is largely isolated from the rich bodies of empir-ical and theoretical work done by social constructionists and evolutionary psychologists. As we saw earlier, the social constructionist argument for the cultural locality of the emo-tions is *entirely independent* of any claims about the psychological mechanisms under-lying the emotions. Thus a social constructionist who accepts a thick description theory of meaning and reference could perfectly well remain agnostic about, *or even endorse*, a model like Levenson's and *still* conclude that the emotions are culturally-local. All that's needed is the premise that ethnopsychologies vary significantly from culture to culture.

---

9. E.g. Braddon-Mitchell and Jackson 1996, Lycan 1988, Griffiths 1997, Recanati 1993.

And this, as we have seen, is not a premise that evolutionary psychologists are in the least inclined to dispute. Quite the opposite; biosocial models like Levenson's are built to accommodate such diversity. But this is no impediment at all to evolutionary psychologists who want to insist on the universality of emotions. For they can simply adopt an account of meaning and reference on which an emotion term in English can refer to mental states in some other culture even if the ethnopsychology in that culture is significantly different from our own. If we are correct, it is the implicit adoption of a thick description theory on one side and an implicit rejection of it on the other which has given rise to the widespread perception that there is a substantial empirical dispute. On our view, this gives rise to the situation depicted in Figure 3.

The second reason why we think it doesn't much matter who's right is that, even on the contested issue of universality, no matter who is right about meaning and reference each side could perfectly well say what it wants to say, with the help of a bit of technical terminology. So, for example, if it turns out that a thick description theory gives the correct account of the reference of ordinary language emotion terms, then evolutionary psychologists must concede that fear and other emotions are not universal. Rather, there is a whole family of distinct emotions which are subserved by the same innate emotion prototype and affect program that subserve fear in us. But if we introduce a technical term to

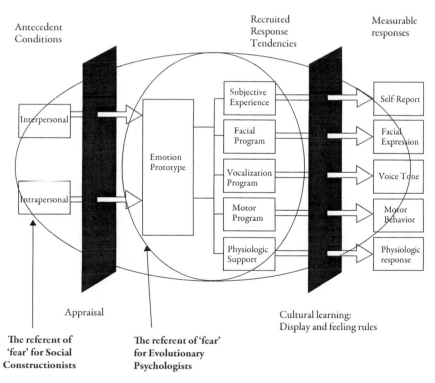

FIGURE 3 Will the *real* fear please stand up?

refer to *all* of these emotions—*core-fear*, perhaps—then the evolutionary psychologists who have conceded that fear is *not* universal can go on to claim that core-fear *is* universal. And that, surely, is all they ever wanted to claim.

Once it is seen how the debate over the universality of the emotions is rooted in a dispute about the meaning and reference of emotion terms, and how little it matters who is right in *that* dispute, it may be much easier for evolutionary psychologists and social constructionists to stop seeing each other as adversaries and start seeing each other as natural allies in the attempt to understand the emotions. We believe it is time for this odd couple to stop the philosophical quarreling and to recognize how compatible their theories are and how nicely they complement each other.

REFERENCES

Armstrong, David (1968), *A Materialist Theory of the Mind*. New York: Humanities Press.

Averill, James (1994), "It's a Small World But a Large Stage," in Ekman and Davidson 1994, 143–45.

Braddon-Mitchell, David and Frank Jackson (1996), *The Philosophy of Mind and Cognition*. Oxford: Blackwell.

Briggs, Jean L. (1970), *Never in Anger: Portrait of an Eskimo Family*. Cambridge, MA: Harvard University Press.

Darwin, Charles (1872 [1998]), *The Expression of the Emotions in Man and Animals*. Paul Ekman (ed.). New York: Oxford University Press.

Devitt, Michael and Kim Sterelny (1987), *Language and Reality*. Cambridge, MA; MIT Press.

Ekman, Paul (1972), "Universals and Cultural Differences in Facial Expressions of Emotion," in James K. Cole (ed.), *Nebraska Symposium on Motivation 1971, vol. 4*. Lincoln: University of Nebraska Press, 207–283.

———. (1994), "All Emotions Are Basic," in Ekman and Davidson 1994, 15–19.

Ekman, Paul and Richard J. Davidson (eds.) (1994), *The Nature of Emotion: Fundamental Questions*. New York: Oxford University Press.

Ekman, Paul and Wallace Friesen (1971), "Constants Across Cultures in the Face and Emotion," *Journal of Personality and Social Psychology* 17: 124–129.

Ekman, Paul, R. Levenson, and Wallace Friesen (1983), Autonomic Nervous System Activity Distinguished Between Emotions," *Science* 221: 1208–1210.

Ekman, Paul and Erika Rosenberg (1997), *What the Face Reveals*. New York: Oxford University Press.

Geertz, Clifford (1973), "Thick Description: Toward an Interpretive Theory of Culture," in *The Interpretation of Cultures: Selected Essays*. New York: Basic Books, 3–32.

Griffiths, Paul E. (1997), *What Emotions Really Are*. Chicago: University of Chicago Press.

Harré, Rom (1986), "An Outline of the Social Construcionist Viewpoint," in Rom Harré (ed.), *The Social Construction of Emotions*. New York: Basil Blackwell, 2–14.

Harré, Rom and Robert Finlay-Jones (1986), "Emotion Talk Across Times: Accidie and Melancholy in the Psychological Context," in Rom Harré (ed.), *The Social Construction of Emotions*. New York: Basil Blackwell, 220–227.

Hochschild, A. (1979), "Emotion Work, Feeling Rules and Social Structure," *American Journal of Sociology* 85: 551–575.

Horgan, Terence and George Graham (1990). "In Defense of Southern Fundamentalism," *Philosophical Studies* 62: 107–134.

Kessler, Suzanne J. and Wendy McKenna (1977), *Gender: An Ethnomethodological Approach*. Chicago: University of Chicago Press.

Lazarus, Richard (1994), "Universal Antecedents of the Emotions," in Ekman and Davidson 1994, 163–171.

Levenson, Robert (1992), "Autonomic Nervous System Differences Among the Emotions," *Psychological Science* 3" 23–27.

———. (1994), "Human Emotion: A Functional View," in Ekman and Davidson 1994, 123–130.

Levy, Robert (1984), "The Emotions in Comparative Perspective," in Klaus Scherer and Paul Ekman (eds.), *Approaches to Emotion*. Hillsdale, NJ: Lawrence Erlbaum.

Lewis, David (1970), "How to Define Theoretical Terms," *Journal of Philosophy* 67: 427–446.

———. (1972), "Psychophysical and Theoretical Identifications," *Australasian Journal of Philosophy* 50: 249–258.

———. (1994), "Reduction of Mind," in S. Guttenplan (ed.), *A Companion to the Philosophy of Mind*. Oxford: Blackwell, 412–431.

Lutz, Catherine (1988), *Unnatural Emotions: Everyday Sentiments on a Micronesian Atoll and Their Challenge to Western Theory*. Chicago: University of Chicago Press.

Lycan, William (1988), *Judgement and Justification*. Cambridge: Cambridge University Press.

Mesquita, B. and N. Frijda (1992), "Cultural Variations in Emotions: A Review," *Psychological Bulletin* 112: 179–204.

Morsbach, H. and W. J. Tyler (1986), "A Japanese Emotion, *Amae*," in Rom Harré (ed.), *The Social Construction of Emotions*. New York: Basil Blackwell, 289–307.

Oberoi, Harjot (1994), *The Construction of Religious Boundaries: Culture, Identity, and Diversity in the Sikh Tradition*. Chicago: University of Chicago Press.

Pinker, Steven (1997), *How the Mind Works*. New York: W. W. Norton and Co.

Recanati, François (1993), *Direct Reference: From Language to Thought*. Cambridge, MA: Basil Blackwell.

Shweder, Richard (1985), "The Social Construction of the Person: How Is It Possible?" in K. Gergen and K. Davis (eds.), *The Social Construction of the Person*. New York: Springer-Verlag, 41–69.

———. (1994), "'You're Not Sick, You're Just in Love': Emotion as an Interpretive System," in Ekman and Davidson 1994, 32–44.

Stich, Stephen (1996), *Deconstructing the Mind*. New York: Oxford University Press.

Tooby, John and Leda Cosmides (1992), "The Psychological Foundations of Culture," in Jerome Barkow, Leda Cosmides, and John Tooby (eds.), *The Adapted Mind*. New York: Oxford University Press, 19–136.

14

DARWIN IN THE MADHOUSE

Evolutionary Psychology and the Classification of Mental Disorders

Dominic Murphy and Stephen Stich

IN RECENT YEARS there has been a ground swell of interest in the application of evolu-tionary theory to issues in psychopathology (Nesse and Williams, 1995; Stevens and Price, 1996; McGuire and Troisi, 1998). Much of this work has been aimed at finding adaptationist explanations for a variety of mental disorders ranging from phobias to depression to schizophrenia. There has, however, been relatively little discussion of the implications that the theories proposed by evolutionary psychologists might have for the classification of mental disorders. This is the theme we propose to explore. We'll begin, in section 1, by providing a brief overview of the account of the mind advanced by evolu-tionary psychologists. In section 2 we'll explain why issues of taxonomy are important and why the dominant approach to the classification of mental disorders is radically and alarmingly unsatisfactory. We will also indicate why we think an alternative approach, based on theories in evolutionary psychology, is particularly promising. In section 3 we'll try to illustrate some of the virtues of the evolutionary-psychological approach to classification. The discussion in section 3 will highlight a quite fundamental distinction between those disorders that arise from the malfunction of a component of the mind and those that can be traced to the fact that our minds must now function in environments that are very different from the environments in which they evolved. This mismatch between the current and ancestral environments can, we maintain, give rise to serious mental disorders despite the fact that, in one important sense, there is nothing at all wrong with the people suffering the disorder. Their minds are functioning exactly as Mother Nature intended them to. In section 4, we'll give a brief overview of some of the ways in which the sorts of malfunctions catalogued in section 3 might arise, and sketch two rather different strategies for incorporating this etiological information in a system for classifying mental disorders. Finally, in section 5, we will explain why an evolutionary approach may lead to a quite radical revision in the classification of certain conditions. From an evolutionary perspective, we will argue, some of the disorders recognized in standard manuals like DSM-IV (American Psychiatric Association, 1994) may turn out not to be disorders at all. The people who have these conditions don't *have* problems; they just *cause* problems!

1   The Evolutionary Psychology Model of the Mind

The model of the mind advanced by evolutionary psychology is built around two central theses which we'll call the *Massive Modularity Hypothesis* and the *Adaptation Hypothesis*. The Massive Modularity Hypothesis maintains that the mind contains a large number of distinct though interconnected information-processing systems—often called 'modules' or 'mental organs.' These modules can be thought of as special-purpose or domain-specific computational mechanisms. Often a module will have proprietary access to a body of information that is useful in dealing with its domain. The information is 'proprietary' in the sense that other modules and non-modular mental mechanisms have no direct access to it.[1] Like other organs, modules are assumed to be innate and (with the possible exception of a few gender-specific modules) they are present in all normal members of the species. Some evolutionary psychologists also assume that there is little or no heritable inter-personal variation in properly functioning mental modules and thus that a given type of module will be much the same in all normal people.[2] Paul Griffiths has dubbed this 'the doctrine of the monomorphic mind.' Both Griffiths and David Sloan Wilson have argued, in our opinion quite persuasively, that this doctrine is very implausible (Wilson, 1994; Griffiths, 1997, sec. 5.5; the point goes back to David Hull, 1989). So, along with Wilson and Griffiths, we will assume that there may be a fair amount of heritable variation in the modules found in the normal population. That assumption will play an important role in section 6, where we argue that some of the conditions that have been classified as mental disorders are not disorders at all.

Since the appearance, in 1983, of Jerry Fodor's enormously influential book, *The Modularity of Mind*, the term 'module' has become ubiquitous in the cognitive sciences. But the sorts of modules posited by the Massive Modularity Hypothesis differ from Fodorian modules in two crucial respects. First, Fodor sets out a substantial list of features that are characteristic of modules, and to count as a Fodorian module a mental mechanism must have most or all of these features to a significant degree. For Fodor, modules are:

---

1. For a much more detailed discussion of the Massive Modularity Hypothesis see Samuels (1998 and 2000).
2. Tooby and Cosmides, who are among the leading advocates of evolutionary psychology, defend this 'psychic unity of mankind' in numerous places including their 1990a, 1990b and 1992.

i. informationally encapsulated
ii. mandatory
iii. fast
iv. shallow
v. neurally localized
vi. susceptible to characteristic breakdown
vii. largely inaccessible to other processes.

The notion of a module invoked in the Massive Modularity Hypothesis is much broader and less demanding. Evolutionary psychologists count as a module any domain-specific computational device that exhibits (i) and (vii), and occasionally even these restrictions are not imposed. The second important way in which Fodorian modules differ from the sorts of modules envisioned by the Massive Modularity Hypothesis is that, for Fodor, modules only subserve 'peripheral' mental processes—those responsible for perception, language processing and the production of bodily movements. Evolutionary psychologists, by contrast, expect to find modules subserving a wide range of other, more 'central' cognitive and emotional processes.

The Adaptation Hypothesis, the second central theme in evolutionary psychology, claims that mental modules are *adaptations*—they were, as Tooby and Cosmides have put it, 'invented by natural selection during the species' evolutionary history to produce adaptive ends in the species' natural environment' (Tooby and Cosmides, 1995, p. xiii). To serve as a reminder of the fact that the modules posited by evolutionary psychology are adaptations, and to distinguish them from Fodorian modules, we will sometimes call them *Darwinian modules*.

The picture of the mind that emerges from the conjunction of the Massive Modularity Hypothesis and the Adaptation Hypothesis is nicely captured by Tooby and Cosmides in the following passage:

> [O]ur cognitive architecture resembles a confederation of hundreds or thousands of functionally dedicated computers (often called modules) designed to solve adaptive problems endemic to our hunter-gatherer ancestors. Each of these devices has its own agenda and imposes its own exotic organisation on different fragments of the world. There are specialised systems for grammar induction, for face recognition, for dead reckoning, for construing objects and for recognising emotions from the face. There are mechanisms to detect animacy, eye direction, and cheating. There is a 'theory of mind' module. . . . a variety of social inference-modules. . . . and a multitude of other elegant machines. (Tooby and Cosmides, 1995, p. xiv)

There are two points that we would add to this colorful account. First, these functionally dedicated computers are linked together in complex networks. The output of one

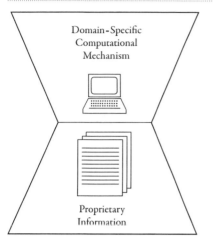

Domain-Specific
Computational
Mechanism

Proprietary
Information

FIGURE 1 Darwinian modules are adaptations that can be thought of as special purpose or domain-specific computational devices which often have proprietary access to a body of information that is useful in dealing with their domain.

module will often serve as the input (or part of the input) for one or more modules that are 'downstream.' Second, there is no reason to suppose that *all* of the mechanisms to be found in the mind are plausibly viewed as modular. In addition to the swarm of modules, the evolutionary psychology model of the mind can accommodate computational devices that are not domain specific, stores of information that are not proprietary, and a variety of other sorts of mechanisms. Figure 2 is a sketch of the sort of mental architecture posited by evolutionary psychology. Figure 3 is a close-up of part of the system portrayed in Figure 2.

2 The Taxonomy Crisis: What's Wrong with the DSM Approach, and Why Taxonomy Matters

In 1964, Carl Hempel thought it very likely 'that classifications of mental disorders will increasingly reflect theoretical considerations' (1964, p. 150). Hempel was a first-class philosopher but an unreliable prophet; the last thirty years have seen the old psychoanalytically based paradigm replaced by an approach to classification which aims to be 'operationalized,' 'a-theoretical' and 'purely descriptive.'[3] Among the most notable products of this approach are DSM-III and its successors DSM-IIIR and DSM-IV (American Psychiatric Association, 1980, 1987, 1994). DSM categories are typically specified by providing a list of sufficient conditions (often disjunctive and with an occasional necessary condition thrown in) stated almost exclusively in the language of 'clinical phenomenology' which draws heavily on folk psychological concepts and protoscientific

---

3. McCarthy and Gerring (1994) is a good brief history.

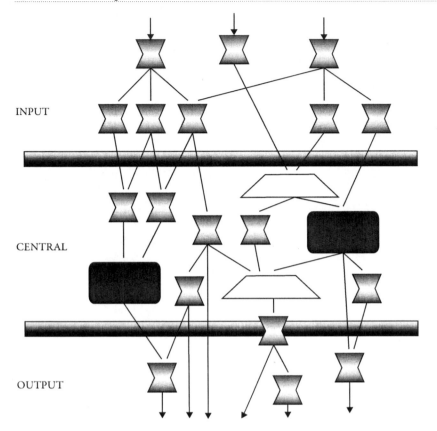

INPUT

CENTRAL

OUTPUT

FIGURE 2 The mental architecture posited by evolutionary psychology includes networks of Darwinian modules subserving central cognitive and emotive processes as well as peripheral processes.

clinical concepts (like self-esteem, delusion, anxiety and depressed mood). The classification systems set out in DSM-III and its successors play a central role in guiding research and clinical practice in the United States and, to a lesser extent, in other countries as well. Moreover, as Poland *et al.* note (1994, p. 235), 'DSM Categories play pivotal roles in financing mental health care, maintaining hospital and clinical records, administering research funds, and organizing educational materials . . . concerned with psychopathology.' Poland and his colleagues go on to claim—and we agree—that the DSM approach 'is deeply flawed and not doing the work it should be doing' and that as a result, the current situation regarding the classification of mental disorders 'involves a crisis' (p. 255).

According to Poland *et al.*, a classification scheme in psychopathology has two primary purposes. It should enhance the effectiveness of clinical activity, and it should facilitate scientific research concerned with psychopathology and its treatment. The DSM approach, they argue, does neither. Though Poland and his colleagues offer a

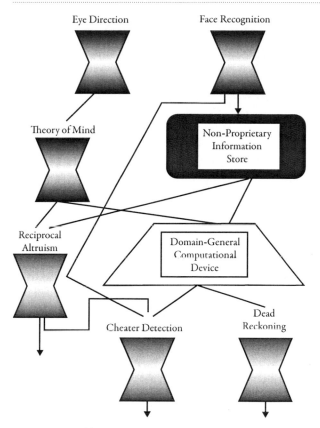

FIGURE 3 In addition to Darwinian modules, the evolutionary psychology model of the mind can accommodate computational mechanisms that are not domain specific and stores of information that are not proprietary.

number of reasons for their deeply sceptical and rather disquieting conclusion, we think that one of these is central. The DSM approach is alleged to be a-theoretical, thus allowing clinicians from different theoretical backgrounds to agree on a diagnosis. But in fact the DSM approach is far from a-theoretical. Rather, it embraces the highly problematic theory that there exist, in the domain of psychopathology, a substantial number of what Poland *et al.* call 'syndromes with unity.' These are clusters of associated attributes, characterized in the folk psychological and proto-scientific language of clinical phenomenology

> that exhibit such dynamic characteristics as typical course, outcome and responsiveness to treatment, and that are related to underlying pathological conditions and etiological factors of development (e.g. genetic and environmental factors). . . . [T]he operationally defined categories within the DSM system are supposed to be *natural kinds* with a characteristic causal structure (i.e. a core pathology) that

underwrites the various lawful regularities characteristic of the disorder (e.g. association of criteria features, dynamic properties of the syndrome). (Poland *et al.*, p. 241)[4]

The problem with all of this is very simple: the theory is false. Though there may be a few syndromes with unity in psychopathology, it is unlikely that there are very many. One reason for this is the all but exclusive reliance on the concepts and categories of clinical phenomenology to characterize syndromes. These concepts are notoriously vague, imprecise and unqualified. Moreover, since highly subjective judgements about their application to a particular case must typically be made in emotionally charged settings in which hidden agendas abound, these judgements are often biased. By limiting the data gathered in diagnosis to the salient and easily identifiable signs and symptoms of clinical phenomenology, the DSM scheme fails to attend to a wide range of other data about mental functioning that can be gathered by psychometric techniques and by methods used in cognitive science and neuroscience.

Another, closely related, reason to think that there are relatively few psychopathological syndromes with unity is the fact that the DSM approach to classification is not guided by any theory about the structure and functioning of normal minds and makes no attempt to uncover and use facts about the underlying psychological, biological and environmental mechanisms and processes that give rise to symptoms. Imagine for a moment trying to construct a classification system for malfunctions in some complex and well-engineered artefact which is built from numerous carefully designed components—a television set, perhaps, or a computer network. Imagine further that the classification system must be based entirely on clusters of user-salient symptoms, without any inkling of how the mechanism was designed to operate and without any theory about its component parts and their functions. The result, almost certainly, would be a set of categories that are *massively heterogeneous* from the point of view of someone who understands how the system works. It would classify together problems which are caused by totally different underlying mechanisms or processes and which require totally different remedies. It would also fail to classify together problems with the same underlying cause (and requiring the same remedy) if they manifest themselves in different ways under slightly different conditions. This, near enough, is just what we should expect in a DSM-style classification of mental disorders. For surely the mind, too, is a complex and well-engineered

---

4. Some advocates of the DSM approach would grant that many currently recognized DSM classifications fail to pick out natural kinds, though they expect that with more research, based on existing assumptions, operationally defined DSM-style diagnoses will converge on natural kinds. The basic 'syndromes with unity' theory is assumed to be correct and in need of more empirical elaboration, rather than conceptual overhaul. See, for example, Goodwin and Guze (1995).

system in which many well designed components interact.[5] Thus, as Poland and his colleagues conclude:

> It appears *unlikely* that the domain of psychopathology is best conceived of in terms of syndromes with unity or that natural kinds will be discovered at the level of clinical phenomenology. There is simply no reason to suppose that the features of clinical phenomenology that catch our attention and are the source of great human distress are also features upon which a science of psychopathology should directly focus when searching for regularities and natural kinds. Human interests and saliencies tend to carve out an unnatural domain from the point of view of nomological structure. Hence the relations between the scientific understanding of psychopathology and clinical responsiveness to it may be less direct than is commonly supposed. In insisting that classification be exclusively focused on clinical phenomenology, DSM not only undermines productive research but also undermines the development of effective relations between clinical practice and scientific understanding. (Poland *et al.*, p. 254)

The remedy that Poland *et al.* propose is one that we strongly endorse. There is a need for a new approach to the classification of mental disorders that is 'based on a more intimate relationship with basic science than is DSM' (p. 255). In trying to construct this new taxonomy, a natural first step is to ask: *which science or sciences are the appropriate ones?* We don't think there is any single right answer to this question. Many sciences can contribute to the construction of a taxonomy that will serve the needs of clinical practice and scientific research into the causes and treatments of mental disorders. But it is our contention that evolutionary psychology has a natural and quite central role to play in this scientifically based reconstruction of the classification system for mental disorders. Evolutionary psychology, as we have seen, seeks to explain how the mind works by characterizing the many computational mechanisms from which it is constructed and attempting to discover the function for which these mechanisms were designed. That sort of account of the mind and its working looks to be just what is needed if we are to take seriously the analogy with a malfunctioning well-engineered artefact. Of course evolutionary psychology is not alone in viewing the mind as made up of lots of components that were designed by natural selection. Neuroscience, at various levels of analysis from the molecular to the computational, takes much the same view. And while we certainly

5. This heterogeneity in DSM classifications is magnified by the fact that actual DSM categories often group together very different symptom profiles as manifestations of the same disorder. Thus, for example, according to the DSM criteria, one can qualify as having a Major Depressive Episode even though one does not experience a depressed mood, provided that one does exhibit a markedly diminished interest in daily activities (DSM-IV, p. 327). And by one reckoning, there are fifty-six different ways to satisfy the criteria for Borderline Personality Disorder! (Clarkin *et al.*, 1983.) As one might expect, these heterogeneous categories are poor predictors of the patients' future trajectory or of their response to treatment, and thus the vast majority of DSM categories remain 'unvalidated.'

don't want to deny that these sciences will be of enormous importance in working toward a new taxonomy, it is our prediction that, in the short run at least, classifications based on evolutionary psychological theories will be particularly useful for clinicians, since they will be at a level of analysis that meshes comfortably with current clinical practice.

Our goal in the remainder of this chapter is to make this prediction plausible. To do this we propose to explore some of the problems that might befall a mind that is structured in the way sketched in section 1 and that contains some of the mechanisms posited by evolutionary psychologists. In many cases, as we shall see, those problems offer plausible explanations for the sorts of troubling symptoms that manuals like DSM-III and its successors take to indicate the presence of a mental disorder. However, it will often be the case that the classification suggested by evolutionary psychological theories recognizes several distinct disorders where current diagnostic manuals see only one. Thus there is reason to hope that a classification system that takes account of theories in evolutionary psychology will begin to reduce the massive heterogeneity that plagues DSM-style classifications. Another virtue of taxonomizing disorders along the lines suggested by evolutionary psychology is that it pulls apart two very different sorts of disorders: those in which components of the mind are malfunctioning and those attributable to a mismatch between the environment in which we live and the environment in which we were designed to live. A third virtue of the evolutionary-psychological approach is that it provides a clear theoretical framework in which we can ask one of the most vexing questions that the study of psychopathology must face: what conditions count as disorders at all?[6]

Before setting out our taxonomic proposals we should stress that evolutionary psychology is still very much in its infancy, and the theories about mental mechanisms that we will invoke are all both speculative and controversial. We don't pretend to be offering a set of diagnostic categories that mental health professionals might use in preference to those in DSM-IV. Rather, our aim is to begin to explore the ways in which evolutionary psychology can contribute to the elaboration of a taxonomy of the sort that Poland *et al.* advocate—one that is 'based on a more intimate relationship with basic science.'

3 A Taxonomy of Disordered Minds

The range of symptoms recognized by modern diagnoses is very broad. To begin with there are cognitive symptoms with highly salient phenomenologies, such as delusions and unwelcome or obsessive thoughts. There are also feelings of 'thought disorder,' in which patients report thinking someone else's thoughts or having their own thoughts

---

6. For reasons that we'll set out in section 6, we are inclined to think that this is best understood as a *pair* of questions: namely, (i) What conditions count as *mental disorders?* and (ii) What conditions count as *problems that may beset an evolved mind (or 'E-M problems' as we'll sometimes say)?* The category of mental disorders, we'll argue, is a subset of the category of E-M problems. The taxonomy that we are about to sketch, in section 4, should be read as an account of the broader category—the category of E-M problems, though for ease of exposition we propose not to emphasize the distinction until section 6.

controlled by another. Other cognitive symptoms include such incapacities as the amnesias, agnosias and aphasias. Then we have behavioral problems, including voluntary patterns of antisocial action and involuntary problems such as drug dependence, motor retardation, sleep disorders and disruptions to the autonomic nervous system like irregular heartbeat. There are also more intuitively qualitative symptoms; some of these are relatively prolonged, such as low affect ('feeling blue'), and others are transitory, such as dizziness, nausea and feelings of anxiety. So there are a great many kinds of symptoms to explain. The exciting thing about evolutionary psychology is the theoretically motivated range of explanatory resources it brings to bear on all this diverse symptomatology.

The evolutionary perspective enables us to make a number of important distinctions among problems that may lead to symptoms of mental disorder. The most theoretically interesting and novel of these is the distinction between problems which are internal to the person and problems which lie in the environment surrounding the person. This marks the first major break in our taxonomy.

Problems which are internal to the person are what we commonly think of when we envisage mental disorders. The official orthodoxy, enshrined in DSM-IV, views mental illness as Janus-faced, with socially disvalued or disabling symptoms being produced by an underlying *malfunction*. (The extent to which this conception is honored in the discussion of particular disorders is another matter—Wakefield, 1997.) However, it is important to recall that the evolutionary perspective on the mind stresses that our psychological mechanisms originated in a past environment, and although those mechanisms may have been adaptive in that past environment, it is entirely possible that the environment has changed enough to render aspects of our cognitive architecture undesirable or obsolete in the modern world. We will discuss this in more detail below. To begin with, though, we'll focus on cases of disorders which are internal to the person.

3.1 DISORDERS WITHIN THE PERSON

As we've seen, the evolutionary-psychology model recognizes several different sorts of mental structures—modules, stores of non-proprietary information, computational devices that are not domain specific, and pathways along which information can flow from one mechanism to another—and since all of these can break down in various ways, the model will admit of a number of different sorts of disorders. However, since Darwinian modules are the most prominent structures in the evolutionary-psychology model it is natural to begin our taxonomy of disordered minds with them. The most obvious sort of difficulty that can beset a mind like the one depicted in Figures 2 and 3 is that one of the modules can behave problematically, producing output which directly or indirectly leads to the symptoms on which diagnoses of mental disorder depend.

There are two very different reasons why a Darwinian module may produce such symptoms, and this distinction generates a first major divide in within-person cases.

Sometimes when a Darwinian module generates problematic output the trouble is *internal* to the module—its special-purpose computer is malfunctioning or its proprietary store of information is not what it should be (or both). In other cases the problem will be *external* to the module. In these cases something has gone amiss earlier on in the causal network and 'upstream' in the flow of information, with the result that the module which is producing problematic output is being given *problematic input*. In the colorful language of computer programmers, 'garbage in, garbage out.'

3.1.1 Disorders Resulting from Module-Internal Problems: Some Examples

Perhaps the best known example of a disorder which has been much studied as a case of modular breakdown is autism (Baron-Cohen *et al.*, 1985; Leslie, 1987, 1991; Frith, 1989; Leslie and Thaiss, 1992; Baron-Cohen, 1995). Recent work has suggested that autism is best explained as a breakdown in the module or system of modules that handle 'theory-of-mind,' the capacity of all normal adults to attribute intentional states like beliefs and desires to other people and to explain their behavior in terms of the causal powers of beliefs and desires. One widely used test of whether a person has a normal adult theory-of-mind module is the ability to pass the false-belief task, at which autistic children are spectacular failures.[7] They do worse at the false-belief task than do children with Down's Syndrome, even though in general their grasp of causal cognition exceeds the latter's (Baron-Cohen *et al.*, 1986). Some people diagnosed with Asperger's Syndrome—high functioning autistic people whose IQs are normal or higher—have offered quite moving accounts of their puzzlement when they realized how much more normal people seemed to know about what others were thinking in social situations. One example, made famous by Oliver Sacks, is Temple Grandin's comment that her social experience in adolescence was like being 'an anthropologist on Mars' (Grandin and Scariano, 1986; Frith, 1989; Sacks, 1995).

A similar explanation in terms of a broken module occurs in Blair's discussion of psychopathy. Three core features in the characterisation of psychopathy are (i) early onset of extremely aggressive behavior; (ii) absence of remorse or guilt; and (iii) callousness and a lack of empathy. Blair (1995) explains psychopathic behavior as due to the absence or malfunctioning of a module which he calls the *violence inhibition mechanism* (VIM). The central idea was borrowed from ethology, where research had long suggested the existence of a mechanism which ended fights in response to a display of submission. A well-known example is the canine tendency to bare the throat when attacked by a stronger conspecific. The assailant then ceases the attack, rather than taking advantage of the

---

7. False-belief tasks are intended to evaluate whether or not experimental subjects understand when someone might hold a false belief. One standard version of the task–sometimes called the 'Sally-Ann Task—involves watching Sally put a piece of chocolate in one place (location A) and later, while Sally is away, Ann moving the chocolate elsewhere (location B). The subject is then asked 'Where will Sally look for her chocolate?' In order to answer this question correctly, the subject needs to appreciate that, since Sally was absent when her chocolate was moved from A to B, she will have the false belief that it is at A (Baron-Cohen, 1995, p. 70).

opportunity to press it home. Blair hypothesizes that a similar mechanism exists in humans, activated by the perception of distress in others. When the VIM is activated it causes a withdrawal response which people experience as aversive. Following Mandler, Blair suggests that this aversive experience is one of the building blocks for such moral emotions as guilt and remorse.

On Blair's account, the VIM acquires new triggers via classical conditioning. Since engaging in aggressive activity will often lead the victim to exhibit distress cues, aggressive activity becomes a conditioned stimulus for the aversive response. Distress cues are also typically paired with the construction of a mental representation of the victim's suffering, and as a result these thoughts also become triggers for the VIM. This linkage, Blair maintains, is a crucial step in the development of empathy. Since psychopaths do not have a properly functioning VIM, they do not experience the effects of their violence on others as aversive, and this explains why psychopathy is associated with an increase in violent tendencies at an early age. Their deficit does not lead psychopaths to become aggressive, but when they do, they are much less inclined to stop. Blair's model also explains why psychopaths fail to develop the moral emotions and fail to experience any empathic response to the suffering of others. The most intriguing part of Blair's theory is his argument that people lacking a properly functioning VIM would not be able to recognize the distinction between moral transgressions which cause other people to suffer and other social transgressions which do not. This prediction was confirmed in a study comparing the moral cognition of psychopathic murderers with the moral cognition of murderers who were not diagnosed as psychopaths.

Since the publication of Robert Trivers' seminal paper on reciprocal altruism (Trivers, 1971), the capacity to engage in reciprocal exchanges has played an important role in the thinking of socio-biologists and evolutionary psychologists. More recently a number of theorists, including Cosmides, Tooby and Gigerenzer, have argued that this capacity is subserved by a module or a cluster of modules designed to compute what is and is not required in reciprocal exchange arrangements and to detect 'cheaters' who fail to reciprocate (Cosmides, 1989; Cosmides and Tooby, 1992; Gigerenzer and Hug, 1992). If the module that computes what is required in reciprocal altruism malfunctions, the likely result will be that the module's owner will systematically misunderstand what is expected in co-operative behavior and reciprocal exchanges. Such a person might regularly overestimate the value or importance of his own contribution in a reciprocal relationship and/or regularly underestimate the value or importance of the other party's contribution.[8] From the point of view of the person with a malfunctioning reciprocal altruism module (though not from the point of view of those he interacts with), he would be regularly exploited or cheated in social exchanges, and this might well lead him to avoid social interaction and to be in a depressed mood for extended periods.

---

8. Of course, the mere fact that the reciprocal altruism module malfunctions does not entail that a person will over-value his own contribution and under-value the other party's. Various other patterns are possible. And if the first pattern is typical, some further explanation is needed for this fact.

In an important series of publications, McGuire and his colleagues have argued that this sort of malfunction may be a central factor in many individuals who fit the DSM criteria for dysthymia, which is an affective disorder characterized by persistent depressed mood for over two years, but without major depressive or manic episodes. In one study, McGuire and his colleagues found that dysthymic patients had a notable deficit in their ability to achieve social goals and carry out simple social tasks. They tended to blame others for their dissatisfactions, rather than considering their own behavior (as did a matched control group). Dysthymic patients were also less likely than controls to interact socially with others. Perhaps the most striking finding of the study was that dysthymic subjects 'believed that they helped others *significantly more* than they were helped by others. Thus, by their own reckoning, they were co-operators.' However, 'a detailed analysis of their social interactions, which involved collecting data from siblings or friends, strongly suggested otherwise.' Subjects with dysthymic disorder 'not only tended to exaggerate their helpfulness to others, but they also downplayed the value of others' help . . . In addition, they were sceptical of others' intentions to help as well as to recipro-cate helping that [they] might provide. For the majority of [dysthymic subjects], these views began *prior* to adolescence . . .' (p. 317).

A defective module (or 'algorithm') for computing what is expected or required in re-ciprocal relations is not the only sort of defect that might lead dysthymic persons to exag-gerate their own helpfulness and downplay the helpfulness of others. Though the basic principles of reciprocal exchange may be universal, the value of specific acts varies enor-mously from culture to culture. In one culture giving your neighbor a hot tip on a stock counts as a valuable favor, while paying a shaman to chant secret prayers for his child who is down with the flu does not. In other cultures this pattern is reversed. A person who had failed to master the local culture's value system might well end up thinking that he helped others vastly more than they helped him. It is plausible that information about the value that one's culture assigns to various actions is not proprietary to any given module, but is stored in a location to which many mental mechanisms have access. If that is right, then dysthymia may be a heterogeneous category since the tendency of dysthymic people to misunderstand reciprocity relationships might have two quite different causes. This suggests an intriguing hypothesis. Suppose that some people diagnosed as dysthymic have defective reciprocal altruism modules, while others have normal modules and have simply failed to master the prevailing principles of social value. If so, it might well be the case that this latter group, but not the former, could be treated effectively by a regimen of cognitive psychotherapy that sought to inculcate the social codes they have failed to internalize.

In the preceding cases we have focused on modules for whose existence we have some independent empirical or theoretical support. Some of the symptoms that characterize the disorders we've considered are those we would expect when these modules malfunc-tion. Indeed, in the case of autism the clinical data have been taken to provide important additional support for the hypothesis that a theory-of-mind module exists. Especially noteworthy in this connection is the double-dissociation evidence provided by studies of

Williams' Syndrome patients (Karmiloff-Smith *et al.*, 1995; Bellugi *el al.*, 1997). For the reasons set out in section 3, it is probably unwise to expect the fit between hypothetical mechanisms and currently recognized symptomatologies to be too exact. In some cases— autism is one—the hypothesized modular deficit does not generate all the symptoms which current clinical thinking takes to characterize the disorder. In these cases there are at least the following two possibilities when it comes to mapping the diagnosis onto the architecture. In many cases the full suite of recognized symptoms is not necessary for the diagnosis at all—a subset of the recognized symptoms will do. When it comes to relating the current diagnosis to our mental architecture, we can isolate a broken module which might explain a subset of the symptomatology which is sufficient for diagnosis. Further clusters of symptoms could be due to other causes. In such cases it is possible that what we are dealing with is actually several disorders, represented by the different sets of symptoms which are currently thought to be variant forms of one disorder. This is the first possibility we have in mind. These different conditions might co-occur due to a common cause which disrupts several mechanisms. The second possibility is that this co-occurrence is more coincidental, and that the different disorders sometimes just happen to occur to- gether. Since the DSM categories are not validated, it probably happens quite often that DSM picks out symptom clusters that are not in fact all that reliably linked with one an- other. It is even possible that the cause of some of the unexplained symptoms may not be a disorder at all. They may, for example, just represent the stress of being in treatment for a different condition, or be responses to what are termed 'problems in living.' Evolutionary psychology offers a model of the mind which allows us to disentangle one set of symp- toms from the wider collection and recognize it as a distinct condition.

Though the modules that have played a role in our discussion thus far are ones which we have non-clinical reasons for recognizing, there have been cases, especially in the neu- ropsychological literature, in which the discovery of particular deficits has led investiga- tors to argue for the presence of specialized systems or modules in the mental architecture. For example, dorsal simultanagnosics can recognize the spatial relations among parts of an object but are unable to compute the spatial relations between objects. This suggests that there are separate systems underlying these two forms of spatial perception (Farah, 1990). It is noteworthy that in this case the symptoms that led to a hypothesis about the underlying mechanism are not among the standard items of clinical phenomenology that loom so large in DSM-III and its successors. Indeed, for a variety of historical and prac- tical reasons, the agnosias, amnesias and aphasias are not even in DSM-IV as conditions, although some of their characteristic symptoms are.

3.1.2 Disorders Resulting from Upstream Problems in the Cognitive System

As we noted earlier, when a module behaves problematically, there can be two very dif- ferent sorts of reasons. In some cases, the module itself is to blame. In other cases, the trouble is further upstream. Many modules receive input from other modules, so it will

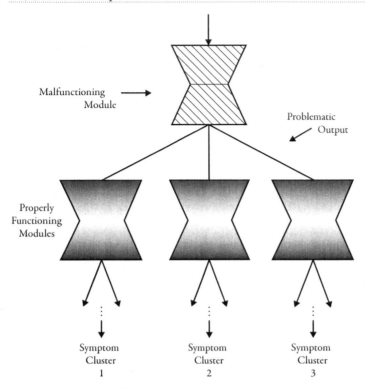

Malfunctioning Module

Problematic Output

Properly Functioning Modules

Symptom Cluster 1

Symptom Cluster 2

Symptom Cluster 3

FIGURE 4 When a malfunctioning module provides information to several separate downstream systems, the upstream problem can result in several quite distinct clusters of symptoms.

often be the case that if an upstream module is malfunctioning, one or more of the modules to which it is supposed to provide information will also produce output that yields symptoms of mental disorder. If the broken upstream module provides information to several separate downstream systems, an upstream problem can result in several quite different clusters of symptoms (see Figure 4). The possibility that a single malfunctioning module may cause several other modules to produce problematic outputs may provide a partial explanation for the very high rate of comorbidity that is found in psychiatric patients. A lot of people have more than one disorder at the same time. The National Comorbidity Survey concluded that 'more than half of all lifetime disorders occurred in the 14% of the population who had a history of three or more comorbid disorders' (Kessler *et al.*, 1994).[9]

Our picture does not mandate that if one module feeds information to another it must always be the case that the second will produce problematic output as a result of a

9. It is worth stressing that this is only one sort of explanation for comorbidity, even at the architectural level. For example, if there are domain-general systems, then if these systems are damaged we might get a general reduction of functioning which causes problems in several areas.

breakdown in the first. There are typically several ways in which a single module can malfunction, and each of these is a matter of degree. So it may happen that a malfunction upstream produces problems in a second module in some people, while in other people it does not. All of this can be iterated for modules which are further downstream. The result is that the profile for a specific patient is likely to be quite complex.

This suggests a way of classifying mental disorders which are internal to the subject. The idea would be that such disorders are to be identified with a chain or network of modules each of which is producing problematic outputs. Those outputs in turn are responsible for a suite of symptoms that is characteristic of the disorder. The canonical specification of a disorder would also include, for each module in the network, an indication of whether it is itself broken or whether it is receiving tainted input from elsewhere in the network. This cuts things up rather finely, but it does allow for some important theoretical distinctions. Suppose that two modules are each delivering problematic outputs, but only the first is actually malfunctioning. The second is producing problematic output because it is downstream from the first and is being provided with problematic input. In this case the solution to the problem lies in repairing the upstream module that is the source of the trouble. However, if both modules are malfunctioning then both will have to be repaired if the disorder is to be dealt with. Merely noting that in each case the two modules form the network underlying the disorder is insufficient to direct therapeutic interventions (Figure 5).

An example of a disorder which may be caused by problems upstream in the flow of information is the Capgras Delusion. Patients with Capgras believe that someone close to them—typically a spouse—has been replaced by an exact replica. Recent work suggests that part of the explanation for the delusion is that the face recognition system appears to have the structure of an and-gate; it requires two sorts of input. The first sort is the input which is absent in prosopagnosics, who are unable to recognize the faces of close relatives, or even their own face in a mirror. It has been suggested that the mechanism which produces this input is either a template-matching system or a constraint-satisfaction network (Farah, 1990), However, it appears that there is also an affective response needed to underwrite face recognition, a neural pathway that gives the face you see its emotional significance. Only if both these sorts of inputs feed into the face recognition gate does full recognition take place. Several authors have suggested that it is the system subserving this affective response that is disrupted in Capgras patients. As a result, these patients have an experience analogous to seeing an identical twin of one's best beloved. The visual match is there but not the emotional response.

This cannot be the whole story, however. Most of us would think that the trouble lay within ourselves if we started having such an experience. It appears that in Capgras the facial recognition system, getting only one sort of appropriate information, sends this on to more central systems which are also in trouble. Stone and Young (1997) argue that in

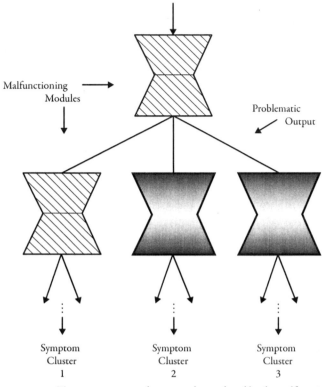

Malfunctioning Modules

Problematic Output

Symptom Cluster 1

Symptom Cluster 2

Symptom Cluster 3

FIGURE 5 The same symptom clusters can be produced by the malfunction of a single module (as in Figure 4) and by the malfunction of two modules. But if two modules are malfunctioning then both will have to be repaired if the disorder is to be dealt with.

addition to their agnosia, Capgras' patients have a belief system which is too heavily weighted towards observational beliefs at the expense of background knowledge. Another possibility is that normal subjects have a mechanism which sets an upper boundary on the weirdness of permissible beliefs, and that in Capgras subjects this is absent, or at least very permissive. Stone and Young argue that similar combinations of disordered affective response and belief-formation problems may underlie Cotard's Delusion, in which one forms the belief that one is dead. If these speculations are correct, then there is, in Capgras' Delusion, a part of the visual system that is working as designed, but receiving only one of the two sorts of input that it needs and passing its own output on to a central system which is also, perhaps, abnormal.

Since the Darwinian modules posited by evolutionary psychology can utilize input from non-proprietary stores of information, it can also happen that a module produces a problem generating output because the non-proprietary information it needs is incorrect. A clear example of this is one of the hypotheses we have already mentioned—the idea that some dysthymic people may have a normally functioning reciprocal altruism module which is being fed with inappropriate data about the values of various acts in the patient's culture.

3.2 DISORDERS THAT RESULT FROM AN ENVIRONMENT DIFFERENT FROM WHAT MOTHER NATURE INTENDED

Natural selection has no foresight; it is concerned only with what works in the here and now. A central tenet of evolutionary psychology is that the human mind is designed to work in our ancestral, hunter-gatherer environment. Natural selection did not design it for the contemporary world. But, of course, a system may function admirably in one environment and work rather poorly in another. So it is entirely possible that the mind contains modules or other sorts of systems which were highly adaptive in the ancestral environment but which do not lead to functional behavior in our novel modern environments.

For example, the social competition theory of depression (Price *et al.*, 1994; Nesse and Williams, 1994) is based on the idea that depression is an evolved response to loss of status or to an unsuccessful attempt to gain status. In response to such a loss, it might be adaptive to abandon the strategy you were previously using in your attempts at status enhancement. Similarly, perhaps you should change behaviors if your previous behaviors were tied to reproductive potential you have now lost. The social competition theory claims that depression provides an introspectable marker which indicates when switching strategies to seek another niche is in order. If you are living in a small group, as our ancestors typically did, switching strategies might well result in considerably greater success. Depressed mood is nature's way of telling you to accept that your current behavior will not improve your reproductive lot and motivating you to try behaving differently. In the circumstances, you should evaluate your behavior thoroughly, dwelling on the negative.[10] In addition, you might try to stay out of social situations altogether if you think you lack the resources to do well in them, and indeed we find that 'depressed individuals report being uncomfortable in interactions with others, often perceiving these interactions as unhelpful, or even as unpleasant or negative' (Gottlib, 1992, p. 151).

The social competition hypothesis sees our ancestral communities as miniature ecosystems in which individuals strive to find niches where they can excel and make a good living. In modern societies, though, your chance of excelling—of being the best at anything, or indeed anywhere near the best—are remote. If we have inherited a mechanism which is triggered when we believe ourselves to be outcompeted, then that

---

10. There seems to be good evidence that this happens in depression. In a review article, Pyszczynski and Greenberg (1987) found support for the idea that depressed individuals have elevated levels of self-focus and that self-focus increases following a loss in the personal, social or employment spheres. In addition, depressives have elevated levels of 'negative self-complexity' and lowered levels of 'positive self-complexity' (Woolfolk *et al.* 1995). That is, depressives tend to think of themselves unfavorably in many different ways, and are quite sophisticated at drawing distinctions among different ways of not being terribly good; whereas they think with a very broad brush when assessing themselves in positive terms.

mechanism will fire frequently as we are inundated with information about accomplished people. But, of course, in the modern world it is far more likely that the mechanism will fail to achieve the goal it was selected to attain. If the mechanism is set off by the realization that one is not even close to being the best at anything in the global village of the information age then getting depressed is not likely to be an effective reaction. For it is typically the case that there is no other strategy to adopt—no other niche one could fill—which would do significantly better than the present one in that global competition. Moreover, the mechanism will frequently be set off even though its owner is actually doing very well in the *local* environment. You can be the most respected and admired real estate developer in Sioux Falls without being Donald Trump.[11]

The social competition hypothesis is not the only explanation for depression which sees it as a formerly adaptive trait which causes problems in our current environment. The defection hypothesis, proposed by Watson and Andrews (1998), Hagen (1998, MS) and others maintains that in the ancestral environment postpartum depression was an adaptive response which led women to limit their investment in the new child when, because of social, biological or environmental factors, a major investment in the infant would be likely to reduce the total number of offspring produced by that woman during her lifetime who would reach reproductive age and reproduce successfully. Among the social conditions in the ancestral environment that would have been good cues for triggering a sharply reduced maternal investment would be insufficient investment from the father and/or other appropriate kin. Biological cues would include problems with the pregnancy or birth, or other visible indications that the infant was not likely to be viable and healthy. Environmental cues would include harsh winters, famine conditions and other indications that material resources would be inadequate. In modern societies, with elaborate support systems provided by the state and other organizations, it may be much less likely that these cues are reliable indicators that a mother who 'defects' and sharply reduces her investment in her baby will increase her own reproductive fitness. But there is a growing body of evidence suggesting that these situations are indeed significantly correlated with postpartum depression (Hagen, 1998, MS). So it may be that postpartum depression is yet another example of a condition produced by an adaptive mechanism that is functioning just as

---

11. One question often asked about the social competition hypothesis is why it does not entail just about everyone in modern societies should be depressed, since almost all of us are aware that there are lots of people who are better than us in just about anything that we do. Part of the answer, we think, is that different individuals will have different levels of sensitivity to the cues that trigger this sort of depression. We will say a bit more about individual differences in 'trigger' sensitivity in our discussion of panic disorders at the end of this section. Another factor that might be relevant is that in some important ways modern societies may not be all that different from ancestral communities. For as Dunbar (2000) has shown, the social networks that individuals maintain in contemporary societies are similar in size to the social networks of individuals in surviving hunter-gatherer communities.

it was designed to function, though in an environment that is quite different from the one in which it evolved.[12]

One of the morals to be drawn from these two hypotheses about depression is quite general. The environment in which selection pressures acted so as to leave us with our current mental endowment is not the one we live in now. This means that any mental mechanism producing harmful behavior in the modern world *may* be fulfilling its design specifications to the letter, but in an environment it was not designed for. In the disorders that result, there is nothing in the mind which is malfunctioning.

Some anxiety disorders provide another possible example of disorders that result from a mismatch between the contemporary environment and the environment in which our minds evolved. Marks and Nesse (1994) note that in the ancestral environment fear of public places and fear of being far from home might well have been adaptive responses 'that guard against the many dangers encountered outside the home range of any territorial species' (p. 251). Similarly, a fear of heights accompanied by 'freezing instead of wild flight' (p. 251) would have had obvious adaptive value to our hunter-gatherer forebears. Moreover these traits, like most traits, could be expected to show considerable phenotypic variation even in a population of individuals who are genotypically identical with respect to the relevant genes. Individuals who are toward the sensitive end of these distributions—those who become anxious more readily when far from home or when they find themselves in high places—might well have functioned quite normally in ancestral environments. In a modern urban environment, however, people who become extremely anxious when they are away from home or when they are in public places will find it all but impossible to lead a normal life. And people who become extremely anxious in high places will find it difficult or impossible to travel in airplanes, ride in glass-enclosed elevators or work on the higher floors of modern buildings. Thus, because the modern environment is so different from the ancestral

---

12. Some theorists have proposed generalizing the defection hypothesis to cover many more (perhaps *all*) cases of depression. On this account, the adaptive function of depression is to negotiate a greater investment from other people with whom one is engaged in collective activities when one's own investment seems unlikely to have a positive payoff. Depression, on this view, functions a bit like a labor strike. The depressed person withdraws his or her services in an effort to get a better deal in some co-operative enterprise. It is our view—though at this point it is little more than a guess—that it is counterproductive to seek a single account of the adaptive function of depression. Rather, we suspect, there may be several quite different kinds of depression, each with its own set of triggers and its own characteristic symptomatology. Thus, for example, we noted earlier that Woolfolk *et al.* (1995) found that people who are depressed have elevated levels of 'negative self-complexity.' This is a symptom that makes perfect sense if the episode of depression is triggered by the sort of perceived failure or loss of status that plays a central role in the social competition account of depression. People in that situation need to think hard about what they are doing wrong. But the symptom makes less sense if the episode is triggered by a situation in which an individual's reproductive interests require re-negotiation of the expected levels of investment in a collective activity. It would be very interesting indeed to know whether women suffering from postpartum depression exhibit negative self-complexity. On the pluralistic account of depression that we favor, it would be predicted that episodes of postpartum depression triggered by inadequate paternal and family investment are not marked by high levels of negative self-complexity.

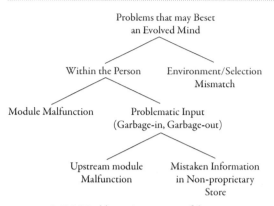

FIGURE 6 E-M Problems. A taxonomy of the main categories of problems that may beset an evolved mind.

environment, people who are towards the sensitive end of the distribution of phenotypic variation may be incapable of coping with many ordinary situations despite the fact that all of their mental mechanisms are functioning in just the way that natural selection designed them to function.

Figure 6 indicates the main categories in our proposed taxonomy of problems that may beset an evolved mind.

4 The Causes of Disorder

In the previous section we saw how the evolutionary psychology model of the mind suggests a theoretically motivated strategy for classifying mental disorders. We also noted some of the ways in which this taxonomy might prove useful in planning therapeutic interventions. In our taxonomy, the notion of a module malfunction played a central role. In this section we want to consider some of the factors that can *cause* a module to malfunction. The discussion will illustrate some of the ways in which an evolutionary motivated taxonomy of disorders can integrate with a variety of scientifically promising approaches to mental disorder.

When considering the causes of module malfunction, it is, we think, both convenient and theoretically well motivated to distinguish two importantly different kinds of case: (i) those in which a fully developed, normally functioning module begins to malfunction and (ii) those in which, as the result of some problem in the course of development, the module in question never functions in the way that it was designed to. We will consider these two kinds of case in turn.

4.1 HOW CAN A NORMAL MODULE BECOME PATHOLOGICAL?

Modules are computers and hence require some kind of physical substrate; in human beings, this substrate is the brain. Psychological disturbances may be a result of damage to the brain caused by strokes or injuries or by other kinds of physical trauma. Apperceptive agnosia, for instance, has often been noted in subjects who have undergone carbon monoxide poisoning (Farah, 1990). Various physical disorders can also cause fully developed minds to malfunction. Metabolic disorders which interfere with the synthesis of neurotransmitters are an obvious example. Autoimmune responses of the sort believed to be responsible for Multiple Sclerosis can lead to the demyelination of nerve tissue which slows up the transmission of impulses. Late-onset genetic disorders are still another example. Huntington's disease (a DSM-IV diagnosis) is a late-onset neurodegenerative disorder caused by an abnormally long CAG trinucleotide repeat in a dominant gene close to the tip of chromosome 4.

Earlier we urged adopting the idea that a disorder should be identified with a network of problematic modules. The physiological causes we have just discussed might have implications for more than one network. Indeed cognitive neuropsychology is bedevilled by the problem of understanding how to apportion to their proper diagnoses the variety of symptoms which typically follow one injury to the brain. How should our taxonomy take these causal factors into account? We propose a *two-dimensional* classification of disorders that arise from problems within the person. One dimension is the network of problematic modules, the other dimension is the aetiology of the malfunction—physiological, developmental and so on. It may seem that the two-dimensional approach generates disorders beyond necessity. However, aetiology is always important in medicine, which tends to regard information about causal history as vital to accurate diagnosis. The other possibility is to opt for a *one-dimensional* classification that identifies disorders with a network of problematic modules (and other sorts of mental mechanisms) and to note in addition that some disorders can be caused in quite distinct ways. The two-dimensional picture is richer and probably more in keeping with medical practice generally, but the question whether to adopt a one- or two-dimensional picture should be decided on grounds of utility. Whichever emerges as the more useful approach should be adopted.

4.2 PROBLEMS THAT CAN PREVENT A MODULE FROM DEVELOPING PROPERLY

In the last section we briefly considered some of the causes that might lead to a malfunction in a fully developed Darwinian module that was functioning normally to begin with. All of the factors we mentioned—brain damage, stroke, physical trauma, physical disorders and genetic disorders—can also occur in infancy or childhood. However, when a module functions improperly in the course of development, it can lead to a suite of problems that are quite different from the sorts of problems that would arise if the same module were damaged in an adult. One reason for this is that modules may require appropriate input to develop normally. Thus if a downstream module is supposed to be getting input from another module further upstream, and if the upstream module is damaged and fails to provide appropriate input, the downstream module may never develop properly. By contrast, damage to the upstream module in an adult might leave the downstream module unscathed.

In a series of recent publications, Baron-Cohen has proposed a theory of the origin of autism that fits this pattern (Baron-Cohen, 1995; Baron-Cohen and Swettenham, 1996). On Baron-Cohen's account, normal development of the theory-of-mind module (ToMM) requires that three upstream systems be in place: an Intentionality Detector, an Eye Direction Detector, and a Shared-Attention Mechanism. In autism, a variety of biological hazards, most notably prenatal problems, damage the Shared-Attention Mechanism. As a result, the downstream ToMM is deprived of the input it needs to develop properly.

Blair's theory of psychopathy provides another illustration of the way in which a malfunction of one mechanism early in development can prevent other mechanisms from developing properly. In Blair's theory, the Violence Inhibition Mechanism (VIM) generates an aversive affective response to signs of pain or distress, and this response is required if the systems responsible for empathy and for moral emotions such as guilt and remorse are to develop properly. Blair claims that in psychopaths the VIM is absent, due to a physiological deficit or poor socialization early in development, and as a result young psychopaths never acquire a capacity for empathy and are never able to experience the moral emotions.

There is another reason why module malfunction early in development can lead to problems that are quite different from those that result when a functional adult module is damaged. To see this, we must first explain a distinction between two importantly different sorts of modules. All of the modules that we've considered so far have, as their main function, subserving some capacity which, once in place, will typically remain intact for the rest of a person's life. Following Segal (1996) we will call these *synchronic modules*. However, theorists who advocate a highly modular account of mental architecture also posit a quite different sort of module which, again following Segal, we will call *diachronic modules*. The computational program and proprietary information embedded in some synchronic modules may be largely insensitive to environmental variation. Synchronic modules of this sort will end up with the same program and information in any normal environment. In many other cases, however, natural selection has found methods of exploiting information available in the environment to fine-tune the workings of a synchronic module in a way that would be adaptive in the environment in which our minds evolved. Thus some synchronic modules can develop in a variety of different ways, resulting in adult modules that compute different functions or use different proprietary information. Diachronic modules are one of the mechanisms responsible for this process of fine-tuning. Many diachronic modules function only in development, though others may be operative throughout life. Their job is to monitor the environment and to set the switches and dials of developing synchronic modules in appropriate ways. Perhaps the best-known example of a diachronic module is the Language Acquisition Device (LAD) posited by Chomsky and his followers. Its job is to set the parameters of the Language Competence System thereby determining which of the large number of languages compatible with Universal Grammar the child will come to know. If a diachronic module malfunctions in the course of development, the synchronic module that it services may be set improperly or, in extreme cases, it may not function at all.

Though there is still much research to be done, Specific Language Impairment might well turn out to be a developmental disorder that results from a malfunctioning diachronic module (Gopnik, 1990a, 1990b; Gopnik and Crago, 1991).

In a well-known series of experiments, Mineka *et al.* (1980, 1984, 1989) showed that young rhesus monkeys who have never seen snakes are not afraid of them, though they develop an enduring fear of snakes after only a few observations of another rhesus reacting fearfully to a snake. Rhesus monkeys do not, however, develop fear of flowers when they see another rhesus reacting fearfully to flowers. This suggests that rhesus may have a diachronic module (a Fear Acquisition Device, if you will) whose function it is to determine which of the switches on an innately prepared fear system get turned on. It is entirely possible that humans have a similar Fear Acquisition Device (FAD). If we do, then it may well be the case that some phobias (or some characteristic symptoms of phobias) are caused by a malfunction in the device which toggles an enduring terror of snakes or spiders, say, despite the fact that the person with the phobia has never seen anyone injured or frightened by snakes or spiders. In other cases phobias may arise when a properly functioning FAD is triggered inappropriately. If, for example, a child sees his parent reacting fearfully in response to something that looks like a snake or a spider, he may acquire a phobia even if the parent's fear was feigned or provoked by something else entirely. Still another intriguing possibility is that there are people whose FAD is defective in the other direction; instead of being too active, it is not active enough. These people would fail to develop fears or anxieties that they ought to develop (cf. Marks and Nesse, 1994). They would be unlikely to come to the attention of psychiatrists or clinical psychologists, though they might be more likely to come to the attention of coroners, since the disorder may have a negative impact on their life expectancy.

5 Disorders That May Not Be

We noted above that the environment, especially the social environment, may change in ways which render well-designed systems pathological. However, an important possibility is that certain forms of what we currently take to be pathology are in fact straightforwardly adaptive in the current environment, just as they were in the ancestral environment in which our minds evolved. To put the point starkly, some people may be designed to be antisocial.

Personality disorders are patterns of experience and behavior which are culturally very deviant, persistent, inflexible, arise in adolescence or early adulthood and lead to distress or impairment. However, it is not clear that antisocial behavior of this sort is always bad for the individual who engages in it, rather than the people who are on the receiving end. McGuire *et al.* (1994) suggest that two personality disorders in particular may represent adaptive deviant behavioral strategies. The first, antisocial personality disorder, is characterized by a disregard for the wishes, rights or feelings of others. Subjects with this disorder are impulsive, aggressive and neglect their responsibilities. 'They are frequently deceitful and manipulative in order to gain personal profit or pleasure (e.g. to obtain money, sex or power).' Typically, they show complete indifference to the harmful consequences of their actions and 'believe that everyone is out to "help number one"' (DSM-IV, p. 646).

The second disorder McGuire and his colleagues discuss is histrionic personality disorder. Subjects diagnosed as having this disorder are attention-seeking prima donnas. Often lively and dramatic, they do whatever is necessary to draw attention to themselves. Their behavior is often sexually provocative or seductive in a wide variety of inappropriate situations or relationships (DSM-IV, p. 655). They demand immediate satisfaction and are intolerant of or frustrated by situations which delay gratification. They may resort to threats of suicide to get attention and coerce better caregiving (DSM-IV, p. 656). Both antisocial and histrionic personality disorders are characterized by manipulativeness, although antisocial subjects manipulate others in the pursuit of material gratification and histrionics manipulate to gain nurture.

Now, on the face of it you might think that being able to manipulate other people so that they nurture you or further your material ends would be quite a useful trait to have, moral qualms aside. And of course one of the more annoying facts about such people is that they don't have moral qualms about their behavior. That makes it easier for them to commit the sorts of acts which occasionally lead to their arrest or undoing. To be classified as suffering from the relevant personality disorder, people must manifest a pattern of behavior that involves these undesirable social acts, though to satisfy the diagnostic criteria set out in DSM-IV their behavior must also 'lead to clinically significant distress or impairment in social, occupational, or other important areas of functioning' (DSM-IV, p. 633). To put the point more colloquially, their behavior has to get them in trouble. However, it is quite likely that there are many people who are just as unsavory and manipulative but who do not get in trouble or suffer adverse consequences. It is estimated, for instance, that fewer than 25% of those who commit non-violent crimes are apprehended (McGuire *et al.*, 1994). Such folk may cheat, deceive and manipulate but be good enough at reading social cues and understanding the structure of reciprocal exchange that they can exploit the social system successfully.

The natural way for philosophers to understand the function of a psychological mechanism, according to the conception of the mind we have presented, is in causal-historical terms (Neander, 1991; Millikan, 1993). This influential view construes the function of a psychological unit as the effect it has in virtue of which it is copied in successive generations. Now if it is indeed true that the disorders we have been considering are adaptive strategies, then we can give precisely this causal-historical explanation of the existence of the mechanisms which generate the antisocial behavior of sociopaths. Antisocial behavior is the proper function of these mechanisms. That pattern of behavior enables enough sociopaths to make a good enough living to ensure that antisocial mechanisms are copied in subsequent generations. On the standard causal-historical view of functions, then, the antisocial behaviors of the sociopathic are produced as the proper, selected functions of their peculiar psychological mechanisms. So these people are, in this respect, functioning as they should; they do not have a broken module or any other sort of malfunctioning mental mechanism. Nor is there reason to believe that the environment has changed in relevant ways since the time when the system was selected. The relevant environment in this case is social, and the current social environment, like the ancestral one, offers many opportunities to cheat and exploit one's fellows.

It is true that some sociopathic individuals spend their best reproductive years incarcerated. However, statistically it may be that other things being equal (general intelligence, normal childhood environments and so on) sociopathic behavior is quite adaptive—it is an effective way of getting one's genes into the next generation. Indeed, a population with a minority of sociopaths may be in an evolutionarily stable state. Skyrms has shown how this is mathematically possible for apparently bizarre strategies such as 'Mad Dog,' which rejects a fair division of resources but accepts a grossly unfair one (1996, pp. 29–31); that is, Mad Dogs punish those who play fair. It is not hard to imagine the survival of more complex strategies which unfairly manipulate others.

These strategies will be useful provided two conditions apply. First, the subjects must often be able to disguise their cheating and deception, perhaps by exploiting and mimicking the signals which others use to convey co-operativeness (Frank, 1988). Second, the antisocial behaviors must be maintained at a comparatively low level in the population. If there are too many people who refuse to co-operate and deal fairly with others, then refusing to co-operate will gain one no dividends. We can expect an arms–race as sociopathic cheaters evolve to be even better at exploiting others, and the others evolve to become better at detecting cheaters and avoiding them.[13]

As we suggested earlier (footnote 6), we think there is an important distinction to be drawn between mental disorders and what, for want of a better term, we call *E-M problems* (problems that may beset an evolved mind). To count as an E-M problem, a condition must be located somewhere in the taxonomic structure sketched in Figure 6. And having an E-M problem is, we maintain, a *necessary* condition for having a mental disorder. But not all cases of E-M problems are or ought to be counted as mental disorders. Mental disorder is a partly normative notion; to count as a mental disorder a condition must cause problems for the people who have it or for those around them. A brain lesion that disrupts the normal function of some mental mechanism, but whose only enduring result is that those with the lesion develop an intense interest in gourmet food, would produce an E-M problem but not be a mental disorder.[14] In other cases, E-M problems do not count as

---

13. McGuire *et al.* are not the only theorists to have tried explaining a disorder in this way. Mealey (1995) thinks that primary sociopathy or psychopathy is an adaptive strategy. Her account is straightforwardly sociobiological, and, in contrast with Blair's theory, it neglects to go into any detail on cognitive mechanisms (Blair and Morton, 1995). However, the two are not entirely incompatible, Blair thinks that the VIM is missing due to neurological impairment or poor early socialization. Mealey can be read as offering an alternative reason for the absence of the VIM; some people are just not designed to have one. The developmental consequences might then unfold as Blair envisages. We could treat Mealey as giving the 'ultimate' explanation and Blair the 'proximate' one (Mayr, 1976).

14. This is not merely a hypothetical case. See Regard and Landis (1997).

mental disorders for a variety of historical, social or practical reasons. Thus, as we mentioned earlier, Huntington's disease is a disorder included in DSM-IV, but Multiple Sclerosis is not, nor are various agnosias and aphasias. If, as McGuire and others have suggested, the mechanisms underlying various sorts of personality disorders are adaptations that evolved in environments which were relevantly similar to the modern environment, then people with these conditions do not have E-M problems, and thus, we maintain, *they do not have mental disorders.*

These people are problems, of course. But they are problems to us, and so are lots of other people who do not receive diagnoses of psychopathology. We might perhaps be able to drug them into submission, but that is best viewed as punishment or pre-emptive social control, not therapy. Similarly, if we could devise ways of restructuring their motivational system, it would be inappropriate to call the process 'therapy.' Rather, we should simply recognize that we are trying to manipulate behavior in the interests of social harmony. Unless we want to medicalize all deviant behavior, we must acknowledge the possibility that apparently disordered behavior, which receives a DSM diagnosis, can be produced by a psychological endowment functioning exactly as it was designed to, in just the environment it was picked to work in. One of the virtues of the evolutionary approach to psychopathology is that, in some cases at least, it provides a principled way of drawing the distinction between mental disorders and patterns of antisocial behavior produced by people whose evolved minds are beset by no problems at all.

REFERENCES

American Psychiatric Association (1980). *Diagnostic and Statistical Manual of Mental Disorders,* 3rd ed. Washington, D.C.: American Psychiatric Association. (DSM-III).

American Psychiatric Association (1987). *Diagnostic and Statistical Manual of Mental Disorders,* 3rd ed. revised. Washington, D.C.: American Psychiatric Association. (DSM-IIIR).

American Psychiatric Association (1994). *Diagnostic and Statistical Manual of Mental Disorders,* 4th ed. Washington, D.C.: American Psychiatric Association. (DSM-IV).

Baron-Cohen, S. (1995). *Mindblindness: An Essay on Autism and Theory of Mind.* Cambridge, MA: MIT Press.

Baron-Cohen, S., Leslie, A. & Frith, U. (1985). Does the autistic child have a theory of mind? *Cognition,* 21, 37–46.

Baron-Cohen, S. & Swettenham, J. (1996). The relationship between SAM and ToMM; two hypotheses. In P. Carruthers & P. Smith (eds.), *Theories of Theories of Mind.* Cambridge: Cambridge University Press.

Bellugi, U., Klima, E. & Wang, P. (1997). Cognitive and neural development: Clues from genetically based syndromes. In Magnusson, D. et al. (eds.), *The lifespan development of individuals: Behavioral, neurobiological, and psychosocial perspectives: A synthesis.* New York: Cambridge University Press. Pp. 223–243.

Blair, R. (1995). A cognitive developmental approach to morality: investigating the psychopath. *Cognition,* 57, 1–29.

Blair, R. & Morton, J. (1995). Putting cognition into sociopathy. *Behavioral and Brain Sciences*, 18, 548.

Clarkin, J., Widiger, T., Frances, A., Hurt, S., & Gilmore, M. (1983). Prototypic typology and the borderline personality disorder. *Journal of Abnormal Psychology*, 92, 263–275.

Cosmides, L. (1989). The logic of social exchange: Has natural selection shaped how humans reason? Studies with Wason Selection Task. *Cognition*, 31, 187–276.

Cosmides, L. & Tooby, J. (1992). Cognitive adaptations for social exchange. In J. Barkow, L. Cosmides, & J. Tooby (eds.), *The Adapted Mind: Evolutionary Psychology and the Generation of Culture*. Oxford: Oxford University Press. 163–228.

Dunbar, R. (2000). On the origin of the human mind. In P. Carruthers & P. Chamberlain (eds.), *Evolution and the Human Mind: Modularity, Language and Meta-Cognition*. Cambridge: Cambridge University Press.

Farah, M. (1990). *Visual Agnosia*. Cambridge, MA: MIT Press.

Fodor, J. (1983). *The Modularity of Mind*. Cambridge, MA: MIT Press.

Frank, R. (1988). *Passions Within Reason*. New York: W.W. Norton.

Frith, U. (1989). *Autism: Explaining the Enigma*. Oxford: Blackwell.

Gigerenzer, G. & Hug, K. (1992). Domain-specific reasoning: Social contracts, cheating and perspective change. *Cognition*, 43, 127–171.

Goodwin, D. & Guze, S. (1995). *Psychiatric Diagnosis*, 5th ed. New York: Oxford University Press.

Gopnik, M. (1990a). Dysphasia in an extended family. *Nature*, 344, 715.

Gopnik, M. (1990b). Feature blindness: A case study. *Language Acquisition*, 1, 139–164.

Gopnik, M. & Crago, M. (1991). Familial aggregation of a developmental language disorder. *Cognition*, 39, 1–50.

Gottlib, I. (1992) Interpersonal and cognitive aspects of depression. *Current Directions in Psychological Science*, 1, 149–154.

Grandin, T. & Scariano, M. (1986). *Emergence Labelled Autistic*. Tunbridge Wells: Costello.

Griffiths, P. (1997). *What Emotions Really Are*. Chicago: University of Chicago Press.

Hagen, E. (1998). The functions of postpartum depression and the implications for general depression. Paper presented at the Tenth Annual Meeting of the Human Behavior and Evolution Society, Davis, CA, July 8–12, 1998

Hagen, E. (Undated MS). The functions of postpartum depression.

Hempel, C. (1965). Fundamentals of taxonomy. In C. Hempel, *Aspects of Scientific Explanation*. New York: The Free Press.

Hull, D. (1989). On human nature. In D. Hull, *The Metaphysics of Evolution*. Albany: SUNY Press.

Karmiloff-Smith, A., Klima, E., Bellugi, U., Grant, J. et al. (1995). Is there a social module? Language, face processing, and theory of mind in individuals with Williams syndrome. *Journal of Cognitive Neuroscience*, 7, 2, 196–208.

Kessler, R., McGonagle, K., Zhao, S., Nelson, C., Hughes, M., Eshleman., W. & Kendler, K. (1994). Lifetime and 12-month prevalence of DSM-III-R psychiatric disorder in the United States. *Archives of General Psychiatry*, 51, 8–19.

Leslie, A. (1987). Pretense and representation: The origins of "theory of mind." *Psychological Review*, 94, 412–426.

Leslie, A. (1991). The theory of mind impairment in autism: evidence for a modular mechanism of development? In A. Whiten (ed.) *Natural Theories of Mind*. Oxford: Blackwell.

Leslie, A. & Thaiss, L. (1992). Domain specificity in cognitive development; neuropsychological evidence from autism. *Cognition*, 43, 225–251.

Marks, I.M. & Nesse, R.M. (1994). Fear and fitness: An evolutionary analysis of anxiety disorders. *Ethology and Sociobiology*, 15, 247–261.

Mayr, E. (1976). Cause and effect in biology. In E. Mayr, *Evolution and the Diversity of Life: Selected Essays*. Cambridge, MA: Harvard University Press.

Mayr, E. (1982). *The Growth of Biological Thought*. Cambridge, MA; Harvard University Press.

McCarthy, L. & Gerring, J. (1994). Revising psychiatry's charter document DSM-IV. *Written Communication*, 11, 147–192.

McGuire, M., Fawzy, F., Spar, J., Weigel, R. & Troisi, A. (1994). Altruism and mental disorders. *Ethology and Sociobiology*, 15, 299–321.

McGuire, M. & Troisi, A. (1998). *Darwinian Psychiatry*. New York: Oxford University Press.

Mealey, L (1995). The sociobiology of sociopathy; an integrated evolutionary model (with commentary). *Behavioral and Brain Sciences*, 18, 523–599.

Millikan, R. (1993). *White Queen Psychology and Other Essays for Alice*. Cambridge, MA: MIT Press.

Mineka, S., Keir, R. & Price, V. (1980). Fear of snakes in wild and laboratory-reared rhesus monkeys. *Animal Learning and Behavior*, 8, 653–663.

Mineka, S., Davidson, M., Cook, M. & Keir, R. (1984). Observational conditioning of snake fear in rhesus monkeys. *Journal of Abnormal Psychology*, 93, 355–372.

Mineka, S. & Tomarken, A. (1989). The role of cognitive biases in the origins and maintenance of fear and anxiety disorders. In L. Nilsson & T. Archer (eds.), *Aversion, Avoidance, and Anxiety: Perspectives on Aversely Motivated Behavior*. Hillsdale, NJ: Erlbaum.

Neander, K. (1991). Functions as selected effects; the conceptual analysts defense. *Philosophy of Science*, 58, 168–184.

Nesse, R.M. & Williams, G.C. (1995). *Why We Get Sick*. New York: Times Books.

Poland, J., Von Eckardt, B. & Spaulding, W. (1994). Problems with the DSM approach to classifying psychopathology. In G. Graham & G.L. Stephens (eds.), *Philosophical Psychopathology*. Cambridge, MA: MIT Press.

Price, J., Sloman, L., Gardner, R., Gilbert, P. & Rohde, P. (1994). The Social Competition Hypothesis of Depression. *British Journal of Psychiatry*, 164, 309–315

Pyszczynski, T. & Greenberg J. (1987). Self-regulatory perseveration and the depressive self-focussing style: a self-awareness theory of reactive depression. *Psychological Bulletin*, 102, 122–138.

Regard, M. & Landis, T. (1997). "'Gourmand Syndrome': Eating passion associated with right anterior lesions." *Neurology*, May 1997.

Sacks, O. (1995). *An Anthropologist on Mars: Seven Paradoxical Tales*. New York: Knopf.

Samuels, R. (1998). Evolutionary Psychology and the Massive Modularity Hypothesis. *British Journal for the Philosophy of Science*, 49, 575–602.

Samuels, R. (2000). Massively modular minds: the evolutionary psychological account of cognitive architecture. In P. Carruthers & P. Chamberlain (eds.), *Evolution and the Human Mind: Modularity, Language and Meta-Cognition*. Cambridge: Cambridge University Press.

Segal, G. (1996). The modularity of theory of mind. In P. Carruthers & P. Smith (eds.), *Theories of Theories of Mind*. Cambridge: Cambridge University Press.

Skyrms, B. (1996). *Evolution of the Social Contract*. Cambridge: Cambridge University Press.

Stevens, A. & Price, J. (1996). *Evolutionary Psychiatry: A New Beginning*. London: Routledge.

Stone, T. & Young A. (1997). Delusions & brain injury: The philosophy and psychology of belief. *Mind and Language*, 12, 327–64.

Tooby, J. & Cosmides, L. (1990a). On the universality of human nature and the uniqueness of the individual: The role of genetics and adaptation. *Journal of Personality*, 58, 17–67.

Tooby, J. & Cosmides, L. (1990b). The past explains the present: Emotional adaptations and the structure of ancestral environments. *Ethology and Sociobiology*, 11, 375–424.

Tooby, J. & Cosmides, L. (1992). The psychological foundations of culture. In J. Barkow, L. Cosmides, & J. Tooby (eds.), *The Adapted Mind: Evolutionary Psychology and the Generation of Culture*. Oxford: Oxford University Press. 19–136.

Tooby, J. & Cosmides, L. (1995). Foreword. In Baron-Cohen (1995), xi–xviii.

Trivers, R. (1971). The evolution of reciprocal altruism. *Quarterly Review of Biology*, 46, 35–57.

Wakefield, J. (1997). Diagnosing DSM IV, part 1: DSM and the concept of disorder. *Behavior Research and Therapy*, 35, 633–49.

Watson, P. & Andrews, P. (1998). An evolutionary theory of major depression. Paper presented at the Tenth Annual Meeting of the Human Behavior and Evolution Society, Davis, CA, July 8–12, 1988

Wilson, D. (1994). Adaptive genetic variation and human evolutionary psychology. *Ethology and Sociobiology*, 15, 219–235.

Woolfolk, R., Novalany, J., Gara, M., Allen, L. & Polino, M. (1995). Self-complexity, self evaluation and depression: An examination of form and content within the self-schema. *Journal of Personality and Social Psychology*, 68, 1108–1120.

15

FOLK PSYCHOLOGY

Stephen Stich and Shaun Nichols

1 Why Does Folk Psychology Play an Important Role in the Philosophy of Mind?

To appreciate philosophers' fascination with folk psychology, it will be useful to begin with a brief reminder about the two most important questions in the philosophy of mind, and the problems engendered by what was for centuries the most influential answer to one of those questions. The questions are the mind–body problem, which asks how mental phenomena are related to physical phenomena, and the problem of other minds, which asks how we can know about the mental states of other people. On Descartes's proposed solution to the mind–body problem, there are two quite different sorts of substance in the universe: physical substance, which is located in space and time, and mental substance, which is located in time but not in space. Mental phenomena, according to Descartes, are events or states occurring in a mental substance, while physical phenomena are events or states occurring in a physical substance. Descartes insisted that there is two-way causal interaction between the mental and the physical, though many philosophers find it puzzling how the two could interact if one is in space and the other isn't. Another problem with the Cartesian view is that it seems to make the other minds problem quite intractable. If, as Descartes believed, I am the only person who can experience my mental states, then there seems to be no way for you to rule out the hypothesis that I am a mindless zombie—a physical body that merely behaves as though it was causally linked to a mind.

In the middle of the twentieth century the verificationist account of meaning had a major impact on philosophical thought. According to the verificationists, the meaning of an empirical claim is closely linked to the observations that would verify the claim. Influenced by verificationism, philosophical behaviorists argued that the Cartesian account of the mind as the "ghost in the machine" (to use Ryle's (1949) memorable image) was profoundly mistaken. If ordinary mental state terms such as "belief," "desire," and "pain" are to be meaningful, they argued, they can't refer to unobservable events taking place inside a person (or, worse still, not located in space at all). Rather, the meaning of sentences invoking these terms must be analyzed in terms of conditional sentences specifying how someone would behave under various circumstances. So, for example, a philosophical behaviorist might suggest that the meaning of

(1) John believes that snow is white

could be captured by something like the following:

(2) If you ask John, "Is snow white?" he will respond affirmatively.

Perhaps the most serious difficulty for philosophical behaviorists was that their meaning analyses typically turned out to be either obviously mistaken or circular—invoking one mental term in the analysis of another. So, for example, contrary to (2), even though John believes that snow is white, he may not respond affirmatively unless he is paying *attention*, *wants* to let you know what he thinks, *believes* that this can be done by responding affirmatively, etc.

While philosophical behaviorists were gradually becoming convinced that there is no way around this circularity problem, a very similar problem was confronting philosophers seeking verificationist accounts of the meaning of scientific terms. Verificationism requires that the meaning of a theoretical term must be specifiable in terms of observables. But when philosophers actually tried to provide such definitions, they always seemed to require additional theoretical terms (Hempel 1964). The reaction to this problem in the philosophy of science was to explore a quite different account of how theoretical terms get their meaning. Rather than being defined exclusively in terms of observables, this new account proposed, a cluster of theoretical terms might get their meaning collectively by being embedded within an empirical theory. The meaning of any given theoretical term lies in its theory-specified interconnections with other terms, *both observational and theoretical*. Perhaps the most influential statement of this view is to be found in the work of David Lewis (1970, 1972). According to Lewis, the meaning of theoretical terms is given by what he calls a "functional definition." Theoretical entities are "defined as the occupants of the causal roles *specified by the theory* . . . ; as *the* entities, whatever those may be, that bear certain causal relations *to one another* and to the referents of the O[bservational]-terms" (1972: 211; first and last emphases added).

Building on an idea first suggested by Wilfrid Sellars (1956), Lewis went on to propose that ordinary terms for mental or psychological states could get their meaning in an entirely analogous way. If we "think of commonsense psychology as a term-introducing scientific theory, though one invented before there was any such institution as professional science," then the "functional definition" account of the meaning of theoretical terms in science can be applied straightforwardly to the mental state terms used in common-sense psychology (Lewis 1972: 212). And this, Lewis proposed, is the right way to think about common-sense psychology:

> Imagine our ancestors first speaking only of external things, stimuli, and responses . . . until some genius invented the theory of mental states, with its newly introduced T[heoretical] terms, to explain the regularities among stimuli and responses. But that did not happen. Our commonsense psychology was never a newly invented term-introducing scientific theory—not even of prehistoric folk-science. The story that mental terms were introduced as theoretical terms is a myth.
>
> It is, in fact, Sellars' myth. . . . And though it is a myth, it may be a good myth or a bad one. It is a good myth if our names of mental states do in fact mean just what they would mean if the myth were true. I adopt the working hypothesis that it is a good myth. (Ibid.: 212–13)

In the three decades since Lewis and others[1] developed this account, it has become the most widely accepted view about the meaning of mental state terms. Since the account maintains that the meanings of mental state terms are given by functional definitions, the view is often known as *functionalism*.[2] We can now see one reason why philosophers of mind have been concerned to understand the exact nature of common-sense (or folk) psychology. According to functionalism, *folk psychology is the theory that gives ordinary mental state terms their meaning.*

A second reason for philosophers' preoccupation with folk psychology can be explained more quickly. The crucial point is that, according to accounts such as Lewis's, folk psychology is an *empirical* theory which is supposed to explain "the regularity between stimuli and responses" to be found in human (and perhaps animal) behavior. And, of course, if common-sense psychology is an empirical theory, it is possible that, like any empirical theory, it might turn out to be *mistaken*. We might discover that the states and processes intervening between stimuli and responses are not well described by the folk theory that fixes the meaning of mental state terms. The possibility that

---

1. Though we will focus on Lewis's influential exposition, many other philosophers developed similar views, including Putnam (1960), Fodor and Chihara (1965), and Armstrong (1968).
2. Though beware. In the philosophy of mind, the term "functionalism" has been used for a variety of views. Some of them bear a clear family resemblance to the one we've just sketched, while others do not. For good overviews, see Lycan (1994) and Block (1994).

common-sense psychology *might* turn out to be mistaken is granted by just about every-one who takes functionalism seriously. However, for the last several decades a number of prominent philosophers of mind have been arguing that this is more than a *mere* possibility. Rather, they maintain, a growing body of theory and empirical findings in the cognitive and neurosciences strongly suggest that common-sense psychology *is* mistaken, and not just on small points. As Paul Churchland, an enthusiastic supporter of this view, puts it:

> FP [folk psychology] suffers explanatory failures on an epic scale . . . it has been stagnant for at least twenty-five centuries, and . . . its categories appear (so far) to be incommensurable with or orthogonal to the categories of the background physical sciences whose long term claim to explain human behavior seems undeniable. Any theory that meets this description must be allowed a serious candidate for outright elimination. (1981: 212)

Churchland does not stop at discarding (or "eliminating") folk psychological theory. He and other "eliminativists" have also suggested that because folk psychology is such a seriously defective theory, we should also conclude that the theoretical terms embedded in folk psychology don't really refer to anything. Beliefs, desires, and other posits of folk psychology, they argue, are entirely comparable to phlogiston, the ether, and other posits of empirical theories that turned out to be seriously mistaken; like phlogiston, the ether, and the rest, *they do not exist*. Obviously, these are enormously provocative claims. De-bating their plausibility has been high on the agenda of philosophers of mind ever since they were first suggested.[3] Since the eliminativists' central thesis is that folk psychology is a massively mistaken theory, philosophers of mind concerned to evaluate that thesis will obviously need a clear and accurate account of what folk psychology is and what it claims.

2   What is Folk Psychology? Two Possible Answers

Functionalists, as we have seen, maintain that the meaning of ordinary mental state terms is determined by the role they play in a common-sense psychological theory. But what, exactly, is this theory? In the philosophical and cognitive science literature there are two quite different approaches to this question.[4] For Lewis, and for many of those who have followed his lead, common-sense or folk psychology is closely tied to the claims about mental states that almost everyone would agree with and take to be obvious.

> Collect all the platitudes you can think of regarding the causal relations of mental states, sensory stimuli, and motor responses. . . . Add also the platitudes to the effect

---

3. For an overview of these debates, see Stich (1996: ch. 1).
4. The distinction was first noted in Stich and Ravenscroft (1994).

that one mental state falls under another—"toothache is a kind of pain" and the like. Perhaps there are platitudes of other forms as well. Include only platitudes that are common knowledge among us—everyone knows them, everyone knows that everyone else knows them, and so on. For the meanings of our words are common knowledge, and I am going to claim that *names of mental states derive their meaning from these platitudes.* (1972: 212; emphasis added)

So, on this approach, folk psychology is just a collection of platitudes, or perhaps, since that set of platitudes is bound to be large and ungainly, we might think of folk psychology as a set of generalizations that systematizes the platitudes in a perspicuous way. A systematization of that sort might also make it more natural to describe folk psychology as a theory. We'll call this the *platitude account* of folk psychology.

The second approach to answering the question focuses on a cluster of skills that have been of considerable interest to both philosophers and psychologists. In many cases people are remarkably good at *predicting* the behavior of other people. Asked to predict what a motorist will do as she approaches the red light, almost everyone says that she will stop, and fortunately our predictions are usually correct. We are also often remarkably good at *attributing* mental states to other people[5]—at saying what they perceive, think, believe, want, fear, and so on, and at *predicting* future mental states and *explaining* behavior in terms of past mental states.[6] In recent discussions, the whimsical label *mindreading* has often been used for this cluster of skills, and since the mid-1980s developmental and cognitive psychologists have generated a large literature aimed at exploring the emergence of mindreading and explaining the cognitive mechanisms that underlie it.

The most widely accepted view about the cognitive mechanisms underlying mindreading (and until the mid-1980s the *only* view) is that people have a rich body of mentally represented information about the mind, and that this information plays a central role in guiding the mental mechanisms that generate our attributions, predictions, and explanations. Some of the psychologists who defend this view maintain that the information exploited in mindreading has much the same structure as a scientific theory, and that it is acquired, stored, and used in much the same way that other common-sense and scientific theories are. These psychologists often refer to their view as *the theory theory* (Gopnik and Wellman 1994; Gopnik and Meltzoff 1997). Others argue that much of the information utilized in mindreading is innate and is stored in mental "modules" where it can only interact in very limited ways with the information stored in other components of the mind (Scholl and Leslie 1999). Since modularity theorists and theory theorists agree that

---

5. Though not always, as we'll see in section 10.4.

6. Eliminativists, of course, would not agree that we do a good job at attributing and predicting mental states or at explaining behavior in terms of past mental states, since they maintain that the mental states we are attributing do not exist. But they would not deny that there is an impressive degree of *agreement* in what people say about other people's mental states, and that that agreement needs to be explained.

mindreading depends on a rich body of information about how the mind works, we'll use the term *information-rich theories* as a label for both of them. These theories suggest another way to specify the theory that (if functionalists are right) fixes the meaning of mental state terms—it is the theory (or body of information) that underlies mindreading. We'll call this the *mindreading account* of folk psychology.

Let's ask, now, how the platitude account of folk psychology and the mindreading account are related. How is the mentally represented information about the mind posited by information-rich theories of mindreading related to the collection of platitudes which, according to Lewis, determines the meaning of mental state terms? One possibility is that the platitudes (or some systematization of them) is near enough *identical* with the information that guides mindreading—that mindreading invokes little or no information about the mind beyond the common-sense information that everyone can readily agree to. If this were true, then the platitude account of folk psychology and the mindreading account would converge. But, along with most cognitive scientists who have studied mindreading, we believe that this convergence is *very* unlikely. One reason for our skepticism is the comparison with other complex skills that cognitive scientists have explored. In just about every case, from face recognition (Young 1998) to decision-making (Gigerenzer et al. 1999) to common-sense physics (McCloskey 1983; Hayes 1985), it has been found that the mind uses information and principles that are simply not accessible to introspection. In these areas our minds use a great deal of information that people cannot recognize or assent to in the way that one is supposed to recognize and assent to Lewisian platitudes. A second reason for our skepticism is that in many mindreading tasks people appear to attribute mental states on the basis of cues that they are not aware they are using. For example, Ekman has shown that there is a wide range of "deception cues" that lead us to believe that a target does not believe what he is saying. These include "a change in the expression on the face, a movement of the body, an inflection to the voice, a swallowing in the throat, a very deep or shallow breath, long pauses between words, a slip of the tongue, a micro facial expression, a gestural slip" (1985: 43). In most cases, people are quite unaware of the fact that they are using these cues. So, while there is still much to be learned about mental mechanisms underlying mindreading, we think it is very likely that the information about the mind that those mechanisms exploit is substantially richer than the information contained in Lewisian platitudes.

If we are right about this, then those who think that the functionalist account of the meaning of ordinary mental state terms is on the right track will have to confront a quite crucial question: which account of folk psychology picks out the theory that actually determines the meaning of mental state terms? Is the meaning of these terms fixed by the theory we can articulate by collecting and systematizing platitudes, or is it fixed by the much richer theory that we can discover only by studying the sort of information exploited by the mechanisms underlying mindreading?

We don't think there is any really definitive answer to this question. It would, of course, be enormously useful if there were a well-motivated and widely accepted general theory of meaning to which we might appeal. But, notoriously, there is no such theory. Meaning is a topic on which disagreements abound even about the most fundamental questions, and there are many philosophers who think that the entire functionalist approach to specifying the meaning of mental state terms is utterly wrongheaded.[7] Having said all this, however, we are inclined to think that those who are sympathetic to the functionalist approach should prefer the mindreading account of folk psychology over the platitude account. For on the mindreading account, folk psychology is the theory that people actually use in recognizing and attributing mental states, in drawing inferences about mental states, and in generating predictions and explanations on the basis of mental state attributions. It is hard to see why someone who thinks, as functionalists do, that mental state terms get their meaning by being embedded in a theory would want to focus on the platitude-based theory whose principles people can easily acknowledge, rather than the richer theory that is actually guiding people when they think and talk about the mind.

3 The Challenge from Simulation Theory

Let's take a moment to take stock of where we are. In section 1 we explained why folk psychology has played such an important role in recent philosophy of mind: functionalists maintain that folk psychology is the theory that implicitly defines ordinary mental state terms, and eliminativists (who typically agree with functionalists about the meaning of mental state terms) argue that folk psychology is a seriously mistaken theory, and that both the theory and the mental states that it posits should be rejected. In section 2 we distinguished two different accounts of folk psychology, and we argued, albeit tentatively, that functionalists should prefer the mindreading account on which folk psychology is the rich body of information or theory that underlies people's skill in attributing mental states and in predicting and explaining behavior. In this section, we turn our attention to an important new challenge that has emerged to all of this. Since the mid-1980s a number of philosophers and psychologists have been arguing that it is a mistake to think that mindreading invokes a rich body of information about the mind. Rather, they maintain, mindreading can be explained as a kind of *mental simulation* that requires little or no information about how the mind works (Gordon 1986; Heal 1986; Goldman 1989; Harris 1992) If these simulation theorists are right, and if we accept the mindreading account of folk psychology, then *there is no such thing as folk psychology*. That would be bad news for functionalists. It would also be bad news for eliminativists, since if there is no such thing as folk psychology, then their core argument—which claims that folk psychology is a seriously mistaken theory—has gone seriously amiss.

---

7. See, for example, Fodor and LePore (1992). For a useful overview of many of the disputes about the theory of meaning, see Devitt (1996).

How could it be that the mental mechanisms underlying mindreading do not require a rich body of information? Simulation theorists often begin their answer by using an analogy. Suppose you want to predict how a particular airplane will behave in certain wind conditions. One way to proceed would be to derive a prediction from aeronautical theory along with a detailed description of the plane. Another, quite different, strategy would be to build a model of the plane, put it in a wind tunnel that reproduces those wind conditions, and then simply observe how the model behaves. The second strategy, unlike the first, does not require a rich body of theory. Simulation theorists maintain that something like this second strategy can be used to explain people's mindreading skills. For if you are trying to predict what another person's mind will do, and if that person's mind is similar to yours, then you might be able to use components of your own mind as models of the similar components in the mind of the other person (whom we'll call the "target").

Here is a quick sketch of how the process might work. Suppose that you want to predict what the target will decide to do about some important matter. The target's mind, we'll assume, will make the decision by utilizing a decision-making or "practical reasoning" system which takes his relevant beliefs and desires as input and (somehow or other) comes up with a decision about what to do. The lighter lines in figure 1 are a sketch of the sort of cognitive architecture that might underlie the normal process of decision-making. Now suppose that your mind can momentarily take your decision making system "off-line" so that you do not actually act on the decisions that it produces. Suppose further that in this off-line mode your mind can provide, your decision-making system with some hypothetical or "pretend" beliefs and desires—beliefs and desires that you may not actually have but that the target does. Your mind could then simply sit back and let your decision-making system generate a decision. If your decision-making system is similar to the target's, and if the hypothetical beliefs and desires that you've fed into the off-line system are close to the ones that the target has, then the decision that your decision-making system generates will be similar or identical to the one that the target's decision-making system will produce. If that off-line decision is now sent on to the part of your mind that generates predictions about what other people will do, you will predict that that is the decision the target will make, and there is a good chance that your prediction will be correct. All of this happens, according to simulation theorists, with little or no conscious awareness on your part. Moreover, and this of course is the crucial point, the process does not utilize any theory or rich body of information about how the decision-making system works. Rather, you have simply used your own decision-making system to *simulate* the decision that the target will actually make. The dark lines in figure 1 sketch the sort of cognitive architecture that might underlie this kind of simulation-based prediction.

The process we have just described takes the decision-making system off-line and uses simulation to predict decisions. But much the same sort of process might be used to take the inference mechanism or other components of the mind off-line, and thus to make predictions about other sorts of mental processes. Some of the more enthusiastic

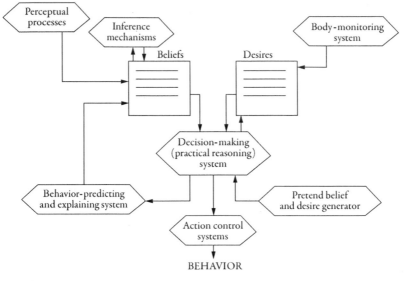

FIGURE I

defenders of simulation theory have suggested that *all* mindreading skills could be accomplished by something like this process of simulation, and thus that we need not suppose that folk psychological theory plays *any* important role in mindreading. If this is right, then both functionalism and eliminativism are in trouble.[8]

4 Three Accounts of Mindreading: Information-rich, Simulation-based, and Hybrid

Simulation theorists and advocates of information-rich accounts of mindreading offer competing empirical theories about the mental processes underlying mindreading,[9] and much of the literature on the topic has been cast as a winner-takes-all debate between

---

8. Robert Gordon is the most avid defender of the view that all mindreading skills can be explained by simulation. Here is a characteristic passage:

> It is . . . uncanny that folk psychology hasn't changed very much over the millennia. . . . Churchland thinks this a sign that folk psychology is a bad theory; but it could be a sign that it is no theory at all, not, at least, in the accepted sense of (roughly) a system of laws implicitly defining a set of terms. Instead, it might be just the capacity for practical reasoning, supplemented by a special use of a childish and primitive capacity for pretend play. (1986: 71)

> Of course, an eliminativist might object that the simulation theorist begs the question since the simulation account of decision prediction presupposes the existence of beliefs, desires and other posits of folk psychology, while eliminativists hold that these common-sense mental states do not exist. Constructing a plausible reply to this objection is left as an exercise for the reader.

9. Though Heal (1998) has argued that there is one interpretation of simulation theory on which it is true a priori. For a critique, see Nichols and Stich (1998).

these two groups.[10] In recent years, however, there has been a growing awareness that mindreading is a complex, multifaceted phenomenon and that some aspects of mind-reading might be subserved by information-poor simulation-like processes, while others are subserved by information-rich processes. This hybrid approach is one that we have advocated for a number of years (Stich and Nichols 1995; Nichols et al. 1996; Nichols and Stich, 2003), and in this section we will give a brief sketch of the case in favor of the hybrid approach.[11] We will begin by focusing on one important aspect of mindread-ing for which information-rich explanations are particularly implausible and a simula-tion-style account is very likely to be true. We will then take up two other aspects of mindreading where, we think, information-rich explanations are clearly to be preferred to simulation-based explanations.

4.1 INFERENCE PREDICTION: A MINDREADING SKILL SUBSERVED BY SIMULATION

One striking fact about the mindreading skills of normal adults is that we are remarkably good at predicting the inferences of targets, even their obviously *non-demonstrative* infer-ences. Suppose, for example, that Fred comes to believe that the President of the United States has resigned, after hearing a brief report on the radio. Who does Fred think will become President? We quickly generate the prediction that Fred thinks the Vice-President will become President. We know perfectly well, and so, we presume, does Fred, that there are lots of ways in which his inference could be mistaken. The Vice-President could be assassinated; the Vice-President might resign before being sworn in as Presi-dent; a scandal might lead to the removal of the Vice-President; there might be a coup. It is easy to generate stories on which the Vice-President would not become the new Presi-dent. Yet we predict Fred's non-demonstrative inference without hesitation. And in most cases like this, our predictions are correct. Any adequate theory of mindreading needs to accommodate these facts.

Advocates of information-rich approaches to mindreading have been notably silent about inference prediction. Indeed, so far as we have been able to determine, no leading advocate of that approach has even *tried* to offer an explanation of the fact that we are strikingly good at predicting the inferences that other people make. And we are inclined to think that the reason for this omission is pretty clear. For a thorough-going advocate of the information-rich approach, the only available explanation of our inference predic-tion skills is *more information*. If we are good at predicting how other people will reason, that must be because we have somehow acquired a remarkably good theory about how

---

10. Many of the important papers in this literature are collected in Davies and Stone (1995a, 1995b).

11. We have also argued that some important aspects of mindreading are subserved by processes that can't be comfortably categorized as either information-rich or simulation-like. But since space is limited, we will not try to make a case for that here. See Nichols and Stich (2003).

people reason. But that account seems rather profligate. To see why, consider the analogy between predicting inferences and predicting the grammatical intuitions of someone who speaks the same language that we do. To explain our success at this latter task, an advocate of the information-rich approach would have to say that we have a *theory* about the processes subserving grammatical intuition production in other people. But, as Harris (1992) pointed out, that seems rather far-fetched. A much simpler hypothesis is that we rely on *our own* mechanisms for generating linguistic intuitions, and having determined our own intuitions about a particular sentence, we attribute them to the target.

Harris's *argument from simplicity*, as we shall call it, played an important role in convincing us that a comprehensive theory of mindreading would have to invoke many different sorts of process, and that simulation processes would be among them. However, we don't think that the argument from simplicity is the only reason to prefer a simulation-based account of inference prediction over an information-rich account. Indeed, if the argument from simplicity were the only one available, a resolute defender of the information-rich approach might simply dig in her heels and note that the systems produced by Mother Nature are often far from simple. There are lots of examples of redundancy and apparently unnecessary complexity in biological systems. So, the information-rich theorist might argue, the mere fact that a theory-based account of inference prediction would be less simple than a simulation-style account is hardly a knock-down argument against it. There is, however, another sort of argument that can be mounted against an information-rich approach to inference prediction. We think it is a particularly important argument since it can be generalized to a number of other mindreading skills, and thus it can serve as a valuable heuristic in helping us to decide which aspects of mindreading are plausibly treated as simulation-based.

This second argument, which we will call the *argument from accuracy*, begins with the observation that inference prediction is remarkably accurate over a wide range of cases, including cases that are quite different from anything that most mindreaders are likely to have encountered before. There is, for example, a rich literature in the "heuristics and biases" tradition in cognitive social psychology chronicling the ways in which people make what appear to be very bad inferences on a wide range of problems requiring deductive and inductive reasoning.[12] In all of this literature, however, there is no suggestion that people are bad at *predicting* other people's inferences, whether those inferences are

---

12. Among the best known experiments of this kind are those illustrating the so-called *conjunction fallacy*. In one quite famous experiment, Kahneman and Tversky (1982) presented subjects with the following task.

Linda is 31 years old, single, outspoken, and very bright. She majored in philosophy. As a student, she was deeply concerned with issues of discrimination and social justice, and also participated in anti-nuclear demonstrations.
Please rank the following statements by their probability, using 1 for the most probable and 8 for the least probable.

good or bad. This contrasts sharply with the literature on desire-attribution that we discuss below, where it is often remarked how surprising and *un*predictable people's desires and decisions are. Although it hasn't been studied systematically, we think it is quite likely that people typically predict others will make just those bad inferences that they would make themselves, even on problems that are quite different from any they have encountered before. If that is indeed the case, it poses a problem for information-rich accounts: How do ordinary mindreaders manage to end up with such an *accurate* theory about how people draw inferences—a theory which supports correct predictions even about quite unfamiliar sorts of inferences? The problem is made more acute by the fact that there are other sorts of mindreading tasks on which people do very badly. Why do people acquire the right theory about inference and the *wrong* theory about other mental processes? A simulation-based account of inference prediction, by contrast, has a ready explanation of our accuracy. On the simulation account, we are using the same inference mechanism for both *making* and *predicting* inferences, so it is to be expected that we would predict that other people make the same inferences we do.

Obviously, the argument from accuracy is a two-edged sword. In those domains where we are particularly good at predicting or attributing mental states in unfamiliar cases, the argument suggests that the mindreading process is unlikely to be subserved by an information-rich process. But in those cases where we are *bad* at predicting or attributing mental states, the argument suggests that the process is unlikely to be subserved by a *simulation* process. We recognize that there are various moves that might be made in response to the argument from accuracy, and thus we do not treat the argument as definitive. We do, however, think that the argument justifies a strong initial presumption that accurate mindreading processes are subserved by simulation-like processes and that inaccurate

---

(a) Linda is a teacher in elementary school.
(b) Linda works in a bookstore and takes Yoga classes.
(c) Linda is active in the feminist movement.
(d) Linda is a psychiatric social worker.
(e) Linda is a member of the League of Women Voters.
(f) Linda is a bank teller.
(g) Linda is an insurance sales person.
(h) Linda is a bank teller and is active in the feminist movement.

In a group of naive subjects with no background in probability and statistics, 89 percent judged that statement (h) was more probable than statement (f) despite the obvious fact that one cannot be a *feminist* bank teller unless one is a *bank teller*. When the same question was presented to statistically sophisticated subjects— graduate students in the decision science program of the Stanford Business School—85 percent gave the same answer! Results of this sort, in which subjects judge that a compound event or state of affairs is more probable than one of the components of the compound, have been found repeatedly since Kahneman and Tversky's pioneering studies, and they are remarkably robust. For useful reviews of research in the heuristics and biases tradition, see Kahneman et al. (1982), Nisbett and Ross (1980), Baron (2001), and Samuels et al. (2003).

ones are not. And if this is right, then there is a strong presumption in favor of the hypothesis that inference prediction is simulation based.

4.2 DESIRE-ATTRIBUTION: A MINDREADING SKILL THAT CANNOT BE EXPLAINED BY SIMULATION

Another quite central aspect of mindreading is the capacity to attribute desires to other people. Without that capacity we would not know what other people want, and we would be severely impaired in trying to predict or explain their actions. There are a number of processes that can give rise to beliefs about a target's desires. In some cases we use information about the target's verbal and non-verbal behavior (including their facial expressions) to determine what they want. In other cases we attribute desires on the basis of what other people say about the target. And in all likelihood a variety of other cues and sources of data are also used in the desire-attribution process. It is our contention that these desire-attribution skills do not depend on simulation, but rather are subserved by information-rich processes. We have two quite different reasons for this claim.

First, desire-attribution exhibits a pattern of systematic inaccuracy and that supports at least an initial presumption that the process is not simulation-based. One very striking example comes from what is perhaps the most famous series of experiments in all of social psychology. Milgram (1963) had a "teacher" subject flip switches that were supposed to deliver shocks to another subject, the "learner" (who was actually an accomplice). For each mistake the learner made, the teacher was instructed to deliver progressively stronger shocks, including one labeled "Danger: Severe Shock" and culminating in a switch labeled "450-volt, XXX." If the teacher subject expressed reservations to the experimental assistant, he was calmly told to continue the experiment. The result of the experiment was astonishing. A clear majority of the subjects administered *all* the shocks. People often find these results hard to believe. Indeed, the Milgram findings are so counterintuitive that in a verbal re-enactment of the experiment, people still didn't predict the results (Bierbrauer 1973, discussed in Nisbett and Ross 1980: 121). One plausible interpretation of these findings is that in the Milgram experiment the instructions from the experimenter generated a desire to comply, which, in most cases, overwhelmed the subject's desire not to harm the person they believed to be on the receiving end of the electric shock apparatus. The fact that people find the results surprising and that Bierbrauer's subjects did not predict them indicates an important limitation in our capacity to determine the desires of others.

There is a large literature in cognitive social psychology detailing many other cases in which desires and preferences are affected in remarkable and unexpected ways by the circumstances subjects encounter and the environment in which they are embedded. The important point, for present purposes, is that people typically find these results surprising and occasionally quite unsettling, and the fact that they are surprised (even after seeing or getting a detailed description of the experimental situation) indicates that the mental mechanisms they are using to predict the subjects' desires and preferences are systematically inaccurate. Though this is not the place for an extended survey of the many examples in the literature, we cannot resist mentioning one of our favorites.[13]

Loewenstein and Adler (1995) looked at the ability of subjects to predict *their own* preferences when those preferences are influenced by a surprising and little-known effect. The effect that Loewenstein and Adler exploit is the *endowment effect*, a robust and rapidly appearing tendency for people to set a significantly higher value for an object if they actually own it than they would if they did not own it (Thaler 1980). Here is how Loewenstein and Adler describe the phenomenon:

> In the typical demonstration of the endowment effect . . . one group or subjects (sellers) are endowed with an object and are given the option of trading it for various amounts of cash; another group (choosers) are not given the object but are given a series of choices between getting the object or getting various amounts of cash. Although the objective wealth position of the two groups is identical, as are the choices they face, endowed subjects hold out for significantly more money than those who are not endowed. (1995: 929–30)

In an experiment designed to test whether "unendowed" subjects could predict the value they would set if they were actually to own the object in question, the experimenter first allowed subjects (who were members of a university class) to examine a mug engraved with the school logo. A form was then distributed to approximately half of the subjects, chosen at random, on which they were asked "to imagine that they possessed the mug on display and to predict whether they would be willing to exchange the mug for various amounts of money" (ibid.: 931). When the subjects who received the form had finished filling it out, *all* the subjects were presented with a mug and given a second form with instructions analogous to those on the prediction form. But on the second form it was made clear that they actually could exchange the mug for cash, and that the choices they made on this second form would determine how much money they might get. "Subjects were told that they would receive the option that they had circled on one of the lines— which line had been determined in advance by the experimenter" (ibid.). The results showed that subjects who had completed the first form substantially underpredicted the amount of money for which they would be willing to exchange the mug. In one group of subjects, the mean predicted exchange price was $3.73, while the mean actual exchange price for subjects (the *same* subjects who made the prediction) was $5.40. Moreover, there seemed to be an "anchoring effect" in this experiment which depressed the actual exchange price, since the mean actual exchange price for subjects who did not make a prediction about their own selling price was even higher, at $6.46. Here again we find

13. For an excellent review of the literature, see Ross and Nisbett (1991).

that people are systematically inaccurate at predicting the effect of the situation on desires, and in this case the desires they fail to predict are their own. If these desire predictions were subserved by a simulation process, it would be something of a mystery why the predictions are systematically inaccurate. But if, as we believe, they are subserved by an information-rich process, the inaccuracy can be readily explained. The theory or body of information that guides the prediction simply does not have accurate information about the rather surprising mental processes that give rise to these desires.

Our second reason for thinking that the mental mechanisms subserving desire-attribution use information-rich processes rather than simulation is that it is hard to see how the work done by these mechanisms *could* be accomplished by simulation. Indeed, so far as we know, simulation theorists have made only one proposal about how some of these desire detection tasks might be carried out, and it is singularly implausible. The proposal, endorsed by both Gordon (1986) and Goldman (1989), begins with the fact that simulation processes like the one sketched in figure 1 can be used to make behavior predictions, and goes on to suggest that they might also be used to generate beliefs about the desires and beliefs that give rise to observed behavior by exploiting something akin to the strategy of analysis-by-synthesis (originally developed by Halle and Stevens (1962) for phoneme recognition). In using the process in figure 1 to predict behavior, hypothetical or "pretend" beliefs and desires are fed into the mindreader's decision-making system (being used "off-line" of course), and the mindreader predicts that the target would do what the mindreader would decide to do, given those beliefs and desires. In an analysis-by-synthesis account of the generation of beliefs about desires and beliefs, the process is, in effect, run backwards. It starts with a behavioral episode that has already occurred and proceeds by trying to find hypothetical beliefs and desires which, when fed into the mindreader's decision mechanism, will produce a decision to perform the behavior we want to explain.

An obvious problem with this strategy is that it will generate too many candidates, since typically there are endlessly many possible sets of beliefs and desires that might lead the mindreader to decide to perform the behavior in question. Gordon is well aware of the problem, and he seems to think he has a solution:

> No matter how long I go on testing hypotheses, I will not have tried out all candidate explanations of the [target's] behavior. Perhaps some of the unexamined candidates would have done at least as well as the one I settle for, if I settle: perhaps indefinitely many of them would have. But these would be "far fetched," I say intuitively. Therein I exhibit my inertial bias. The less "fetching" (or "stretching," as actors say) I have to do to track the other's behavior the better. I tend to feign only when necessary, only when something in the other's behavior doesn't fit. . . . This inertial bias may be thought of as a "least effort" principle: the "principle of least pretending." It explains why other things being equal, I will prefer the less radical departure from the "real" world—i.e. from what I myself take to be the world. (Gordon 1986: 164)

Unfortunately, it is not at all clear what Gordon has in mind by an inertial bias against "fetching." The most obvious interpretation is that attributions are more "far-fetched" the further they are, on some intuitive scale, from one's own mental states. But if that's what Gordon intends, it seems clear that the suggestion won't work. For in many cases we explain behavior by appealing to desires or beliefs (or both) that are *very* far from our own. I might, for example, explain the cat chasing the mouse by appealing to the cat's desire to eat the mouse. But there are indefinitely many desires that would lead me to chase a mouse that are intuitively much closer to my actual desires than the desire to eat a mouse. Simulation theorists have offered no other proposal for narrowing down the endless set of candidate beliefs and desires that the analysis-by-synthesis strategy would generate, and without some plausible solution to this problem the strategy looks quite hopeless. So it is not surprising that accounts of this sort have largely disappeared from the simulation theory literature over the last decade. And that, perhaps, reflects at least a tacit acknowledgement, on the part of simulation theorists, that desire-attribution can only be explained by appealing to information rich processes.

4.3 DISCREPANT BELIEF-ATTRIBUTION: ANOTHER MINDREADING SKILL THAT CANNOT BE EXPLAINED BY SIMULATION

Yet another important aspect of mindreading is the capacity to attribute beliefs that we ourselves do not hold—*discrepant beliefs*, as they are sometimes called. There are a number of processes subserving discrepant belief-attribution, some relying on beliefs about the target's perceptual states, others exploiting information about the target's verbal behavior, and still others relying on information about the target's non-verbal behavior. All of these, we suspect, are subserved by information-rich mechanisms, rather than by a mechanism that uses simulation. Our reasons are largely parallel to the ones we offered for desire-attribution. First, there is abundant evidence that the discrepant belief-attribution system exhibits systematic inaccuracies of the sort we would expect from an information-rich system that is not quite rich enough and does not contain information about the process generating certain categories of discrepant beliefs. Second, there is no plausible way in which prototypical simulation mechanisms could do what the discrepant belief-attribution system does.

One disquieting example of a systematic failure in discrepant belief-attribution comes from the study of belief-perseverance. In the psychology laboratory, and in everyday life, it sometimes happens that people are presented with fairly persuasive evidence (e.g. test results) indicating that they have some hitherto unexpected trait. In light of that evidence people typically form the belief that they do have the trait. What will happen to that belief if, shortly after this, people are presented with a convincing case discrediting the first body of evidence? Suppose, for example, they are convinced that the test results they relied on were actually someone else's, or that no real test was conducted at all. Most people expect that the undermined belief will simply be discarded. And that view was

316 Collected Papers, Volume 1

shared by a generation of social psychologists who duped subjects into believing all sorts of things about themselves, often by administering rigged psychological tests, observed their reactions, and then "debriefed" the subjects by explaining the ruse. The assumption was that no enduring harm could be done because once the ruse was explained the induced belief would be discarded. But in a widely discussed series of experiments, Ross and his co-workers have demonstrated that this is simply not the case. Once a subject has been convinced that she has a trait, showing her that the evidence that convinced her was completely phony does not succeed in eliminating the belief (Nisbett and Ross 1980: 175–9). If the trait in question is being inclined to suicide, or being "latently homosexual," belief perseverance can lead to serious problems. The part of the discrepant belief-attribution system that led both psychologists and everyone else to expect that these discrepant beliefs would be discarded after debriefing apparently has inaccurate information about the process of belief-perseverance and thus it leads to systematically mistaken belief-attributions.

Another example, with important implications for public policy, is provided by the work of Loftus (1979) and others on the effect of "post-event interventions" on what people believe about events they have witnessed. In one experiment subjects were shown a film of an auto accident. A short time later they were asked a series of questions about the accident. For some subjects, one of the questions was: "How fast was the white sports car traveling when it passed the barn while traveling along the country road?" Other subjects were asked: "How fast was the white sports car traveling while traveling along the country road?" One week later all the subjects were asked whether they had seen a barn. Though there was no barn in the film that the subjects had seen, subjects who were asked the question that mentioned the barn were five times more likely to believe that they had seen one. In another experiment, conducted in train stations and other natural-istic settings, Loftus and her students staged a "robbery" in which a male confederate pulled an object from a bag that two female students had temporarily left unattended and stuffed it under his coat. A moment later, one of the women noticed that her bag had been tampered with and shouted, "Oh my God, my tape recorder is missing." She went on to lament that her boss had loaned it to her and that it was very expensive. Bystanders, most of whom were quite cooperative, were asked for their phone numbers in case an account of the incident was needed for insurance purposes. A week later, an "insurance agent" called the eyewitnesses and asked about details of the theft. Among the questions asked was "Did you see the tape recorder?" More than half of the eyewitnesses remem-bered having seen it, and nearly all of these could describe it in detail—this despite the fact that *there was no tape recorder*. On the basis of this and other experiments, Loftus concludes that even casual mention of objects that were not present or of events that did not take place (for example, in the course of police questioning) can significantly increase the likelihood that the objects or events will be incorporated into people's beliefs about what they observed. A central theme in Loftus's work is that the legal system should be much more cautious about relying on eyewitness testimony. And a major reason why the legal system is *not* as cautious is it should be is that our information-driven discrepant belief-attribution system lacks information about the post-event processes of belief-formation that Loftus has demonstrated.

As in the case of desire-attribution, we see no plausible way in which the work done by the mental mechanisms subserving discrepant belief-attribution *could* be accomplished by simulation. Here again, the only proposal that simulation theorists have offered is the analysis-by-synthesis account, and that strategy won't work any better for belief-attribution than it does for desire-attribution.

5 Conclusion

In the previous section we sketched some of the reasons for accepting a hybrid account of mindreading in which some aspects of that skill are explained by appeal to information-rich processes, while other aspects are explained by simulation. Though we only looked at a handful of mindreading skills, we have argued elsewhere (Nichols and Stich, 2003) that much the same pattern can be found more generally. Mindreading is a complex and multifaceted phenomenon, many facets of which are best explained by an information-rich approach, while many other facets are best explained by simulation. If this is correct, it presents both functionalists and eliminativists with some rather awkward choices. Functionalists, as we have seen, hold that the meaning of ordinary mental state terms is determined by folk psychology, and eliminativists typically agree. In section 2 we argued that functionalism is most plausible if folk psychology is taken to be the information-rich theory that subserves mindreading. But now it appears that only *parts* of mindreading rely on an information-rich theory. Should functionalists insist that the theory underlying these aspects of mindreading fixes the meaning of mental state terms, or should they retreat to the platitude account of folk psychology? We are inclined to think that whichever option functionalists adopt, their theory will be less attractive than it was before it became clear that the platitude approach and the mindreading approach would diverge, and that only part of mindreading relies on folk psychology.

REFERENCES

Armstrong, D. (1968). *A Materialist Theory of the Mind*. New York: Humanities Press.
Baron, J. (2001). *Thinking and Deciding*, 3rd edn. Cambridge: Cambridge University Press.
Bierbrauer, G. (1973). *Effect of Set, Perspective, and Temporal Factors in Attribution*, unpublished doctoral dissertation, Stanford University.
Block, N. (1994). "Functionalism," In S. Guttenplan (ed.), *A Companion to the Philosophy of Mind*. Oxford: Blackwell: 323–32.
Churchland, P. (1981). "Eliminative Materialism and Propositional Attitudes." Journal of Philosophy, 78: 67–90. Reprinted in W. Lycan (ed.), *Mind and Cognition*. Oxford: Blackwell (1990): 206–23. Page reference is to the Lycan volume.

Davies, M. and Stone, T. (1995a). *Folk Psychology*. Oxford; Blackwell.

Davies, M. and Stone, T. (1995b). *Mental Simulation*. Oxford: Blackwell.

Devitt, M. (1996). *Coming to Our Senses: A Naturalistic Program for Semantic Localism*. Cambridge: Cambridge University Press.

Ekman, P. (1985). *Telling Lies: Clues to Deceit in the Marketplace, Politics, and Marriage*. New York: W.W. Norton and Co.

Fodor, J. and Chihara, C. (1965). "Operationalism and Ordinary Language." *American philosophical Quarterly*, 2 (4). Reprinted in J. Fodor, *Representations*. Cambridge, MA: MIT Press (1981): 35–62.

Fodor, J. and LePore, E. (1992). *Holism: A Shopper's Guide*. Oxford: Blackwell.

Gigerenzer, G., Todd, P. and the ABC Research Group (1999). *Simple Heuristics that Make Us Smart*. Oxford: Oxford University Press.

Goldman, A. (1989). "Interpretation Psychologized." *Mind and Language*, 4: 161–85.

Gopnik, A. and Meltzoff, A. (1997). *Words, Thoughts and Theories*. Cambridge, MA: MIT Press.

Gopnik, A. and Wellman, H. (1994). "The Theory-Theory," In I. Hirschfeld and S.Gelman (eds.), *Mapping the Mind: Domain Specificity in Cognition and Culture*. New York: Cambridge University Press: 257–93.

Gordon, R. (1986). "Folk Psychology as Simulation." *Mind and Language*, 1: 158–70. Reprinted in Daivies and Stone (1995a). Page reference is to the Davies and Stone volume.

Halle, M. and Stevens, K. (1962). "Speech Recognition: A Model and a Program for Research." In J. Fodor and J. Katz (eds.), *The Structure of Language: Readings in the Philosophy of Language*. Englewood Cliffs, NJ: Prentice-Hall.

Harris, P. (1992). "From Simulation to Folk Psychology: The Case for Development." *Mind and Language*, 7: 120–44.

Hayes, P. (1985). "The Second Naive Physics Manifesto." In J. Hobbs and R. Moore (eds.), *Formal Theories of the Commensense World*. Norwood, NJ: Ablex: 1–36.

Heal, J. (1986), "Replication and Functioinalism." In J. Butterfield (ed.), *Language, Mind and Logic*. Cambridge: Cambridge University Press: 135–50.

—— (1998). "Co-cognition and Off-line Simulation: Two Ways of Understanding the Simulation Approach." *Mind and Language*, 13: 477–98.

Hempel, C. (1964), "The Theoretician's Dilemma; A Study in the Logic of Theory Construction." In C. Hempel, *Aspects of Scientific Explanation*. New York: The Free Press: 173–226.

Kahneman, D. and Tversky, A. (1982). "The Psychology of Preferences." *Scientific American*, 246(1): 160–73.

Kahneman, D., Slovic, P., and Tversky, A. (eds.) (1982). *Judgment Under Uncertainty: Heuristics and Biases*. Cambridge: Cambridge University Press.

Lewis, D. (1970). "How to Define Theoretical Terms." *Journal of Philosophy*, 67: 17–25.

—— (1972). "Psychophysical and Theoretical Identifications." *Australasian Journal of Philosophy*, 50: 249–58. Reprinted in N. Block (ed.), *Readings in the Philosophy of Psychology*. vol. 1. Cambridge, MA: Harvard University Press: 207–15. Page references are to the Block volume.

Loewenstein, G. and Adler, D. (1995). "A Bias in the Prediction of Tastes." *The Economic Journal: The Quarterly Journal of the Royal Economic Society*, 105: 929–37.

Loftus, E. (1979). *Eyewitness Testimony*. Cambridge, MA: Harvard University Press.

Lycan, W. (1994). "Functionalism." In S. Guttenplan (ed.), *A Companion to the Philosophy of*

Mind. Oxford: Blackwell: 317–23.

McCloskey, M. (1983). "Intuitive Physics." *Scientific American*, 248(4): 122–9.

Milgram, S. (1963). "Behavioral Study of Obedience." *Journal of Abnormal and Social Psychology*, 67: 371–8.

Nichols, S. and Stich, S. (1998). "Rethinking Co-cognitions: A Reply to Heal." *Mind and Language*, 13: 499–512.

—— (2003). Mindreading. Oxford: Oxford University Press.

Nichols, S., Stich, S., Leslie, A., and Klein, D. (1996). "Varieties of Off-line Simulation." In P. Carruthers and P. Smith (eds.), *Theories of Theories Mind*. Cambridge: Cambridge University Press: 39–74.

Nisbett, R. and Ross, L. (1980). *Human Inference*. Englewood Cliffs, NJ: Prentice-Hall.

Putnam, H. (1960). "Minds and Machines." In S. Hook (ed.), *Dimensions of Mind*. New York: New York University Press: 138–64.

Ross, L. and Nisbett, R. (1991). *The Person and the Situation: Perspectives of Social Psychology*. Philadelphia: Temple University Press.

Ryle, G, (1949). *The Concept of Mind*. London: Hutchinson.

Samuels, R., Stich, S., and Faucher, L. (2003). "Reasoning and Rationality." In L, Niiniluoto, M. Sintonen, and J. Wolenski (eds.), *Handbook of Epistemology*. Dordrecht: Kluwer: 1–50.

Scholl, B. and Leslie, A. (1999). "Modularity, Development, and 'Theory of Mind'." *Mind and Language*, 14: 131–53.

Sellars, W. (1956). "Empiricism and the Philosophy of Mind." In H. Feigl and M. Scriven (eds.), *The Foundations of Science and the Concepts of Psychology and Psychoanalysis: Minnesota Studies in the Philosophy of Science* vol. 1. Minneapolis: University of Minnesota Press: 253–329.

Stich, S. (1996). *Deconstructing the Mind*. Oxford: Oxford University Press.

Stich, S. and Nichols, S. (1995). "Second Thoughts on Simulation." *In Davies and Stone* (1995b): 86–108.

Stich, S. and Ravenscroft, I. (1994). "What *is* Folk Psychology?" *Cognition*, 50: 447–68. Reprinted in Stich (1996).

Thaler, R. (1980). "Toward a Positive Theory of Consumer Choice." *Journal of Economic Behavior and Organization*, 1: 39–60.

Young, A. (1998). *Face and Mind*. Oxford University Press.

SEMANTICS, CROSS-CULTURAL STYLE

Edouard Machery, Ron Mallon, Shaun Nichols, and Stephen Stich

1 Introduction

Theories of meaning and reference have been at the heart of analytic philosophy since the beginning of the twentieth century. Two views, *the descriptivist view of reference* and *the causal-historical view of reference*, have dominated the field. The reference of names has been a key issue in this controversy. Despite numerous disagreements, philosophers agree that theories of reference for names have to be consistent with our *intuitions* regarding who or what the names refer to. Thus, the common wisdom in philosophy is that Kripke (1972/1980) has refuted the traditional descriptivist theories of reference by producing some famous stories which elicit intuitions that are inconsistent with these theories. In light of recent work in cultural psychology (Nisbett, Peng, Choi, & Norenzayan, 2001; Weinberg, Nichols, & Stich, 2001), we came to suspect that the intuitions that guide theorizing in this domain might well differ between members of East Asian and Western cultures. In this paper, we present evidence that probes closely modeled on Kripke's stories elicit significantly different responses from East Asians (EAs) (Hong Kong undergraduates) and Westerners (Ws) (American undergraduates), and we discuss the significance of this finding for the philosophical pursuit of a theory of reference.

I.I TWO THEORIES OF REFERENCE

Theories of reference purport to explain how terms pick out their referents. When we focus on proper names, two main positions have been developed, *the descriptivist view of reference* (e.g. Frege, 1892/1948; Searle, 1958) and *the causal-historical view* associated with Kripke (1972/1980).

Two theses are common to all descriptivist accounts of the reference of proper names:[1]

D1. Competent speakers associate a *description* with every proper name. This description specifies a set of properties.

D2. An object is the referent of a proper name if and only if it *uniquely or best satisfies* the description associated with it. An object uniquely satisfies a description when the description is true of it and only it. If no object entirely satisfies the description, many philosophers claim that the proper name refers to the unique individual that satisfies most of the description (Lewis, 1970; Searle, 1958). If the description is not satisfied at all or if many individuals satisfy it, the name does not refer.

The causal-historical view offers a strikingly different picture (Kripke, 1972/1980):[2]

C1. A name is introduced into a linguistic community for the purpose of referring to an individual. It continues to refer to that individual as long as its uses are linked to the individual *via a causal chain* of successive users: every user of the name acquired it from another user, who acquired it in turn from someone else, and so on, up to the first user who introduced the name to refer to a specific individual.

C2. Speakers may associate descriptions with names. After a name is introduced, the associated description *does not play any role* in the fixation of the referent. The referent may *entirely* fail to satisfy the description.

1.2 THE GÖDEL CASE AND THE JONAH CASE

There is widespread agreement among philosophers on the methodology for developing an adequate theory of reference. The project is to construct theories of reference that are consistent with our intuitions about the correct application of terms in fictional (and non-fictional) situations.[3] Indeed, Kripke's masterstroke was to propose some cases that elicited widely shared intuitions that were inconsistent with traditional descriptivist theories. Moreover, it has turned out that almost all philosophers share the intuitions

1. There are a variety of ways of developing description–theoretic accounts (e.g. Frege, 1892/1948; Garcia-Carpintero, 2000; Jackson, 1998; Lewis, 1970; Loar, 1976; Searle, 1958, 1983).

2. This picture has been refined in various ways (e.g. Devitt, 1981; Devitt & Sterelny, 1999; Salmon, 1986; Soames, 2001).

3. Philosophers typically assume that speakers know (perhaps implicitly) how the reference of proper names is picked out. The intuitive judgment of the speakers are supposed somehow to reflect that knowledge (Kripke, (1972/1980, pp. 42, 91; Segal, 2001).

elicited by Kripke's fictional cases, including most of his opponents. Even contemporary descriptivism allow that these intuitions have falsified traditional forms of descriptivism and try to accommodate them within their own sophisticated descriptivist frameworks (e.g. Evans, 1973, 1985; Jackson, 1998).

To make all of this a bit clearer we present two of Kripke's central cases in greater detail and describe the corresponding descriptivist[4] and causal-historical intuitions.

1.2.1 The Gödel Case (Kripke, 1972/1980, pp. 83–92)

Kripke imagines a case in which, because of some historical contingency, contemporary competent speakers associate with a proper name, "Gödel," a description that is entirely false of the original bearer of that name, person a. Instead, it is true of a different individual, person b. Descriptivism implies that the proper name refers to b because b satisfies the description. The descriptivist intuition is that someone who uses "Gödel" under these circumstances is speaking about b. According to the causal-historical view, however, the name refers to its original bearer, since contemporary speakers are historically related to him. The Kripkean intuition is that someone who uses "Gödel" under these circumstances is speaking about a. According to Kripke (and many other philosophers), our semantic intuitions support the causal-historical view:

> Suppose that Gödel was not in fact the author of [Gödel's] theorem. A man called 'Schmidt' (. . .) actually did the work in question. His friend Gödel somehow got hold of the manuscript and it was thereafter attributed to Gödel. On the [descriptivist] view in question, then, when our ordinary man uses the name 'Gödel,' he really means to refer to Schmidt, because Schmidt is the unique person satisfying the description 'the man who discovered the incompleteness of arithmetic.' (. . .) But it seems we are not. We simply are not. (Kripke, 1972/1980. pp. 83–84)

1.2.2 The Jonah Case (Kripke, 1972/1980, pp. 66–67)

Kripke imagines a case in which the description associated with a proper name, say "Jonah," is not satisfied at all. According to descriptivism, "Jonah" would then fail to have a referent. The descriptivist intuition is that someone who uses the name under these circumstances isn't speaking about any real individual.[5] On the contrary, on the causal-historical view, satisfying the description is not necessary for being the referent of a name.

---

4. We use "descriptivism" to refer to the simple, traditional versions of descriptivism, and not to its recent, sophisticated elaborations. We call intuitions that are compatible with the causal-historical theory and incompatible with the traditional versions of descriptivism *Kripkean intuitions*. In contrast, we call those that are compatible with the traditional descriptivist theories and incompatible with the casual-historical theory *descriptivist intuitions*.

5. Or that the statement "Jonah exists" is false (given that the name has no referent).

The Kripkean intuition is that someone can use the name to speak about the name's original bearer, whether or not the description is satisfied.[6] Again, our intuitions are supposed to support the causal-historical view:

> Suppose that someone says that no prophet ever was swallowed by a big fish or a whale. Does it follow, on that basis, that Jonah did not exist? There still seems to be the question whether the Biblical account is a legendary account of no person or a legendary account built on a real person. In the latter case, it's only natural to say that, though Jonah did exist, no one did the things commonly related to him. (Kripke, 1972/1980, p. 67)

1.3 CULTURAL VARIATION IN COGNITION AND INTUITIONS

Philosophers typically share the Kripkean intuitions and expect theories of reference to accommodate them. As we discuss more fully in Section 3, we suspect that most philosophers exploring the nature of reference assume that the Kripkean intuitions are universal. Suppose that semantic intuitions exhibit systematic differences between groups of individuals. This would raise questions about whose intuitions are going to count, putting in jeopardy philosophers' methodology.[7]

As researchers in history and anthropology have long maintained, one should be wary of simply assuming cultural universality without evidence. Recent work in cultural psychology has provided experimental results that underscore this cautionary note. In an important series of experiments, Richard Nisbett and his collaborators have found large and systematic differences between EAs and Ws on a number of basic cognitive processes including perception, attention and memory.[8] These groups also differ in the way they go about describing, predicting and explaining events, in the way they categorize objects and in the way they revise beliefs in the face of new arguments and evidence (for reviews, see Nisbett, 2003; Nisbett et al., 2001). This burgeoning literature in cultural psychology suggests that culture plays a dramatic role in shaping human cognition. Inspired by this research program, Weinberg et al. (2001) constructed a variety of probes modeled on thought experiments from the philosophical literature in epistemology. These thought experiments were designed to elicit intuitions about the appropriate application of epistemic concepts. Weinberg et al. found that there do indeed seem to be systematic cross-cultural differences in epistemic intuitions. In light of these findings on epistemic intuitions, we were curious to see whether there might also be cross-cultural differences in intuitions about reference.

---

6. Or that Jonah might have existed, whether or not the description is satisfied.

7. A few philosophers have acknowledged the possibility that there is variation in semantic intuitions (e.g. Dupré, 1993; Stich, 1990, 1996) but this possibility has not previously been investigated empirically.

8. The East Asian participants were Chinese, Japanese, and Korean.

We lack the space to offer a detailed account of the differences uncovered by Nisbett and his colleagues. But it is important to review briefly some of the findings that led to the studies we will report here. According to Nisbett and his colleagues, the differences between EAs and Ws "can be loosely grouped together under the heading of holistic vs. analytic thought." Holistic thought, which predominates among EAs, is characterized as "involving an orientation to the context or field as a whole, including attention to relationships between a focal object and the field, and a preference for explaining and predicting events on the basis of such relationships." Analytic thought, the prevailing pattern among Ws, is characterized as "involving detachment of the object from its context, a tendency to focus on attributes of the object in order to assign it to categories, and a preference for using rules about the categories to explain and predict the object's behavior" (Nisbett et al., 2001, p. 293).

One range of findings is particularly significant for our project. The cross-cultural work indicates that EAs are more inclined than Ws to make categorical judgments on the basis of similarity; Ws, on the other hand, are more disposed to focus on causation in describing the world and classifying things (Norenzayan, Smith, & Kim, 2002; Watanabe, 1998, 1999). This differential focus led us to hypothesize that there might be a related cross-cultural difference in semantic intuitions. On a description theory, the referent has to satisfy the description, but it need not be causally related to the use of the term. In contrast, on Kripke's causal-historical theory, the referent need not satisfy the associated description. Rather, it need only figure in the causal history (and in the causal explanation) of the speaker's current use of the word.

Given that Ws are more likely than EAs to make causation-based judgments, we predicted that when presented with Kripke-style thought experiments, *Ws would be more likely to respond in accordance with causal-historical accounts of reference, while EAs would be more likely to respond in accordance with descriptivist accounts of reference.*[9] To test this hypothesis, we assembled a range of intuition probes to explore whether such differences might be revealed. The probes were designed to parallel the Jonah case and the Gödel case.

2 Experiment

2.1 METHOD

2.1.1 Participants
Forty undergraduates at Rutgers University and 42 undergraduates from the University of Hong Kong participated. The University of Hong Kong is an English speaking

---

9. There is a common concern that the labels 'East Asian' and 'Western' are too rough to do justice to the enormous diversity of cultural groups such labels encompass. We are sympathetic to this concern. However, the crudeness of these groupings does nothing to undermine the experiment we present. On the contrary, if we find significant results using crude cultural groupings, there is reason to believe more nuanced classifications should yield even stronger results.

university in Hong Kong, and the participants were all fluent speakers of English. A standard demographics instrument was used to determine whether participants were Western or Chinese. Using this instrument, nine non-Western participants were excluded from the Rutgers sample, leaving a total of 31 Western participants from Rutgers (18 females, 13 males). One non-Chinese participant was excluded from the Hong Kong sample, leaving a total of 41 Chinese participants from Hong Kong (25 females, 16 males). One additional Hong Kong participant was excluded for failure to answer the demographic questions.

2.1.2 Materials and procedure

In a classroom setting, participants were presented with four probes counterbalanced for order. The probes were presented in English both in the USA and in Hong Kong. Two were modeled on Kripke's Gödel case, and two were modeled on Kripke's Jonah case. One probe modeled on Kripke's Gödel case and one probe modeled on Kripke's Jonah case used names that were familiar to the Chinese participants. One of the Gödel probes was closely modeled on Kripke's own example (see Appendix A for the other probes):

> Suppose that John has learned in college that Gödel is the man who proved an important mathematical theorem, called the incompleteness of arithmetic. John is quite good at mathematics and he can give an accurate statement of the incompleteness theorem, which he attributes to Gödel as the discoverer. But this is the only thing that he has heard about Gödel. Now suppose that Gödel was not the author of this theorem. A man called "Schmidt," whose body was found in Vienna under mysterious circumstances many years ago, actually did the work in question. His friend Gödel somehow got hold of the manuscript and claimed credit for the work, which was thereafter attributed to Gödel. Thus, he has been known as the man who proved the incompleteness of arithmetic. Most people who have heard the name "Gödel" are like John; the claim that Gödel discovered the incompleteness theorem is the only thing they have ever heard about Gödel. When John uses the name "Gödel," is he talking about:

> (A) the person who really discovered the incompleteness of arithmetic?

> or

> (B) the person who got hold of the manuscript and claimed credit for the work?

2.2 RESULTS AND DISCUSSION

2.2.1 Scoring

The scoring procedure was straightforward. Each question was scored binomially. An answer consonant with causal-historical accounts of reference (B) was given a score of 1; the other answer (A) was given a score of 0. The scores were then summed, so the

TABLE 1

Mean scores for experiment 1 (SD in parentheses)

	Score (SD)
Gödel cases	
Western participants	1.13 (0.88)
Chinese participants	0.63 (0.84)
Jonah cases	
Western participants	1.23 (0.96)
Chinese participants	1.32 (0.76)

cumulative score could range from 0 to 2. Means and standard deviation for summary scores are shown in Table 1.

An independent samples t-test yielded a significant difference between Chinese and Western participants on the Gödel cases ($t(70) = -2.55$, $P < 0.05$) (all tests two-tailed). The Westerners were more likely than the Chinese to give causal-historical responses. However, in the Jonah cases, there was no significant difference between Chinese and Western participants ($t(69) = 0.486$, n.s.). In light of the dichotomous nature of the underlying distributions, we also analyzed each Gödel case non-parametrically, and the results were largely the same. Western participants were more likely than Chinese participants to give causal-historical responses on both the Tsu Ch'ung Chih probe ($\chi^2(1, N = 72) = 3.886$, $P < 0.05$) and on the Gödel probe ($\chi^2(1, N = 72) = 6.023$, $P < 0.05$).[10]

Thus, we found that probes modeled on Kripke's Gödel case (including one that used Kripke's own words) elicit culturally variable intuitions. As we had predicted, Chinese participants tended to have descriptivist intuitions, while Westerners tended to have Kripkean ones. However, our prediction that the Westerners would be more likely than the Chinese to give causal-historical responses on the Jonah cases was not confirmed. There are a number of possible explanations for this. Setting out the Jonah cases precisely requires a lengthy presentation (see Appendix A), so it is possible that our probes were simply too long and complex to generate interpretable data. Another, more interesting possibility hinges on the fact that in the Jonah cases, the descriptivist response is that the speaker's term fails to refer. It might be that for pragmatic reasons, both the Westerners and the Chinese reject the uncharitable interpretation that the speaker is not talking about anyone.

---

10. It is worth noting that this result replicated an earlier pilot study in which we used two different cases modeled on Kripke's Gödel case. In the pilot study, we found that Western participants (at the College of Charleston, $N = 19$, $M = 1.42$, SD = 0.77) were more likely than Chinese participants (at Hong Kong University, $N = 32$, $M = 0.65$, SD = 0.75) to give causal-historical responses ($t(43) = -3.366$, $P < 0.01$, two-tailed). The results of the pilot study were also significant when analyzed non-parametrically.

3 The End of the Innocence

Our central prediction was that, given Westerners' greater tendency to make causation-based judgments, they would be more likely than the Chinese to have intuitions that fall in line with causal-historical accounts of reference. This prediction was borne out in our experiment. We found the predicted systematic cultural differences on one of the best known thought experiments in recent philosophy of language, Kripke's Gödel case. However, we have no illusions that our experiment is the final empirical word on the issue. Rather, our findings raise a number of salient questions for future research. For instance, we predicted that the Westerners would be more likely than the Chinese to have Kripkean intuitions *because they are more likely to make causation-based judgments*. Although our results are consistent with this hypothesis, they fail to support it directly. They do not establish unequivocally that the cultural difference results from a different emphasis on causation. In future work, it will be important to manipulate this variable more directly. Further, our experiment does not rule out various pragmatic explanations of the findings. Although we found the effect on multiple different versions of the Gödel case, the test question was very similar in all the cases. Perhaps the test question we used triggered different interpretations of the question in the two different groups. In addition, our focus in this paper has been on intuitions about proper names, since proper names have been at the center of debates about semantics. However, it will be important to examine whether intuitions about the reference of other sorts of terms, for example natural kind terms (see, e.g. Putnam, 1975), also exhibit systematic cross-cultural differences. We hope that future work will begin to address these questions.

Although there are many empirical questions left open by the experiment reported here, we think that the experiment already points to significant philosophical conclusions. As we noted above, we suspect that philosophers employing these thought experiments take their own intuitions regarding the referents of terms, and those of their philosophical colleagues, to be universal. But our cases were modeled on some of the most influential thought experiments in the philosophy of reference, and we elicited culturally variable intuitions. Thus, the evidence suggests that it is wrong for philosophers to assume a priori the universality of their own semantic intuitions. Indeed, the variation might be even more dramatic than we have suggested. While our focus has been on cultural differences, the data also reveal considerable intra-cultural variation. The high standard deviations in our experiment indicate that there is a great deal of variation in the semantic intuitions within both the Chinese and Western groups. This might reflect smaller intra-cultural groups that differ in their semantic intuitions. A more extreme but very live possibility is that the variability exists even at the individual level, so that a given individual might have causal-historical intuitions on some occasions and descriptivist intuitions on other occasions. If so, then the assumption of universality is just spectacularly misguided.

Perhaps, however, philosophers do not assume the universality of semantic intuitions. In that case, philosophers of language need to clarify their project. One possibility is that philosophers of language would claim to have no interest in unschooled, folk semantic intuitions, including the differing intuitions of various cultural groups. These philosophers might maintain that, since they aim to find the *correct* theory of reference for proper names, only *reflective* intuitions, i.e. intuitions that are informed by a cautious examination of the philosophical significance of the probes, are to be taken into consideration.

We find it *wildly* implausible that the semantic intuitions of the narrow cross-section of humanity who are Western academic philosophers are a more reliable indicator of the correct theory of reference (if there is such a thing, see Stich, 1996, Chap. 1) than the differing semantic intuitions of other cultural or linguistic groups. Indeed, given the intense training and selection that undergraduate and graduate students in philosophy have to go through, there is good reason to suspect that the alleged *reflective* intuitions may be *reinforced* intuitions. In the absence of a principled argument about why philosophers' intuitions are superior, this project smacks of narcissism in the extreme.

A more charitable interpretation of the work of philosophers of language is that it is a proto-scientific project modeled on the Chomskyan tradition in linguistics. Such a project would employ intuitions about reference to develop an empirically adequate account of the implicit theory that underlies ordinary uses of names. If this is the correct interpretation of the philosophical interest in the theory of reference, then our data are especially surprising, for there is little hint in philosophical discussions that names might work in different ways in different dialects of the same language or in different cultural groups who speak the same language. So, on this interpretation, our data indicate that philosophers must radically revise their methodology. Since the intuitions philosophers pronounce from their armchairs are likely to be a product of their own culture and their academic training, in order to determine the implicit theories that underlie the use of names across cultures, philosophers need to get out of their armchairs. And this is far from what philosophers have been doing for the last several decades.

Acknowledgements

We are grateful to Vivian Chu, Max Deutsch, Tim German, Chad Hansen, Ping Lau, Philippe Schlenker, and an anonymous referee for advice, discussion and helpful comments.

Appendix A

A.1 GÖDEL CASE

Ivy is a high-school student in Hong Kong. In her astronomy class she was taught that Tsu Ch'ung Chih was the man who first determined the precise time of the summer and winter solstices. But, like all her classmates, this is the only thing she has heard about Tsu

Ch'ung Chih. Now suppose that Tsu Ch'ung Chih did not really make this discovery. He stole it from an astronomer who died soon after making the discovery. But the theft remained entirely undetected and Tsu Ch'ung Chih became famous for the discovery of the precise times of the solstices. Many people are like Ivy; the claim that Tsu Ch'ung Chih determined the solstice times is the only thing they have heard about him. When Ivy uses the name "Tsu Ch'ung Chih," is she talking about:

(A) the person who really determined the solstice times?

or

(B) the person who stole the discovery of the solstice times?

A.2 JONAH CASES

In high-school, German students learn that Attila founded Germany in the second century A.D. They are taught that Attila was the king of a nomadic tribe that migrated from the east to settle in what would become Germany. Germans also believe that Attila was a merciless warrior and leader who expelled the Romans from Germany, and that after his victory against the Romans, Attila organized a large and prosperous kingdom.

Now suppose that none of this is true. No merciless warrior expelled the Romans from Germany, and Germany was not founded by a single individual. Actually, the facts are the following. In the fourth century A.D., a nobleman of low rank, called "Raditra," ruled a small and peaceful area in what today is Poland, several hundred miles from Germany. Raditra was a wise and gentle man who managed to preserve the peace in the small land he was ruling. For this reason, he quickly became the main character of many stories and legends. These stories were passed on from one generation of peasants to the next. But often when the story was passed on the peasants would embellish it, adding imaginary details and dropping some true facts to make the story more exciting. From a peaceful nobleman of low rank, Raditra was gradually transformed into a warrior fighting for his land. When the legend reached Germany, it told of a merciless warrior who was victorious against the Romans. By the eighth century A.D., the story told of an Eastern king who expelled the Romans and founded Germany. By that time, not a single true fact remained in the story.

Meanwhile, as the story was told and retold, the name "Raditra" was slowly altered: it was successively replaced by "Aditra," then by "Arritrak" in the sixth century, by "Arrita" and "Arrila" in the seventh and finally by "Attila." The story about the glorious life of Attila was written down in the eighth century by a scrupulous Catholic monk, from whom all our beliefs are derived. Of course, Germans know nothing about these real events. They believe a story about a merciless Eastern king who expelled the Romans and founded Germany.

When a contemporary German high-school student says "Attila was the king who drove the Romans from Germany," is he actually talking about the wise and gentle nobleman, Raditra, who is the original source of the Attila legend, or is he talking about a fictional person, someone who does not really exist?

(A) He is talking about Raditra.
(B) He is talking about a fictional person who does not really exist.

Lau Mei Ling is a high-school student in the Chinese city of Guangzhou. Like everyone who goes to high-school in Guangzhou, Mei Ling believes that Chan Wai Man was a Guangdong nobleman who had to take refuge in the wild mountains around Guangzhou in the eleventh century A.D., because Chan Wai Man was in love with the daughter of the ruthless Government Minister Lee, and the Minister did not approve. Everyone in Lau Mei Ling's high-school believes that Chan Wai Man had to live as a thief in the mountains around Guangzhou, and that he would often steal from the rich allies of the Minister Lee and distribute their goods to the poor peasants.

Now suppose that none of this is true. No Guangdong nobleman ever lived in the mountains around Guangzhou, stealing from the wealthy people to help the peasants. The real facts are the following. In one of the monasteries around Guangzhou, there was a helpful monk called "Leung Yiu Pang." Leung Yiu Pang was always ready to help the peasants around his monastery, providing food in the winter, giving medicine to the sick and helping the children. Because he was so kind, he quickly became the main character of many stories. These stories were passed on from one generation of peasants to the next. Over the years, the story changed slowly as the peasants would forget some elements of the story and add other elements. In one version, Leung Yiu Pang was described as a rebel fighting Minister Lee. Progressively the story came to describe the admirable deeds of a generous thief. By the late fourteenth century, the story was about a generous nobleman who was forced to live as a thief because of his love for the Minister's daughter. At length, not a single true fact remained in the story.

Meanwhile, the name "Leung Yiu Pang" was slowly altered: it was successively replaced by "Cheung Wai Pang" in the twelfth century, "Chung Wai Man" in the thirteenth, and finally by "Chan Wai Man." The story about the adventurous life of Chan Wai Man was written down in the fifteenth century by a scrupulous historian, from whom all our beliefs are derived. Of course, Mei Ling, her classmates and her parents know nothing about these real events. Mei Ling believes a story about a generous thief who was fighting against a mean minister.

When Mei Ling says "Chan Wai Man stole from the rich and gave to the poor," is she actually talking about the generous monk, Leung Yiu Pang, who is the original source of the legend about Chan Wai Man, or is she talking about a fictional person, someone who does not really exist?

(A) She is talking about the generous monk, Leung Yiu Pang.
(B) She is talking about a fictional person who does not really exist.

REFERENCES

Devitt, M. (1981). *Designation*. New York: Columbia University Press.

Devitt, M., & Sterelny, K. (1999). *Language and reality: an introduction to the philosophy of language* (2nd ed.). Cambridge, MA: MIT Press.

Dupré, J. (1993). *The disorder of things: metaphysical foundations of the disunity of science*. Cambridge, MA: Harvard University Press.

Evans, G. (1973). The causal theory of names. *Supplementary Proceedings of the Aristotelian Society*, 47, 187–208. Reprinted in Evans (1985) and Ludlow (1997).

Evans, G. (1985), *Collected papers*. Oxford: Oxford University Press.

Frege, G. (1892/1948). On sense and reference (M. Black, Trans.). *The Philosophical Review*, 57, 207–230. Reprinted in Ludlow (1997).

Garcia-Carpintero, M. (2000). A presuppositional account of reference fixing. *Journal of Philosophy*, 97(3), 109–147.

Jackson, K. (1998). Reference and description revisited. In J. Tomberlin (Ed.), *Language, mind, and ontology (12)* (pp. 201–218). *Philosophical perspectives*, Oxford: Blackwell.

Kripke, S. (1972–1980). *Naming and necessity*. Cambridge, MA: Harvard University Press.

Lewis, D. (1970). How to define theoretical terms. *Journal of Philosophy*, 67, 427–446.

Loar, B. (1976). The semantics of singular terms. *Philosophical Studies*, 30, 353–377.

Nisbett, R.E. (2003). *The geography of thought: how Asians and Westerners think differently. . . and why*. New York: Free Press.

Nisbett, R.E., Peng, K., Choi, I., & Norenzayan, A. (2001). Culture and systems of thought: holistic vs. analytic cognition. *Psychological Review*, 108, 291–310.

Norenzayan, A., Smith, E., & Kim, B. (2002). Cultural preferences for formal versus intuitive reasoning. *Cognitive Science*, 26, 653–684.

Putnam, H. (1975). The meaning of "meaning." In H. Putnam (Ed.), *Mind, language, and reality (2)*. *Philosophical papers*, New York: Cambridge University Press.

Salmon, N. (1986). *Frege's puzzle*. Cambridge, MA: MIT Press.

Searle, J. (1958). Proper names. *Mind*, 67, 166–173. Reprinted in Ludlow (1997).

Searle, J. (1983). *Intentionality: an essay in the philosophy of mind*. Cambridge: Cambridge University Press.

Segal, G. (2001). Two theories of names. *Mind and Language*, 16(5), 547–563.

Soames, S. (2001). *Beyond necessity: the unfinished semantic agenda of naming and necessity*. New York: Oxford University Press.

Stich, S. (1990). *The fragmentation of reason*. Cambridge, MA: MIT Press.

Stich, S. (1996). *Deconstructing the mind*. Oxford: Oxford University Press.

Watanabe, M. (1998). *Styles of reasoning in Japan and the United States: logic of education in two cultures*. Paper presented at the American Sociological Association annual meeting, San Francisco, CA.

Watanabe, M. (1999). *Styles of reasoning in Japan and the United States: logic of education in two cultures*. Unpublished PhD thesis, Columbia University, New York.

Weinberg, J., Nichols, S., & Stich, S. (2001). Normativity and epistemic intuitions. *Philosophical Topics*, 29(1&2), 429–459.

17

AGAINST ARGUMENTS FROM REFERENCE

Ron Mallon, Edouard Machery, Shaun Nichols, and Stephen Stich

INTEREST IN THEORIES of reference is not limited to the philosophy of language. In fact, assumptions about theories of reference figure crucially in nearly every corner of philosophy, including the philosophy of mind, the philosophy of science, the philosophy of race, and meta-ethics, and it is widely agreed that identifying a correct theory would have far-reaching philosophical implications. In what follows, we focus on arguments that derive philosophically significant conclusions from the assumption of one or another theory of reference—what we call 'arguments from reference.' We review a recent empirical challenge to the project of finding a correct theory of reference (Machery et al. 2004). At the core of that challenge are data that suggest strong variation in the intuitions used to find the correct theory of reference. We consider several ways that theorists of reference might accommodate this variation in intuitions about reference, and we show that arguments from reference are undermined on all of these options.

Here is how we proceed. In Section 1, we consider the structure of arguments from reference, and review a number of projects in several areas of philosophy that employ such arguments. Then, in Section 2, we show that while intuitions about reference are central in the philosophy of language for finding the correct theory of reference, the recent empirical work of Machery and colleagues suggests that intuitions about reference vary both within and across cultures. In Section 3, we take the variation suggested by this

We would like to thank Elizabeth Harman, Jonathan Weinberg, and Wayne Wu for helpful comments on previous drafts.

empirical work for granted and consider its implications for arguments from reference. We conclude that arguments from reference ought to be relinquished.

1 Arguments from Reference

Arguments from reference are common in projects throughout philosophy. These arguments can be analyzed into three stages. In the first, philosophers implicitly or explicitly adopt a substantive theory of the reference of a term *t* (or of a class of terms *T*, such as theoretical terms).[1] In the second stage, they claim that the reference of *t* or of members of *T* has some specific properties. For instance, in some arguments from reference, philosophers argue that the reference relation obtains or fails to obtain—that is, that *t* refers or fails to refer. Or, in other arguments from reference, they argue that the reference of *t* has changed. Finally, a philosophically significant conclusion is drawn. These conclusions include metaphysical conclusions—conclusions to the effect that the referent of *t* exists or does not exist (e.g. Stich 1983; Zack 1993)—and epistemological conclusions—conclusions about the nature of our knowledge about the referent of *t* (e.g. Boyd 1983, 1988; Kitcher 1993).

Where can we find such arguments from reference? Everywhere in philosophy, it would seem. We begin by reviewing how arguments from reference play a key role in the philosophy of mind, then we suggest they play a similarly important role in other areas including the philosophy of science, social theory, and metaethics.

1.1 THE PHILOSOPHY OF MIND: THE DEBATE
OVER ELIMINATIVE MATERIALISM

Eliminativists in the philosophy of mind (Churchland 1981; Stich 1983) defend the surprising claim that the propositional attitudes like beliefs and desires that figure in the explanations of behavior offered by folk psychology literally do not exist. Eliminativists argue that these propositional attitudes are posits of a folk theory of mind that is spectacularly false in light of the emerging sciences of the mind and brain. They conclude that the posits of this theory—beliefs and desires—don't exist.

Consider how this argument fits the three steps of the arguments from reference.

(Step 1) Assumption of a substantive theory of reference: Eliminativists propose that mental state terms like 'belief' and 'desire' are defined by their role in a folk theory, namely the folk theory of mind. They assume that if these terms have referents, they must be entities that satisfy (or come close to satisfying) the relevant definitions. That is, eliminativists assume some version of a descriptivist theory of reference for mental state terms

---

1. We use the term "substantive" to rule out deflationary accounts of reference such as those suggested by Field (1986, 1994) and Horwich (1990).

like 'belief' and 'desire.' While such theories may take a variety of forms, they typically agree on the following points:

D1. Competent speakers associate a description with a term *t*. This description specifies a set of properties.

D2. An object is the referent of *t* if and only if it uniquely or best satisfies the description associated with it.

In the absence of an entity that satisfies the description (or at least comes close), the term is empty.

(Step 2) Claim about reference: Eliminativists claim that the emerging scientific facts suggest that nothing satisfies the descriptions folk psychology associates with 'belief' and 'desire.' Thus, 'belief' and 'desire' do not refer.

(Step 3) Philosophically significant conclusion: Eliminativists conclude that, since 'belief' and 'desire' do not refer, beliefs and desires do not exist.

How does this eliminativist argument fare? As William Lycan (1988) has pointed out, the eliminativist conclusion follows from the falsity of folk psychology only on the assumption of some descriptivist theory of reference (in step 1).[2] But descriptivist theories of reference have been sharply contested by causal-historical theories of reference, such as those defended by Kripke (1972/1980) and Putnam (1975). Like descriptivist theories, causal-historical theories of reference may take a variety of forms. However, they typically agree on the following points:

C1. A term *t* is introduced into a linguistic community for the purpose of referring to a particular thing (e.g. a person or a property). The term continues to refer to that thing as long as its uses are linked to the thing via an appropriate causal chain of successive users: every user of the term acquired it from another user, who acquired it in turn from someone else, and so on, back to the first user who introduced the term.

C2. Speakers may associate descriptions with terms. But after the term is introduced, the associated description does not play any role in the fixation of the referent. The referent may entirely fail to satisfy the description.

If, like Lycan, one adopts some causal-historical theory of reference, the eliminativist conclusion does not follow. Here is how Lycan makes the point:

---

2. In this article, we take for granted that if 'belief' and 'desire' refer descriptively and if the folk theory of mind is massively erroneous, then beliefs and desires do not exist. However, it is worth noting that this inference has been contested. Bishop and Stich (1998) have argued that one needs an additional premise to get from the claim that 'belief' does not refer to the desired conclusion that beliefs do not exist. Moreover, they claim that it is not clear how any of the premises that might fill the gap could be defended. We argue that even if Bishop and Stich's (1998) challenge were met, arguments from reference *still* wouldn't work.

I am entirely willing to give up fairly large chunks of our commonsensical or platitudinous theory of belief or desire (or of almost anything else) and decide that we
were just wrong about a lot of things, without drawing the inference that we are no
longer talking about belief or desire. To put the matter crudely, I incline away from
Lewis's Carnapian and/or Rylean cluster theory of reference of theoretical terms,
and toward Putnam's (1975) causal-historical theory. (Lycan 1988, 31–32)

So, by assuming a different theory of reference than the eliminativist, Lycan draws the
opposite conclusion, viz. that beliefs and desires *do* exist.

Of course the simple descriptivist and causal-historical theories we sketch here do not
exhaust options for specifying a substantive theory of reference. But the moral we want
to draw is quite general: depending on the substantive theory of reference one assumes
about a term or a class of terms, one can draw different metaphysical conclusions.

1.2 OTHER ARGUMENTS FROM REFERENCE

Arguments from reference have played an important role in metaphysical debates in the
philosophy of mind, but their influence is much more widespread—reaching into almost
every corner of philosophy. In the remainder of this section, we note three other important debates that look to hang on arguments from reference.

Consider first the debate in the philosophy of science over scientific realism. Several
influential philosophers of science have defended the surprising claim that there is no
scientific progress, thereby denying a key component of scientific realism (e.g. Feyerabend 1962; Kuhn 1970). They assume that theoretical terms like 'mass' or 'energy' are
defined by their role in scientific theories. Because the role of these terms is fundamentally modified during scientific revolutions, such as Einstein's revolution in physics, these
philosophers of science conclude that the reference of theoretical terms changes during
scientific revolutions. They conclude that there is no scientific progress.

But this conclusion follows from claims about scientific change only on the assumption of some descriptivist theory of the reference of theoretical terms (in step 1). If the
causal-historical theory is the correct theory of the reference of theoretical terms (e.g.
Putnam 1975), the inference from scientific change to the non-existence of scientific
progress is blocked. Thus, Richard Boyd notes the crucial role causal-historical theories of reference have played in the defense of scientific realism against various stripes
of anti-realism:

The anti-realist consequences which Kuhn (and Hanson) derived from descriptiv-
ist conceptions led to the articulation by realists of alternative theories of reference.
Characteristically, these theories followed the lead of Kripke (. . . 1972) . . . and
Putnam (. . . 1975 . . .) . . . . Each of them advocated a "causal" theory of reference . . .
It is by now pretty well accepted that some departure from analytic descriptivism,

involving some causal elements, is a crucial component of a realist approach to scientific knowledge. (2002, sect 4.1)

While the moves and countermoves here can get very complex, the general point is quite simple: some important arguments regarding scientific realism and anti-realism are arguments from reference—they derive significant metaphysical and epistemological conclusions from a specific theory of reference.

Theories of reference have also played a key role in contemporary debates over the reality of race, with a number of theorists explicitly or implicitly adverting to such theories.[3] Like eliminativists about propositional attitudes, race skeptics argue that race does not exist by denying that there is anything that satisfies the beliefs ordinary people hold about race (e.g. Appiah 1995; Zack 1993). As Robin Andreasen (2000, S661ff) notes, however, this conclusion tacitly depends on the endorsement of some descriptivist theory of reference. Andreasen goes on to point out that other theories of reference, like causal-historical theories, allow that the referent of a term may not satisfy much of the description common sense associates with the term, and she uses this strategy to defend her own account of race against the challenge of the race-eliminativists. Again we see that different metaphysical conclusions depend crucially upon the particular assumptions made about the theory of reference.

Finally, consider an example of the role that theories of reference have played in recent ethical theorizing. Robert Merrihew Adams (1979) and Richard Boyd (1988) have proposed that our ethical knowledge is similar to our scientific knowledge in some key respects: our knowledge about the nature of the good is a posteriori, it can progress, and our commonsensical ethical beliefs might turn out to be prejudices. They derive these surprising conclusions from the extension of the causal-historical theory of reference from scientific terms to moral terms. If moral terms, for instance 'good,' refer in a causal-historical manner, then it is an empirical question what the referents of these moral terms, for instance, the property *good*, are. Thus, a significant epistemological position in ethics is derived from a specific theory about the reference of a class of terms—i.e., moral terms.

2 Semantics, Cross-Cultural Style

2.1 FINDING THE CORRECT THEORY OF REFERENCE: THE METHOD OF CASES

The arguments sketched in the previous section all hinge on what the correct theory of reference is. But how do we know which theory of reference is correct? Unfortunately, philosophers of language have rarely addressed this methodological issue explicitly. However, it is clear from the arguments for and against specific theories of reference that the

---

3. E.g. Andreasen 1998, 2000; Appiah 1996; Glasgow 2003; Kitcher 1999; Mills 1998; Zack 1993, 2002; for a critical discussion, see Mallon 2006.

correct theory of reference for a term (or for a class of terms such as proper names) is commonly thought to be constrained by our intuitions about the reference of this term (or about the reference of the members of a given class of terms) in actual and fictional cases. For instance, according to Evans (1973), people have the intuition that nowadays the proper name 'Madagascar' refers to the large island near the south of Africa, even when they learn that the term was historically used to refer to a region on the mainland of Africa.

We propose that to find the correct theory of reference, philosophers of language are committed to using what is sometimes called 'the method of cases':

The method of cases: The correct theory of reference for a class of terms T is the theory which is best supported by the intuitions competent users of T have about the reference of members of T across actual and possible cases.

The method of cases has played a crucial role in the challenge posed to traditional descriptivist theories of reference by the causal-historical theories championed by Kripke and others. Indeed, Kripke's masterstroke was to propose a number of cases that elicited widely shared intuitions that were inconsistent with traditional descriptivist theories (Kripke 1972/1980).[4]

It will be useful to briefly review one of Kripke's most widely discussed cases involving the reference of proper names. In this case ('the Gödel case'), Kripke imagines a scenario in which a name is widely associated with a description that is false of the original bearer of that name a, but true of some other person, b. Because descriptivist theories of reference hold that a term refers to the thing that (uniquely or best) satisfies the description associated with the term, a descriptivist theory of reference would seem to hold that the name in Kripke's example refers to b, the satisfier of the description. But, Kripke maintains, this is just wrong.

Suppose that Gödel was not in fact the author of [Gödel's] theorem. A man called 'Schmidt' . . . actually did the work in question. His friend Gödel somehow got hold of the manuscript and it was thereafter attributed to Gödel. On the [descriptivist] view . . . when our ordinary man uses the name 'Gödel,' he really means to refer to Schmidt, because Schmidt is the unique person satisfying the description 'the man who discovered the incompleteness of arithmetic.' . . . But it seems we are not. We simply are not. (Kripke 1972/1980, 83–84)

In contrast, a causal-historical theory of the reference of proper names is consistent with the intuition that the name continues to refer to its original bearer a, because a is the

---

4. In his reply to Kripke, Evans (1973) also relies on intuitions about the reference of proper names, such as 'Madagascar.' Putnam (1973, 1975) relies on intuitions about the reference of natural kind terms such as 'gold.' See also Schwartz (1978, 1980) and Devitt (1981).

person causally-historically linked with contemporary uses of the name. Many contemporary descriptivists allow that these intuitions have falsified traditional forms of descriptivism and try to accommodate these intuitions within more sophisticated descriptivist theories (Evans 1973; Jackson 1998b).

A plausible justification for the method of cases might be the assumption that language users have an implicit theory of reference that produces intuitions about reference. The project for reference theorists can then be conceived by analogy with the Chomskyan project in linguistics. Philosophers of language use people's intuitions about reference to reconstruct the implicit theory that is part of each speaker's cognitive endowment (Segal 2001).

Despite agreement on the method of cases and agreement on many of the intuitions about the cases used in the philosophical literature, a consensus on the correct theory of reference remains elusive.[5] As this paper goes to press, intuitions about cases continue to underdetermine the selection of a correct theory of reference. However, our argument is based not on the diversity of theories that may be constructed around the same set of intuitions, but on the possibility of variation in the intuitions themselves. Philosophers interested in reference are well aware that intuitions might differ for different classes of terms (e.g. natural kind terms, names, artifact terms, etc.). For instance, cases involving natural kind terms might elicit causal-historical intuitions, while cases involving artifact terms might elicit descriptivist intuitions (e.g. Schwartz 1978, 1980). Because intuitions might differ for different classes of terms, philosophers interested in reference are willing to allow different accounts of reference for different classes of terms (e.g. Devitt and Sterelny 1999). However, as we have previously noted (Machery et al. 2004), the possibility of diverse intuitions about the same cases, for instance about Kripke's Gödel case, plays little role in the contemporary search for a theory of reference. Indeed, contemporary participants in semantic debates seem to assume that the relevant intuitions about cases are more or less universal, and that exceptions can be explained away. As to why we should believe this, little is said. Just what happens to the search for a theory of reference (and the arguments that depend on it) if this assumption is mistaken, is a subject we turn to below. First, however, we consider a fledgling empirical program that casts doubt on this assumption, suggesting systematic diversity in intuitions about reference.

2.2 CULTURAL VARIATION IN INTUITIONS ABOUT REFERENCE

Recent work in cultural psychology and empirical philosophy has suggested the existence of real and systematic differences in philosophical intuitions. In an important series of

---

5. Recanati 1993; Abbott 1997, 1999, 2002; Jackson 1998a, b; Devitt and Sterelny 1999; Geurfs 1997, 2002; Garcia-Carpintero 2000; Segal 2001; Soames 2002; Reimer 2002, 2004; Jeshion 2004.

experiments, Richard Nisbett and colleagues found large and systematic differences between people in East Asian cultures and people in Western cultures on a number of basic cognitive processes including perception, attention and memory. This burgeoning research program has also discovered group differences in describing, predicting and explaining events, in categorization of objects and in belief revision in the face of new arguments and evidence (for review, see Nisbett and Miyamoto 2001; Nisbett 2003; Nisbett and Miyamoto 2005). These findings suggest a dramatic role for culture in shaping human cognition. Inspired by this research program, Weinberg et al. (2001) decided to explore cultural differences in intuitions about cases drawn from philosophical epistemology. These cases were designed to elicit intuitions about the appropriate application of the concept of knowledge, and Weinberg et al. found that there are indeed systematic cross-cultural differences in epistemic intuitions.

The success of Nisbett's research program and Weinberg et al.'s results suggested that other philosophical intuitions, including intuitions about reference, might also admit of systematic cultural differences. In an earlier paper (Machery et al. 2004), we set out to explore this possibility. We began by noting that existing cross-cultural work suggests that East-Asians' categorization judgments depend heavily on similarity while Westerners are more inclined to focus on causation in classification (Watanabe 1998, 1999; Norenzayan et al. 2002), and we hypothesized that this emphasis on causation might make Westerners more likely to rely on causation in linking terms with their referents, favoring the sort of intuitions that Kripke used in support of his causal-historical theory. In fact, this is just what we found.

We constructed a set of vignettes suggested by Kripke's Gödel case, discussed above (Kripke 1972/1980, 93–92). The vignettes were presented in English to American and Chinese subjects.[6] One of the vignettes was closely modeled on Kripke's own Gödel case (see Machery et al. 2004 for more details on the experiment):

Suppose that John has learned in college that Gödel is the man who proved an important mathematical theorem, called the incompleteness of arithmetic. John is quite good at mathematics and he can give an accurate statement of the incompleteness theorem, which he attributes to Gödel as the discoverer. But this is the only thing that he has heard about Gödel. Now suppose that Gödel was not the author of this theorem. A man called "Schmidt" whose body was found in Vienna under mysterious circumstances many years ago, actually did the work in question. His friend Gödel somehow got hold of the manuscript and claimed credit for the work, which was thereafter attributed to Gödel. Thus he has been known as the man who proved the incompleteness of arithmetic. Most people who have heard the name

6. The Chinese subjects were students at the University of Hong Kong where the language of instruction is English: all participants were fluent speakers of English.

'Gödel' are like John; the claim that Gödel discovered the incompleteness theorem is the only thing they have ever heard about Gödel. When John uses the name 'Gödel,' is he talking about:

(A) the person who really discovered the incompleteness of arithmetic?

or

(B) the person who got hold of the manuscript and claimed credit for the work?

In two separate studies using four different vignettes, we found that Americans were more likely than Chinese to give causal-historical responses. Thus, we found that probes modeled on Kripke's Gödel case (including one that used Kripke's own words) elicit culturally variable intuitions. As we had predicted, Chinese participants tended to have descriptivist intuitions, while Americans tended to have Kripkean intuitions.

It is important to note that we found significant intra-cultural differences as well. While for each vignette a majority of Americans gave causal-historical responses, in each case a sizable minority of the population (as high as 45% in one case) gave descriptivist responses. Similarly for the Chinese population, for each vignette, a majority of Chinese participants gave descriptivist responses, but in each case a sizable minority (in some cases over 30%) gave causal-historical responses.

2.3 SIGNIFICANCE OF THESE FINDINGS

We have no illusions that our experiments are the final empirical word on the issue. This is a newly emerging type of research, and obviously it is too early to draw any definite conclusion about the variation of intuitions about reference.[7] Nonetheless, our results already point toward some significant conclusions. Our findings suggest that some well-known semantic intuitions about proper names vary within and across cultures. If that conclusion is judged to be premature, at least our findings show that philosophers cannot simply *assume* that intuitions about reference are universal. Intra-cultural and cross-cultural variation in intuitions about reference is a live possibility.

Since intuitions about reference are used to support theories of reference, proponents of the arguments from reference should be eager to explore what consequences would

---

7. Further empirical investigation should explore whether semantic intuitions about proper names elicited by other cases and semantic intuitions about other types of words, particularly natural kind terms, also vary across cultures. It is commonly assumed that the semantics of proper names and the semantics of natural kind terms are similar, in contrast with the semantics of other predicates such as artifact terms (e.g. Schwartz 1978; Devitt and Sterelny 1999). Furthermore, natural kind terms and proper names elicit similar intuitions about their reference from philosophers (Kripke 1972/1980; Putnam 1973, 1975).

follow for these arguments if intuitions about reference do indeed vary both within and across cultures.

3 Against Arguments from Reference

While the empirical results reviewed in Section 2 are still preliminary, they constitute a strong prima facie case that intuitions about reference used to construct theories of reference might vary from culture to culture and person to person. In the remainder of this paper, we will *assume* that such variation does exist, and we will explore its implications both for the theory of reference and for arguments from reference. We consider a number of ways that theorists of reference might accommodate this variation in intuitions about reference, but argue that none of them salvages arguments from reference.

3.1 GIVING UP ON SUBSTANTIVE THEORIES OF REFERENCE

A first response to the diversity in intuitions about reference is to give up on the idea that the search for a substantive theory of reference is a viable enterprise.[8] While such an abandonment might take a variety of forms, for present purposes we need only note that if there is no correct substantive theory of references, there can be no arguments from reference.

3.2 DOWNPLAYING THE METHOD OF CASES

A second response to variation in intuitions about reference is to downplay the role of intuitions in choosing a theory of reference in favor of other theoretical considerations.[9] Philosophers could adopt a theory of reference on the grounds that it has some desirable philosophical consequences, independent of their intuitions about reference. For instance, a proponent of scientific realism might endorse a causal-historical theory of reference, on the grounds that it gives support to scientific realism.

But however well this approach to reference works, it is not our concern here.[10] Arguments from reference *begin* with a theory of reference that is *independently* motivated, and *proceed* to philosophically significant conclusions. And the dominant way of independently motivating a theory of reference among philosophers of language is by appeal to intuitions about whether or how terms refer in various cases. Arguments that assume a theory of reference that is not independently motivated are not arguments from reference, as we use the term.

---

8. This is a strategy that would be endorsed by deflationists like Field (1986, 1994) and Horwich (1990), albeit for other reasons.
9. Dennett (1996), Papineau (1996) and Laurence and Margolis (2003) have suggested intuitions are only one among several factors in choosing the correct theory of reference.
10. For doubts about this approach, see Mallon (2007).

One might reply that besides the method of cases and the appeal to the philosophical consequences of theories of reference, some other considerations might be used to justify these theories. In reply, we first note that this move would involve breaking with the dominant tradition of employing the method of cases in the philosophy of language. More important, we have no idea what other considerations philosophers of language might appeal to. Thus, in the absence of concrete suggestions, we remain skeptical of the proposal to downplay the role of intuitions in choosing a theory of reference.

3.3 ENDORSING REFERENTIAL PLURALISM

Yet another option for accommodating the variation in intuitions about reference in order to construct a theory of reference is to hold that differences in intuitions about the reference of a word t (or a class of words T) indicate that t (or every member of T) refers differently for different groups, just as different grammatical intuitions among members of different linguistic groups indicate different grammars for their languages.

In order to state this third option more precisely, we introduce the notion of an *intuition group*. An intuition group is simply a group of persons who share intuitions about a set of cases. Put in these terms, the apparent assumption of philosophers of language that intuitions about a type of case are universal amounts to the assumption that there is only one intuition group (or at least that there is only one for a given language). But the data we present above suggest that not everyone belongs to the same intuition group (because intuitions differ systematically), that intuition groups cross-cut language groups (because speakers of English can have systematically different intuitions), and that intuition groups cross-cut cultural groups (because significant minorities of both American and Chinese cultural groups have intuitions matching the majority of the other cultural group).

Like traditional philosophers of language, the referential pluralist holds that the correctness of a theory of reference for a class of terms is determined by the intuitions of the appropriate intuition group, but unlike them, the referential pluralist allows that there may be more than one intuition group. Referential pluralists thus hold the following:

> *The pluralist method of cases:* The correct theory of reference for a class of terms T employed by members of intuition group G is the theory which is best supported by the intuitions that competent members of G have about the reference of members of T across actual and possible cases.

In the remainder of this section, we argue that referential pluralism is an implausible way of accommodating the variation in intuitions about reference.

3.3.1 Are Referential Intuitions Evidence for Reference?

Referential pluralism assumes that speakers' intuitions about reference provide evidence about reference. This assumption would be quite plausible if variation in intuitions about reference mapped onto variation in languages or dialects. Similarly, we are confident that intuitions about the grammaticality of sentences provide evidence about grammatical properties, because variation in these intuitions map onto variation in languages or in dialects. People who have different intuitions about the grammaticality of sentences tend to speak different languages or different dialects.[11] The same is true of other linguistic intuitions, such as intuitions about synonymy, antonymy or polysemy. Now, consider the situation in which people who evidently speak the same dialect have different intuitions about the grammaticality of sentences. Plausibly, this would cast doubt on the assumption that intuitions about grammaticality provide reliable evidence about the grammatical properties of the dialect they speak. At the very least, syntacticians would be hard-pressed to find a justification for this assumption. Our data seem to show that two individuals can belong to two distinct intuition groups despite evidently speaking the same dialect (because they speak the same language, belong to the same culture and have much the same socio-economic status). Faced with this variation, it is very tempting to abandon the assumption that intuitions about reference provide evidence about reference all together. Instead, one might, for example, propose that a speaker's intuitions about reference are caused by a variety of factors that turn out to have nothing do with reference, including her culture and perhaps her philosophical commitments (Stich 1996, 85, fn. 35). But referential pluralism is committed to the method of cases, and so must make this assumption, despite the fact that it is an assumption that is in dire need of justification.

3.3.2 From Referential Pluralism to Referential Relativism

For argument's sake, let's grant that proponents of arguments from reference can justify the assumption that intuitions about reference provide evidence about reference, even though variation in intuitions about reference does not map onto variation in dialects or languages. Then, according to the referential pluralist, the correct theory of reference for interpreting a person's utterance is the theory of reference supported by the intuitions of the intuition group to which the person belongs.

How does referential pluralism affect arguments from reference? Consider the argument for the elimination of propositional attitudes.[12] Suppose that members of Group A have descriptivist intuitions about predicates such as 'belief,' while members of Group B have causal-historical intuitions. The referential pluralist concludes that predicates such as 'belief' refer differently when they are used by members of Group A and by members of Group B. They refer descriptively when used by members of Group A, and they refer in a causal-historical manner when used by members of Group B. Suppose also that the

---

11. There are some tricky issues involved in identifying languages and dialects, but for present purposes they can safely be ignored.

12. The same line of argument applies, mutatis mutandis, to the other arguments from reference.

description associated with 'belief' is derived from a theory that is massively erroneous and thus that the description is satisfied by nothing. Because 'belief' refers descriptively when used by members of Group A and because the description associated with 'belief' is satisfied by nothing, when a member of Group A says 'Beliefs do not exist,' the referential pluralist concludes that what this person says is true. However, because 'belief' refers causal-historically when used by a member of Group B, when a member of B says 'Beliefs do exist,' the referential pluralist concludes that what this person says is also true. But these two conclusions seem to flatly contradict one another. Surprisingly, referential pluralism seems to lead to contradictions.

The referential pluralist need not be daunted, however, for he can simply argue that there is no contradiction when a member of A says truly 'Beliefs do not exist' and when a member of B says, also truly, 'Beliefs do exist.' Consider the following situation. John and Jean are talking to each other by phone. John is in New York, while Jean is in Paris. It's noon in New York and 6 pm in Paris. John says truly 'It's noon,' while Jean says truly 'It's not noon.' It's raining in New York, but not in Paris. John says truly 'It's raining,' while Jean says truly 'It's not raining.' John and Jean are not contradicting each other, and it is clear to them that they are not. For the truth of what John and Jean say when they say 'It's noon' and 'It's raining' depends upon the contexts of use of the two sentences 'It's noon' and 'It's raining.' And the context of use is not the same for Jean's utterances and for John's utterances. The context of use for Jean's utterance of 'It's noon' and 'It's raining' involves the weather and the time *in Paris* when the phone conversation takes place, while the context of use for John's utterance of 'It's noon' and 'It's raining' involves the weather and the time *in New York* when the phone conversation takes place. Relativization to a context of use is extremely common in natural languages.

The referential pluralist might simply argue that a similar phenomenon is going on when our imaginary member of Group A says truly 'Beliefs do not exist,' while our imaginary member of Group B says, also truly, 'Beliefs do exist.' The context of use for our member of A's utterance of 'Beliefs do not exist' and the context of use for our member of B's utterance of 'Beliefs do exist' are not the same. When the member of A says 'Beliefs do not exist,' the context of use includes how terms such as 'belief' refer when they are used by members of Group A, which itself depends, according to the referential pluralist, on what kind of intuitions about reference members of Group A have. When a member of B says 'Beliefs do exist,' the context of use includes how terms such as 'belief' refer when they are used by members of Group B, which in turn depends on what kind of intuitions about reference members of Group B have. The truth of what a speaker says when she utters 'Beliefs do exist' or 'Beliefs do not exist' is relativized to the intuition group of this speaker. And similarly for every utterance. Like John and Jean, members of Group A and Group B do not contradict each other, for their utterances are evaluated according to the distinct contexts appropriate to their respective groups.

3.3.3 Relativizing Assertions in Philosophy and Beyond

All this has very far-reaching implications for how we carry on discourse, ordinary and philosophical. To see why, recall that while our data suggest systematic differences in philosophical intuitions between Hong Kong and U.S. students, they also suggest a high degree of *intra-cultural variation*. So, while our data suggest that culture has a systematic effect on the intuition group to which one belongs, they also indicate that intuition groups cross-cut cultural groups. Call this the *ubiquity of variation*. As we have seen, our referential pluralist argues that because individuals may belong to different intuition groups, we should relativize their utterances to the theories of reference appropriate to their intuition groups. And while this allows the referential pluralist to resolve apparent contradictions, when combined with the ubiquity of variation, referential pluralism entails that conclusions of the arguments within cultural groups must be similarly relativized. In philosophy, this means that arguments over the existence of beliefs (or the existence of races, the progress of science, the nature of our epistemic access to moral properties and so on for the conclusions of every other argument from reference) have to be relativized. Thus, suppose that Kuhn and Feyerabend were right that the role of theoretical terms is fundamentally changed by scientific revolutions. Philosopher A might truly say that 'science progresses' because she has causal-historical intuitions about theoretical terms and Philosopher B might truly say that 'science does not progress' because she has descriptivist intuitions, and according to the referential pluralist, the two philosophers *would not disagree*. Similar considerations apply to the case of philosophical agreement. When asserting or denying that beliefs exist or that science progresses (or the conclusion of any other argument from reference), philosophers A and B *would agree or disagree only if* they belonged to the same intuition group. If, for example, Churchland and Fodor both belonged to an intuition group whose intuitions about reference support a descriptivist theory of reference for mental state terms, then they might genuinely disagree about whether beliefs exist.

We take it that these conclusions are very surprising and would involve a very substantial revision of philosophical methodology. For they suggest that philosophical disagreement and agreement among even speakers of the same language, who belong to the same culture, have the same socio-economic status, and even attended the same graduate program in philosophy may be illusory if the speakers have different intuitions about how terms refer in actual and fictional cases. Moreover, this conclusion is not limited to philosophical debate, but appears to extend to all discourse. And there is worse to come. For, as we now argue, when combined with an additional (we think very plausible) premise, referential pluralism has conclusions that are far more absurd than any we have suggested so far.

3.3.4 The Uncertain Membership of Intuition Groups

This additional premise is, simply, that we do not really know to which intuition groups any of us belongs. Before arguing for it, we point out that this premise, combined with referential pluralism and the ubiquity of variation, leads to the *prima facie* absurd conclusion that we do not really know, of any of our discourse, whether it agrees or disagrees with the discourse of anyone else. Consider how this applies to a philosophical case. Suppose that there are a number of different intuition groups and that it is unclear what intuition group philosophers A and B belong to. Then, if referential pluralism is correct, when philosopher A says 'Beliefs exist' and philosopher B says 'Beliefs do not exist,' it is unclear whether philosophers A and B disagree or whether they are speaking at cross-purposes. Thus, if it is unclear which intuition group we belong to, far from salvaging the arguments from reference, referential pluralism leads to the absurd conclusion that we simply have no idea when proponents of these arguments agree, when they disagree and when they talk past each other. And again, this conclusion is not limited to debates in philosophy, but rather extends quite generally to discourse about anything at all!

So, the question is pressing: Do we know which intuition group each of us belongs to? We think the answer is no: Our knowledge of the intuitions each of us has about the relevant cases is very far from complete. A series of considerations suggest why this is the case:

1. Every speaker must be considered because of the ubiquity of variation.

As we have already mentioned, intuitions even about the simple cases we have tested vary within cultural and language groups. It follows that one cannot assume that people who share a language and a culture are members of the same intuition group. This means every speaker must be considered individually!

2. Because lots of cases are relevant, intuition groups must be fine-grained.

Above we said an intuition group was a group of persons who shared intuitions about a set of cases. Since we are interested in theories of reference, the relevant intuitions are all those judgments about cases that decide between distinct theories of reference. For example, Machery et al. (2004) considered hypothetical cases that have been used to test whether descriptivist or causal-historical theories of reference better comport with our intuitions. But this is only the tip of the iceberg of relevant intuitions for there are many varieties of descriptivist theories, causal-historical theories, and blends of such theories that might be best supported by different sets of intuitions.

Moreover, the schematic theories of reference we have discussed must be accompanied by *auxiliary assumptions* in order to apply the theories, assumptions that themselves are typically justified in part by appeal to intuitions. For example, causal-historical theorists must decide exactly *what individual or thing is picked out by the historical introduction of a term*, and *whether any "switching" to another individual or thing has occurred along the way* (Evans 1973). And descriptivists must decide on *what the reference-fixing description is*, and *how closely a thing must satisfy it* in order to qualify as a referent.

But do intuitions that are needed to determine the right auxiliary assumptions really vary in ways similar to the intuitions tested by Machery et al. (2004)? While evidence is limited, there is every indication that the answer is yes. Consider, for example, the extensive literature on what knowledge is. Much of this literature employs the method of cases in order to elicit judgments about whether there is knowledge in various counterfactual cases in the hopes of arriving at an understanding of knowledge. In recent decades, a vast amount of work has been driven by responses to Edmund Gettier's (1963) thought experiments. Famously, Gettier suggested that certain sorts of justified true beliefs (for example, those that were accidentally true) did not intuitively count as knowledge, and so the search has gone on for additional conditions that would allow a statement of the necessary and sufficient conditions of knowledge. Other work on knowledge has also employed the method of cases. Keith Lehrer (1990) employed the 'Truetemp' case to explore intuitions regarding the internalism/externalism debate—a debate about whether factors external to a subject's introspective access are relevant to the application of epistemically normative concepts like *justification*.

As we mentioned above, Weinberg et al. have found variation in judgments about whether cases count as instances of knowledge. In particular, they found variation regarding *both* Gettier cases and Truetemp cases, and they found it *both within* and *across cultures*. This suggests that the ubiquity of variation may well extend to judgments elicited to determine the right auxiliary assumptions to make. For example, these results suggest there may well be variation in judgments about what the right description to associate with the term 'knowledge' is.

Because it takes a great many assumptions to determine and apply a theory of reference, and because the intuitive judgments required to decide which of these assumptions is correct for a person likely vary within and across cultures, it follows that the sorts of intuition groups into which people must be divided in order to determine full-fledged theories of reference will be very fine-grained.

3. Numerous cases must be considered for each speaker.

It seems to follow from 1 and 2 that assigning every speaker to the correct intuition group would require a vast amount of careful work. Numerous cases, actual and fictional, would have to be considered for every speaker. Nothing of this kind has ever been attempted.

4. Explicit views are not a good guide to intuition group membership.

It remains open to a referential pluralist to insist that at least philosophers have considered a wide range of actual and fictional cases in deciding what their own intuitions are. And, as we noted above, some philosophers are explicitly committed to descriptivist or to causal-historical theories of reference for specific classes of words (e.g., proper names). It therefore seems open to the referential pluralist to contend that a philosopher's explicit commitments are good evidence about the intuition group she belongs to. For instance, if a philosopher endorses a descriptivist theory of the reference of theoretical terms, this could be taken to be evidence that she has descriptivist intuitions about the reference of theoretical terms. If so, the referential pluralist could insist that, at least for philosophers, we can have some idea about whether they agree and disagree.

Call this assumption that a philosopher's explicit views are a guide to her intuition group membership *the limpidity assumption*. We think the limpidity assumption is eminently questionable. Remember that prior to Kripke and Putnam, pretty much everyone was a descriptivist. But as soon as Kripke proposed his famous cases, including the Gödel case, many philosophers discovered that they had intuitions that were incompatible with descriptivist theories of reference and adopted some version of the causal-historical theory of reference. It is overwhelmingly plausible that the distribution of intuitions elicited by these cases would have been much the same ten or fifty years before Kripke and Putnam. That is, had Anglo-American philosophers been asked about the Gödel case in 1931 rather than in 1971, many would have had causal-historical intuitions. But almost nobody was committed to the causal-historical theory of reference before Kripke and Putnam. They simply hadn't considered a relevant case.

Indeed, many philosophers of language are implicitly committed to denying the limpidity assumption. In debates about what the right theory of reference is, philosophers of language often contend that their opponents have failed to consider the cases that would have elicited intuitions inconsistent with the theory held by their opponents. That is, they contend that their opponents have ignored some of their own intuitions, by failing to consider the whole gamut of actual and fictional cases. Thus, philosophers of language take for granted that their opponents might hold a theory of reference that is not supported by their opponents' intuitions. This is tantamount to denying the limpidity assumption.

Because philosophers represent the most plausible candidates for persons whose explicit views about reference track their intuition group membership, the failure of the limpidity assumption for philosophers is very bad news for any suggestion that each of us knows which intuition group she belongs to. Furthermore, while the limpidity assumption is implausible for philosophers, it is of no use at all in considering discourse among ordinary people who typically have neither considered their intuitions about actual and fictional cases nor explicitly endorsed a theory of reference.

Together, these considerations strongly support the view that we simply do not know to which intuition group any of us belongs. And that completes our reductio, for since it is unclear which intuition group each of us belongs to, and because we may well belong to different groups (even if we share, e.g., a language, culture, and socio-economic group), referential pluralism leads to the absurd conclusion that no one knows when proponents of arguments from reference agree, when they disagree, and when they speak at cross-purposes. This conclusion is so bizarre that we ought to abandon the referential pluralism that leads to it.

4 Metaphysics without Arguments from Reference

Arguments from reference are a basic philosophical currency, used to establish philosophically significant conclusions in a variety of areas. But if we are right, arguments from reference have to be rejected, given the plausible (but, by no means, conclusively established) assumption that the intuitions many take to be important in finding the correct theory of reference are themselves diverse. The three ways we have considered of accommodating the diversity in intuitions about reference in order to build a theory of reference undermine these arguments from reference.

(i) If philosophers give up on substantive theories of reference, then, obviously, they ought to give up on arguments from reference, since arguments from reference begin with a substantive theory of reference.

(ii) If philosophers endorse a theory of reference because it gives support to their metaphysical commitments, then they do not need arguments from reference. And absent concrete proposals for the justification of theories of reference on the basis of something other than the method of cases, we remain skeptical of this response to the variation in intuitions about reference.

(iii) If philosophers endorse referential pluralism, then they must justify the assumption that intuitions about reference provide evidence about reference, although variation in these intuitions do not map onto variation in languages or dialects. Supposing this can be done, philosophers must accommodate a relativization of the conclusion of the arguments from reference to intuition groups that may cross cut languages, cultural groups, and so forth. This might be a way to accommodate the variation in intuitions about reference provided that we know which intuition group a person belongs to. However, we do not know. Without this knowledge referential pluralism leads to the absurd view that we do not know when people agree, when they disagree and when they speak at cross-purposes.

So philosophers must choose. They can abandon arguments from reference. Or they can hold on to the hope that, despite evidence to the contrary, variation in intuitions about reference does not really exist. One of these is clearly a safer bet.

REFERENCES

Abbott, B. 1997. A note on the nature of 'water.' *Mind* 106: 311–319.
———. 1999. Water = H$_2$O. *Mind* 108: 145–148.
———. 2002. Definiteness and proper names: Some bad news for the description theory. *Journal of Semantics* 19: 191–201.

Adams, R. M. 1979. Divine command ethics modified again. *Journal of Religious Ethics* 7(1): 66–79.

Andreasen, R. O. 1998. A new perspective on the race debate. *British Journal for the Philosophy of Science* 49: 199–225.

———. 2000. Race: Biological reality or social construct? *Philosophy of Science* 67: S653–S666.

Appiah, K. A. 1995. The uncompleted argument: Du Bois and the illusion of race. In L. A. Bell and D. Blumenfeld (eds.), *Overcoming Racism and Sexism*. Lanham, MD: Rowman and Littlefield, 59–78.

———. 1996. Race, culture, identity: Misunderstood connections. In K. A. Appiah and A. Gutmann (eds.), *Color Conscious: The Political Morality of Race*. Princeton, NJ: Princeton University Press, 30–105.

Bishop, M. and Stich, S. P. 1998. The flight to reference, or how not to make progress in the philosophy of science. *Philosophy of Science* 65: 33–49.

Boyd, R. 1983. On the current status of the issue of scientific realism. *Erkenntnis* 19: 45–90.

———. 1988. How to be a moral realist. In G. Sayre-McCord (ed.), *Essays on Moral Realism*. Ithaca: Cornell University Press.

———. 2002. Scientific Realism. *The Stanford Encyclopedia of Philosophy (Summer 2002 Edition)*, Edward N. Zalta (ed.), http://plato.stan-ford.edu/archives/sum2002/entries/scientific-realism/.

———. 2003a. Finite beings, finite goods: The semantics, metaphysics and ethics of naturalist consequentialism, part I. *Philosophy and Phenomenological Research* 66: 505–553.

———. 2003b. Finite beings, finite goods: The semantics, metaphysics and ethics of naturalist consequentialism, part II. *Philosophy and Phenomenological Research* 67: 24–47.

Churchland, P. M. 1981. Eliminative materialism and the propositional attitudes. *Journal of Philosophy* 78: 67–90.

Dennett, D. 1996. Cow-sharks, Magnets, and Swampman. *Mind & Language* 11(1): 76–77.

Devitt, M. 1981. *Designation*. New York: Columbia University Press.

——— and Sterelny, K. 1999. *Language and Reality: An Introduction to the Philosophy of Language* (2nd ed.). Cambridge, MA: MIT Press.

Evans, G. 1973. The causal theory of names. *Supplementary Proceedings of the Aristotelian Society* 47: 187–208.

Feyerabend, P. K. 1962. Explanation, reduction and empiricism. In H. Feigl and G. Maxwell (eds.), *Minnesota Studies in the Philosophy of Science, vol. 3: Scientific Explanation, Space, and Time*. Minneapolis: University of Minnesota Press, 28–97.

Field, H. 1986. The deflationary concept of truth. In G. MacDonald and C. Wright (eds.), *Fact, Science, and Value*. Oxford: Blackwell, 55–117.

———. 1994. Deflationist views of meaning and content. *Mind* 103: 249–85.

Fodor, J. 1987. *Psychosemantics: the Problem of Meaning in the Philosophy of Mind*. Cambridge, MA: MIT Press.

Garcia-Carpintero, M. 2002. A presuppositional account of reference-fixing. *Journal of Philosophy* 97(3): 109–147.

Geurts, B. 1997. Good news about the description theory of names. *Journal of Semantics* 14: 339–348.

———. 2002. Bad news for anyone? A reply to Abbott. *Journal of Semantics* 19: 203–207.

Glasgow, J. 2003. On the new biology of race. *The Journal of Philosophy* 100: 456–74.

Horwich, P. 1990. *Truth*. Oxford: Blackwell.

Jackson, F. 1998a. *From Metaphysics to Ethics: A Defense of Conceptual Analysis*. Oxford: Oxford University Press.

———. 1998b. Reference and description revisited. In J. Tomberlin (ed.), *Philosophical Perspectives, vol. 12: Language, Mind, and Ontology*. Oxford: Blackwell, 201–218.

Jeshion, R. 2004. Descriptive descriptive names. In A. Bezuidenhout and M. Reimer (eds.), *Descriptions and Beyond*, Oxford: Oxford University Press.

Kitcher, P. 1993. *The Advancement of Science*. Oxford: Oxford University Press.

———. 1999. Race, ethnicity, biology, culture. In Leonard Harris (ed.), *Racism*. New York: Humanity Books, 87–120.

Kripke, S. 1972/1980. *Naming and Necessity*. Cambridge, MA: Harvard University Press.

Kuhn, T. S. 1970. *The Structure of Scientific Revolutions*, 2nd edition. Chicago: University of Chicago Press.

Laurence, S. and Margolis, E. 2003. Concepts and conceptual analysis. *Philosophy and Phenomenological Research* 67: 253–282.

Lycan, W. 1988. *Judgement and Justification*. Cambridge: Cambridge University Press.

Machery, E., Mallon, R., Nichols, S. and Stich, S. 2004. Semantics cross-cultural style. *Cognition* 92: B1–B12.

Mallon, R. 2006. Race: Normative, not metaphysical or semantic. *Ethics* 116(3): 525–551.

———. 2007. Arguments from reference and the worry about dependence. *Midwest Studies in Philosophy* 31(1): 160–183.

Mills, C. 1998. *Blackness Visible: Essays on Philosophy and Race*. Ithaca: Cornell University Press.

Nisbett, R. E. 2003. *The Geography of Thought: How Asians and Westerners Think Differently . . . and Why*. New York: Free Press.

Nisbett, R. E. and Miyamoto, Y. 2005. The influence of culture: holistic versus analytic perception. *Trends in Cognitive Sciences* 9(10): 467–473.

———. 2001. Culture and systems of thought: Holistic vs. analytic cognition. *Psychological Review* 108: 291–310.

Norenzayan, A., Smith, E. and Kim, B. 2002. Cultural preferences for formal versus intuitive reasoning. *Cognitive Science* 26: 653–684.

Papineau, D. 1996. Doubtful intuitions. *Mind & Language* 11(1): 130–2.

Putnam, H. 1973. Explanation and reference. In G. Pearce and P. Maynard (eds.), *Conceptual Change*. Dordrecht: Reidel.

———. 1975. The meaning of 'meaning.' In H. Putnam, *Mind, Language and Reality*. Cambridge: Cambridge University Press.

Recanati, F. 1993. *Direct Reference*. Oxford: Basil Blackwell.

Reimer, M. 2002. Ordinary proper names. In G. Preyer and G. Peter (eds.), *On Logical Form and Language*, Oxford: Oxford University Press.

———. 2004. Descriptive names. In A. Bezuidenhout and M. Reimer (eds.), *Descriptions and Beyond*, Oxford: Oxford University Press.

Schwartz, S. P. 1978. Putnam on artifacts. *Philosophical Review* 87: 566–574.

———. 1980. Natural kind terms. *Cognition* 7: 301–315.

Segal, G. 2001. Two theories of names. *Mind & Language* 16(5): 547–563.

Soames, S. 2002. *Beyond Necessity: the Unfinished Semantic Agenda of Naming and Necessity*. New York: Oxford University Press.

Stich, S. P. 1983. *From Folk Psychology to Cognitive Science*. Cambridge, MA: MIT Press.

———. 1996. *Deconstructing the Mind*. Oxford: Oxford University Press.

Taylor, P. 2000. Appiah's uncompleted argument: DuBois and the reality of race. *Social Theory and Practice* 26: 1 103–28.

Watanabe, M. 1998. *Styles of reasoning in Japan and the United States: logic of education in two cultures*. Paper presented at the American Sociological Association annual meeting, San Francisco. CA.

———. 1999. *Styles of reasoning in Japan and the United States: logic of education in two cultures*. Unpublished PhD thesis, Columbia University, New York.

Weinberg, J., Nichols, S. and Stich, S. 2001. Normativity and Epistemic Intuitions. *Philosophical Topics* 29(1/2): 429–459.

Zack, N. 1993. *Race and Mixed Race*. Philadelphia: Temple University Press.

———. 2002. *Philosophy of Science and Race*. New York: Routledge.

Name Index

Subject Index